New Directions in Scandinavian Studies

Terje Leiren and Christine Ingebritsen, Series Editors

New Directions in Scandinavian Studies

This series offers interdisciplinary approaches to the study of the Nordic region of Scandinavia and the Baltic States and their cultural connections in North America. By redefining the boundaries of Scandinavian studies to include the Baltic States and Scandinavian America, the series presents books that focus on the study of the culture, history, literature, and politics of the North.

KNUT HAMSUN

The Dark Side of Literary Brilliance

Monika Žagar

UNIVERSITY OF WASHINGTON PRESS

Seattle & London

This publication is supported by a grant from
the Scandinavian Studies Publication Fund.

© 2009 by the University of Washington Press
Printed in the United States of America
Design by Thomas Eykemans
14 12 11 10 09   5 4 3 2 1

UNIVERSITY OF WASHINGTON PRESS
PO Box 50096, Seattle, WA 98145 USA
www.washington.edu/uwpress

LIBRARY OF CONGRESS CATALOGING-IN-PUBLICATION DATA
Žagar, Monika.
Knut Hamsun : the dark side of literary brilliance / by Monika Žagar.
  p. cm. — (New directions in Scandinavian studies)
Includes bibliographical references and index.
ISBN 978-0-295-98945-7 (hardback : alk. paper) — ISBN 978-0-295-98946-4
(pbk. : alk. paper)
  1. Hamsun, Knut, 1859–1952—Criticism and interpretation. I. Title.
PT9850.H3Z97 2009
839.8'236—dc22   2009018648

Parts of chapters 3, 4, 5, and 8 were published in somewhat different form in the follow-
ing journals; the material is gratefully used here with permission:
  "Imagining the Red-Skinned Other: Hamsun's Article 'Fra en Indianerleir' (1885),"
      Edda 4 (2001): 385-95.
  "Hamsun's Black Man, or Lament for Paternalist Society: A reading of Hamsun's play
      Livet ivold through Fra det moderne Amerikas aandsliv," Edda 4 (1997): 364-79.
  "*Hamsun's Dronning Tamara,*" *Scandinavian Studies* 70 (1998): 337-58.
  "The Rhetoric of Defense in Hamsun's *Paa gjengrodde stier,*" Edda 3 (1999): 252-61.

CONTENTS

ACKNOWLEDGMENTS

A BOOK LIKE THIS IS ALWAYS A TEAM PROJECT AND A WORK OF LOVE THAT starts at home. I wish first to thank my family and friends for their many years of support and love. Above all, it would have been impossible to write this book without the steady, loving, and insightful support given by my husband, Al, and the teenage inquisitiveness of my daughter, Lena. Their comments, as well as their presence, reminded me that academic research needs to connect to important ethical questions and moral choices taken on a daily basis. I am also deeply grateful to my Global Warming women friends at the University of Minnesota whose solidarity and unflagging belief in me have been enormously helpful over the years.

Many colleagues gave generously of their time in discussing parts, or the entire argument, of this manuscript in its various stages. Some read, critiqued, and suggested changes to individual chapters or the final manuscript. Others provided me with succinct information about topics in their specific fields or with intelligent guidance regarding research and publishing issues. These are: Steven Feinstein, Kaaren Grimstad, Poul Houe, Ruth-Ellen Joeres, Nils Magne Knutsen, Terje Leiren, Arne Lunde, Anne Sabo, Frankie and Jole Schackelford, John Weinstock, and Erik Østerud. Frankie Schackelford was instrumental in crafting the final title. Harald Næss helped untie some of the most resistant research riddles and, above all, reduced the frequency of my library visits by generously giving me all six volumes of Hamsun's correspondence. Marte Kvam Hult edited the next-to-last version of the manuscript, plowing through the English text and the Norwegian quotes, improving the structure and helping me clarify some muddled points. In addition, I am deeply grateful to many colleagues for their encouragement and enthusiasm over the years. I fervently hope that I haven't forgotten anyone.

Inside the University of Washington Press, the professional attitude of all involved in the lengthy process from manuscript to book was simply awesome. My editor, Marilyn Trueblood, oversaw the entire process with intelligence, steady enthusiasm, and an admirable attention to detail. The copyeditor, David Jessup, did a truly remarkable job of meticulously combing through my somewhat baroque manuscript and imposing a consistent, clear, and cogent order from which a leaner and clearer book emerged. Finally, Tom Eykemans provided the overall book design and the stunningly beautiful cover, which includes his original artwork for the evocative portrait of the elderly Hamsun.

I would also like to thank the University of Minnesota for granting me a sabbatical leave during the academic year 2001–2, which made possible the early research and writing on this long-term project. The university also granted me an unpaid leave for the academic year 2004–5, during which time much of the revision of the manuscript was accomplished. In addition, I am very grateful to the following institutions for providing much needed funds for visits and research in Norway during the spring of 2005: the American Scandinavian Foundation, for a fellowship; the Norge-Amerika Foreningen, for a research grant; the Norwegian Ministry of Culture as well as the Norwegian Information Office in New York, for travel grants that enabled me to travel to Norway for additional research. NORTANA provided assistance by letting me stay in their subsidized housing in Oslo in June 2005. The helpful staff at the Resistance Museum in Oslo assisted me during my research in their library.

Finally, Gunnar Sønsteby in Norway and Reidar Dittmann in Minnesota, two World War II resistance fighters and truly inspirational individuals, reminded me, in spirited conversations and at crucial intervals, that Hamsun, the novelist, was also a person who played an active role in a historic time.

KNUT HAMSUN

The Dark Side of Literary Brilliance

INTRODUCTION

IN DECEMBER OF 1947, KNUT HAMSUN (1859–1952), THE CRITICALLY ACCLAIMED Norwegian novelist and Nobel laureate, was convicted by a municipal court in Norway of being a member of the Nasjonal Samling (NS) party and thus of supporting the Nazi occupation. He was fined the large sum of 425,000 kroner, an amount that was later substantially reduced upon appeal. The extraordinary mix, in one man, of brilliant art and repugnant politics has produced a continuing fascination with Hamsun's life and writings; his example, indeed, compels us to ask the question: how could a literary genius of his stature fall so low as to become a political collaborator with the National Socialist regime?

Over the past few decades, interest in Hamsun's life and work has increased and intensified both within academic circles and among broader audiences. This interest has spawned a full-length feature film, *Hamsun* (1996), directed by the Swedish filmmaker Jan Troell and starring Max von Sydow as the elderly Hamsun; a Norwegian television miniseries, *The Enigma of Knut Hamsun* (1997); numerous republications and new translations of Hamsun's works in both Scandinavia and abroad; and new and exciting scholarly discussions of his texts. I cherish this renewed interest in Hamsun and his art, but the early impetus for the present book emerged from my astonishment over the reception of the 1996 film, which professed admiration and compassion

for the frail old writer. The movie portrays Hamsun as a complex but ultimately sympathetic old man, and his wife, Marie, as the Nazi in the family.
This apologetic view was based on the work of Thorkild Hansen, the Danish
novelist. His 1978 book was heavily indebted to Hamsun's own version of
events as he described them in his last book, *Paa gjengrodde stier* (On overgrown paths).[1] The movie, however, distorts matters even further by transforming the obfuscations and omissions of Hamsun's book into pure truth. It
is here, with Hamsun's own text as the underpinning, that fiction takes over
and becomes reality and pushes historical facts into oblivion. Hamsun's collaboration was reduced to an insignificant trifle, a research project for some
dusty history buffs perhaps, while new Internet sites bemoaned the incredibly
cruel treatment that the "innocent" Hamsun had to endure after the war.

A quick review of the body of work on Hamsun created between the
1950s and the early 1990s reveals that the majority of critics and scholars,
their personal lenses notwithstanding, have either tacitly ignored Hamsun's
ideological tendencies or expressly come to his defense (for example, Sten
Sparre Nilson and, in a more skewed way, Thorkild Hansen).[2] The critics
most often point out Hamsun's hatred of the Anglo-Saxon worldview and his
gratitude toward Germany (where he enjoyed early literary success), his aversion to modern progress, his unique sensitive personality, and his political
naiveté. There have also been, however, a handful of articles and books that
have accused Hamsun of being a fascist writer. Of these, the most resonant
are Leo Löwenthal's discussion of Hamsun in his book *Literature and the
Image of Man* (1956); Morten Giersing et al., *Det reaktionære oprør: Om
fascismen i Hamsuns forfatterskap* (The reactionary revolt: About fascism in
Hamsun's authorship; 1975); and Allen Simpson's 1977 essay, "Knut Hamsun's Anti-Semitism."[3]

A number of other important Hamsun studies have appeared as well, but
they focus primarily on such issues as Hamsun's modernist, stream-of-con-
sciousness writing style, his ambivalent narrative voice, or simply his eloquence and do not address the ways in which his personal political philosophy
is reflected in his writing. While scholars who concentrate on Hamsun's modernism do acknowledge his support of the Nazi regime, they tend to dismiss
it as an expression of his private opinion, something separate from his fiction.
Of these discussions, perhaps the most prominent is Atle Kittang's *Luft, vind,
ingenting: Hamsuns desillusjonsromanar fra* Sult *til* Ringen sluttet (Air,
wind, nothing: Hamsun's novels of disillusionment from *Hunger* to *The Ring
Is Closed*), a Lacanian interpretation of Hamsun's novels of disillusionment.[4]

Robert Ferguson's by now standard biography of Hamsun, *Enigma: The Life of Knut Hamsun* (1987), presents Hamsun as a creative genius and an innocent victim of Nazi propaganda who ultimately remains a mystery.[5]

Yet the modernist-oriented critical stance has gradually started to shift; there is less emphasis on Hamsun's writings as self-contained texts and a renewed interest in coupling his life and opinions with the explicit and implicit messages of his fictional and nonfictional writings. Ståle Dingstad's *Hamsuns strategier: Realisme, humor og kynisme* (2003) is a good example of this shift, as are my own previous articles on Hamsun.[6] Dingstad's important book examines Hamsun's texts from the twentieth century with a close focus on the period between 1927 (when *Landstrykere* [Wayfarers] was published) and 1949 (when *Paa gjengrodde stier* appeared). The most important aspect of Dignstad's book is his argument that Hamsun's novels from this period are a contribution to realism rather than to modernism, and as such offer rich indications of how Hamsun's writings intersect with his politics.[7] As still another Hamsun scholar, Petter Aaslestad, writes: "I will claim that the I-narrator in Hamsun's short stories now and then comes closer to the real Knut Hamsun than we present it when we treat the text as an autonomous unit."[8] In addition, in Lars Frode Larsen's last volume on the young Hamsun, this tireless biographer presents an argument for reading *Sult* (Hunger) as autobiography rather than as a novel, thus returning, at least to some degree, to a formerly discredited positivistic interpretation of Hamsun's texts.[9]

The discussions that arose in the aftermath of the 1996 film, among both the general public and academics, ranged from expressions of pity for a great writer, who at the age of eighty-seven was compelled to face a court trial, to insistence on Hamsun's conservatism and patriotism. Yet another view was expressed by Øystein Rottem, one of Norway's leading literary critics prior to his early death in 2004. In an article in the newspaper *Dagbladet*, he argued that Hamsun's Nazi sympathies were a logical extension of his conservative, traditionalist, and patriotic views.[10] Rottem refreshingly contextualizes Hamsun's Nazi sympathies, rising above the "He is a fascist" / "No, he is not a fascist" sentiments that have generally prevailed. He concludes, however, that in light of Hamsun's consistent political views, his Nazism is a "banality" that has been over-researched, while it is Hamsun's writing that is the real miracle.[11]

It is impossible to provide an overview of all the books and articles published these days on Hamsun. It is, rather, an endless game of catch-up against a continuous stream of publications. Two recent ones, Gunvald Hermundstad's *Hamsuns polemiske skrifter* (Hamsun's polemical writings; 1998) and

Ingar Sletten Kolloen's two-volume biography (2003–4), categorically avoid pronouncing judgment on Hamsun's political activities.[12] Kolloen, in spite of his rigorous research on Hamsun's activities and writings, falls prey in the end to Hamsun's seductive prose, very much as Thorkild Hansen did in 1978. Jørgen Haugan, a Norwegian scholar working in Denmark, published his own critical assessment of Hamsun titled *Solgudens fall: Knut Hamsun, en litterær biografi* (The fall of the Sun God: Knut Hamsun, a literary biography; 2003).[13] Haugan's is a scholarly volume that is critical of academia's apologias on behalf of Hamsun's politics. The most recent publication (at the time of my writing) is by the Swedish novelist Sigrid Combüchen, *Livsklättrare: En bok om Knut Hamsun* (The climber of life: A book about Knut Hamsun; 2006). Combüchen's novelistic text reflects on and intertwines Hamsun's literary prose and achievements with facts from Hamsun's life, without passing judgment. On a final note, in the 2005 English-language analysis of Hamsun's literary texts, *Knut Hamsun, Novelist: A Critical Assessment*, Sverre Lyngstad mitigates his analysis with the following statement: "However awkward it may be to split an individual into different personae, it is necessary to do so in Hamsun's case if we want to insure a fair judgment of his literary achievement."[14] Here fairness is equated with isolating the novels from their historical context; such fairness to Hamsun ultimately elevates his literary achievements while ignoring their rootedness in contemporary culture and their political context, as if Hamsun were writing in a vacuum.

All of these publications have contributed to a renewed debate on art and politics in Norway, a positive step. And it is obvious that Hamsun is not being ignored as a writer, or even as a literary genius, although the troubling part of such qualified debates is the whitewashing of Hamsun's political collaboration, which tends to make it seem insignificant and irrelevant, when, in fact, it is not.

The issue of Hamsun's collaboration ought not to be overshadowed by the writer's genius and should certainly not be ignored. As recently as the fall of 2004, the debate over the writer's collaborationist activities received new impetus when Norway's Riksteatret decided to stage a play about Hamsun entitled *Jeg kunne gråte blod* (I could cry blood), written by Ingar Sletten Kolloen, the author of the most recent Hamsun biography. Historian Hans Fredrik Dahl of the University of Oslo was invited to write an essay for the theater program. The essay, "Marie, Knut og de 55000 andre" (Marie, Knut, and the 55,000 others), is essentially an apologia that sees the Hamsun family's questionable activities during the occupation as little more than contributions to a cultural debate, hardly Nazi propaganda. Dahl concludes that the family was punished much too severely. "Was not the Hamsun family hard hit? None of them had damaged a hair on anybody's head," Dahl asks, and then continues: "Weren't their activities in 1940–45 really more like a contribution to the cultural debate than an evil contribution to war and violence?"[15] Another red flag in Dahl's article is his description of Hamsun as a "dissident"—a word that today generally carries a positive connotation. Given that historians do not dispute Hamsun's support for the Nazi authorities, it is hard to see Dahl's essay as anything but an attempt to manipulate the attitudes of theater audiences. Such manipulations are deplorable: readers of Dahl's essay might draw a conclusion that Hamsun's actions were, after all, unfortunate but acceptable.[16]

It comes as no surprise that Dahl, an expert on World War II and the Nazi occupation of Norway, should argue as he does. His 1996 article, "Hamsun, Quisling og det norske rettsoppgjøret" (Hamsun, Quisling, and the Norwegian post-war trials), compares the legal proceedings against Hamsun with those against Vidkun Quisling. Dahl writes as if the majority of the populace and most experts agree that the verdict against Hamsun was too severe and that the proceedings themselves were inhumane and unjust.[17] Rather misleadingly, he uses the vague expression *det vanlige syn* ("the usual opinion"), while the experts he mentions in Hamsun's defense—Sten Sparre Nilson, Thorkild Hansen, Sigrid Stray (Hamsun's defense lawyer), and Tore Hamsun (his son)—have all been shown to be biased. Their "clear apologias" (*klare apologier*), as Dahl calls them, have been shown to be little more than wishful thinking based on admiration for Hamsun, whether as a person or a writer. Dahl seems to dismiss Hamsun's trial as a case of emotionally charged excess typical of the post-war years, but he does not stop there. He goes on to speculate whether the public will one day be able to visit the small cell where Hamsun was held while awaiting trial—like those prison cells that once held the working-class organizer Marcus Thrane and the visionary preacher Hans Nielsen Hauge—as a monument to the madness of the past. Here, I will say only that such statements are entirely misleading; fuller discussion of these views, including the faulty comparison of Hamsun to Thrane and Hauge, I reserve for my final chapter. But Dahl's conclusion about "the usual opinion" deserves a closer look. He writes:

> In any case, it must be said to be now the general opinion that our grand writer did make atonement for his sins—if it was at all a sin

in Hamsun's case that he stuck to what the court called "his own special opinion about the political questions" in a world that by 1940 had become for him both too foreign and too complicated.[18]

Any consideration that ignores Hamsun's actions in clear support of Nazi Germany's occupation of Norway, as Dahl's essay does, can hardly be considered good scholarship. What is more, Hamsun would surely have been offended by the allegation that he was somehow not up to dealing with the affairs of a world "too foreign and too complicated." On the contrary, he was an alert old man who was, in spite of his medical problems, keenly interested in world events.

My own research, which stresses the importance of interdisciplinary insights gleaned from such fields as history, women's studies, anthropology, and race research, has focused on Hamsun's conservative principles, especially when it comes to his representation of women. My conclusions differ substantially from Rottem's. Far from being merely "banal," Hamsun's support for the Nazis is an embodiment of, and integral to, his long-held conservative worldview. I would counter Rottem's exculpatory comments by pointing out the unfortunate fact that it was often ordinary, "banal" bystanders who enabled the Nazi regime to function as efficiently and for as long as it did. Furthermore, my response to Dahl is that Hamsun was not just an innocent cultural commentator; he was a Nobel Prize–winning author whom the Nazis eagerly exploited in their propaganda. Rather than pass over or dismiss the context in which Hamsun worked, my investigation situates the established view of Hamsun's articles and novels within a broader cultural framework. It takes into account West European imperialist expansion to other continents. If such an approach seems far-fetched, let me point out that Hamsun lived during the last decades of European expansion and consolidation of colonial rule. "The colonial project," in Susanne Zantop's words, "from its very inception in the imaginary, encompassed both the foreign and the domestic sphere."[19] Nazi Germany's takeover of other territories, which Hamsun supported, can be viewed as a delayed imperialist thrust into non-German areas and non-Germanic cultures.

My inspiration originally came from Edward Said's monumental rethinking of the colonial project and its consequences, as well as his development of the postcolonial discourse in *Orientalism* (1978) and *Culture and Imperialism* (1994). Said's approach is particularly relevant to my investigation of Hamsun as novelist and cultural critic because of his insistence on the complicity between literature and imperialism. As he puts it, "cultural forms like the novel . . . were immensely important in the formation of imperial attitudes, references, and experiences."[20] Exposing the powerful connection between culture and politics, he argues against reducing colonialism to economic exploitation or political domination and for a closer investigation of how culture molds imperial discourse. At the same time, while postcolonial discourse has been extremely enlightening as an umbrella approach, I felt that it had to be grounded more narrowly in the historical specificities and political nuances of Norway in particular and Scandinavia in general, and in their relations to other parts of the world. As Anne McClintock has observed in her book *Imperial Leather,* Said left the issue of gender undertheorized and often viewed sexuality as a metaphor for more general power relations. McClintock argues persuasively that gendered dynamics need to be examined more closely as an integral part of imperial enterprise rather than as a theoretical add-on. She writes: "Imperialism cannot be fully understood without a theory of gender power."[21] For my own investigation, this required being informed by parallel approaches grounded in a variety of gender studies subfields. I found it imperative to look at the historical circumstances of women's lives, on the one hand, and, on the other, to examine the imaginary that shaped female protagonists in texts. I concur with McClintock's claim that "gender is not synonymous with women" and that there needs to be an acknowledgment that "gender is as much an issue of masculinity as it is of femininity."[22] Throughout my study, I have endeavored to strike a balance between insistence on women's visibility and agency—often a blind spot in Hamsun scholarship—and the conviction that gender configuration at the turn of the century impacted both men and women in fundamental ways. In addition to the work of several Nordic critics, studies by Elaine Showalter and Rita Felski have been influential in my research.[23] Finally, feminism is, as so aptly articulated by McClintock, "as much about class, race, work, and money as it is about sex."[24] Gender issues were an important part of the cultural and political realignment in the interwar period in Norway, and they became even more relevant as an element of Nazi policies after 1933.

Like many of his contemporaries, Hamsun observed the momentous changes modern development brought to Scandinavia (and particularly Norway) with a skepticism tinged with fear. While embracing such technological innovations as automobiles, his is a reactionary worldview within modernity, one that rejects emerging forms of industrialization, metropolitan growth, materialism, socialism, and women's suffrage. For Hamsun, there was nothing more lamentable than an urban wageworker uprooted from the land or a childless woman in search of an education. Yet Hamsun the modernist writer, deeply aware of modernity's newly created sense of homelessness, invented a series of de-centered and complex modern protagonists who perfectly echo their rapidly changing environment. My study acknowledges the tension between Hamsun's condemnation of modernity's too rapid progress and his role as a pioneer of modernist style. It charts the transformation of the writing process, the dissolution of the writing subject, and the absence of a coherent spiritual force. I want to position Hamsun's texts at the intersection of modernity (economic and social development) and modernism (the artistic and literary response to change), much the same way that Marshall Berman charts the experience of modernity in his 1982 book *All That Is Solid Melts into Air*. Berman, who borrowed the title from the 1848 *Communist Manifesto*, writes: "To be modern, I said, is to experience personal and social life as a maelstrom, to find one's world and oneself in perpetual disintegration and renewal, trouble and anguish, ambiguity and contradiction: to be part of a universe in which all that is solid melts into air. To be a modern*ist* [italics in original] is to make oneself somehow at home in the maelstrom, to make its rhythms one's own, to move within its currents in search of the forms of reality, of beauty, of freedom, of justice, that its fervid and perilous flow allows."[25] Hamsun's project was indeed to express the anxiety of the maelstrom and to attempt to create a sense of home, a sense of stability.

Standard approaches to modernity have, until recently, been blind to issues of race and gender, especially in Scandinavia.[26] But as Zantop writes in her study of pre-colonial Germany, it was "in the late 1700s . . . that 'race' became defined as a series of immutable physical properties, accompanied by equally immutable intellectual and moral characteristics, and that 'gender' was constituted as a naturally hierarchical difference between the sexes. This construction of a race-gender model occurred within a decidedly 'colonial' context."[27] I focus on a less frequently investigated aspect of modernity, namely, the increased contact among different peoples resulting from an increase in their mobility. As a seafaring nation with a long western coastline, Norway has always had a fair amount of contact with other peoples, which resulted in rich images of Others in Norwegian folklore and texts. This contact intensified during the second half of the nineteenth century. Increased knowledge and speculation about other peoples resulted in numerous scientific and ethnographic studies, museum displays, and a great variety of travelogues and fiction writing. Increased mobility created new hybrid identities and challenged or reinforced older identities. An examination of the tropes concerning various kinds of Others illuminates modernity in a new light. Neil Kent's book, *The Soul of the North*, for instance, reminds us of the Scandinavians' complicated relationship with other peoples.[28] Modernity exerted influence on traditional family bonds, offered women greater opportunities for paid employment, and led women to demand more rights and greater visibility. As two elements that influenced Hamsun's perception of the world, as well as his own self-perception, race and gender offer us new and surprising insights into Hamsun's writings and actions. As Patricia Szobar has convincingly argued in her essay "Telling Sexual Stories in the Nazi Courts of Law: Race Defilement in Germany, 1933 to 1945," the successful enforcement of various laws regarding race and sex during the short lifetime of the Third Reich must have rested upon "older, existing patterns of explanation and control, most prominently, the sexual monitoring of women and of racial 'others.'"[29] My book investigates some of these older patterns of control as applied to women and racial Others as Hamsun perceived and understood them.

As early as 1890, in his literary manifesto "Fra det ubevidste Sjæleliv" (From the unconscious life of the soul), Hamsun stressed instinctual writing, what has become known conventionally as the "whisper of the blood, the pleading of the bone."[30] Opposing the predominantly realistic fiction of the 1870s and 1880s, Hamsun boldly posited a subjective, instinctual style of writing that would track minute shifts in the landscape of the mind instead of charting social evils or political causes. This focus on interior processes made him initially indifferent and later hostile to modern industrial development, which he viewed as, at best, a necessary evil and, at worst, the root cause of all misfortune.

My primary goal in the present study—and what I hope to contribute to our understanding of Hamsun—is to demonstrate the interconnectedness of his extraordinary writerly imagination and his political and cultural opinions, especially as examined through the bifocal lens of race and gender. I do not intend to probe in detail the complex intricacies of his novels, much as I admire them. Many fine analyses of Hamsun's novels exist. What interests me is unearthing Hamsun's views on race and gender—views often well disguised in his canonical work but revealed clearly in his correspondence, articles, and plays. Hamsun lived and developed as a writer at a time when emergent modern trends engaged society in a major reexamination and reevaluation of both race and gender. In that, my approach echoes that of McClintock who writes: "This, then, is a central theme of this book: as domestic space became racialized, colonial space became domesticated."³¹ Whereas Hamsun's personal experiences and values resonated with the popular and scientific thinking about race, they diverged from modernity's view of the expanding role for women.

While Hamsun's ideas about race and women are often intertwined, his concerns are manifestations of a white man's fear of being displaced by the developments of modernity. A close reading of his texts reveals how he establishes a dichotomy between the traditional white patriarch, in one positively marked category, and all others, who are lumped together in an opposing category. My research centers on the way Hamsun, a white male artist, viewed and portrayed people different from himself, people who were, in one way or another, exotic: Africans, Orientals, American Indians, Sami and, not least, women.³² The divide between the patriarchal white man on the one hand and women and exotic groups on the other runs deep and constant through Hamsun's life and work. It is this divide, I believe, that eventually led him to support Norway's inclusion in the Third Reich, which he saw as a fortress of Germanic tradition against the encroachment of modern ideas and foreign peoples. It needs to be stressed that the complexity of Hamsun's protagonists in many of his texts richly complicates this dichotomy.

It is often argued that both racism and misogyny were such prevalent attitudes in Europe and the United States toward the end of the nineteenth century and into the early twentieth century that there seems little point in investigating these issues, and that such an exercise would, moreover, be quite reductive. Hamsun, however, was hardly conventional in his overall views; indeed, he took special delight in challenging the establishment, be it literary, religious, or moral. Since he had himself been a struggling artist, at least for a time, one might have reason to expect him to be rather sympathetic to marginalized groups. We need, then, to ask the logical questions: Why did he not question racial stereotypes and sexual norms? Why did he not align himself with progressive movements for the cultural and political rights of women and minorities? Although Hamsun usually loved to provoke the so-called silent majority, on these two issues he sided with it. Why was this so? A closer look at Hamsun's texts sheds light on his often complex but fundamentally socially conservative positions.

The chapters of this book dealing with race seek to situate Hamsun and his texts within a racialized discourse that extends from the last decades of the nineteenth century through the early decades of the twentieth, that is, the period during which Hamsun first became an established and then acclaimed writer. The most radical forms of this racialized discourse eventually deteriorated into Nazi expansionism and the politics of extermination. The critical issue here, of course, is to distinguish appropriately and fairly between the commonplace views (and stereotypes) of race that Hamsun shared with many other educated as well as uneducated people and our own—hopefully more enlightened—views based on respect for universal human rights and the rejection of racial discrimination. We must recognize that the development of racial tolerance has occurred primarily during the second half of the twentieth century and was not especially widespread in Hamsun's time. It is also important to acknowledge some of the ideological distinctions between Hamsun and those of his contemporaries who, while sharing his Eurocentric views, chose not to support the Nazi ideology of the pure Aryan race.

In addition, Hamsun's enthusiastic support of Norway's political independence in 1905 was bound up with his sense of national identity and the modern notion of race, which was based on the scientific conception of biological heredity. This notion was, as Kwame Anthony Appiah wrote, "interwoven with a new understanding of a people as a nation and of the role of culture—and crucially for our purposes, of literature—in the life of nations."[33]

Given the centrality, within the scientific and semi-scientific debates of the period, of such issues as degeneration, demographics, fertility and, by implication, interracial relationships, a chapter on women's roles and experience in modernity became pivotal. Hamsun was enormously troubled by feminist demands on behalf of women: demands for better education, access to politics, economic power, control over their own bodies, and recognition as artists. A significant portion of this book, then, investigates and documents Hamsun's belief that a woman's primary duty is motherhood—a belief reflected in his fiction through positive portrayals of women as mothers—as well as his opposition to women's education and their involvement in political or artistic activities. A similarly traditional portrayal of women was a cornerstone of Nazi propaganda. Hamsun fears both exotic peoples and women, and he fears especially sexual contacts between nonwhite men and white women as a source of degeneracy. He perceives liberal democracy as enabling both women and minorities to assert rights they had never previously enjoyed.

It is not possible to discuss in a single volume the whole of Hamsun's huge corpus. Instead, I focus on a specific selection of his texts—articles, essays, plays, novels, poems, and book reviews—that include Others in one way or another. I attempt to show that there are, to a certain extent at least, a number of constants that underlie his work and relate to significant issues in his personal life. In addition to several of his exotic protagonists, I examine closely a limited number of his female protagonists, taken from all of the main periods in his writing, showing how Hamsun presents them as out of control and in need of taming.

Since Hamsun's nonfiction often expresses his racist and misogynist views quite clearly, the chapters open with discussions of selected passages from Hamsun's polemical writings and from his voluminous correspondence. These are followed by an examination of the novels, paying special attention to his narrative strategies. His depiction of exotic races is explored as a double metaphor: signifying, on the one hand, repulsive and animalistic dangers but, on the other, fertile inspiration and invigorating difference. In his fiction, images of darkness, exoticism, and eroticism are especially complex and challenging, but our understanding of these will be supplemented by a consideration of Hamsun's relevant opinions as articulated in his articles and essays. In his resentment of progress, Hamsun searched nostalgically for uncontaminated regions and peoples. The primitivism he promoted was an antidote to modernity's materialism and spiritual alienation, but he could promote this remedy only half-heartedly, since he remained divided between the claims of nature and culture.

With his portrayal of primitive cultures, Hamsun achieved two goals. First, he satisfied his desire to find an artistic means of criticizing the contemporary state of affairs, and second, he established the difference between primitive peoples, malodorous and filthy, and himself, a representative of the civilized. This served as a way of strengthening his own identity, which he felt to be threatened by modernity's permanent flux. The paradox is succinctly described by Fred R. Myers in an essay on primitivism and modernism. Noting that "the contribution of the primitivism debates to theorizing modernity has been the recognition of the role of the Primitive (external or internal) in constituting the modern,"[34] Myers goes on to comment on the trope of the Primitive and its relation to fragmented contemporary life. He writes:

> The Primitive Other—as evidence of the existence of forms of humanity that are integral and cohesive, that work as a totality—functions not merely as the critical opposite to such an experienced world. Such a figure and its represented reality also permit the very characterization of the 'modern' as fragmented, and a sense of contemporary mass culture as "spurious" and somehow "inauthentic."[35]

One of Myers's aims is to investigate whether "the figures of the Primitive and their deployments can illuminate the larger movement of 'anti-modernism'—the recoil from an 'over-civilized' modern experience to more intense forms of physical or spiritual experience."[36] The primitive man, as well as the white man "gone native" (as, for instance, Gauguin in Tahiti), lives in a state of regenerating communion with animals and, indeed, with Nature itself. Thus, the Primitive has provided a starting point for investigating Western categories through the attempt to define difference, yet this has been done, Myers writes, "within the ideological function of Western cultural systems."[37] More important, the primitive or primitive societies become a place, as Marianna Torgovnick writes, "to project feelings about the present and to draw blueprints of the future."[38]

Additionally, Myers reminds us that postmodernist criticism demonstrates how modernism's definitions of form and content, and by extension, modernist canons, were established at least in part as exclusionary and defensive strategies in response to low art's encroachment upon high art. In my view, Hamsun critics and scholars have adopted precisely such a defensive position and, consequently, have created a much too narrow canon. The established Hamsun canon consists only of novels. It starts with the acclaimed modernist novel *Hunger* (1890), proceeds through *Mysterier* (Mysteries; 1892) and *Pan* (1894), then embraces the regressive-utopian *Markens grøde* (Growth of the soil; 1917), and culminates with his vast epic novels of the twenties and thirties, that is, the so-called August Trilogy and such works as *Konerne ved vandposten* (The women at the pump; 1920). These canonical Hamsun novels, which are set in quintessentially Norwegian locations, do indeed provide excellent illustrations of various aspects of modernity, for instance, modern alienation and the dissolution of the self. But if we broaden the canon to include Hamsun's travel writing, selected plays, and relevant articles, our view of his world becomes much more diverse, inhabited by a greater number of nontraditional characters and displaying features borrowed from popular dime novels, serialized novels, and so forth.

In the process of rethinking the Hamsun canon, folklore research came to my aid. Kathleen Stokker's book *Folklore Fights the Nazis: Humor in Occupied Norway, 1940–1945*, which looks at the jokes, puns, and cartoons about Nazis and native collaborators circulating in Norway during the occupation, includes many jokes about Hamsun, who was the most visible and most famous Norwegian supporter of the Germans.[39] In the section of the book "Jokes about the Food Shortages," Stokker describes jokes about

Hamsun as "among the most popular witticisms of 1941."[40] His outspoken support of the National Socialist cause in numerous articles and speeches naturally caused him to be embraced by the occupiers, who responded by issuing reprints of several of his novels. A popular joke, which circulated widely in several variants and was printed in underground newspapers, reflected this fact. Here is the version printed by *Hjemmefronten* on August 9, 1941, and quoted by Stokker:

> The Germans have decided to divide Hamsun's works between themselves and the Norwegians. The Germans will get *The Growth of the Soil* and *Victoria*, while Norwegians will keep *Hunger*.[41]

The main point of the joke illuminates a bitter everyday reality, namely, that a large portion of Norway's economic output, in particular its food production, was diverted to Germany. As a result of German economic policies, the Norwegian population had to endure all kinds of shortages, especially in winter clothing and food. As a mountainous country with only 3 percent of its land arable, Norway has always had difficulty providing enough food for its people. With many food staples going to Germany or to German troops, and despite Germany's reciprocal supplies of various goods to Norway, popular sentiment against the Germans escalated throughout the occupation.

The jokes spurred my interest as to why there was such a wide discrepancy between the general public's straightforward response to Hamsun's collaboration and academics' willingness to look the other way. True, Norwegian writers who had agreed not to publish during the occupation had many bitter complaints about Hamsun. But soon after 1945, a rehabilitation of sorts of the famous author emerged on two fronts. The first was a direct denial or whitewashing of Hamsun's actions during the war (as, for instance, in the writings of Sten Sparre Nilson), while the second was the decision on the part of literary critics to focus exclusively on Hamsun as a writer, on narrative issues, psychoanalytical analysis, and so forth, when discussing Hamsun's works (examples include Sigurd Hoel, one of the first writers to initiate a discussion of Hamsun after the war, and, more recently, Atle Kittang). Was it that the intellectual elite wanted, at all costs, to make sure that Norway's Nobel laureate remained just as famous, and as pure, as he had been before the war? Or was it that, indeed, the complexity of issues and the narrative form in Hamsun's works lend themselves solely to academic interpretation? In my view, such an attitude constitutes a gross underestimation of the broader public and its reading of Hamsun.

Still, to try to come to terms with Hamsun's collaboration and to appreciate his genius as a writer is not an easy matter. Even more difficult is to find one definitive reason for his collaboration, because there is no one narrow answer. His motives were drawn from somewhere between his often simplified and hastily formed political convictions and his writerly ambitions, his distaste for Great Britain and his affection for Germany, his aversion to America and his admiration of primitive regions, his patriotism and traditionalism, and his fear of modernity in general and Bolshevism in particular. These were all molded by the idiosyncrasies of his unique mind. However, what we can do is to take a fresh look at the cultural baggage, never far from his political decisions, that he possessed as a white European writer who lived and wrote during one of the most intense periods of expansion in terms of both geographic migration and scientific invention.

I WILL CONCLUDE THIS INTRODUCTION WITH SOME THOUGHTS ABOUT HOW I see my own work within the general discussion about Knut Hamsun. First, as I have suggested, my research is a step toward a broadened definition of the Hamsun canon. When defined narrowly as a set of novels, Hamsun's canon lends itself easily to a number of critical approaches; for example, the investigation of narrative similarities, the comparison of various male protagonists, the mapping of the concept of modernism, etc. But such a formulation of the canon offers little when it comes to a deeper understanding of the relationship between Hamsun's art and his politics, which seems to me one of the crucial questions in Hamsun scholarship and one which I explore in depth in this study. In order to focus on Hamsun's portrayal of other racial and ethnic groups, I found it necessary to examine texts, such as his travel writings, that have usually fallen outside of the canon because they include many nonwhite protagonists.

What is more, a fuller understanding of the reasons behind Hamsun's collaboration with the German occupiers can provide material for fruitful comparisons based on our knowledge about collaborators elsewhere in Europe, a continent where even today divisions between those who fought the Nazis and those who supported them have not been erased. And, finally, the issue of collaboration remains an extremely important existential and moral question, highlighting the kinds of crucial decisions any one of us might be compelled to make under adverse circumstances or during times of war. Additional questions present themselves: Why would Hamsun, a proud patriot, ignore the recommendations of his own government to resist the German occupiers? Why did he not change his stance after the Germans started executing Resistance fighters and imprisoning their families? Why did he completely disregard the opinions and feelings of the majority of Norwegians? How could he refrain from asking whether or why he, the great artist, could be so at odds with his neighbors? — or wondering whether he could actually be wrong? He neither probed any of these questions nor regretted any of his actions. While I cannot with certainty claim how I would act during a five-year long occupation of my country, I am certain of one thing: had I been honored with the Nobel Prize for Literature, I would never have given my Nobel medal as a personal gift to Joseph Goebbels, the man serving as Hitler's Propaganda and Enlightenment Minister. Hamsun did this.[42] The symbolic value of this one gesture on Hamsun's part, in which literature is subsumed into politics, is simply overhelming and must have felt like a monumental betrayal to his countrymen. It can only be understood as a gesture of deep admiration and shared values. Goebbels' response to Hamsun, dated June 23, 1943, supports such an interpretation. Goebbels deemed it an expression of Hamsun's commitment to Germany's fight for a new Europe. Unfortunately for those of us who love literature, not only was Hamsun a great writer, he was also an enthusiastic supporter of the Third Reich.

1
DISCOURSES OF RACE AND
PRIMITIVISM IN SCANDINAVIA

But Greenland is Norwegian land, from times immemorial a Norwegian crown
colony, where Norwegians have colonized and later had their bounty as hunters. The island was plundered from us by Denmark in 1814 with the Kiel Agreement and it has since been impossible to wrench it from Denmark.
　　　　　　　　　—Knut Hamsun to Reichkomissar Josef Terboven, June 8, 1940

Well, but the Eskimos are not civilized people. They are animals in the woods,
animals on the ocean beaches. If they lived as civilized people on Greenland,
they would die.
　　　　　　　　　—Knut Hamsun, "August Strindberg," 1889

BEGINNING IN THE LATE EIGHTEENTH CENTURY AND INCREASINGLY OVER THE
course of the nineteenth century, a great deal of scientific research in Europe
focused obsessively on race and biological degeneration. The topic of degeneration had by the middle of the century become a central concern not only
in race biology but also in medical pathology, psychiatry, and criminology,
as Nancy Stepan writes in her article "Biological Degeneration: Races and
Proper Places."[1] Citing Charles Rosenberg, Stepan stresses that "the idea
that social context, not empirical research or internal logic, determined the

contours of hereditarian thought can well be applied to the entire story of biological, racial degenerationism."[2] While the amount of material available on the topic of race research during this era is vast, the insights made by many contemporary theorists reveal the sort of worldview shared by Hamsun and other writers in Scandinavia.[3] As is clear in the epigraphs to this chapter, Hamsun, very much in line with prevailing attitudes on race, made a clear distinction between the Inuit (Eskimos), whom he characterized as animals, and "civilized people." At the same time, he expressed an awareness of the need for adapting to a particular environment. His understanding of survival in the extreme North may be best understood in light of the debates about the survival of the fittest in various global environments both in the scientific literature of the time and in the popular press. Furthermore, he had no appreciation of what we would today call the indigenous territorial rights of the Inuit. The only concern Hamsun had in the 1940s was which European state was going to control Greenland; the Inuit are not even in the picture.

Stepan's essay shows how race biology appropriated the language and methodology of racist discourse in order to justify slavery, colonization, and the marginalization of people of African descent. She also discusses how nineteenth-century scientists theorized about the relationship of people to climate and geography in ways that sought to explain why people of different races thrived in particular regions and why, consequently, the races should not mix. The temperate, civilized world of Europe was, for instance, deemed to be the proper place for the white race. If whites moved away from Europe, the race would start to degenerate biologically and become "tropicalized." While the inability of whites to survive new diseases bolstered the biologists' claims, European colonization remained justified as long as the white colonists maintained close ties with their homelands and as long as new whites continued to move to "tropical" zones. As Stepan summarizes the theories of the time, the removal of Africans from their "proper" place, namely, the tropics, had led to the degeneration of the race, which now manifested itself in disease and depravity among Africans outside of Africa. She details how "the thesis of primordial racial distinctions and noncosmopolitanism provided support for the theory that blacks were fundamentally 'out of place' in the Americas and were doomed to degenerate as they moved northward into white, temperate territory, and as they moved socially and politically into freedom. . . . It helped perpetuate the status quo at a time when emancipation threatened to change it."[4] The stereotype which held that emancipated blacks were the most degenerate of all of their race and were, indeed, beyond redemption, was now given a scientific rationale. When Hamsun, in his book *Fra det moderne Amerikas aandsliv* (From the cultural life of modern America), writes in condescending terms about emancipated black slaves, his attitude is in line with that of many progressives of the time.[5]

Eugenics emerged as a logical extension of the research on, and the preoccupation with, the issue of racial degeneration. A strong element behind the development of eugenics was the increasing knowledge of the laws of human heredity. The term "eugenics," from the Greek word *eugenes* (wellborn) was, in fact, coined by the British scientist Francis Galton in 1883 to describe social actions and policies that attempted to apply the new scientific understanding of human heredity to the goal of improving a population's hereditary composition. In light of today's generally negative outlook on eugenics, a view strongly colored by the horrific acts of the Nazis, it is interesting to observe how the ideas of eugenics were widely applied to social planning in Europe between roughly 1880 and 1950. Eugenics programs were promoted by well-respected doctors, scientists, and social workers of all political persuasions. Laws and social ordinances based on eugenic principles were seen as integral to public health policies. In Norway, for instance, one of the most vocal advocates of the idea of shaping human abilities through eugenic methods was Karl Evang, a medical doctor and socialist who served as the director of Norway's public health service from 1938 to 1940 and again from 1945 to 1972. In that capacity, Evang was a leading advocate of a centrally planned state-run welfare system. The influence of eugenic theory, in other words, preceded its monstrous application by the Nazis in the Holocaust. The appeal of this theory can tell us much about the cultural ideas of past generations.

Radical racist eugenics, moreover, may be viewed as modernity's attempt not only to come to terms with a visually and culturally radical otherness but also to discredit it. Increased knowledge of and contact among different peoples—through travel, colonial expansion, ethnographic studies, and museum displays—either challenged established beliefs in stable identities or had the backlash effect of strengthening same. Soon, the fundamental concern in this debate became, to paraphrase Nancy Stepan, the determination of "the proper place" of each of the world's peoples on the racial black-and-white scale. The discourse of race became a powerful tool for framing historical changes, present events, and future predictions. When we examine the eugenic practices of the past, it is useful to keep in mind the distinction between "mainline" ("old style") eugenics and "reform" ("new style") eugenics.[6] While both were originally linked to progressive social practices, mainline eugenics, before "the advent of classical genetics," first emerged from the field of anthropology and its reflections on the differences between—and perceived deficiencies of—various races.[7] Reform eugenics, on the other hand, which developed around 1930, was based on new advances in classical genetics. Practiced mainly by socialist or left-leaning health officials, this new approach to eugenics discredited much of the earlier research. The racial boundaries supported by ideas from eugenics were especially relevant to European societies fearful of colonial rebellion and racial degeneration. It is useful to see race research as part and parcel of a larger discussion on enlightenment and human evolution, especially in light of Darwin's monumental *On the Origin of Species* (1859). This larger framework, however, is beyond the scope of the present study.

In Norway, as in the rest of Europe, race issues were researched and debated in both popular and academic circles.[8] Jon Alfred Mjøen (1860–1939) was an early popularizer of eugenic principles and an acquaintance of Knut Hamsun. In 1905, the year Norway became an independent state, Mjøen founded an international eugenics organization, the Vindern Biological Laboratory, together with Alfred Ploetz, a physician from Dresden, and Leonard Darwin, who in addition to being Charles Darwin's son was also a major in the British army and chairman of the British Eugenics Society between 1911 and 1928. Mjøen's laboratory operated from 1905 to 1939. Mjøen was the author of the controversial book *Racehygiene* (1914), as well as numerous other writings, in which he expressed the fears of many Norwegians that, thanks to increased mobility, the best Norwegians were emigrating overseas while inferior races were migrating to Norway, resulting in an unfortunate mingling of races.[9] In 1908, Mjøen proposed the biological registration of foreigners, which, as he expressed it succinctly years later, was a way of "making it easier for us to prevent undesirable elements, especially strange races, from entering our Scandinavian countries."[10] He also advocated the prohibition of immigration and the institution of programs designed to increase the number of children born to the healthiest Norwegian farmers—suggestions that echoed the popular sentiments of the time. Mjøen later suggested compulsory segregation and voluntary sterilization for certain groups. As historian Nils Roll-Hansen explains: "There was at this time [the 1910s] a strong tendency to explain social phenomena in biological terms. This was not peculiar to the scientific community but part of a generally held worldview."[11] One of Mjøen's particular interests was research into the heredity of musical talent in families, talent that Hamsun explores, at roughly the same time, in his Segelfoss novels.

Mjøen was not alone in his fears. In 1934, the Norwegian Parliament, citing the degeneration of healthy Norwegian stock, passed—with only one dissenting vote—a sterilization law that promoted the voluntary, if coercive, sterilization of the mentally ill, those with serious hereditary diseases, and criminals. The goal was to improve the country's gene pool and reduce sex crime. Nils Roll-Hansen describes the 1934 sterilization law as a "consensus law" representing "the least common denominator of public opinion," implying that eugenic measures were supported evenly across the political spectrum.[12] Mjøen's political position—he was a member of the progressive Liberal Party, which formed the government from 1913 to 1920—should remind us that eugenics was not the sole property of conservative or far-right politicians. Indeed, it constituted an integral element in government planning and scientific research.

"Racehygiene," or "samfunnshygiene," as eugenics was called in Norway, was central to emerging attitudes inspired by ideas from continental Europe, mainly Germany, as well as from the United States. The premises of eugenics fit well into the Norwegian rational worldview in the early twentieth century: this was a time, especially in the interwar period, marked by intense debate and activity among "economists, eugenicists, and engineer-architects [who formed] an ideological avant-garde," as Rune Slagstad describes in his book *De nasjonale strateger* (The national strategists).[13] The so-called Neue Sachlichkeit (New Objectivity) cultural movement swore by progressive, positivistic ideas and rational planning and was hostile to metaphysics. Knut Hamsun fundamentally positioned himself against such currents, deeming them mechanical and dry.

"Positive eugenics," as it was termed, aspired to create better hygienic, sexual, and social behavior, while "negative" eugenics focused mainly on two goals: the segregation of men and women who should not procreate and the sterilization of those with unwanted medical or social traits. Norway's 1934 sterilization law had been preceded by Denmark's in 1929, while Sweden and Finland passed similar laws a year after Norway, with Iceland following suit in 1938. In Germany, Hitler's government passed its sterilization law in 1933 and embarked on its implementation almost immediately.[14] Although not anti-Semitic per se, it became so after the Nürnberg laws of 1935.

In Norway, the other leading supporter of the sterilization law, besides Mjøen, was Johan Scharffenberg, a psychiatry professor and the head doctor at Botsfengelset, a prison in Oslo. While his 1932 book *Hovedpunkter i Arvelæren* (Main points in the principles of heredity) did not declare any particular race superior to others and used the term *slektshygiene* (family hygiene) instead of *racehygiene*, Scharffenberg's scientific approach neverthe-less emphasized the quality of hereditary material and expressed optimism regarding the success of eugenics-inspired social reforms.[15] Scharffenberg believed that research findings on the scientific principles of heredity in ani-mals and plants should be applied to people. He proposed laws for limiting procreation in individuals with hereditary diseases and advocated the incar-ceration and compulsory sterilization of the insane and the feebleminded. A marriage, he emphasized, should be viewed as a union of two families and not just of two individuals. Today, Scharffenberg is perhaps best known for his tireless campaign in favor of the sterilization law, as well as for a series of newspaper articles published in 1933, in which he proclaimed Hitler a psy-chopath. He was critical of the German sterilization law because it permit-ted sterilization only on eugenic or medical grounds to the exclusion of any social rationale. Scharffenberg's nuanced positions regarding various facets of hereditary research illustrate well the complexities and contradictions of wider debates about biology, society, and public policy.

Ragnar Vogt (1870–1943) was another vocal Norwegian proponent of eugenics. Vogt, who today is known primarily as the founder of modern psy-chiatry in Norway, was critical of many popular prejudices concerning biolog-ical heredity; nevertheless, he held both racist and sexist views. For example, he "took it for granted that blacks were biologically inferior to whites, in par-ticular to Nordics, and that women were made for the tasks of the home and procreation," as Roll-Hansen points out.[16] Another academic, Carl Schiøtz, who was a professor of hygiene (today we might say public health) from 1931 until his death in 1938, contributed to the eugenics debate with his book *Lærebok i hygiene* (Teaching manual in hygiene), which explored the influ-ence of aspects of the social environment (such as class, nutrition, education, and health care) on children's health and the national gene pool.[17] One of his favorite expressions, "the plus variants" (*plusvariantene*), referred to individ-uals or families who had extraordinary talents. He later became very involved in developing ways to encourage the "plus variants" to have more children.

It was Otto Lous Mohr, appointed professor of anatomy at the Univer-sity of Kristiania in 1919, who led the professional opposition to the kind of mainstream popular eugenics advocated by Mjøen.[18] As early as 1915, Mohr had attacked Mjøen's *Racehygiene* as dilettantish and unscientific; he also attacked Mjøen for exaggerating the projected eugenic results of his proposed policies.[19] In Mohr's own book, *Arvelærens grundtrek* (The fun-damentals of heredity), he expressed doubt about the widely believed "fact" that the European race was degenerating. "We have no scientific proof that this is the case," he wrote.[20] He restated this position in his influential article "Menneskeavlen under kultur" (Human reproduction in culture), although here the focus was more on the issues of overpopulation and immigration in Europe.[21] Mohr was of the opinion that for contemporary people, as creatures of culture, it would be most rational to limit the number of births so as to avoid overpopulation. He argued on behalf of women and children, noting the detrimental health effects suffered by women who bear multiple children. Interestingly, Mohr here challenged the alarmist view, expressed in some circles in Norway and elsewhere in Europe, that a temporary demographic decrease would mean that some nations were headed toward extinction. Mohr's skepticism about degeneration contributed substantially to softening the final wording of the sterilization law.

Another vocal opponent of eugenics, as it was popularly interpreted, was the cytogeneticist Kristine Bonnevie. Not only was she the first female professor in Norway, in 1916 she was appointed by the Norwegian parliament to head the Institute of Genetics, founded the previous year at the University of Kristiania. Mjøen was excluded from consideration for this position because of the controversial nature of *Racehygiene*. In essence, however, the division between Mjøen and the scientific community regarding eugenics was one of degree. The establishment's rejection of Mjøen's book represented a rejection of the excesses of eugenics rather than of its basic premises.

The prominent women's rights activist Katti Anker Møller also contributed to the eugenics debate insofar as her efforts in educating women about sexually transmitted diseases, contraception, and abortion, were intended to improve the health and well being of women and children. Together with the politician Johan Castberg, she was instrumental in conceiving and drafting the so-called Castberg Law (1915), which gave children born outside of marriage the right to their father's surname, the right to economic support from their father, and the right to an inheritance equal to that of the father's other children. Her daughter Tove, a medical doctor who in 1914 married Otto Louis Mohr, continued her work on behalf of women and children.

In his advocacy of eugenics as a tool for public health, Karl Evang was primarily inspired by the public health policies of the Soviet Union and served as the president of Norway's Union of Socialist Doctors. Evang was instrumental in incorporating public hygiene issues into the Labor party platform both before and after World War II. In the introduction to his book *Rasepolitik og reaksjon*, Evang pointed out a certain discrepancy between eugenics efforts and capitalism: "Eugenicists demand large flocks of children. The capitalist system allows very little space for children."[22] He further discussed the exploitation of colonized peoples and stressed that colonial expansion was predicated on social Darwinism, especially on the conviction that the ruling classes (and certain nations) were biologically superior, thus warning of the connection between reactionary political forces and notions of race-based eugenics.[23]

Tirelessly defending his conviction that no race was pure, Evang, like Mohr, disputed the idea that degeneration was actually taking place in Europe. He writes: "The claim that the quality of population in general is constantly declining, that it is 'degenerating' in modern society, is held by practically every modern eugenicist and constitutes the central point in their entire thinking. . . . But they are unable to present any proof for this claim."[24] Evang warns against blurring the boundaries separating biological research, philosophy, and politics and is extremely critical of the Nazi takeover in Germany.[25]

It is interesting to note that Evang warned of two possible intertwined consequences of radical eugenicist politics, namely the systematic suppression of women's rights and the strengthening of the patriarchal family as the core social unit. Certainly, if women must conform to gender-role expectations and live under constant pressure from their environment to be good mothers and supporting wives, their own desires and talents will, and almost certainly did, come last. Children, family, husband, and the welfare of the state were the declared or implied goals foisted upon women, and in such an environment women's often modest wishes and desires for public success and personal happiness were frowned upon, resisted, or ridiculed, and very rarely supported. The newly emerging medical sciences might be fairly viewed as, more often than not, imposing additional restraints on women. While imparting knowledge about health in general and healthy procreation in particular, the medical profession educated women about their reproductive rights. Still, it incessantly emphasized the importance of motherhood for women, and, in the process, also warned against procreation with nontraditional, non-Norwegian partners.

Last but not least, I should mention one of the most important contributors to the race debates of the twentieth century in Norway, Andreas M. Hansen. In 1899, he published *Norsk folkepsykologi* (Norwegian folk psychology), wherein he attempted to analyze recent parliamentary election results using racial demographics. Influenced by the popularity of Darwinism, Hansen applied the contemporary scientific discourses of evolution and race to Norwegian circumstances, dividing people into round-skulls (in the western part of the country) and long-skulls (in the eastern part), claiming that the long-skulled inhabitants of eastern Norway were liberal and voted for left-to-moderate candidates, while round-skulled voters in the western parts of Norway chose conservatives. Hansen, although not a scientist, was a skilled writer who knew how to appropriate scientific research and popularize it according to his own interpretation. His writing was so compelling, in fact, that his views were taken seriously even by the scientific community. The long-skulled people with narrow faces, white skin, blue eyes, light hair, and tall and narrow body frames were described by Hansen as psychologically aggressive and ready to fight for their convictions. In addition to being courageous, independent, and respectful of women, their gaze was steady and full of energy. Hansen further believed that they were the offspring of never-defeated ancestors. Round-skulls, who were characterized as conservative, had a round face, a shorter and broader nose, darker skin, and dark hair. Hansen also "established" that the round-skulled, west-coast inhabitants were lazy and slow, suspicious, and believed in supernatural forces. One of the consequences of his influential book was that it reinforced and legitimized existing attitudes toward nonethnic Norwegians using quasi-scientific claims. In his later book, *Landnåm i Norge* (Settlement of Norway; 1904), Hansen extends his reflection on the two races to include the Sami (Lapps). According to Hansen, the Sami were descendents of the round-skulls rather than the indigenous people of the Scandinavian Peninsula, and thus they were relatively recent newcomers to the area. Since their status as an indigenous people was central to the negotiation of their rights with the Norwegian and Swedish governments, Hansen's claims were extremely detrimental to their cause. The book constituted one element in an extensive network of prejudice; in the two decades following the book's original publication, discrimination against the dark-haired, short-skulled 'conservatives'—often conflated with the Sami—escalated noticeably.[26]

Some of Hansen's ideas later found their way into one of the largest anthropological studies undertaken in Norway, the mapping of physical and racial traits of nearly twelve thousand military recruits in the 1920s. The project was directed by a team composed of the military doctor Halfdan Bryn, University of Oslo anatomy professor Kristian Emil Schreiner, and medical doctor and writer Alette Schreiner (Kristian Schreiner's wife). The results were published in 1929 in four large volumes. When establishing a methodological approach to the mapping of various traits, Bryn and the Schreiners often relied on the work of the German scientists Rudolf Martin and Eugen Fischer. Martin, for instance, had established a classification scheme for eye color variations, while Fischer had done similar work on hair color. As some of Hansen's ideas were closely connected to the concept of the Nordic Race, they proved attractive to the framers of German Nazi thought, who incorporated them as pillars of party ideology in the twenties and early thirties.

For all the profusion of different and sometimes conflicting views on eugenics in Norway in the early twentieth century, eugenics was popularly and scientifically accepted as a legitimate approach to improving the human race. The significant differences of opinion were over the selection of desirable characteristics and over which social engineering methods were acceptable to employ. Several participants in this debate (such as Dr. Karl Evang and Otto Lous Mohr) argued that objective scientific methods should be strictly observed and that race should not be a factor of any weight in eugenics. Jon Mjøen, on the other hand, championed more extreme criteria and methods, including such measures as segregating certain races, i.e., those considered inferior. Regardless of these differences, there was broad political and professional support for moderate approaches to eugenics. Moderate eugenicists distanced themselves from racist concepts, while at the same time denying the existence of socially important differences among races.[27]

It would be incorrect to claim that all racial stereotypes developed from the social changes effected by modernity. As even a cursory glance at history shows, Norwegians (and Scandinavians in general) have always viewed with suspicion people who looked or behaved differently from themselves, whether they were indigenous peoples, gypsies, foreigners, or pagans. The attitudes of ethnic Norwegians toward other ethnic groups who have resided in Norway for centuries, such as the Sami, Finns, and Jews, are in many ways—condescending and ignorant at best, and prejudicial and discriminatory at worst—similar to those that colored Scandinavians' perception of the original inhabitants of other continents.[28] Indeed, examples of such attitudes may be found as far back as the period of the Viking voyages and early settlements of Iceland and other territories.

Centuries of Meeting the Other

AS THE TWENTIETH CENTURY DREW NEAR, NORWAY WAS DEVELOPING INTO A modern state, with political independence on the horizon, and the concept of "Norwegianness" was very much in vogue. To judge by the alarmist rhetoric of some of the eugenicist warnings of the time about dangers to the purity of the white Nordic race, one might think that for the first time in their history, the homogenous peoples of Scandinavia were mingling with non-Nordic, usually darker skinned peoples, and in disturbing numbers. But nothing could be further from the truth. Scandinavians had, in fact, been in contact with other peoples for centuries, as research in Old Norse texts and folklore reveals. In her 1999 essay, "Race and Ethnicity in the Old Norse World," Jenny Jochens writes about early interactions, including intermarriage, between Norwegians and Celts (who often had darker hair and complexions, or were perceived to have) during the period of Icelandic settlement and beyond. Jochens researched the problems of self-perception, awareness of 'the other,' naming patterns, and cooperation among different ethnic groups, including marital and reproductive strategies. More specifically, she writes:

> It needs to be noted that in Norse texts a "black man" (*maðr svartr*) does not refer to an African but indicates an individual with a darker complexion than others. Nordic people distinguished between dark and black. On their travels Vikings had encountered Negroes whom they designated, not as *svartir menn*, but as *blámenn* (blue men). In other words, although *svartr* does not refer to race in the generally accepted modern sense, it nonetheless demonstrates an awareness of physical differences based on color.[29]

Using the *Landnámabók* (The book of settlements) and Icelandic family sagas as sources, Jochens establishes that physical diversity existed in the North as evidenced most clearly from the epithets "white" (*hvíti*) and "black" (*svartr*). Dark features and complexion could have native roots or could be the result of genetic mixing of ancient Norwegians and Celts. The accepted ideal of beauty was linked with light, while darkness was often associated with supernatural trolls and giants, and was often linked with the adjective "ugly." During the settlement of Iceland, the empty island "became a veritable melting pot, as blond Nordic colonists received heavy doses of settlers originating in the Celtic world." In addition, the Norse, who raided the British Isles, brought captured Celtic slaves to Iceland. Many of these Celtic slaves, or freedmen, ended up with the personal name of "Svartr," referring to their Celtic origin and lower-class status. More important, "since the Norse brought only few women from Norway," Jochens emphasizes, "female slaves from the Celtic world were valued both for the physical labor and their sexual services."[30] This early intermingling between Norse and Celt contributed to the first generation of Icelanders. Still, Jochens notes that the sagas often record a general aversion to dark looks, as well as "discomfort perhaps tinged with an element of fear."[31] In her discussion of personal names in Icelandic family sagas and of two protagonists from *Njal's Saga*—a worker named Svartr and a manager named Kolr—Jochens argues that "medieval Icelanders still linked dark features with lower-class people and violent acts."[32] Over time, however, and especially with the establishment of patronymics, both Svartr and Ljótr declined and are almost nonexistent in today's Iceland.[33]

Jochens's research led her to conclude that "dark features were considered less objectionable in Celtic women," presumably because women in general did not inspire fear in the way that men did and because there was a general shortage of fertile women on Viking expeditions.[34] In another essay, however, Jochens comes to a slightly different conclusion. In "Vikings Westward to Vínland," in which she focuses on reasons for the failure of the Vikings' North American settlement, she concludes that because Norse men were unaccustomed to interacting with different-looking people, especially the Indians, they would have refrained from sexual encounters with them.[35] The Norse bias against the dark features of the *skrælingjar*—a term of disparagement that suggests people who are "wizened and dried up"—coupled with the shortage of Norsewomen in the New World, proved stronger than the Norsemen's sexual frustration and the reproductive needs of the colony. Alongside more established theories as to why the Vikings never settled permanently in America, such as lack of support from the home base in Greenland and Indian hostility, Jochens adds the important factors of sexuality and reproduction.[36]

In the Greenland colony, in contrast to earlier colonized territories, the Norsemen considered the importation of Scandinavian women to be the only viable option, and Jochens found no record whatsoever of sexual mingling with the Inuit. But there were sufficient numbers of Norse women to sustain a settlement for five hundred years, and here, too, female infanticide was curbed. In Vínland, Jochens argues, the situation was difficult from the beginning: "by provoking hostile relations with the Indians, the colonists made sexual contacts difficult and remained limited to their own women."[37] Jochens questions whether or not the Norse would ever have mixed with the Indians. There were far too few Nordic women to ensure the survival of the colony into the next generation, nor were their numbers sufficient to alleviate the male colonists' sexual frustration. For the Norsemen, intimacy with the natives in Greenland and Vínland would have involved dealing with more significant physical differences than simply complexion and hair color. The physical differences their forefathers had encountered in the Western islands with the Celts and Picts were relatively minor in comparison. But, Jochens observes, "sexual encounters with the Inuit and Indians necessitated mingling of peoples with completely different physiques. Without doubt, like other medieval people, the Norse were racist and felt revulsion at the mere sight of the natives."[38] Shunning the natives significantly reduced the Vikings' chances of establishing a permanent colony in the New World.

Scandinavia's perception of itself, its worldview, and its thinking about outside ethnic groups were relatively stable from the time of the Old Norse sagas to the beginning of the twentieth century—possibly even longer, as John Lindow argues in his 1995 article, "Supernatural Others and Ethnic Others."[39] Lindow cites evidence of supernatural-ethnic "Othering" in "Ynglingatal," a Norwegian poem traditionally ascribed to the late ninth century. The Scandinavian worldview was distinguished by a certain overlap between ethnic and supernatural beings. Thus, the primary boundary ran between one's own group and everybody outside the group. The earliest outsiders, the *blámenn* and *skrælinger*, were most often assigned supernatural properties. Later the Sámi and Finns, the Gypsies and tinkers were all ascribed similar attributes, or emblems, of contrast. For example, the belief that these ethnic groups were associated with shamanism, witchcraft, and an "unnatural" connection to animals has survived for centuries in Scandinavian literature and folklore. For the most part, that is how Hamsun describes them as well. In his own life, Hamsun's fundamental complaint about modernity was that political democracy gave some of these traditionally outsider groups the right to cross the prescribed boundaries.

Meeting the Native Americans in *Amerika*

EMIGRATION TO THE UNITED STATES PROVIDED AN IMPORTANT SOURCE OF new ideas for Norwegians at home. They were exposed to immigration recruitment literature, read letters and diaries from relatives who had emigrated, listened to the tales of returnees and of sailors who made repeated journeys to the United States, and read literary texts about the New World. In addition, there were official church documents and missionary reports from the New World. These texts collectively illuminate for modern readers the attitudes and mindset of early immigrants and help us understand ideas about America that circulated in Norway long before Hamsun's travels to Wisconsin and Minnesota in the 1880s. Certainly, many preconceived notions about the New World must have accompanied him on his journey.

In the Scandinavian imagination of the time, America was not just a real destination for emigrants but also the so-called "New Continent," offering the utopian promise of a richer life and a new beginning. Paradoxically, it also offered an authentic experience of living off the land, which for many in Norway was no longer possible, given the lack of good arable land. This put immigrants in direct conflict with Native Americans, who were forced to leave the lands the immigrants occupied. Yet in Norwegian texts about America, the Native Americans are largely, although not always, ignored. When they are portrayed, they appear as "noble savages" at best, or are demonized as wild beasts; this was especially true after the Dakota Uprising in 1862.[40] Until Betty Bergland identified it in her research, this aspect of relations between Scandinavian immigrants and Native Americans remained unexplored, and our knowledge of historical patterns was meager and fragmented.[41]

In addition to contributions by well-known Norwegian writers and politicians, scholars have unearthed a wealth of information in the immigrants' letters, diaries, and manuals from and about the New Continent, predominantly focusing on the immigrants' daily lives. Betty Bergland, for instance, researched the major sources of information about North America available to Norwegians between 1825 and 1862. Her findings on Scandinavian immigrants' interaction with Native Americans as they established settlements in the midwestern United States demonstrate that while most texts simply ignored the issue of the dispossessed Indians, some were sympathetic to them, and even critical of the government's policies toward the tribes. The Lutheran church, with its view of Native Americans as heathens, must have influenced the immigrants' perception of the indigenous population, making it easier to dispossess them of their land.[42] On the whole, Bergland writes, even the most educated and compassionate writers eventually succumbed to romanticized images of the Indians as noble savages; more important, they never called into question the land-taking itself.[43]

In general, Scandinavians' depiction of the United States as a whole remained positive and sentimental. In his essay "The Image of the United States in Danish Literature," Sven Rossel dates the earliest mention of Amerika in Scandinavian literature to 1608. He focuses in particular on the swell of information about the United States in the nineteenth and twentieth centuries, reminding us that "literary expression can in this way serve as a barometer, registering the ever-changing political and aesthetic views of various literary periods."[44] The Norwegian authors Bjørnstjerne Bjørnson, Alexander Kielland, Jonas Lie, and Henrik Ibsen all saw the United States' political model as one worth pursuing, and Ibsen's 1877 play, *Samfundets Støtter* (Pillars of society), is a good example of this view. In the 1800s, America was seen as the land of liberty and of the future, writes Rossel, but as mass emigration continued, a much more realistic narrative emerged, describing also the experiences of those who failed to achieve the American dream. Rossel estimates that the sentimental success story nevertheless survived well into the twentieth century. Travelogues from the United States were also common.[45] After his stay in Wisconsin among the Chippewa (1872–74), the Danish writer Wilhelm Dinesen (1845–95) published his *Jagtbreve*, describing the experiences.[46] In Norway, Bjørnson's journalistic letters circulated in the liberal press and popularized his ideas and perceptions of America. The letters recounted Bjørnson's experiences and extremely positive impressions as he traveled in 1880–81 from the East Coast of the United States through the Norwegian settlements in the Midwest.

Hamsun's early articles on America are an important contribution to shedding some light on the mindset of Norwegian immigrants and their conceptualization of the New Continent and Native Americans. Hamsun, however, was one of America's harshest critics, portraying the country as a place of material greed and mass mediocrity, of shallow values and shallow roots and suffering from a general lack of creativity—in short, as the epitome of the dark side of modernity. Hamsun visited America twice in the 1880s, hoping to become famous and wealthy. Disillusioned, he finally returned to Scandinavia and vented his disappointment in a series of lectures on the New World. These lectures eventually became his book on America, *Fra det moderne Amerikas aandsliv* published in 1889. In Hamsun's mid-career novels, America was where he dispatched useless characters, and it was the land from which immigrants returned, restless and changed, transplanting their restlessness to small Norwegian communities.[47] In contrast to the more or less race-blind depictions of America by most Nordic settlers, who tended to congregate with other Scandinavians in the New World, Hamsun's America is multicolored, as he writes about both blacks and Native Americans.

Knut Hamsun and Jon Alfred Mjøen

ALTHOUGH RACE ISSUES WERE "IN THE AIR" SO TO SPEAK, JON ALFRED MJØEN himself most likely had a very specific influence on Hamsun's views on race, since Hamsun was a frequent guest in the Mjøen household for social and professional reasons. Mjøen's German wife, Claire Greverus Mjøen, a respected translator of Norwegian literature into German, translated Hamsun's travel account *I Æventyrland* (In wonderland), a number of his short stories, and some of his correspondence. The compliment Hamsun paid her—"Mrs. Claire is certainly a master!" (*Fru Claire er jo en mester!*)—has often been quoted. Claire Mjøen also translated texts by Bjørnstjerne Bjørnson, Georg Brandes, Barbara Ring, Nordahl Grieg, and several other Norwegian writers.

Soon after her move to Norway, this talented and well-educated woman, with the encouragement of her husband, became involved in various women's causes. Her speech "Kvinnenes oppgaver i kampen mot tuberkulose" (Women's tasks in the struggle against tuberculosis), which she delivered at the Students' Society Hall in Kristiania, put her in touch with the most important Norwegian women lobbyists. She soon became the general secretary of the National Council of Norwegian Women. A well-known peace activist, Claire Mjøen met with the 1905 Peace Prize recipient, Bertha von Suttner, when she came to Kristiania in 1906 to receive the award.

Despite her work on behalf of women, Claire Mjøen did not approve of women's suffrage and regretted that the "motherly element," as she called it, was disappearing from families. On this point, she differed greatly from Katti Anker Møller, the outspoken suffragist, whom she knew well. Nevertheless, Claire supported Møller's and Castberg's ideas and the eventual law establishing illegitimate children's rights, because she believed it improved the position of single mothers and their children. As her daughter, Sonja Mjøen, writes in her memoir of her mother, Claire Mjøen believed that women were better caregivers and nurturers than men were, and consequently they should focus primarily on the family.[48] In her book, which pays tribute to her mother, her father, and her childhood home, Sonja mentions briefly her father's work in the eugenics laboratory and his research on the heredity of musical talents. She writes that, while his work received much appreciation abroad, Jon Alfred Mjøen was often criticized in Norway, and she remembers how he once shed tears over a bad review.[49]

Sonja describes the Mjøen estate at Gjøvik as a lively gathering place for writers, intellectuals, and politicians. The Mjøen family alone included a writer, a doctor, a musician, an actor, and several politicians, and they often hosted interesting guests. The writers Bjørnstjerne Bjørnson and Nils Kjær and the critic Carl Nærup visited frequently, and Bergljot and Sigurd Ibsen were good acquaintances.[50] Georg Brandes stayed with the Mjøens when he visited Norway. Edvard Grieg and Ole Bull were regular visitors, if not close friends. The lawmaker Johan Castberg used to play music with the Mjøens. The editors from Hamsun's Munich-based publishing house, Langen Verlag, were also welcome guests. It was Langen that published most of the new and radical Scandinavian literature in German. When Knut Hamsun visited Gjøvik, he would, like other guests, often stay for several days and, as Sonja Mjøen recalls in her memoir, he would read to the others from his books.[51] This list of names reveals two things: first, that the Norwegian intellectual elite was a small and intertwined group, and second, that it maintained fruitful connections with similar circles in Germany. Sonja Mjøen gives an interesting description of how Jon Alfred Mjøen would lecture his guests in his laboratory about his research and related scientific questions:

> When people came to visit, or at festive occasions, the guests first had to gather in the large lab that he had constructed as an addition to the villa. Before they sat down to dinner, he would give them a lecture on heredity research and would explain his views on the future, his new ideas. . . . In addition, what most of the guests found instructive were universal problems and popular science ideas.[52]

In 1921, Sonja accompanied her father to the International Eugenics Congress in New York. In his presentation, Jon Alfred Mjøen talked about the increased risk of mental and physical pathologies in the offspring of parents of widely disparate races. Although Mjøen cautioned against drawing rash conclusions, he went ahead and drew them anyway. He claimed that the children of mixed-race liaisons had a higher likelihood of handicaps in comparison to those of same-race parents. Focusing predominantly on what he called the "unbalanced mind," he titled his paper "Harmonic and Disharmonic Race-crossings." He supported his conclusions with two kinds of "evidence," the first based on research into mixed Sami-Norwegian families, the second deriving from experiments in the breeding of two varieties of rabbits.[53] He found a higher occurrence of both unbalanced minds and tuberculosis in the progeny of mixed-race unions. As Mjøen claims in his paper, it was among the Sami of northern Norway that he first formulated his theory of harmonious and disharmonious crossings, based on his observation of numerous hybrids (as he called them) produced by Norwegian-Sami unions. He states that due to the hybrids' "unbalanced minds," which resulted in disharmonic attitudes, morals, and even appearance (large heads, for example), these people were shunned by the Sami. Among them, he found many with a propensity for stealing, lying, and drinking. But tellingly, upon finding a significant number of hybrids who were taller than their progenitors and smarter than their Sami neighbors, he contended that tall stature does not always signify strength, health, and vigor, nor does intellectual superiority always translate into superior morals.[54] His initial biological argument gave way to random conclusions, and, ultimately, to his own prejudice. He could equally have concluded, after all, that the results of such crossings are positive. Moreover, he could have given some weight to social circumstances as possible causes for the alleged difference in the rate of occurrence of "unbalanced minds."

Mjøen ends his paper with a twelve-point summary in which he claims that "crossings between widely different races can lower the physical and mental level [of offspring or of society as a whole],"[55] that deficiencies increase as additional races are mixed in. He found that tuberculosis and prostitution occur most frequently among people of mixed races and in areas inhabited by mixed-race people. Diseases against which people of a single race have developed immunity, he argued, often reappear in racially mixed populations. He concluded that until more is known about race-crossing, it should be avoided, and he urges people to "nourish and develop a strong and healthy race instinct." He also notes that "by removing the bilinguistic barrier (for example, compelling the Laps [sic] to learn Norwegian and Swedish), *we are building the first bridge, safe and sure, to a blood mixture between the two races which we will deplore and regret when it is too late.*"[56] What is striking about Mjøen's argument is its random logic and lack of awareness of any possible cause but a racial one to explain laziness, prostitution, disease, and so on. Mjøen concludes his article with mixed messages: he issues a lofty warning against persecuting any race and urges compassion, but at the same time he makes a careful distinction between "the right to live" and "the right of other races to mix their blood with ours and—give life." The latter, "to give life," is without doubt a warning against mixed-race offspring, later echoed in the Nasjonal Samling (NS) party's family policies and attitudes. It is no coincidence that Mjøen has been referred to as the spiritual father of the NS.[57]

In the article, Mjøen also describes the pedigree of one of these disharmonic hybrids, a certain Ingwill-Ola. His four grandparents were tinker, Finnish, Norwegian, and Sami. Mjøen writes:

Although Ingwill-Ola had great difficulty in understanding the difference between mine and thine and found much more interest in telling a story than telling the truth, and although Ingwill-Ola could not see why he should not empty the whole brandy bottle at once, he was the most beloved man in the little town of Rorøs in Norway. His prison-terms were short and he had a rather jolly and innocent character. And when he died the whole town was mourning because they had lost the best topic of conversation that they had had at the family table for more than thirty years. He was somewhat of an historical personage.[58]

Essentially describing Ingwill-Ola as a drinker and a thief, Mjøen adds some redeeming features to Ingwill-Ola's character. Casting him as the villagers' most beloved fool and conversation piece, Mjøen does not notice his own patronizing and demeaning tone. There are certainly parallels to be drawn between Mjøen's and Hamsun's thoughts regarding hybrids. Fundamentally, they agree that races should be kept apart and that hybrids are an unfortunate and deplorable consequence of modernity. Although they came from different fields—the sciences and literature—they both could appreciate an exceptional individual. Mjøen's sympathetic, if condescending, depiction of Ingwill-Ola's creativity in telling stories overlaps with Hamsun's thoughts on what constitutes an interesting, nonconformist, and ultimately creative personality. The "disharmonious" life, as opposed to that of a settled bourgeois, was in Hamsun's view most conducive to creativity. Yet both Mjøen and Hamsun viewed modern changes through the lens of blood-mixing, which genuinely alarmed them. At times, Mjøen can sound very much like Hamsun, who, in his book on America, wrote about how the population of the United States was made up of "trash" immigrants from all regions of the world. Regarding race-crossings, Mjøen writes:

It is a fact that during the last decades an unfortunate mingling of races has increased to an enormous degree as the result of new communications (railroad, steamship lines and autos) and our . . . tendency to immigration. The migrations of nations in former times were, biologically regarded, harmless in comparison with those of the last ten or twenty years. Over the German frontier there have come in from the East 600,000 people of by no means the best racial elements, while the United States have had to accept a migration almost three times as large within a corresponding period of years.[59]

Knut Hamsun was acquainted with race-crossings in two regions: first, in the northern parts of Norway where he grew up and where Norwegians, Sami, Finns, and Russians often lived in close proximity, and second, in the United States where he lived from 1882 to 1884 and from 1886 to 1888. His American experience, though it was predominantly among Scandinavian immigrants in the Midwest, resulted in several texts in which he mentions or reflects on questions of race and race-crossing. These include his short semi-fictional account of visiting with American Indians, "Fra en Indianerleir" (From an Indian camp; 1885), which Hamsun sold as investigative reporting, and his first book, the cultural critique *Fra det moderne Amerikas aandsliv*, where he attacks and ridicules the offspring of white women and black men as the result of "mulatto stud farms." In his description of "half-breeds," or mulattos, Hamsun's ideas about both races overlap to create an image of general degeneration. He views the black race as underdeveloped, closer to apes than to humans, and generations away from reaching a decent human level. He considers the white race, especially its women, to be degenerating, as manifested in its low birth rate. White women refused to have children in favor of education, while educated white men conducted research into forms of birth control. Underdeveloped and oversexed blacks, he argues, were mixing with overeducated and promiscuous white women. Hamsun's American experience made a life-long impression on him, and its influence can be felt, in one way or another, in almost every book he wrote, including his next to last novel, *Ringen sluttet* (The ring is closed).

Hamsun did not directly participate in the scientific debate on various facets of race or biology, yet as a lifelong avid reader, he must have followed such discussions in the daily press. In addition to the strictly scientific debate among scientists like Mohr, Bonnevie, Scharffenberg, Evang, and Mjøen, the popular press carried articles and discussions on such issues as marriage, children, the hereditary nature of talent and intelligence, and the mixing of races. A woman's fertility, as well as her choice of a partner, became paramount concerns in the debate over family, health, public policy, and national identity.

One book that presented the general public with many of the ideas debated in scientific circles was *Den moderne mennesketype* (The modern human type; 1917), by the Danish doctor Konrad Simonsen.[60] The book comprises five lectures Simonsen gave at the universities of Copenhagen and Kristiania, which, as Simonsen notes in his preface, were extremely well attended. Because of its great popularity—it went through ten printings during its first year—and because of Hamsun's strong commendation of it, it is worth looking at this book in some detail. Hamsun first praised Simonsen's book in the short story "Nabobyen" (The neighboring town), which appeared in 1917. In the 1930s, Hamsun more than once urged the directors of the Aschehoug and Gyldendal publishing houses to reissue the book, speaking of it in the most positive terms.[61] Clearly, ideas from Simonsen's book resonated with Hamsun over several decades.

Konrad Simonsen (1877–1945) was known in Scandinavia primarily for his opposition to the ideas of the critic Georg Brandes[62] and for his popularization of the ideas of the German intellectual, industrialist, and writer Walter Rathenau.[63] In his book, Simonsen presents an "analysis" of southern and northern peoples and a discussion of the consequences of modern mobility that in many points recall Mjøen's research. Simonsen's book, which closely follows Rathenau's cultural critique, condemns the alleged myth of Western progress and material wealth. Simonsen's argument is based on two fundamental premises. The first is that material gains in Western modernity entailed a loss in intuition and soul, transforming forever the character of mankind—a lament often voiced in Europe at the time; modern Western man is a restless, empty, and soul-less creature who reacts automatically and mechanically to stimuli from material reality. In the Orient, so Simonsen claims, a lack of concern with accumulating capital and a robust intuitive wisdom result in a simpler, happier, and more authentic life. Simonsen's list of modern technological inventions represents a litany of complaints against the institutions and achievements of democracy, including such things as public libraries, museums, legally ensured and protected leisure time, and so forth.[64]

The book's second premise expresses the belief that the mixing of the healthy, noble Germanic race with other races, deemed inferior, has brought about the decline of the Germanic civilization, through the gradual process of "de-Germanization" (*Afgermanisering*). Everywhere, he writes, the conquering Germanic peoples had a fairer complexion than their conquered primitive slaves, who were "stocky, sturdy, with a broad face, short limbs, low forehead, small eyes and most often had dark hair and darker skin."[65] Simonsen includes Jews in the primitive category.[66] While a certain amount of contact between some races was still acceptable, there was, according to Simonsen, an insurmountable abyss between the white man and the Indians, the Dravidians, and the Negroes. He cites with approval the English saying: "God created the white man, and God created the black man, but Satan created the Eurasian."[67] Certainly one way to interpret the message contained in this expression is that races are acceptable as long as they are kept apart, while the worst "sin" is for members of different races to engage in sexual encounters with each other. Race mixing was most prevalent in cities, Simonsen writes, but not even the countryside—not even remote Norway—was immune from this modernizing process. The Germanic peoples, who once cherished the inherent challenge of victory, had turned into hunters of material gain, with all of their activities focused on the shallow goal of achieving importance through wealth and social status.

Simonsen closes the book on an optimistic note. He expresses the belief that the horrors of World War I (then still raging) would force people to adopt stronger moral, ethical, and spiritual values in their actions. In 1917, the same year in which Simonsen's book came out, Hamsun wrote his widely read novel *Markens grøde* (The growth of the soil), in which he offers a somewhat comparable hope that mankind might be saved through hard work on the soil and such efforts as settling the wilderness. Simonsen's optimistic vision of the future includes scientific race research. He writes: "By means of science, through race studies and the observation of man's exterior, by which we can so easily learn about his talents and limitations, we will further develop our so far quite primitive knowledge of man."[68]

Simonsen here touches on what at the time was a popular concept: that a person's external appearance can tell us about his or her level of intelligence. While the efforts and conclusions of eugenic research varied greatly, this particular approach represents one of eugenics' cruder yet most accessible forms. This conception is echoed also in the Nordic "theory" that divided people into round skulls, with lower intelligence and weaker morals, and long skulls, with higher intelligence and better moral judgment.[69] It is easy enough to dismiss Simonsen's book as "a witless, racist and anti-Semitic glorification of the German soul," as Professor Allen Simpson did in his article "Knut Hamsun's Anti-Semitism."[70] But the book's enthusiastic reception and great popularity reveal the overlap between Simonsen's ideas about race and popular attitudes toward those perceived as outsiders. In fact, Simonsen's book reflects the contemporary medical and scientific debates over what today we call genetics and family traits. It contains much the same racial imaginary that informs Hamsun's texts, an imaginary that attributes sexuality, promiscuity, and a lack of civilized self-restraint, as well as slyness and cunning, to so-called primitives.

Simonsen quotes extensively from Hamsun's 1915 novel *Segelfoss by* (Segelfoss town), which he understands to be a cultural critique of materialistic values as the root cause of the destruction of the traditional, noble community. Yet, it is precisely in *Segelfoss by* and its predecessor, *Børn av tiden* (Children of the age), that Hamsun creates Mariane Holmengrå, the daughter of a Norwegian father and a Mexican-Indian mother. Mariane is an endearing and complex female character who belies the opinion that blood-mixing causes degeneration. On the contrary, she can be seen as an invigorating exotic Other.[71]

Norway Becomes a Modern State

WHILE MY STUDY OF HAMSUN FOCUSES MAINLY ON THE LAST DECADES OF THE nineteenth century and the early part of the twentieth century, it is important to review what transpired in prior decades within Scandinavia so as to understand how Norway arrived at the state of self-awareness reflected in the thoughts and values of intellectuals like Knut Hamsun. The end of the Napoleonic Wars in 1814 brought many changes to Norway, as it did for all of Scandinavia. Norway's status changed from that of a Danish province—some called it a colony—to that of a partner in a union with Sweden. The Norwegian constitution of 1814, the so-called Eidsvoll Constitution, strengthened Norway's position in the union and guaranteed a certain amount of independence in domestic affairs. Norwegian intellectuals and politicians set about defining and promoting the concept of Norwegian identity, "Norwegianness," in a movement that eventually led to full political independence in 1905.

During the latter half of the nineteenth century, Norway enjoyed a period of rapid if uneven economic growth and cultural change that resulted in a permanent shift in attitudes about both domestic conditions and the outside world. Entry into modernity meant, among other things, increased contact with other peoples and cultures, along with intensified attempts to describe and classify these new experiences, providing the tinder for a fierce debate over race and racial degeneration. At the same time, there was renewed interest in indigenous peoples. The fundamental concern in this Norwegian debate, as well as in the more general European discussion, was the "proper place" of the world's races on a scale that ranged from the most primitive to the most developed.

Economic growth in Norway had been hampered by harsh terrain, low capital investment, and a lack of affordable energy, but the construction of railroads and the introduction of regular steamboat routes increased the pace of change. The development of a reliable transportation system added to the overall sense of progress. Between 1854 and 1868, Christiania was linked by rail to Hamar via Eidsvoll. By 1877, this line had been pushed as far north as Støren, near Trondheim. In 1902, Kristiania (with its post-1877 spelling) was connected to Gjøvik, and by 1909 the link to Bergen completed the rail connection to the western coast over the most demanding terrain. In 1893, the establishment of a year-round coastal steamboat (the *Hurtigruta*) route meant reliable connections between settlements along the long and treacherous western coastline.

Industrialization accelerated after 1850, when the export of fish and timber and shipping industry services began to generate much-needed capital for investment in other industries, mainly in the textile and paper industries. Eventually, it was the shipping and merchant marine industry that provided the backbone for expansion in the late nineteenth century. When, around the turn of the century, the latest hydroelectric technology became readily available, power plants harnessed Norway's rivers as a principal source of energy for the larger industrial enterprises. Along with these important industrial changes came changes in societal structures. Expansion in certain areas, combined with the pressures of rapid population growth, caused significant internal migration, as well as emigration to the United States. As much as one fourth of the population would ultimately emigrate from Norway. These migrations, both internal and external, were unprecedented in Norway's history and contributed to a new feeling of rootlessness.

The sharp rise in industrial fortunes that generally characterized Europe in the 1870s and 1880s also took place in Scandinavia, although at a somewhat later date and on a smaller scale. The population of Christiania more than doubled between 1865 and 1885 (from 57,000 to 130,000), creating enormous pressure on the housing and job markets. Especially affected were the neighborhoods of Akerselva and Sagene, which attracted working-class families drawn by industries that had developed in these districts because of the cheap waterpower. The textile and paper mills continuously expanded and modernized. In the 1870s, the first urban public transportation system in Norway was introduced in Christiania, as was gas and then electric street lighting. The first department stores in Christiania offered a new kind of employment and introduced mass advertising on walls and kiosks throughout the city. The situation was similar in other Nordic capitals.[72] And just as on the continent, the eastern districts of the Scandinavian capitals were marked by urban decay and viewed as degenerated: the poor working class, the unemployed, alleged and real criminals, and alleged and real prostitutes inhabited the eastern suburbs, which were sometimes labeled "jungle districts."

Native Primitivism

IF AMERICA REPRESENTED THE MODERN WORLD OF BUSINESS OPPORTUNITY and technological invention on an unprecedented scale, it was at the same time a wild, largely uncharted continent that fit well into the European idea of the primitive. Hamsun, too, shared the Euro-centric fantasies of the American wilderness. In his article about his visit to Native Americans in Wisconsin, for instance, he reflects on the contrast between the native way of life and modern civilization. Hamsun's views may be seen as part of an international critical (and nostalgic) reaction to the modern changes taking place in western Europe and parts of North America, especially its East Coast. His emerging anti-modernism constituted not only a general response to the encroachments of modern life, but also a response to the perceived loss of authentic connection and experience.

Anti-modernism advocated the "authentic" as the vehicle of redemption amidst rapid social and economic changes and their attendant anxieties. For anti-modernists, the authentic could still be found, or constructed, in pre-industrial societies or geographically remote areas, such as the Orient, Africa, or America. Europeans often saw the distinct cultures of these places as pure and primitive. Hamsun, like many other artists and intellectuals, was involved in the examination, construction, reproduction, and dissemination of these ideas.

The discourse of primitivism is fundamental to the Western sense of Self and the Other, as Fred R. Myers, among others, has claimed. Myers points out how the primitive is conceptualized as coherent and wholesome, which allows for a critique of the West as fragmented and split. Similarly, Marianne Torgovnick, in her 1990 study *Gone Primitive*, develops a compelling argument for the close interrelation of modernity and primitivism. Within the Scandinavian field, Michelle Facos's research on late nineteenth-century Swedish painting, published as *Nationalism and the Nordic Imagination*, illuminates this relationship,[73] while Nina Witoszek develops her own, highly original understanding of the connection between culture and nature in Norway, in her book *Norske naturmytologier* (Norwegian mythologies about nature). Here the Norwegian worldview is shown to consist of the interrelationship between culture and nature in a holistic cosmology.[74] Indeed,

Norway's geographically marginal position and delayed industrialization and modernization fostered a close entwinement of nature and people. In addition, Norway's explorations of the far North, the barren inhospitable tracts of Lappland, Spitzbergen, Greenland, and the arctic regions, provided the occasion for personal duels with nature, far from urban civilization. The harsh climate and forbidding landscape did not offer relaxed communion with nature, as was the case in warmer, southern climates; consequently, Norway developed its own particular version of wholesomeness. Nature in Norway has, since the mid-nineteenth century, represented an important element in the country's self-perception and national identity—even in its national political program—while other ethnicities and races presented a contrast to Norwegians' own image of themselves. The Norwegians were free, then, to position themselves as civilized, but at the same time, and just as importantly, they could invoke their natural, instinctual, and "authentic" side.

With only a handful of urban centers at the turn of the twentieth century, the country had a sparsely populated landscape in which most Norwegians lived in close proximity to nature. When the dissolution of the union with Sweden occurred in 1905, Norwegians suddenly perceived this natural way of life as robust and authentic and connected with the country's unique dramatic topography. In this way, national independence, nature, and primitivism became interlinked. The gradual shifts in Hamsun's focus—from foreign lands to his homeland, from traveling in America and the Orient to traveling to the Norwegian North, and from modernism to anti-modernism—are all part of his attempt to anchor his restless modernist experience in a home-based version of wholesomeness.

Despite its Germanic cultural roots, Norway, like Scandinavia in general, was very different from the countries on the European continent; it was geographically remote and socioculturally distinct. The post-1814 movement that united artists, writers, politicians, and educators in their pursuit of a unique Norwegian identity developed alongside an emerging, politically progressive democracy (led by the Venstre political party) and ultimately led to political independence from Sweden in 1905. In this effort, Norway and Norwegianness were often perceived and constructed, by Norwegians and foreigners alike, as wholesome and in harmony with nature. This development represents a successful blend of progressive politics and traditional cultural ideas. As folklore research also has shown, Scandinavian society remained intimately connected with nature and its imagined inhabitants, such as the *huldrer* and *nisser*, far into the twentieth century. Hamsun, in his short story

"Nabobyen," implies that *nisser* inhabit a barn right in the middle of an otherwise very normal small town.[75]

The Nordic landscape, viewed from the nineteenth-century continental perspective, seemed as unspoilt and majestic as India, Africa, or the South Sea islands; this perception of wildness only intensified during the second half of the century. Travel in the northernmost regions of Europe became a fashionable pastime among English, German, and Italian socialites and early eco-tourists.[76] Mary Wollstonecraft published her account of travels through Denmark, Norway, and Sweden as early as 1796. With a condescending attitude, she describes the backwardness of Scandinavians, but she is impressed by the sublime beauty of Norwegian nature. It is striking how Wollstonecraft's travelogue, like other early accounts, reflects what Mary Louise Pratt has aptly called "imperial eyes." The attitudes of these early travelers toward Norway were similar to those of their compatriots in regard to Britain's overseas colonies. Nevertheless, travel accounts were consistently enthusiastic in their praise of Norway's natural beauty.

For those who lived outside of cities, however, day-to-day life—survival, really—in the inhospitable Norwegian landscape left neither time nor energy for appreciating natural beauty.[77] A handful of Norwegian intellectuals began to travel around the country, recording their impressions and collecting folklore material: songs, stories, proverbs, and legends they deemed authentically Norwegian. The country's topography and the inhabitants of its inaccessible valleys became building blocks used by a wealthy, educated, urban, and politically patriotic elite to construct the image of a healthy, invigorating, and mystical Nordic landscape, one that stood in sharp contrast to that of continental Europe. The image of Nature became part and parcel of the movement toward cultural, and eventually political, independence from Denmark and Sweden—a process that required a mechanism and a symbolism that would unite divergent, isolated, and distinctive populations as Norwegian citizens. As Marte Hvam Hult aptly notes, "mountain ranges and often barely arable land had to be redefined as positive symbols rather than as the often bleak and inhospitable tracts that they actually were."[78] While Hult correctly claims that "it is a long journey from the irrational terror of the natural world felt by medieval man to the modern Norwegian's relationship with nature,"[79] some irrationality in Norwegians' relationship to nature has survived well into the twentieth century, as folklore scholars Henning Sehmsdorf, John Lindow, and Nina Witoszek have shown.

Scandinavia, then, requires a nuanced study as to how it has resembled and differed from the continent in general, and certain countries in particular, in its attitudes toward various exotic locations. Scandinavians often became acquainted with places such as China, Persia, and Africa via other European countries, notably France and Germany; and Scandinavian descriptions of these distant locales often included a comment on the mediating nation as well. At the same time, Scandinavia developed its own version of primitivism in the North. If Norwegian artists viewed and presented themselves as Others with respect to the continent, or sometimes viewed visitors from the continent as Others, how did that complicate their understanding of concepts such as race? Certainly, this insistence of alterity implies an unstable identity that shifts with the angle of perception. Hence, it is interesting to observe a primitivist hierarchy of locations. Can one be more primitive, more authentic than one's neighbors? Swedish artists, for instance, would sometimes present themselves as primitive vis-à-vis the continent, and at other times as civilized, especially when looking down on, or seeking inspiration from, the rugged, dramatic, and unspoiled landscape of Norway. Would a Norwegian writer from Kristiania construct a civilized identity vis-à-vis the inhabitants of the North, but when in Paris construct himself as a wild Nordic? And if so, what would that mean for his sense of identity?

European colonial enterprise offered the most immediate confrontation between cultures and peoples, and thus identities. Scandinavian participation in Europe's overseas expansion was limited, especially in comparison to that of France, Britain, Spain, or Portugal. Seventeenth-century Scandinavian colonial endeavors included a short-lived Swedish settlement in modern-day Delaware, forts established by both Sweden and Denmark-Norway on the Guinea Coast of Africa for facilitating commerce in slaves, the formation of the Danish East India Company and the Swedish East India Company, and Caribbean colonies like the Danish West Indies (now the U.S. Virgin Islands).[80]

Slavery, a major component of the colonial project, was a North American institution for two centuries, from 1639 to the middle of the nineteenth century. Serfdom was still thriving in seventeenth-century Denmark, but black slaves were occasionally brought to Copenhagen for prestige, entertainment, or novelty, if not for labor. Scandinavians did, however, use slave labor on their overseas sugar plantations and actively participated in the Caribbean slave trade. The Danes maintained their Caribbean colony in the Virgin Islands from 1666 until 1917, when they sold their holdings to the United States under pressures related to World War I. In 1784, King Gustaf III of Sweden acquired colonies on the Caribbean islands of St. Barthelemy and

St. Martin from France. Although these islands proved less prosperous than the Danish acquisitions, St. Barthelemy was, at least for a while, a lucrative trading port. In 1877, Sweden sold the island back to France, having found it difficult to maintain ties with the colony and ensure its economic self-sufficiency.[81]

The Scandinavian role in the larger colonial project, and especially the slave trade, was relatively minor compared to that of other European nations or the United States—less than half a percent of the Africans who survived the Middle Passage had been transported on Danish ships. Nevertheless, this amounted to approximately 50,000 Africans.[82] As part of the legacy of Scandinavian colonialism, Nordic painters recorded not only the landscapes of Africa and the Caribbean, but also such items as parrots, palm trees, and scantily clad Africans. A seventeenth-century portrait of Queen Sofie Amalie of Denmark, for instance, depicts her with "her Negro boy and other Exotic Accoutrements," as the painting's title denotes.[83] Neil Kent rightly notes a "general amnesia about Nordic involvement in the trans-Atlantic slave trade."[84] Indeed, much of the world seems to share this amnesia, as more recent images of an egalitarian, peace-loving, and liberal Nordic society tend to dominate. Hamsun's reflections on other races may serve as an intriguing and enlightening window on Scandinavians as participants in the European colonial expansion.

Toward the indigenous peoples of the Arctic and Subarctic—the Sami and the Inuit— Scandinavians behaved no less imperialistically than they did with their overseas possessions, or than the continental powers did with their respective colonies. In Hamsun's texts, the original inhabitants of the glorious Arctic landscape are either largely invisible or portrayed through stereotypes. In *Markens grøde*, for instance, Hamsun creates a hierarchy that sets the hard-working ethnic Norwegians settled on the Sellanraa farm against the nomadic Sami, depicted as sly beggars and/or purveyors of gossip and evil spells. While the Norwegian Isak bonds reverently with nature even as he tames it, the Sami, with their black magic, blend into the background as part of the natural scenery.

Scandinavian Expatriate Artists and Their Arts

WHEN REFLECTING ON THE CHANGING PERCEPTIONS OF SCANDINAVIA among continentals and Scandinavians alike, Scandinavian expatriate artists provide an instructive case in point.[85] Having absorbed the tenets of naturalist concepts and techniques while studying in cities like Paris or Berlin in the 1880s, they soon rediscovered their native countries and landscapes.[86] While these diasporic artists initially admired what they perceived as the continent's more civilized society, and lamented their homelands' shortcomings, they gradually began to appreciate the Nordic way of life as something authentic, healthy, and vigorous. They positioned themselves as wholesome naturals without need of a healing rebirth, unlike the continental modernists. The overdeveloped and over-civilized continent, this picture suggests, was rapidly approaching the point of physical and mental exhaustion, the symptoms of which—alcoholism, madness, and degeneration—were already visible in modern cities.

Among the first Scandinavian intellectuals to return home from Paris in the mid-1880s were the Norwegian painters Erik Werenskiold and Christian Krohg.[87] By 1890, most of the other expatriate Scandinavian painters would also leave the continent to return to Scandinavia. After Gauguin's exploration of the rugged landscape of Brittany, and especially after his departure for Tahiti in 1891, it seemed appropriate to seek a lost paradise not only in the exotic South but also in the equally exotic North. Art historian Roald Nasgaard claims that Gauguin was "the spiritual father of many of the Northern Symbolist landscape painters."[88] In fact, he was a personal mentor to several of them, and his work was often exhibited in Copenhagen, his wife, Mette, being Danish. Once back in Scandinavia, several of these former expatriate painters became part of national revival movements in art and culture. Politically social democrats, they articulated a unique response to, and confirmation of, the continental cultural notion that a spiritual and artistic rebirth would come from the North. Landscape painting played the most prominent role in this rebirth, with artists like Harald Sohlberg and Nikolai Astrup (and to a certain extent Edvard Munch) of Norway, Jens Ferdinand Willumsen of Denmark, Akseli Gallen-Kallela of Finland, and Karl Nordström of Sweden mapping the territory. It is telling, in this context, that the wild forests of Karelia, which Finnish artists visited and explored in search of mystical experience and reconnection with their primeval roots, could be considered a kind of domestic Tahiti.[89]

As Marte Hvam Hult has noted, as late as 1949 Per Arneberg used a comparison of Norway and Tibet to illustrate the remoteness of the Norwegian landscape of the 1850s to the average Christiania resident, describing it as "Nordic Tibet."[90] In retracing writer and legend collector Per Christian Asbjørnsen's journey to the mouth of the Maridals River in the 1820s, Arneberg finds Nature still intact, completely untouched by time. This place, he writes, should be a "national shrine" (*nasjonalhelligdom*), a sort of "Mecca for the national soul" (*et folkesjelens Mekka*). Arneberg invokes both the artistic construction of a timeless North, where natural beauty is a kind of home, and the appeal of an infinitely mysterious invisible world. Arneberg's 1949 text, reprinted in 1958, testifies to the strength of the idea of natural wholeness and reinforces the parallels between Scandinavian primitivism and that projected onto the Orient and other exotic locales.

In addition, the *Lysaker* circle of Norwegian artists and intellectuals—which included such influential figures as the scientist, explorer, politician, and sportsman Fridtjof Nansen, the brothers Ernst and Ossian Sars (a historian and a zoologist, respectively), the painters Erik Werenskiold and Gerhard Munthe, and the pedagogue and writer Nordahl Rolfsen, the author of an immensely influential and popular school reader or *lesebok*—promoted the tradition of native forms in the visual arts and architecture as yet another expression of the organic ties between natural and cultural patterns. The establishment of open-air museums, with their explicit message of preserving the authentic architecture that had grown out of the local topography was also part of this primitivist movement.[91]

In this process of building Norwegian national identity, led mainly by well-educated and privileged elites from the capital, Hamsun participated from his own constantly shifting position. He was neither from a prominent family nor formally educated, still relatively poor, and certainly ambivalent about the social elite. Along with Nils Kjær, Jens Tiis, and Christian Krohg (to name a few of his closest colleagues at the time), Hamsun opposed the *Lysaker* circle on several issues. It is well known, for example, that Hamsun ridiculed the national euphoria over Fridtjof Nansen's triumphs in Greenland and at the North and South Poles, deploring the hero-worship of sports and adventure and the simultaneous decline of a reading culture.[92] On the other hand, by defending the use of Riksmål, the Dano-Norwegian language, on the grounds that it had become the preferred and natural choice for writing, and opposing the recently created Landsmål, he was at odds with equally influential rural leaders.[93] For a while, Hamsun felt most at home in bohemian café circles, but his awareness of the idle, "degenerate" side of artistic life, and his insistence on hard work, soon made him skeptical of that lifestyle as well.

The artists whose primary impulse in the late 1870s was to escape barbarian Scandinavia and explore the civilized culture of the continent ended up rediscovering the lands of their birth—the unique topography and remarkable quality of light, the mountains and fjords and desolate high plateaus—and endowing these landscapes with special invisible powers and symbols. Often they would employ typical Scandinavian subjects in their paintings (birch trees, folk costumes, typical seashores, regional animals) but would elevate them to the level of symbols. This was quite a shift in perspective to have transpired over roughly ten years. Hamsun was part of this shift, in both geography and paradigm: he returned from the United States in 1888, settled in Copenhagen for a while, and lived in Paris from the spring of 1893 to the summer of 1896, when he finally returned to Norway for good. Hamsun's novel *Pan*, so often described as a hymn to Norway's northern landscape, was written mostly in the urban environment of Paris, where Hamsun by all accounts had a miserable experience, living in poverty and relative social isolation while romanticizing his homeland.

Like most artists of his time, Hamsun believed that the artist was an exceptional being, who for brief moments could experience and record his bliss in nature and thus present a hidden yet somehow more authentic reality beyond the concrete world. The artist's inspiration, it was thought, came from his immediate contact with a mystical yet distinct environment. The aim of the artist was to establish links with the original, primitive culture of the region in order to preserve or embolden his creativity and communicate his experience to audiences. In the final analysis, however, unity with nature is revealed as an impossibility. Highly sophisticated artists and intellectuals, while enjoying the privileges of modern education and technology, were both consciously and instinctively promoting primitivism as a model for entire nations. Yet all the artist could strive for was the worship and preservation of nature, and perhaps short moments of ecstasy and bliss to be captured and conveyed to readers. In this way, modernity, tradition, modernism and anti-modern sentiment all worked hand in hand, in complex and unexpected ways. And so it was with Hamsun: primitivism attracted him because he saw in it a promise of ecstatic bliss and creative renewal, but the attraction was complicated by his cultural beliefs and self-perception. He could not imagine himself "going native," as his contemporary Gauguin had done. In his writing, however, Hamsun toys with this very idea and examines the increasing industrialization and modernization of a typical Norwegian small town against the background of a simpler yet coherent, even primitive, way of life.

2

HAMSUN'S WOMEN AS SCAPEGOATS FOR MODERNITY'S SINS

I also want to live in the countryside so that you won't have so many opportunities to fall back on if you one day become bored with me. In the city you could merely stand motionless in the street for a moment, and men would come, that is not *so* easy in the countryside.

—Knut Hamsun writing to his new bride, Marie (1909)

KARL EVANG, THE NORWEGIAN DOCTOR AND ADVOCATE FOR SOCIALISM, speculated as to whether eugenics research would lead to an erosion of women's rights and the reinforcement of the patriarchal family as the core social unit (see chapter 1). It is hard to evaluate whether or not deliberately misogynistic goals were behind some of the arguments in the eugenics debate, but Evang touched on what might rightly be called a backlash against the social and political advances Norwegian women were making in the late nineteenth and early twentieth centuries. By 1900, partly because of pragmatic policies and partly because of a growing feminist movement, women were able to own their own businesses, work outside the home, inherit on terms equal to those of their brothers, attend university, and more easily get a divorce. After gaining the right to vote in regional elections, they eventually won the general franchise in 1913.[1]

The general enfranchisement of 1913, however, was merely the tip of the proverbial iceberg, as the right to vote was accompanied by other, equally important measures that benefited women. Collectively, these changes helped to create a cultural climate in which it was easier for a woman to function as a fully realized human being. It is advisable to keep these significant historical advances in mind when analyzing artistic creations of the period. Feminist reforms, or even merely demands for such reforms, challenged the established institutions of family, inheritance, marriage, and work everywhere in Europe. One result was a heightened fear of biological and moral "degeneracy." Metaphors and images of sexual crisis, indeed of an impending collapse of existing social institutions, permeated the arts of the time, not least in Scandinavia.[2] The evolution of women's rights was a crucial part of the political and social background against which Hamsun created his female protagonists.

During the second half of the nineteenth century, the trope of the Nordic Woman acquired popularity, renown, and sometimes notoriety throughout Europe, and not just in reference to such rebellious women protagonists as Henrik Ibsen's Nora from *A Doll's House* (1879) or August Strindberg's Miss Julie from the play of the same name (1888). It also related to women writers like Camilla Wergeland Collett (1813–1895), who in 1855 gained fame when she published the first Norwegian novel, *Amtmandens døttre* (The district governor's daughters), which later inspired Ibsen. A dedicated defender of women's rights, Collett, after the early death of her husband in 1851, led a nomadic existence in Europe, writing short stories, essays, articles, and book reviews. In addition, the Swedish writers Fredrika Bremer (1801–1865) and Ellen Key (1849–1926) and the Norwegian writer Hanna Winsnes (1789–1872) became popular figures both at home and abroad. In the minds of critics and readers, the intellectual power of these women writers was often conflated with the constructed image of the brave and independent Viking Woman, provoking a range of responses from both male and female audiences.[3]

The number of groundbreaking pioneers in Norway was small. Cecilie Thoresen, for instance, was the only female student admitted to Norway's single university in 1882. However, the symbolic implications of the changes then under way were enormous. Demands for greater opportunities for women in the economic, political, and cultural spheres, and the eventual expansion of these opportunities, produced varied reactions on the part of both men and women. Some were ardent defenders of the new movement, while others panicked and resisted. Among prominent Scandinavian men of letters, Henrik Ibsen and Bjørnstjerne Bjørnson supported women's demands for rights and visibility in the public arena, while August Strindberg and Knut Hamsun fiercely opposed them. Caricatures of mannish women taking over jobs, offices, and even parliaments abounded in contemporary literature and the popular press, as did cartoons of emasculated men changing diapers or cleaning houses. The cultural response was not unlike that on the continent, although historical specificities certainly differed among individual countries.

In Scandinavia, the second part of the nineteenth century became culturally defined by what is known as the "great morality debate" over chastity, sexuality, prostitution, sexual diseases, and marital responsibility. The debate affected perceptions of all aspects of life, from family structure to leisure time, and from the growing size of (legal) bordellos to public health measures. Also contributing to the debate were Georg Brandes's 1869 Danish translation of J. S. Mill's *On the Subjection of Women*, Henrik Ibsen's play *Gjengangere* (Ghosts; 1881), Bjørnstjerne Bjørnson's play *En håndske* (Gauntlet; 1883), Hans Jæger's two-volume novel *Fra Kristiania-bohêmen* (From Kristiania's Bohemia; 1885), and Christian Krogh's paintings of prostitutes and novel *Albertine,* also on the theme of prostitution.[4] Amalie Skram's novels about women trapped in unhappy marriages of convenience enraged, provoked, and inspired readers from Kristiania to Vienna. In short, the debates around these texts and the issues they highlighted polarized the public and influenced both private and social behavior. Most of these debates were colored by the changed status of women and fueled by a fear that established traditions were being shattered.

Often, this broadly conceptualized fear erupted around pressing personal crises, such as an impending abortion, battles about the legitimacy of heirs, or despair over infertility. The fear of degeneration and regression was an ever-present concern. Ensuing demands for stricter controls on behavior intensified in a vain attempt to preserve the imagined purity of the family. The logic of the backlash ran as follows: if we can keep the unruly woman (the homosexual, the bohemian, the Negro, the working-class rebel) in her appropriate place, then we can retain a sense of stability and identity. Change was a scary word for many—women and men alike.

Concurrent with the emergence of fears over degeneracy, a sentimentalization of domestic life took shape on the artist's canvas and in the writer's text. At the end of the century, the Swedish painter Carl Larsson (1853–1919) conjured images of idyllic domesticity that continue to enjoy undiminished popularity. "There was even an element of missionary zeal in these images of the wholesome family," Neil Kent writes, "which increasingly found its way into all segments of society. Such images served to inspire others, in turn, to improve the health, morals, nutrition, and general wellbeing of the humblest segments of the population so that they too could enjoy the blessings of a happy and healthy family life."[5] In Norway, the paintings of Gustaf Wentzel (1859–1927) were similar to Larsson's, if somewhat less idyllic. Kent is certainly right when he sees similarities between Hamsun's worship of the healthy family in *Growth of the Soil* and the numerous sculptures by Gustaf Vigeland (1869–1843) that portray the cycle of life and the place of women and men in it.[6]

The formidable resistance of men to women's demands for equality—and of male writers to advances in women's writing—may have made it seem that "victory," that is, something close to equality, was imminent for women. Yet the gap between rhetoric and reality was astounding in every area, particularly in education, employment, politics, and the cultural arena. Still, the new-woman tropes were abundant, and most often used pejoratively or satirically. Only seldom would they be employed as figures of empowering strength. Perceptions of masculinity and femininity were meanwhile being questioned, reconfigured, or reinforced by the new sciences, with voices on both sides of the debate. Post-Darwin science, medicine and psychology in particular, might offer "proof" that supported the importance of traditional roles (women as protective mothers and men as strong providers) or provide arguments for increased equality between the sexes. As more women took seriously the principle of equality as advocated by certain doctors, liberal politicians, and intellectuals, other scientific voices warned them of the potential dangers on their new path; sickness, sterility, and degeneration were potential risks and the price to be paid for nontraditional interests and activities. The consequences of the new ideas and the subsequent cultural questioning and insecurity took several forms: feminism, male-supported feminism, antifeminist backlash, male appropriation of femininity, and the movement for a virile male supremacy.[7]

Critical cultural responses to social change, or to the prospect of social change, included misogynistic portrayals of a devouring femininity, a celebration of traditional gender roles, and ironic portrayals of effeminate men and frigid women. Tales of the downfall of individuals and nations were attributed to the blurring of sexual roles. The upper classes feared that the transgression of class boundaries, which typically occurred in the syphilis-infested bordellos, could bring about annihilation from below. The crossing of racial boundaries further threatened to infect the (white) race and undermine the nation. The arts of the period were filled with images of deviant figures such as the Emancipated or New Woman, the Odd Woman, the dandy and the homosexual, all of whom transgressed the bounds of the normal. Oscar Wilde's notoriety spread across continents, while in Scandinavia, the writers J. P. Jacobsen, Herman Bang, Hans Jæger, and Sigurd Obstfelder represented a new variety of the sensitive, creative (and in some cases gay) male intellectual. In his work, Knut Hamsun cultivated a sort of nervous yet virile image of the creative man.

Many scholars have rightly stressed society's preoccupation with issues of gender and sexuality during the second part of the nineteenth century, and especially around the turn of the century. The idea of "sexual anarchy," which Elaine Showalter uses as the title of her book *Sexual Anarchy: Gender and Culture at the Fin de Siècle,* is an apt metaphor for the way in which the notions of gender governing sexual identity and behavior were redefined and transformed during the fin-de-siècle period in Europe. As Showalter points out, the term "sexual anarchy" was coined by cultural pessimists, traditionalists, and conservatives to describe or represent a civilization facing collapse.[8] Bram Dijkstra has catalogued the ubiquitousness of misogynistic images in nineteenth-century figurative painting, through which artists waged war on women.[9] These were either images of women portrayed in socially prescribed roles as submissive, pale, mute, and childlike or as fertile mothers, or images of predatory, man-eating women who refuse to comply with the roles expected of them. Dijkstra goes even further in his analysis, seeing in the "gynocidal" attitudes of European intellectuals the beginning of the prejudicial attitudes that later enabled the rise of the Third Reich.[10]

In her book *The Gender of Modernity,* Rita Felski echoes Showalter's claims that the alliance between male and female artists was an uneasy one. The male agenda often bordered on appropriation of femininity for the male aesthetic project while neglecting any in-depth exploration of feminine identity. As Felski observes, most male decadent writers played with the performative side of gender, yet simultaneously retained the traditional binary division between men and women, including an essentialist identification of man with rationality, spirit, and self-reflection, and of woman with nature, home, and fertility.[11] It was acceptable for men to rely on intuition for their creative projects, but this was deemed inappropriate for women. Male artifice was welcomed by male artists inasmuch as it represented imagination and creativity, but for actual women, or women artists, such artifice overshadowed and spoiled women's "real" mission: to be mothers and nurturers.

Thus, on the one hand, the male artist of the turn of the century, who often presented himself as decadent or at least as an outsider, represented a challenge to the traditional concept of masculinity as aggressive and entrepreneurial. By rejecting the utilitarian and entrepreneurial achievements of middle-class society, the artist sided with such qualities as intuition and sensitivity, traditionally defined as feminine. On the other hand, many male artists expressed extremely harsh views about women's artistic projects and, in their personal lives, entered into traditional family arrangements. In short, the rebellion of artists against traditional masculinity did not automatically mean support for women's causes, and critique of the traditional society did not automatically translate into lobbying for the rights of women.

Specifically dealing with Scandinavian conditions, Pil Dahlerup's pioneering study *De moderne gennembruds kvinder* (Women of the modern breakthrough) analyzes how gender prejudice influenced male critics—including the key figure of Georg Brandes—during the turbulent and radical period of the Modern Breakthrough.[12] Jørgen Lorentzen shows how the interrogation of traditional male identity is a pivotal obsession of male writers in the period and how the threat, or perceived threat, of a loss of gender identity was extremely problematic for the male writer.[13] Birgitta Holm has presented a new reading of both established and neglected women writers, as well as certain male writers, including Knut Hamsun, showing how gender was an intricate component of their writing.[14] Holm claims that Hamsun was not a feminist in the social sense, that is, he was not a supporter of political emancipation for women, but she continues:

That women should achieve a place in a world where man was the norm, where masculine rationality was in control, did not interest him. "Grand men" were not worth emulating in his world. . . . But he was a feminist in *Mysteries*. A feminist roughly like Irigaray, Hamsun wants to clear space for that which goes against a patriarchal logic: "Contradictions," "The Inconsistencies"—that which is repressed by male rationality and phallic logic.[15]

Holm convincingly demonstrates that Hamsun was aware of the social construct of gender, citing a brief episode in *Mysteries*, in which two lovers disappear into a train station restroom marked "For Women" and later emerge happy and starry-eyed. By focusing on a woman who leads the way (into the restroom) for an amorous encounter, Hamsun chooses real emotions over social norms. Furthermore, *Mysteries* starts and ends with women, while Nagel, the main protagonist, commits suicide defeated and misunderstood. Holm speculates that Hamsun, disappointed over the tepid reception of *Mysteries* and its critique of patriarchal society, may have deliberately changed his (feminist) angle in his later writing.

Hamsun and Modernity

HOW THEN DO WE POSITION HAMSUN AND HIS NOVELS AGAINST THIS RADI- cally changing social and cultural background? Provincial Norway was then in the process of attaining its political independence from Sweden, while Great Britain and France were great empires and Germany was emerging as one. Common topics and trends, including the women's movement, engaged cultural thinkers across Europe. Hamsun was celebrated for having reinter- preted and transgressed the masculinist voice of Scandinavian naturalism and realism, and he was revered for his innovative formal techniques and presentation of fragmented subjectivity—assessments that still hold weight today. Nevertheless, he fundamentally continued to write within the mascu- linist paradigm that seeks to affirm traditional gender categories. The idea and trope of woman are paramount in his texts, as are their variants: the mother, the urban middle-class supported woman, the prostitute, the femme fatale, the innocent country girl, and so forth.

While the depictions of predatory women in Scandinavian art and litera- ture were not as dramatic as those on the continent, some of Hamsun's early texts contain a combination of seductive, vital women and pale, enervated males. Edvard Munch, too, went through a phase during which he intensively investigated the trope of the Dangerous Woman, in part venting his own frus- trations and fears and in part examining stereotypes in the cultural portrayal of women.[16] Just as it would be unfair to consider Munch solely through the narrow lens of misogyny, Hamsun's production should be given fair evalu- ation. Clearly, however, while Hamsun liked his women interesting, erotic, and provocative, this erotic provocation could only go so far, and preferably within the frame of a patriarchal union. Hamsun took women's provocative nonconformity no further than the level of cosmetic performance. That his own wife, or the other women around him, would ever behave like his pro- vocative heroines was out of the question.

Hamsun's early short stories, "Et livsfragment" (A fragment of life),

"Livets kald" (The call of life), and "Kjærlighetens slaver" (Slaves of love), illustrate some of his views on women. While quite different from one another in topic, structure, and form, they describe the basic relationship between men and women as one of opposition, in a pattern that pits vital, successful, and victorious women against victimized men. The coldhearted Nanna from "Et Livsfragment" or the demonic circus lady in the yellow dress from "Kjærlighetens slaver" can be read more as versions of the Femme Fatale, as Dijkstra found her, than as complex protagonists. Hamsun certainly shared his period's stereotypical fears and foibles in many ways, even as he created his own variants of stereotypical images.

Hamsun's fundamental complaint was that many women no longer defined themselves primarily through marriage and motherhood but instead insisted on developing their talents and aspirations. Declining to serve solely as muses, they attempted to be artists and writers, which increased competition for scarce audiences and their money. And while women writers portrayed the New Woman as modest and compassionate—as in the case of Amalie Skram's Else Kant from *Professor Hieronimus* (1895) or Victoria Benedictsson's Selma from *Pengar* (Money; 1885)—in portrayals by Hamsun and Strindberg she was ridiculed and pitied, vilified and exaggerated.

Hamsun is generous in his portrayal of women's sexual desire; women in his works are, more often than not, erotic sexual beings who avidly seek to fulfill their desires. Characters from his novels of the nineties—such as Ylajali from *Sult* (Hunger), Hanka from *Ny jord* (Shallow soil), Edvarda and Eva from *Pan*, as well as women protagonists from his twentieth-century novels and plays, such as Juliane from *Livet ivold* (In the grip of life), Mariane from *Segelfoss by* (Segelfoss town), Lili and Olga from *Ringen sluttet* (The ring is closed)—cannot help but submit to their desire, out of weakness and/or passion. Still, after their stories have been told, women's ultimate role in life, Hamsun insists (either directly or indirectly), is to bear and raise children. Other pursuits—whether education, travel, or creative work—go against their nature and lead to their degeneration and misery.

Common to a number of Hamsun's works from his middle-to-late period are portraits of strong independent women, with aspirations outside of marriage, who undergo transformations into happily tamed wives and mothers. Inger from *Markens grøde* (Growth of the soil) is one such example. Often marriage to a hard-working, dependable man is the conclusion to a disappointed and humbled woman's search for free love, a free union with an artist, or an independent career. Such women, their appetites tamed, come to appreciate the value of a real man. This happens in both *Den sidste glæde* (The last joy; 1912) and *Siste kapittel* (The last chapter; 1923). The title character of *Victoria* (1898) is tamed only through death. Before succumbing to tuberculosis, she confesses that her own stubborn nature is the true cause of her miserable love affair with Johannes. Hamsun's slanted view of women has often, if inconsistently, been noted. James W. McFarlane wrote on the subject as early as 1956.[17] McFarlane stresses that "the reader seeks in vain for any objective or non-partisan picture of women and their modes of thinking and doing; the very structure of the first-person novels prevents it from being otherwise in them; and even where a third-person technique is adopted, the reader is allowed to know of the secret dreams and thoughts of the male hero (including his dreams and thoughts of women) in a way he is denied with the female characters."[18]

It is interesting to follow McFarlane's suggestion and examine some of Hamsun's female protagonists who, freed from the constraints of the first-person male narrator, are, technically, given their own voice. What do they say? In Victoria's famous letter to Johannes—a first-person view in an otherwise omniscient-narrator account—Victoria blames herself and her nature for the failure of the love affair, thus confirming Johannes's presentation of her at the beginning of the novel. Queen Tamara, the title character of the 1903 play, similarly blames herself for an imminent tragedy because of a little pleasure she felt in the presence of the handsome young Muslim Khan of Tovin. In the play *In the Grip of Life*, Juliane ominously announces her final degradation in a union with a black servant, yet is too weak to resist. Both Juliane and Queen Tamara, given voice by Hamsun, are heroines who condemn themselves as both victims and the agents of their own victimhood. Hamsun gives Juliane a strong voice and the somewhat questionable career of an entertainer, only to show where a woman's pursuit of her talents and aspirations takes her: to physical and existential degeneration.[19] Such tragic women stand in for the losses of modernity, as Rita Felski pointedly remarks: "It is often onto the figure of woman that writers project their ambivalence about the path of social progress."[20] This is precisely what Hamsun does in *In the Grip of Life* and *Queen Tamara*. Women who pursue independent professions without strong men to guide them must fail. Queen Tamara regrets her lack of attention to domestic life, and Juliane bemoans how her past has led her to a black man as a kind of punishment for having lived the carefree life of a cabaret performer. Teresita from *Livets spil* (The game of life; 1896) regrets not having found somebody to obey.

The female protagonists Hamsun created after the 1890s are, in general, toned down and more down to earth than those of his earlier works. Juliane is one of the more prosaic characters: a middle-aged woman who formerly entertained audiences from continent to continent, but has ended up without her stage, without her illusions, and without children. Although she can be interpreted as one of Hamsun's many artist-protagonists who battle the issue of creative and existential meaninglessness, Hamsun belittles her art and provides her with no existential or creative opportunities. Although it is now accepted that issues of an existential void and artistic creativity are central to Hamsun's work, the question of how Hamsun gendered creativity remains under-examined. Hamsun's understanding of the connection between creativity and gender is pointedly illustrated by comparing two protagonists whose self-assessments are directly parallel, but whose destinies diverge based on the perceived artistic merits of their gender.

If we compare Juliane's words, "Det går bare nedover med slike some meg" (It only gets worse for people like me), with the lament of the starving protagonist in *Hunger,* "Hvor det hadde gåt jevnt og regelmæssig nedover med mig hele tiden!" (How it has gone steadily downward with me all the time!), it is clear that both protagonists see themselves in dire existential predicaments. Whereas Hamsun allows his hungering hero to counter his existential despair with artistic creativity—of which the prime example is his salvation through the creative invention of a new word, *kuboå,* and the writing of articles—Juliane is not given this option. The possibility that Juliane might be similarly inventive does not occur to Hamsun; her art is, from the very beginning, discredited as "mere" entertainment, and her punishment, a Negro servant as her mate.

Such bias, certainly, extends beyond the level of the text. Applying feminist theory, the Norwegian critic Pål Bjørby has compared the reception of novels by Hamsun and Ragnhild Jølsen, an eloquent female writer of the same period. Glahn, the protagonist from *Pan,* is widely interpreted as a representative of modernist sensibility and social alienation, the novel itself as a modernist classic. However, Jølsen's *Rikka Gan,* a novel that similarly charts the slow dissolution of the protagonist (albeit a woman), has only recently been included in the canon thanks to the deliberate effort of feminist literary scholars.[21] In the traditional view, Jølsen's novel maps a pathological, incoherent female character who deviates from the standard portrayal of Woman. Thus, while Glahn is viewed as a representative of universal modernist change and trauma, Rikka's story is one of personal downfall. Bjørby's analysis provides a good example of how fictional fantasies correlate with real-life values and perceptions.

Personalia

KNUT HAMSUN AND MARIE ANDERSEN MET IN THE SPRING OF 1908 AFTER Hamsun's first marriage to Bergljot Goepfert, née Bech, had dissolved but had not formally ended. Marie was an actress who came to audition for the part of Elina Kareno in Hamsun's play *Livets spil*, which was to be staged by the National Theater in Kristiania. Talented and pretty, Marie was living with a fellow actor, Dore Lavik, at the time. By all accounts it was love at first sight when she met Hamsun, and, after an intense courtship, Marie and Knut married in June of 1909. Their marriage, although stormy and full of tensions, fights, and silences, and despite Knut's escalating mental cruelty toward Marie, lasted until his death in 1952. Marie's last wish, however, was to be buried by the side of her grandson, Espen, rather than with Knut.

Hamsun shared the commonly held view of the time that acting was a questionable profession for a woman. Coerced by Hamsun, who disliked the artificiality and pretense of the stage, Marie Hamsun gave up her acting career. She gave in to Hamsun's numerous other demands and changed her manner of socializing. Robert Ferguson describes Knut's letters to Marie during the period of their courtship as a "sustained assault on Marie's personality."[22] In the years following their marriage, she agreed to move with Knut to various remote locations where he sought to experience his dream of unspoilt nature—a life she eventually enjoyed—only to be left alone, and later alone with their children, for months at a time. Knut, unable to tolerate the interruptions of daily life and the disruptiveness of his young children, preferred to do his writing in hotels and boarding houses. He loved his children and was an attentive father, at least to a point. During his long absences, when he was holed up in a hotel room writing, he remained involved in their upbringing through a copious correspondence with Marie. The monotonous and wearisome work of raising the children was left to the often frustrated Marie. She had her own considerable artistic talents and published several books of her own later in life. Her memoir *Regnbuen* (The rainbow; 1953) enjoyed great success and has become a classic in its genre. Controlled and yet revealing, it is a text that unveils a complicated intimate relationship, passionate and conflicted. Several of her books for and about children also became bestsellers.

From the very beginning, the Hamsuns' relationship was marked by

Knut's extreme jealousy and manipulative behavior. Reading through Knut's correspondence, and Marie's memoir, it becomes clear that Knut's wish to settle in the countryside was quite egotistical. It was motivated by his jealousy and his disgust for the city, which he saw as the locus of erotic and sexual opportunity (as illustrated by the epigraph to this chapter). In a letter dated August 4, 1909, he writes that he does not want to meet Marie in Kristiania but rather in the more provincial Drammen, presumably for similar reasons.[23] On August 12, he writes again, this time fantasizing about an idyllic life on a farm:

> God Almighty, Marie, if you and I had met then and there was not
> such a terrible difference in age and we had fallen in love and mar-
> ried! And gotten each other as often as we wanted. And worked
> outside in the free nature and I was not nervous and grumpy towards
> you. For I would have been the son at the neighboring farm without
> such trifles to do as books and writing. And your and my highest
> goal would have been to run the farm well and beget beautiful strong
> children.[24]

In another letter he muses about Marie's true nature and the pure life she led before she was tainted by the city:

> You were a fabulous child of Østerdal-valley, there was no filth and
> rubbish and trickery there, and you *know* that in your innermost
> thoughts because you have sought back to your original nature. . . .
> That is why I would like it so much for us to no longer stay in the
> city, and instead come here where you had earlier learned to lead a
> good and trustworthy and clean life.[25]

Although obviously captivated by this independent, talented, and beauti-ful woman, Hamsun found it difficult to accept the qualities of independence, talent, and beauty in a wife. It was essential that his wife behave and dress in a dignified way, safeguard her standing in the community, consider her repu-tation, and not talk to just anybody. Marie acted accordingly. It might well be that Knut was particularly aggressive on such points because he viewed the normative patriarchal union as an extremely fragile state of affairs that could dissolve at any given moment, endangered as it was by constant exter-nal temptations and inner passions. *Livet ivold* from 1910 is rightly regarded as as admonition to his wife, an attempt to rein her in and persuade her to abandon her independence and artistic aspirations and to forget her sexual past.[26]

For her part, Marie, when considering the possible publication of her and Knut's love letters, confided to her son Tore:

> I would like to try in my book to give a hint of how his opinion, his will, won out in everything. How he tyrannized me and pushed me from whim to whim in my youth, for in all respects I was dependent on him, which of course was something he made sure I became . . . but I also don't want to give the impression that he deliberately dragged me under the soles of his shoes, held me in constant fear of what he might think up, never in safety, living through all the years with my heart in my throat.[27]

Years later, Marie wrote to her friend, the composer David Monrad Johansen: "I remember that my Knut gave me his 'Feverish' poems one day during our engagement. What stuck most with me were the lines: 'And so it is me who comes, / it is I who comes riding, / and you who run like a dog by my side.' How often did I get the opportunity to remember those words. And yet I do not regret anything."[28]

Knut Hamsun's dream of living on a farm and having lots of children eventually came true. He and Marie had four healthy, talented children and lived in a number of places in the countryside before finally settling at Nørholm, a large and beautiful estate in southern Norway. Hamsun spoke about the value of having children on numerous occasions; a good example is the speech he gave upon accepting the 1920 Nobel Prize in Literature, in which he noted that children provided focus to individuals, families, and nations. In line with turn-of-the-century opinion and the tenets of the larger debate on procreation and degeneration, he saw children as innocent primitives, unspoiled by modern corruption. In Hamsun's universe, in other words, children were an anchor, a blessing, and a miracle.

Family Structure at the Turn of the Twentieth Century

BECAUSE OF THE FEAR OF DEGENERATION, THE PROCREATION OF CHILDREN was considered of utmost importance during this era, and often women were expected to be morally pure in order to bear good children. Ellen Key, the

notable Swedish writer whose ideas on social reform were invoked ubiq-
uitously throughout Europe, particularly in Germany, weighed in on this
debate in many of her writings.[29] In "A New Marriage Law," Key asserts
that the existing marriage law is outdated and not always in the interest of
the wellbeing of children.[30] She argues that while marriage was once a way to
protect children, economically and morally, the society no longer rendered it
impossible for women to protect children through means available outside the
confines of matrimony. Indeed, children would be better protected if dangerous marriages were prohibited or dissolved: "Our time has recognized more
and more the importance of every child as a new member of society and the
right of every child to be born under healthy conditions." A child's worth
should not be determined by his or her legitimacy.[31] She argues that the system in place at the turn of the century "maintains that most crude injustice"
of differentiating between children born in or out of wedlock, which frees
unmarried fathers of their responsibilities and drives unmarried mothers to
commit infanticide or suicide.[32] Hamsun, too, addresses issues pertaining
to illegitimate children in his writings through his own idiosyncratic, but
ultimately positive, lens. For Hamsun, all children are a sign of a vital life,
regardless of their parentage.

What is troubling is Hamsun's disgraceful behavior toward his eldest
child, Victoria, from his first marriage. She was forbidden to visit him and his
new family; her letters to him went unanswered; and most of her efforts to
reach out to him were rejected. Hamsun further exhibited a total disregard for
the disruption that children brought to women's lives. Children arrive with a
balance due—of time, money, and mental energy—that often takes a toll on
the mother's health. Women, far more often than men, have had to make the
hard choice between motherhood and professional activities. Witness how
Hamsun engineered his own family by persuading Marie to give up her acting
career so that he was free to retreat to a hotel—away from the children—to
pursue his writing. More subtle, but no less important, was Hamsun's view
that children were tools for taming women who might otherwise entertain
such outlandish notions as obtaining an education or practicing a profession.

Through the ages, pregnancy and child-rearing have been for women not
only sources of happiness and pride but also of danger and, in many cases,
despair, shame, and poverty. Individuals, interest groups, and the state have
at various times used children as an instrument of pressure and control over
women. In personal relationships, men have often controlled women by keeping them pregnant. States have attempted to regulate women's child-bearing

as a way of dealing with labor shortages, fulfilling military strategies, or meeting farming needs. In other words, having children is not simply a natural process; rather, it is influenced by social conceptions, ideals, and prejudices. In Hamsun's time, marriage was the institution that "sanctioned" the bearing and acceptance of children.[33]

It comes as no surprise that in the late nineteenth century women from all walks of life considered the number of children they would bear as one of the key issues in their lives. It was not just suffragettes who saw birth control as one of the primary tools for women's emancipation. As Sølvi Sogner writes: "Feminist historians have claimed that the drop in birth rates at the end of the nineteenth century was a more important and more meaningful milestone in women's history than the more traditional turning points in political development. When sexuality and reproduction were separated, the situation of women was fundamentally changed."[34] The birth rate in Norway, as well as in the rest of the Western world, decreased markedly around the turn of the twentieth century. As historian Ida Blom writes, "Around the turn of the century we can certainly detect a young generation of women who have a view of marriage different from that which their mothers had accepted. Among the issues the young viewed differently was the question of how many children a woman might have. . . . From 1900 to 1910, the birth rate in the west end of Kristiania decreased by 36 percent."[35] While women have long known secrets for preventing or terminating pregnancies, these methods were unreliable; it was only as the turn of the twentieth century approached that consistent and reliable birth control devices became mass-produced and widely available (in the form of condoms, diaphragms, and pessaries). Blom notes that such prevention methods were used "in a climate where the discussion and practice of contraception were advised against, rather than recommended"; she tentatively concludes that family planning was something decided on between spouses, often in the form of abstinence and interrupted coitus.[36]

Blom also points out, however, that the knowledge and practice of various methods of pregnancy prevention were not confined to Kristiania: "Other studies of birth rates within marriage have shown that by the 1890s birth rates had also declined in the rural districts of Vestlandet and in Northern Norway."[37] While the use of birth control methods started among the higher classes, it soon became common practice. Blom quotes a member of parliament from Tromsø in an 1891 debate, saying that "even in such remote areas as Nordland, I can claim that knowledge about such things (birth control methods) is far from rare."[38] She concludes that, while knowledge of various sorts of modern prevention methods does not necessarily imply their use, "it would be natural to believe, however, that restraint and 'reason'—in the form of interrupted coitus or sexual abstinence—has been a much-used means of limiting the number of pregnancies within a family."[39] When discussing education and employment for married women, Blom draws the conclusion that women's increased professional commitments could not have been a decisive factor in the diminishing birth rates.[40] In her discussion of the importance of education for unmarried women and girls, she notes that the number of girls taking the graduating exam was "microscopic."[41] Nevertheless, by the turn of the century, there was an unmistakable trend in favor of having fewer children, although the underlying reasons varied among the generations: older married women were having fewer pregnancies because more children meant a lower standard of living, while younger women were influenced by ideas of women's emancipation. It was this younger, rapidly expanding group who set the tone for subsequent generations of Scandinavian women.

For the most part, it was well-educated, urban, middle-class women who fought for greater legal and economic equality. It was only women from this tiny social class who did not need to earn a living and therefore had the time to work for reforms. Most women worked extremely hard, either in or outside the home, and emancipation was far from their everyday reality. Thus, women had different experiences depending on their economic status and geography. As Blom writes:

> [F]or all the women who still lived in the countryside, the double
> burden of children and home, on the one side, and the cow barn,
> poultry, water-carrying, berry-picking, etc., on the other, did not lead
> to the same sort of practical and ideological conflicts that their sisters
> faced in the growing cities. In the countryside, the old social form
> continued for a long time, whereas the difference between women's
> and men's work tasks had less importance. But for these women, too,
> it was clearly the case that their formal rights were curtailed by the
> letter of the law.[42]

In this complex historical picture the key word is not (yet) power or change, but visibility. The cultural impact of the visible New Woman, and her childlessness, should not be underestimated; she was the subject of debate in cultural circles, journal editorials, letters to the editor, and in the parliament. While many adjusted to the new reality, as is evident from the practice of birth control by married couples, others were alarmed. Blom concludes: "Some of those who were interested in the question viewed the development, as small as it was, as a threat to women's traditional functions as wives and mothers."[43] Knut Hamsun was certainly among those who saw the new opportunities for women as threatening. He articulated his views on the subject very clearly in his essays, short stories, and plays, and in a more complex way, in his novels.

Hamsun's Views on Women

OF THE NUMEROUS ESSAYS HAMSUN WROTE ABOUT WOMEN, TWO ARE ESPE-cially strident. "Brev om kvinden" (A letter about woman), published in 1896 in *Husmoderen: Tidskrift for hus og hjem* (The homemaker: A journal for house and home), is one long attack on what Hamsun calls development— in quotation marks—for women.[44] Voting rights, women in sports, women's writing, the modern marriage of equal partners, families with fewer chil-dren—he ironizes all the relevant issues for women and dismisses them as fashionable whims. The article contains two cautionary anecdotes. The first concerns a Kristiania wife who allowed an admirer to come home with her and then introduced him to her husband (behavior, Hamsun feels, of which the modern woman is capable). The second describes a bride who made all her furniture herself. The trend, Hamsun concludes, is clear: a woman "lib-erates" herself, has "woken up," but ends up merely imitating men. Men get woodworkers instead of real wives. Hamsun contends that this is only tem-porary: "When those female specimens who emerged in the seventies die out . . . then we'll have reached a new century that will dictate different fashions. Then perhaps it won't be so trendy for women to be mannish."[45] Hamsun would have been utterly dismayed by twenty-first century Norway.

The second essay is Hamsun's text on August Strindberg, a piece first published in 1889 in *Dagbladet* and often reprinted.[46] Hamsun was a great admirer of the Swedish writer, both of his literary works and his worldview, and here he discusses Strindberg's ideas on everything from religion and ancient Greece to the definitions of beauty, science, and art. Although Ham-sun is mildly critical of some of these ideas, it is clear from his enthusiasm that he generally approves of them. Fundamentally, they share the view that nature has been weakened by culture, and man by his focus on science and reading, at the expense of cultivating his body. Hamsun makes a special point in this article of discussing Strindberg's attitudes toward women. Here, too, there are strong parallels with Hamsun's own ideas. Hamsun and Strindberg view women as ignorant, uncreative, and lazy; deem them sly, manipulative, and egotistical; and see them as demanding, despite their hidden and controlling power over men. Hamsun sees in Strindberg's hatred of women both genuine feeling and posturing, and yet he does not question his basic attitude. In fact, it is at times difficult to distinguish here whose ideas are actually being discussed, Strindberg's or Hamsun's.

Hamsun's short story "Kvindeseier" (Woman's victory), which presents a "macabre" reminiscence of Hamsun's days as a Chicago trolley conductor, can also be read as an allegory on the war between the sexes.[47] In this story, a husband's dilettantish attempt to scare his alienated wife into loving him again is outwitted by the wife's murderous plan. The husband, who plans to hide himself in a manhole between the trolley tracks, pays the conductor (Hamsun) to make sure that the trolley will stop just in time. The wife, however, had paid the driver a great deal more money to keep on driving. The husband ends up being decapitated. Given the suggestive way this murder is executed, it makes sense to see the story as a modern variant of the Salome story, a frequent theme of the times.[48] Hamsun continues the war-between-the-sexes motif in his book about America.

The Portrayal of Women in Hamsun's Book on *Amerika*

WHILE IT IS ACCEPTED THAT HAMSUN WAS CRITICAL OF THE AMERICAN DREAM and the American way of life, it is less well known that his book *Fra det moderne Amerikas aandsliv* (From the cultural life of modern America) includes a rabid attack on feminism and feminists. An investigation of the way in which women are represented in this often hilarious work clearly shows Hamsun defending a worldview that is not only anti-democratic and racist but also paternalistic and misogynistic. There are several passages in *Fra det moderne Amerikas aandsliv* where Hamsun makes an explicit connection between women's behavior and the degeneration of morals, culture, and politics. Defending Sarah Bernhardt against a vicious press, Hamsun nevertheless writes the following about women and the arts:

> Much of the prudery in American art can be explained by the fact
> that the great majority of those engaged in painting are *women*. This
> is significant; it is a key explanation for the artistic tastes of the entire
> nation. American women are the leaders of art in their country just
> as the German women now lead *their* literature—and desolate it with

the dexterity of their pens. Either they are rich men's daughters who have learned their art at one of the eighty-eight American academies, or they are married women who on their own initiative, out of boredom and because it is the proper thing to do, have turned to dabbling at home. Making paintings is quite simply feminine handiwork; you do not have to visit very many homes over there before this becomes apparent. It almost seems as if American women feel that they owe it to themselves to bring a couple of hens into the world. The influence of women, which in turn is shaped by the temper of Boston, is so prevalent that it affects all the country's art. And not only the painters and sculptors but also the writers and actors come under its sway. In America the women call the tune.[49]

This might well be Hamsun's idea of satirical wit, but today words like sarcasm and sexism spring to mind more quickly. In a later passage, Hamsun offers the following illuminating comments about women's lives in America:

Truly American women have no house to manage, no husband to help, no children to raise; in the first two years of marriage they may have as many as two children—through carelessness; then they have no more. Sitting there in churches now at the youthful age of thirty to thirty-five, they no longer have any children to look after. They have absolutely nothing to look after; they are unemployed persons. Their cares consist of tending their nerves in the morning, painting works of art until two o'clock, reading *Uncle Tom's Cabin* until six o'clock, and taking a stroll until eight o'clock. The schedule of their daily activities is variable, however. Three or four times a week they may feel impelled—in spite of the great artistic burdens weighing upon them—to steal a modest eight to eleven hours daily for participation in women's congresses. . . . So American women find they are capable of the following occupations in this world: suffering from nerves, painting works of art, enjoying Negro poetry, strolling and participating in congresses. On the other hand, they do not find time to have children.[50]

This is no longer witty by any stretch of the imagination. And while some critics have tried to excuse Hamsun's expression of such attitudes as clever irony, his misogynist message is echoed in the description of several of his women protagonists in later novels. Where is the line drawn on Hamsun's writing on America and its women? Where does it stop being opinion and sarcasm, wrapped in stylistic bravura, and become normative, reductive, and insulting? When do we laugh at Hamsun's puns, and when do we admit that his sense of humor has gone berserk?

Hamsun extrapolated his criticism of women onto American democracy, a political system in which the impulses of women and former slaves ran rampant. Women could easily obtain a divorce, and so dispense with their husbands, Hamsun complained. For him, the best male role model in the United States was the pre–Civil War Southern plantation owner, a kind of Old World patriarch utterly degraded in the post–Civil War era.[51] Hamsun's disdain for American women went beyond simple condescension; his primary concern was their unwillingness to be mothers, and especially their use of birth control:

> They do not find time to have children. By bringing two paper
> hens into the world they feel that they have fulfilled their maternal
> mission. In a way they want to avoid having children; they do not
> want the bother of nursing them; it is too much trouble. As a result
> all the Yankees' ingenuity is set in motion, looking for means of
> preventing childbirth. American women are as thoroughly familiar
> with these measures as ours are with Luther's catechism. If things
> nevertheless go wrong in spite of these measures—through careless-
> ness—there is still a remedy: in the same country where a man in the
> name of morality is condemned to prison for a theory of free love,
> doctors openly advertise their specialty in abortion. . . . American
> women come to them. If it now happens that things still do not go as
> desired—one can of course go to the doctor a small matter of four or
> five months too late—then misfortune has to run its course. A veri-
> table child is born, to put it bluntly, an audaciously real child. And
> that is a misfortune. No chairmanship in a women's congress accom-
> panies such a child. And this the mother rues.[52]

The tirade ends with Hamsun quoting a doctor on the causes of the extremely high mortality rate among American children, supposedly the result of women's refusal to breast-feed their babies. One is reminded of Katti Anker Møller's description of the prevailing expectation that women be "mechanical birthing machine[s]" (*mekanisk fødemaskin*).[53]

The social expectation that women become mothers and criticism of women who deviated from this expectation were widespread. Even so, such views were at times offset by more understanding attitudes among intellectuals. Kristofer Janson, who put Hamsun up at his home in Minneapolis during Hamsun's first American visit, wrote with compassion and understanding about the plight of women and the feminist cause. Janson's wife, Drude, wrote several novels that focused on the lives of women. Hamsun brushed their views aside.

The Portrayal of Women and Children in *Markens grøde* and *Ny Jord*

AGAINST THE BACKDROP OF WORLD WAR I AND A NEWLY INDEPENDENT NOR-way experiencing disillusionment with progress and modernity, Hamsun embarked on a project he described as "a book dedicated to contemporary Norwegian life" (*en Bok til min norske Samtid*).[54] One of its main messages was the value of hard work in settling the wilderness. Like many other Europeans in 1917, Hamsun was looking for a way to end the war and tame progress, and he found it in settlement of the lands in the north. But what contributed significantly to the novel's success was its description of a lasting and harmonious—although hardly frictionless—marital life, far from the poisonous discussion about women's emancipation. The wild and destructive passion for the opposite sex described in Hamsun's earlier novels is replaced here by a shared responsibility for the farm and children. *Markens grøde* appeared only four years after the general franchise was established in Norway in 1913. The message, while aimed at both sexes, is most clearly articulated for women: return to nature and natural cycles, and turn away from so-called progress and the degenerating modern lifestyle. Hamsun turns to the semi-utopian project of living the pioneer life amid the untamed nature of northern Norway, describing in broad strokes how untamed nature is domesticated. The taming of nature parallels the taming of the novel's female protagonists. In *Markens grøde*, Hamsun fundamentally writes against the feminism he had first observed—and detested—in the United States and which he believed had now caught up with him in Norway.

In his novels, Hamsun pushed for what sociologists and demographers have called "natural fertility." The presentation of women, children, and fertility in *Markens grøde* illustrates Hamsun's way of dealing with the modern opportunities available to women. Published in 1917, *Markens grøde* was almost immediately a popular and critical success and enjoyed several printings in numerous European languages. In 1920, it earned Hamsun the Nobel Prize in Literature. The novel may be read as a recipe for taming women's passions and appetites for non-maternal interests. It can also be read as Hamsun's experiment in generosity, as extramarital sexuality is here treated with compassion and, through children, is inserted into something larger and more important, namely, the cycle of life.

Hamsun was convinced that the settlement of the northern region of Norway would stem emigration, while the ensuing return to the traditional values of family and working the soil would strengthen the country. In this picture, men are valued as the tillers of virgin soil, and women as mothers and homemakers. It is therefore important to look closely at how the women in *Markens grøde*—Inger, Barbro, Inger's daughters, and Mrs. Heyerdahl—are portrayed, especially in regard to their motherhood (or lack thereof). Inger is the novel's main female protagonist. Although described as not pretty because of a cleft lip, she is strong, hard working, and attractive, and her fertility has been incorporated into the rhythm of life on the farm. Inger, as a woman who is constantly producing offspring, stands for the overall positive message of the novel as exemplified in the following passage:

And now little Silverhorns had calved, the sheep had lambs, the goats had kids, the young stock fairly swarmed about the place. And what of the people? Eleseus could walk already, all by himself wherever he pleased, and little Sivert was christened. Inger? She was surely getting ready for another child, she was so fertile. Another child—oh, a mere nothing to Inger! . . . now her time has come, she was in full flower and constantly with child.[55]

Inger gives birth to five children over the years and, at the end of the book, is referred to as the mother of her tribe. Time and again, Inger is described as big and beautiful in her strength and raw fertility. Hamsun is here writing in opposition to the predominant contemporary cultural model at a time when "the muscular and robust woman was out of fashion,"[56] having yielded her place to a more middle-class image of the slender, pale, and often helpless urban woman. Hamsun thus grants women healthy bodies and, to a certain extent, partnership with their husbands on the farm. He envisions clearly defined gender roles and expectations as manifested in the respective attitudes of Inger and her husband Isak to children. She has a practical, down-to-earth attitude toward her deliveries, while Isak is overwhelmed by the miracle of childbirth, his sentiment underscored by a poetic textual passage.

While Hamsun detested the notion of intervening in the conception and bearing of children, the novel displays his understanding of eugenic methods. Inger's and Barbro's motherhood strategies, which include pregnancy, prevention of pregnancy, and infanticide, are structuring topoi in the book.[57] Although the novel is a rich tapestry of events, the first part focuses on Inger's story and the second part on Barbro's, both women being infanticidal mothers. In addition, a prominent part of *Markens grøde* deals with Fru Heyerdahl's failed attempts to avoid motherhood. From his conservative viewpoint, Hamsun structured his novel around one of the crucial social issues of the time—the effort of women to regulate their pregnancies and control the number of children they bore.

Hamsun's presentation of Inger's infanticide is compassionate. When her baby girl is born with a cleft lip, Inger strangles her because of her feelings about her own deformity. The murder causes suffering for both Inger and Isak, but it can nevertheless be accepted, explained, and understood. We are told that Isak, although shaken and distressed, pities her, because he connects the crime with Inger's fears of Os-Anders' black magic. When Inger returns from prison in Trondheim, she has changed. Her cleft lip has been corrected with a simple operation. Not only have her looks improved and her lisp vanished, but she now speaks with elegance and style. She has also become restless and impatient with farm chores. She starts a sewing business and wants a maid, just like families in town. She has several affairs with the engineers who work in the area. She becomes religious. All the attributes associated with Inger's new behavior have negative connotations in Hamsun's universe, from modern surgery to religion. And then there is Inger's knowledge about birth control. After Inger's return from Trondheim, she and Oline have a conversation about Os-Anders's black magic, in which we find out that Inger has learned to control her own fertility:

> Said Inger then: "What harm could it do if he did come, anyway? He can't hurt me any more."—Oline pricked up her ears: "Ho, you've learned a trick for that?"—"I shan't have any more children," said Inger.
>
> Why should Inger say that about having no more children? She was not on bad terms with her husband, 'twas no cat-and-dog life

between them—far from it. . . . She might have had children till past fifty; as it was, she was perhaps hardly forty now. She had learned all sorts of things at the institution—had she also learned to play tricks with herself? She had come back so thoroughly trained and educated after her long association with the other murderesses; maybe the men had taught her something too—the wardens, the doctors. She told Isak one day what one young medical man had said of her little crime: "Why should it be a criminal offence to kill children—ay, even healthy children, well-developed children? They were nothing but lumps of flesh after all."[58]

In the spring, however, Inger is pregnant again, in tune with the rhythm of the seasons and content as part of a large rural family. By then, her passion for other men, and perhaps also for Isak, has run its course. Isak looks back nostalgically on times of passion now gone. This is how the novel envisions sexuality and fertility through the prism of Isak's memory:

Oh, it was a good life in those days, he was cutting cordwood, and Inger watched, those were his best days. And when March and April came, he and Inger would be crazy for each other, just like the birds and animals in the forest, and when May came he would sow his corn and plant potatoes, living and thriving from day to dawn. Work and sleep, love and dreams, he was like the first big ox, and that was a miracle, big and shiny as an entering king.[59]

The novel pays tribute to people as part of nature and its cycles. Formal marriage in itself is insignificant; what is important is the relationship between Isak and Inger and their children. Their union is sacred. After their first night together, she is already referred to as his wife, although they do not marry until their child needs to be baptized.

In terms of sexual morality, Hamsun paints a picture of monogamous men and promiscuous women. Isak's sexual and emotional life is centered on Inger and linked to the rhythms of nature and farm work. It is Inger who cannot control herself and falls in and out of love several times. The narrator benevolently grants her the pleasure of these affairs, yet makes several derogatory remarks about women in general and about Inger in particular; for example, he observes that Inger is a woman like other women and the sole reason for her earlier fidelity to Isak was the absence of temptation.[60]

The narrator suggests that a woman's sexual appetite does not necessarily discriminate between men so long as it is satisfied:

Inger? Inger was out plucking berries, had been out plucking berries ever since Isak went to the mountains—she and Gustaf the Swede. Ay, the old woman, all confused and in love. . . . "Come and show me where there's cloudberries," said Gustaf; "hjortron," said he. And how could a woman say no? Inger ran into her little room and was both earnest and religious for several minutes; but there was Gustaf standing waiting outside, the world was at her heels, and all she did was to tidy her hair, look at herself carefully in the glass, and out again. And what if she did? Who would not have done the same? Oh, a woman cannot tell one man from another: not always, not often.[61]

The novel's message of natural procreation is put in relief by the harsher story of Barbro, who is carrying someone else's child when Axel marries her. Barbro and Axel's tug of war provides a considerably less idealized parallel to Inger and Isak's marital disputes. Axel is a solid, stable, and hard-working farmer, while Barbro is described as a pretty country girl with the mentality of a servant girl and a "small pitiful Negro brain," who leads a promiscuous life in Bergen.[62] Hamsun portrays her as quarrelsome, with an unquenchable desire to become part of the Bergen middle class. Her sudden return to the village and her employment at Axel's farm, Måneland, is later explained by the appearance of a dead child's body in Bergen harbor. Wishing to keep her on the farm, Axel hopes that her second unwanted pregnancy will be a sort of leash.[63] However, when Barbro drowns her second child, Axel realizes that "the arrangement has become less of a tie. Barbro felt herself no more at home there now than any other servant-girl, no more bound to the place. Axel could see that his hold on her had relaxed with the death of the child. He had thought to himself so confidently: wait till the child comes! But the child had come and gone."[64]

Axel is no fool; he is a calculating farmer who needs farm hands. Still, he is described as having a basic decency, while she is a murderess without conscience. The text comments: "Infanticide meant nothing to her, there was nothing extraordinary in the killing of a child; she thought of it only with the looseness and moral nastiness that was to be expected of a servant-girl."[65] She does not feel any guilt, justifying her behavior on the grounds that the elites in Bergen and Kristiania do the same, and with doctors' help: "What about all the married people in the towns and the things they did? They killed their children before they were born—there were doctors who managed that. They didn't want to have more than one, or at the most two children, and so the doctor opened the uterus a little bit." [66] Ultimately, with her other possibilities exhausted, she settles into the relationship with Axel on the farm. Barbro is a cold-hearted murderess in contrast to Inger, whose infanticide can be forgiven. In his portrayal of both women, Hamsun describes women who enjoy their sexuality and are reluctant to accept the responsibility of having children, albeit for different reasons. In the course of the novel they are transformed into wives and mothers.

Cultural historian Brit Berggreen sees in traditional agriculture an example of cooperation between men and women in which women's contribution to farming was significant. [67] However, by the late nineteenth century, farming was increasingly perceived as men's work. As Berggren explains, "A picture of the man as field cultivator, stock breeder, and garden tiller was laid over the earlier picture of Norwegian farm culture in which women were active in these roles." [68] In the character of Isak, Hamsun uses precisely this new picture of the male farmer as the planter of grain. In fact, the sower is one of the book's dominant metaphors:

> For generations back, into forgotten time, his fathers before him had
> sown grain; solemnly, on a still, calm evening, best with a gentle fall
> of warm and misty rain, soon after the grey goose flight. Potatoes
> were a new thing, nothing mystic, nothing religious; women and chil-
> dren could plant them—earth-apples that came from foreign parts,
> like coffee; fine rich food, but related to turnips. Grain was bread,
> grain or no grain meant life or death. [69]

Women are here associated with potatoes, a prosaic everyday staple imported from the Americas. With some poetic license, grain is connected to the question of life and death, unlike potatoes, although in fact these lowly tubers saved many a European from starvation. In another passage, Hamsun refers to *den velsignede potet* ("the blessed potato"), in a kind of balancing act with the grain passage above. Still, the narrative weight is clear: the mythological underpinnings of the grain passage are unmistakable, while potatoes, despite their versatility and usefulness, do not quite share in the life-and-death drama. Grain and potatoes mark the male and female worlds, different, and most importantly, different in rank.

When Brit Berggreen writes about the concept of farmer as it was perceived around 1890, she notes that the word "farmer" (*bonde*) included both
the male and female farmer. There was a high degree of equality in the farm
and village community, and the division of labor between women and men
was, for the most part, clear. Before the professionalization of agriculture,
she writes, "there existed a clear understanding about what was men's work
and what was women's work."[70] Under women's responsibilities she lists
work with textiles, care of animals (except for horses), the production of
cheese and butter, and planning the distribution of food over the calendar
year for the entire household. Hamsun, indeed, describes Inger as being well
respected on Sellanraa farm, in the maintenance and expansion of which she
plays an indispensable role. *Markens grøde* is full of clearly differentiated
gender roles. Inger weaves, while Isak chops wood; he takes care of the horse
and she takes care of the child; and so forth. In Hamsun's view, this sort of
patriarchal equality is how the world should be—a way of life different from
what he had observed in cities and seen in the United States.

Despite his being portrayed as a nearly mythological pioneer figure, Isak
is a man of modernity: he acquires the latest model of grass-mower, accepts
money as payment, and deals with state institutions. It is important to note
that one of his conflicts with Inger breaks out over money, a symbol of modern society. In this pivotal scene, which is later described as a turning point
and the most important event of the year, Isak lifts Inger off the floor and
thumps her down with all his strength. This show of force changes Inger back
to the supportive wife she was prior to her imprisonment in Trondheim. The
event was triggered by Inger's trying to take money that Isak considered his.
Thus, although they may be equal as partners on the farm, they are not equal
when it comes to money, and he can dominate her with his sheer physical
strength. Isak's double standards—she cannot have a sewing machine while
he gets a mowing machine—permeates all other aspects of life. While they
may appear to be equals, he is more equal than she is, since he has access to
machinery, advances in technology, money, and other conveniences provided
by the emerging capitalist society. Hamsun's compelling writing makes us
believe that we are reading about a utopian agrarian society, while in reality,
he is describing the accumulation of material wealth and modern technology
that characterizes early capitalism. In contrast to such men of modernity, the
women in Hamsun's universe are supposed to remain mothers and wives, full
of "natural" sex and untainted by money or education.

The text insists that on the cosmic scale, we are all equal, we are all just specks in the universe. Yet here, too, there is a difference: unlike Inger, Isak is portrayed as connected to the mystic power of the universe, power that is eternal and specifically Norwegian. Women remain associated with the prosaic potato, and although they bear and raise children, they are not quite capable of grasping what motherhood means in the vastness of the universe.

Sivert, Inger and Isak's firstborn, is an improved version of Isak, with a jester's touch, who eventually takes over the family farm. Eleseus is the problematic child, damaged and made rootless by the city. A bachelor, he is without a family of his own: "A strange man to live in the wilds, a gentleman with thin writer's hands, and the sense of a woman for finery, for canes and umbrellas and galoshes. Frightened off, and exchanged, an incomprehensible bachelor. Even his upper lip declines to put forth any brutal degree of growth."[71] Given his bad luck with women and his lack of interest in farm work, Eleseus seems surplus material. Indeed, the adjective "exchanged" seems to suggest that he does not really belong biologically to this family. He is off to America one day, an effeminate bachelor going to the woman-friendly New World. He never returns.

Finally, there is Mrs. Heyerdahl, who at one point decides not to have children. In portraying her, Hamsun caricatured the emancipated New Woman. The text tells us: "Lensmand Heyerdahl had married the year before. His wife had no intention of ever being a mother—no children for her, thank you! And she had none."[72] In the end, Heyerdahl becomes a mother in spite of herself, two times, and the community has great fun with this:

> But the Lensmand's lady had had a child after all—in spite of the way she'd spoken at the women's club against the increasing birth-rate among the poor; better give women the franchise and let them have some say in their own affairs, she said. And now she was caught. Yes, the parson's wife had said "She's had some say in lots of things, ha, ha, ha!—but she has not escaped her destiny." These clever words about Mrs. Heyerdahl that went the round of the village, and there were many that understood what was meant—perhaps Inger understood it too; it was only Isak who did not understand.[73]

Before she had children, Fru Heyerdahl lobbied for women's issues. The novel ridicules her as a naive stick-in-the-mud without any common sense, as illustrated by her testimony as a defense witness in Barbro's trial for infanticide. Rarely is Hamsun's text as ironic as in the courtroom passage. While the lawyers and other state representatives are portrayed ironically and the whole trial is called a comedy, the focus rests on Fru Heyerdahl's defense speech. The ability to speak well, a charismatic talent usually praised in Hamsun's male characters, is ridiculed here:

> When her turn came, she stood there before them all and was a great lady indeed; she took up the question of infanticide in all its aspects, and gave the court a long harangue on the subject—it almost seemed as if she had obtained permission beforehand to say what she pleased. Ay, folk might say what they would of Fru Lensmand Heyerdahl, but make a speech, that she could, and she was well educated in politics and questions of society. 'Twas a marvel where she found all her words. Now and again the presiding justice seemed wishful to keep her to the point, but maybe he had not the heart to interrupt, and let her run on.[74]

The Belgian scholar Alex Bolckman argues that the section concerning Fru Heyerdahl is structured as a short story.[75] If Hamsun was willing to interrupt the otherwise carefully arranged structure of the novel in order to include this section, then he must have considered the issue of women in court, indeed, of women's emancipation, a burning one and could not resist mocking a New Woman and her public appearance. Hamsun uses Fru Heyerdahl to exemplify what women should not become. In Hamsun's ideal universe, women should never leave home and family. Yet it is women, with their constant desire to reach beyond their assigned social place, who provide ample material for his fantasies. Nonetheless, his urge to control them always leads him to tame them in one way or another.

If we look at *Ny jord* (Shallow soil), published in 1893, as a story about taming women, it is easy to see it as Hamsun's reply to Ibsen's monumental play *A Doll's House*. Through the story of Hanka, Hamsun reflects on what happens to Ibsen's Nora after she leaves the family, a topic that has preoccupied many later writers and scholars. One can agree with Harald Næss, who deems this lesser known novel a good one.[76] It has been overshadowed by the more experimental modernist novels such as *Mysteries* and *Pan*, but its captivating portrayal of Kristiania as a dynamic modern trade city, sarcastic presentation of Bohemian artists, and two well-developed melodramatic love stories make it an interesting and enjoyable read. The novel's presentation of global trade as positive and merchants as innovative, daring, and mature shows that Hamsun's worldview was not always anti-modern. The two main protagonists, Andreas Tidemand and Ole Henriksen, are entrepreneurial, decent, and hard-working merchants. They generously support Bohemian writers, painters, and journalists, who return the favor by complaining about repressive and boring bourgeois society. The portrayal of artists is caustic: their self-aggrandizement, poor work habits, readiness to be supported by the middle class, and attempts to outmaneuver each other in the race for lucrative state grants are mercilessly portrayed.

In the course of the novel, Irgens, a poet, seduces both Tidemand's wife, Hanka, whom he exploits sexually and financially, and Henriksen's fiancé, Aagot Lynum, whom he eventually marries. While Hanka, the older and smarter of the two women, soon realizes Irgens's deceptiveness and returns to her husband and children, Henriksen commits suicide after Aagot, not yet nineteen, is corrupted by Irgens and his clique into a coarse woman who drinks, smokes, and frequents cafés. Hamsun's disapproval of the Bohemian circle notwithstanding, the weight of his criticism rests on the New Woman, as exemplified by Hanka and Aagot, and their befuddled and immoral lives of newly found freedom.

When the novel opens, Hanka and Andreas Tidemand have been married for four years and have two children. Hanka, lively and popular, is initially described as an artist by nature (*kunstnernatur*) who does not have much sense for keeping house.[77] But a conversation between Andreas and Ole reveals that her failure at housekeeping is not the worst of it. Worse yet is her decision not to have more children:

> This unbearable blessing of a child each year two years in a row
> made her really desperate; God almighty, she was no more than a
> child herself, full of blood and irrationality, she had her youth in
> front of her. She forced herself for a while, it ended that the young
> wife lay crying at night. But following the understanding that the
> couple finally agreed to last year, Hanka did not need to force herself
> any longer.[78]

Hanka resembles the spoilt modern American women, described in *Fra det moderne Amerikas aandsliv*, who simply did not want to bother having more than one or two children. This American trend, Hamsun suggests, has now reached Norway. Andreas further reveals that he must seek her company away from home, at restaurants. "What shall I do at home," he asks. "Hanka is not home, there is no food, I don't see anybody in the rooms. We have closed down our household, through a friendly agreement."[79]

The novel thus sets up a caricature of marriage that to most readers must have appeared extraordinary for the times, an impression confirmed by Ole's reaction, a gaping mouth. Andreas sums up his marriage: "Now and then, she lives where I live, we take care of the children, come in and out of the house, and go our separate ways."[80] Further building his case against modern marriage as he understood it, Hamsun describes Hanka as a woman in search of a professional goal who ignores her two children and the household affairs. To top it off, she has even begun to use her maiden name, calling herself Hanka Lange Tidemand. This is how Hamsun sets up the novel, including all of this information in the Introduction, which ends with Ole bringing his innocent fiancé Aagot to town.

In the main part of the novel, Hanka pursues Irgens, while Irgens, after their brief affair, starts flirting with Aagot and "so Aagot's little goose head was touched."[81] The narrative core is a long monologue by Andreas Tidemand, the cuckolded husband who nevertheless retains his dignity. The monologue spans more than one uninterrupted page.[82] Andreas and Ole, readers are led to understand, are trustworthy, decent men with one fatal flaw: they do not control their women but rather let them make their own decisions. Neither Hanka nor Aagot handle their freedom responsibly, wasting their dignity on undeserving men. This message of poor judgment is reinforced by the comments of Coldevin, a former teacher and a somewhat enigmatic character who shadows Aagot and Hanka around town. During a seventeenth of May celebration, Coldevin offers a long reflection on how home is no longer what it used to be, essentially because of the women's movement.[83] After Aagot and Irgens's upcoming marriage becomes public, Coldevin further reflects on women's deteriorating sense of pride, their poor judgment, and their readiness to be seduced with poor verse.[84] Coldevin's opinion is echoed in one of Ole's last comments before he shoots himself: "How they have corrupted her, how they have corrupted her."[85]

In the meantime, Andreas has agreed to a divorce, but Hanka, now struggling alone and living in a shabby room, slowly realizes what she has abandoned and eventually reunites with her husband and children. This is only possible after he has decided to be the leader in their relationship. Hanka is described with enough depth and complexity to make her decision to return to her family and her newfound happiness with her husband believable. Hamsun certainly knew, from his own experience and from his observation of the Kristiania Bohemians, how difficult it would be for a woman to support herself and lead an independent life. Still, it is simply impossible for Hamsun to imagine a woman alone and content, independent and creative. Instead, the cruel reality of independent life tames Hanka into seeing the benefits of a family and the love of her husband. While Ibsen's play is open-ended as to when the miracle of a partnership between Nora and Helmer, husband and wife, might come into being, Hamsun actually envisions it: a dose of reality reveals to Hanka the value of a partnership of two decent individuals within the confines of a patriarchal marriage. This happy ending privileges marriage and motherhood at the expense of Hanka's *kunstnernatur* on which no more words are wasted.

3

IMAGINING THE INDIANS

Your wife has now written a new book? Will it be out soon? I have heard that it is about Indians. Ugh, why can't you, Mrs. Janson, write a book about yourself? Oh my dear, don't go and waste yourself on such stuff as Indians. You yourself know well enough, when you give it a thought, that the grand poetry of the Indians is a big American lie. The Indians are simply half-apes. I have visited those animals two times. God what a smell! Forgive me for being angry with this desperate attempt of yours.

—Hamsun's letter to Kristofer Janson, circa 1888

IN THIS LETTER TO HIS FORMER EMPLOYER, KRISTOFER JANSON, HAMSUN, with his characteristically blunt arrogance, dismisses Native Americans as "half-apes" and "animals." Such an attitude was neither better nor worse than that of many European visitors to the United States in the late nineteenth century. Hamsun chose to stress the negative aspects of the idea of the Noble Savage, a conception that Philip Deloria aptly describes as "a flexible ideology." Depending on where one placed the emphasis, the meaning and application of the term could, and did, change.[1] A focus on the "nobility" of the Indians underscored the authentic spirit of the New World and implied a critique of old, corrupt Europe.[2] Placing the stress on "savage," however, could form the basis for an argument in favor of eliminating any indigenous tribe that resisted assimilation, acculturation, or western resettlement; in this sense, the term corresponded to the portrayal of Native Americans as cruel, revengeful, bloodthirsty, cheating, unreliable, smelly, and filthy. Hamsun, too, stresses the stench of the savage in his letter to Janson, and he rejects their reputedly noble culture as a lie.

In terms of identity formation, savage Indians enabled the new, predominantly white Americans to see themselves as civilized individuals and members of a civilized nation.[3] Still, constructed as an emblem of freedom in wild nature, the Indians were irresistibly attractive to Europeans, especially those Europeans with a bit of imagination, and triggered contradictory feelings of desire and repulsion.

Just a few years before he wrote this letter, Hamsun described one of his visits to "those animals" in "Fra en Indianerleir" (From an Indian camp), an article published in two installments in the Norwegian daily *Aftenposten* (May 2 and 4, 1885).[4] The article presents his general reflections on the American Indian way of life as well as a detailed portrait of his 1883 visit to an Indian village near Briggsville, Wisconsin, during his first trip to the United States. The core of the article is an account of a purported discussion with two Shawnee chiefs, Yellow Thunder and Broad Shoulder.[5] I have shown elsewhere that these two Native Americans, whom Hamsun portrays with great flair, are to a large extent a fabrication of his lively imagination.[6] On such points as these, my findings contradict established Hamsun scholarship as, for instance, represented by Lars Frode Larsen, who in his discussion of "Fra en Indianerleir" expresses no doubts concerning Hamsun's journalistic integrity; on the contrary, he states that Hamsun's "ideal is faithfulness to reality."[7] In light of the circumstances of this particular article, and Hamsun's nonchalant attitude toward sources in general, my conclusion is that he simply made up some of the things he reports as factual.[8]

In the mixed-genre essay, Hamsun combines journalistic reporting with a freely invented core story. Will T. Ager, whom several sources mention as the friend who took Hamsun to Wisconsin's Lake Mason where the Indians were supposedly setting up their temporary village, does not mention Indians at all in his reminiscence of the event.[9] While it is very likely that Hamsun did indeed come into contact with Native Americans in Wisconsin, his two main protagonists are constructs based on folklore, local stories, popular literature, dime novels, and, probably, photographs. In this context, the photographs depicting Native Americans by Henry Hamilton Bennett come to mind.[10] Bennett's work was widely used to advertise Wisconsin's beautiful scenery, with romantic images of subdued Indians.[11] Further west, the Indian threat was still something to be reckoned with, but Wisconsin was hoping to capitalize on the attraction of its landscape, spiced with exotic yet docile natives. In fact, one of Bennett's widely circulated photos, taken in the early 1870s, showed a certain Chief Yellow Thunder and two other Indians outside a rather shabby tent, a far cry from the majestic teepee of Wild West romance.[12]

Hamsun was a keen reader of popular trivial literature, a fact apparent in his earliest works.[13] Hamsun's later novels, too, borrow from popular genres, as Atle Kittang points out in reference to the 1898 novel, *Victoria*.[14] We also know that James Fennimore Cooper's *The Last of the Mohicans* appeared in Danish as early as 1826 and that by 1861 Cooper's collected works had been published in Denmark in 209 booklets.[15] In addition, Longfellow's *Song of Hiawatha* was translated into Danish five years after its initial publication in English in 1855. Classics such as *Robinson Crusoe* were also popular with Scandinavian readers. A fascination with exotic non-European peoples living in areas as diverse as the South Seas, Egypt, and the United States swept across Europe in the eighteenth and nineteenth centuries. Not only literature, but also museum collections and the visual arts of the era testified to the popular enthusiasm for knowledge of the West.

"Fra en Indianerleir" conveys complex, multilayered attitudes and a wide range of emotions toward the Indians, from empathy and understanding about their vanishing traditions to revulsion at their apparent lack of hygiene. While Hamsun blames external causes for the persistent deterioration of the native peoples' living conditions, he also reveals a racist and condescending attitude, not unlike that of many of his contemporaries. Thus, he participates in what is customarily called colonial ambivalence. Writers like Hamsun engaged in rhetorical conquest, but it was conquest just the same: by providing their own imaginative narratives for the reading audiences of Europe and appropriating the natives' rhetoric and images, they aestheticized the reality of Native Americans instead of providing them with a voice. Hamsun evokes a nostalgic picture of the canoes of the past and invents an interview with the proud savages of the present. He continues a tradition begun centuries earlier by the first conquistadors: he imagines and interprets the natives as objects to be admired and marveled at, feared, reviled, and exhibited as exotic primitives.

Hamsun was just one of many Scandinavian travelers intrigued by American Indians. Besides the now classic three volumes of travel impressions of

America by the Swedish writer Fredrika Bremer, *Hemmen i den nya världen* (The homes of the New World; 1853–1854), there is the well-known memoir *Boganis jagtbreve* (Boganis's hunting stories) by the Dane Wilhelm Dinesen, father of Karen Blixen.[16] Dinesen published the account of his time with the Chippewa in northeastern Wisconsin between 1872 and 1874 under the pseudonym "Boganis," the name given him by the Chippewa.[17] Despite the relative proximity of the Wisconsin locations they describe, the reports of Dinesen and Hamsun differ significantly in their portrayal of the Native Americans. Dinesen's largely positive description of life with the Indians stands in contrast to Hamsun's condescending description of his short encounter with them.

In general, the level of literacy was high in the Scandinavian countries thanks to the efforts of the Lutheran church. Compulsory education had been mandated in Norway in 1739, so it is reasonable to assume that it was not only the urban elites who read the available religious and secular texts, including those about foreign places and peoples.[18] Given the enormous popularity of these texts, it seems likely that Hamsun read some of these stories, as well as emigration pamphlets and letters. Judging from the range of books, journals, and articles Hamsun mentions or reviews in *Fra det moderne Amerikas aandsliv* (1889), it is obvious that he read widely and indiscriminately during his stay in the United States, not only books from Kristofer Janson's library of European classic and contemporary literature but also popular dime novels. The two main Indian protagonists of "Fra en Indianerleir" are probably a kaleidoscopic composition of many different impressions.

Deloria, in *Playing Indian*, explores the way racial imagination has figured into the complex attempt by (mainly) white Americans to define themselves as a nation. Just as blackness, constructed in various cultural and historical representations, is an essential element against which American whiteness has been contrasted, so, too, is Indianness. "The figure of the Indian," Deloria claims, "holds an equally critical position in American culture."[19] American identity has always been in flux and unfinished, and Deloria attributes this in part to the unfinished elimination of, and continuous threat posed by, Indians: "The indeterminacy of American identities stems, in part, from the nation's inability to deal with Indian people. Americans wanted to feel a natural affinity with the continent, and it was Indians who could teach them such aboriginal closeness. Yet, in order to control the landscape they had to destroy the original inhabitants."[20]

In American cultural attitudes, Deloria writes, modernity has constructed

Indianness and Indian play as the experience of the authentic within the context of encroaching industrialization and urban disillusionment.[21] Play, performance, and art were often spaces for fantasy and desire in which primitivism could be idolized. As the landscape became more and more domesticated, reveries of a free and erotic paradise were combined with fantasies of power.

Hamsun was, of course, not an American, nor did he desire to become one. Perceiving America as a new, raw, and in many respects barbaric state, Hamsun's American allegiances rested with the Norwegian or sometimes broader Scandinavian communities of the Midwest. Hamsun participated in many cultural, political, and benevolent activities in the Minneapolis expatriate community.[22] Yet for all his involvement with the Nordic diaspora, Hamsun remained an outsider to the upper echelons of Scandinavian immigrant society, not to mention the American cultural elite. This is in stark contrast to his compatriot Bjørnstjerne Bjørnson, who had visited the United States several years before Hamsun and had access to many important cultural figures. Bjørnson wrote enthusiastically about America, while Hamsun was extremely critical of the country. In *The Cultural Life of Modern America*, for example, he attacked the raw barbaric spirit of the American people and their moralistic and restrictive, if haphazard, application of laws and regulations. Still, when it came to Indians, Hamsun displayed the standard attitudes of white Americans: at best, a melancholy sympathy for the seemingly inevitable decline of a noble race, and at worst, disgust over their supposed body odors and mental atavism. Even if noble and proud, they could not possibly be acculturated to civilization.

"As European immigrants arrived in the New World they were also socialized into racial hierarchies surrounding 'whiteness' that conferred relative status and privilege," writes historian Betty Bergland in her groundbreaking article on Norwegian immigrants' attitudes toward Indians.[23] Despite coming from the margins of Europe, moreover, Norwegians were able to exploit their whiteness since the colonial politics of exclusion was contingent on the construction of racial categories. For those immigrants unable to form elites or shape overall policies, there was always the option of claiming and settling land. Indeed, Norwegian immigrants of the nineteenth century appear to have claimed land in larger numbers than any other immigrant group, choosing to live in small rural settlements rather than cities. Odd Lovoll, who has researched Norwegian immigration patterns, found that Norwegians were "the most rural of any immigrant group in the nineteenth century."[24]

Norwegians also resisted the subsequent urbanization process more than other immigrant groups. According to the 1900 census, only one quarter of Norwegian-born immigrants in America lived in cities with a population of more than twenty-five thousand, "the lowest percentage of any European immigrant group," Lovoll notes elsewhere.[25] In other words, three out of four Norwegian immigrants lived in rural areas or small settlements, a demographic pattern that lasted well into the twentieth century. Given their focus on land ownership as both a form of material security and a cultural value, it comes as no surprise that Norwegians came into direct conflict with Native Americans.

In light of Hamsun's lifelong investigation of the struggle between culture and nature and the ways in which the interconnectedness of the two influences artistic creativity, it is interesting to see how Hamsun was preoccupied, in this early article, with comparing these two categories. He examines the different stages of Shawnee chief Broad Shoulder's life by evaluating the separate influences of both civilized and primitive environments. As a person of mixed-blood, born in the wild and raised by whites, Broad Shoulder is split between his "original" race's instincts and the white man's bookish learning. There are no historical records to be found on Broad Shoulder, although Hamsun's article includes a long footnote about his genealogy, assuring the reader that the discussion with Broad Shoulder is reported as truthfully as possible under the circumstances. It remains highly enigmatic as to why Hamsun added this particular footnote at all, though we can certainly speculate that Hamsun wanted to add an aura of veracity to his article.[26] For contemporary readers, most interesting is Hamsun's reflection on the nature-culture dichotomy and the survival of the races. As Broad Shoulder puts it, "A divide opened up between my aimless original nature and the rituals, the schemes, the liturgies."[27] He is healed when he returns to his original place, to commune with nature and other natives. Thus he concludes:

> And I am delighted with joy and desire on the trackless, wide-open expanses in a nature of which I myself am a living part. And I wash my spear in the breast of the mountain bear, and I eat the buffalo's roasted steaming udder. And I lay down in the coolness of the dew when night falls and the bird is silent in the trees, and I wake when the sentinel's shout signals danger nearby. It is *this* that I call "real" life, because it is natural.[28]

Broad Shoulder's words are a tribute, a hymn, to authentic, natural life and are set into strong relief by his negative experience in the white community. In such phrases as "I wash my spear in the breast of the mountain bear" and "I lay down in the coolness of the dew," one can see Hamsun's attempt to capture the cadences of Indian speech and expression as portrayed in the popular media, including dime novels, of the era. A number of speeches made by various Indian orators were published in English in the 1870s and were available for readers' consumption; it is quite likely that Hamsun came across some of them, either in novels or in the daily press.[29]

"Fra en Indianerlier" also reveals Hamsun's reflections on race and race-crossing, which are fundamentally in agreement with the perceptions of other contemporary European writers and artists. Hamsun has Broad Shoulder himself characterize the Indian race as "hot" and passionate while lamenting the ways in which the white man's knowledge adversely affected him: "I was an Indian and had my hot race's mind and longings. I couldn't tolerate the effect of massive knowledge."[30] He uses strong images when describing how he acquired the teachings of white men's dead books, along with the white man's nervous temperament. He concludes by saying that after many years he could no longer endure the "cultural life's taming discipline."[31] These last observations are especially interesting given Hamsun's own lifelong aversion to academia as well as his ambivalence about written knowledge, including his own writings.

The scientific discourse and public debates of the late nineteenth century (triggered by scientific developments and colonial expansion) often expressed ideas using racial metaphors and the contrast between the primitive and the civilized. Nancy Stepan notes that from the late eighteenth century to well into the twentieth century there existed within the biological sciences a range of discussion focused on issues of degeneracy and race.[32] There was a prolonged discussion, for instance, about whether or not all races would tend to degenerate outside their "proper places" and whether or not whites, when in the tropics or other non-European environments, would succumb to disease or become infertile. Broad Shoulder's belief in the purity of the Indian's primitive way of life and the confining nature of civilization would be well within the parameters of contemporary discourse. Nevertheless, the belief that some races were naturally degenerate and doomed to vanish coexisted alongside the belief that certain nonwhite races were inherently more vital and more fit for survival, with stronger life-drives. Stepan writes: "Racial degeneration was critical to these debates in part because it supplied them, if unconsciously, with their social and political meanings."[33] Echoes from these varied and sometimes contradictory debates are unmistakably present in Hamsun's text.

The first installment of "Fra en Indianerleir" (published on May 2, 1885) is composed of the following sections: "The Indians' Gradual Decline," "Their Daily Life," "Social Circumstances," "Arrival at the Camp," "The Chief and His Squaw," "The White River-Flower."[34] Hamsun begins with a more or less historically accurate two-paragraph summary of the various causes that led to the American Indians being dispossessed of their lands. He cites the accelerated progress of civilization, the development of the land, and the subsequent urbanization. These opening thoughts might well be among Hamsun's earliest reflections on the process by which modernity encroaches on an unspoiled landscape, a subject he would continue to write about throughout his life. The opening paragraph is characterized by a melancholy tone. Hamsun writes nostalgically: "Canoes no longer move, pointed and silent, across the lakes and rivers of the East . . . and their grassy and immense plains and broad forests now lie uprooted by the furrows of the plough or are built over by the settlers' towns and farms."[35] The first paragraph concludes with the observation: "[S]oon the last copper-brown man will stand on his final spot of ground on the Pacific coast and see his sun set for the last time."[36] The second paragraph continues the sad tone, making a distinction between the Noble Savage and the barbaric North Africans: "[B]ut while raw, barbaric tribes down in North Africa flourish and propagate, the Indian is incapable of living in civilization and incapable of living *next* to it. Daily he meets his own demise."[37]

Unlike the vast majority of Scandinavian immigrants to the Midwest, Hamsun clearly links the European colonists' occupation of land with the dispossession of the native peoples. As Bergland points out, such admissions were very rare.[38] Moreover, Robert A. Birmingham and Leslie E. Eisenberg note that such admissions invariably occurred after the fact, when the native peoples had already been subdued and no longer posed any real danger to white settlers. This is true of Hamsun's acknowledgment, too, since in 1882, when he arrived in Wisconsin, the land there had already been taken through a number of treaties and was largely settled.[39] Earlier sources—letters, diaries, missionary texts, and immigrant guidebooks—rarely touched on the issue of land-taking. In general, these texts simply acknowledged that the Indians had been deported and the land was now available to be settled. The rare texts that do portray the Native Americans depict them either as innocent and friendly children or as savages deserving of punishment and even death.

An early immigrant guidebook published in 1838 was Ole Rynning's *Sand-færdig beretning om Amerika*, based on the author's sojourn in Beaver Creek, Illinois.[40] Rynning wrote that his goal was to provide a practical guide, "allay fears," and encourage settlement. Written in simple language that imitated the question-and-answer format of a catechism, Rynning's thirty-nine-page booklet became a bestseller with many reprintings in Christiania.[41] Rynning grouped Indians with wild animals, even as he underscored their "good-natured" demeanor in a way that invoked the Noble Savage. Here is one question-and-answer pairing from Rynning's text:

> [Question:] Is there reason to fear wild animals and the Indians? . . .
> [Answer:] There are no dangerous beasts of prey in this part of the
> country. The prairie wolf is not larger than a fox; but still it is harm-
> ful to the extent that it often destroys pigs, lambs, and chickens.
> *Snakes* are *numerous* here, but small; and few of them are poison-
> ous. The most poisonous kind is the *rattlesnake*; but even that is
> not nearly so venomous as many in Norway believe. I know two
> instances of persons being bitten by rattlesnakes, and in both cases
> the patients were cured by simple household remedies. . . .
>   The *Indians* have now been transported away from this part of
> the country far to the west. Nowhere in Illinois is there any longer
> danger from assault by them. Besides, these people are very good-
> natured, and never begin hostilities when they are not affronted.
> They never harm the Quakers, whom they call *Father Penn's
> children*.[42]

Wild animals and Indians elicit similar concerns and so are addressed together. While Rynning portrays Native Americans as peaceful, he avoids discussing such topics as reservations or persecution, mentioning only that the Indians have been "transported away." It is significant that he uses a passive construction, as this avoids the question of agency and presents the matter as settled for good. To answer the question, "How did the country first become known?" Rynning provides this reply:

> It is clearly shown by the old sagas that the Norwegians knew of
> America before the black death. They called the land *Vinland the
> Good*, and found that it had low coasts, which were everywhere
> overgrown with woods. Nevertheless there were human beings there

even at that time; but they were savage, and the Northmen had so little respect for them as to call them *"Skrellings"* . . . a disparaging epithet, meaning inferior people, i.e., savages.[43]

This passage links nineteenth-century Norwegian immigration with the Vikings' tenth-century landing in Newfoundland and so establishes a centuries-old Scandinavian presence in the New World. At the same time, it reinforces the image of Native Americans as savages. Rynning's *True Account*, Bergland writes, laid the groundwork for a "structure of knowledge about Native Americans."[44]

Not long after Rynning's guidebook became popular reading, Johan Reinert Reiersen published his *Veiviser for norske emigranter til de forenede Nordamerikanske stater og Texas* (Pathfinder for Norwegian emigrants to the United States of America and Texas), an account of his search for land for a prospective settlement in the Mississippi Valley, the Great Lakes region, and Texas. While Rynning was educated at the University of Christiania and addressed better-educated readers, Reiersen was a journalist who wrote for the common people. With his unquestioning approval of U.S. federal policies, he made it easier for prospective immigrants to accept with equanimity the removal of Native Americans. He writes: "The red man was a monopolist. He took possession of more land than could be reconciled with the welfare of the human race. And he was a barbarian, hostile to the useful occupations and fair arts of a civilized life."[45]

Many of the letters Norwegians wrote home from America were read aloud in their target communities or published in newspapers. Of special importance were those written in 1847 and 1848 by Ole Munch Ræder and published in the Christiania newspaper *Den norske rigstidende*.[46] Here, too, Norwegians could learn about the Indians from a well-educated source, Ræder having been sent by the Norwegian government to the United States to study its jury system. Ræder draws parallels between the Pottawatomie tribe of Wisconsin and two groups in Norway: the Sami, who shared similar features and clothing with the Indians, and the northern Norwegians, who, in Ræder's view, were exploited by Bergen merchants in ways that resembled the exploitation of Indians by traders.[47]

As a wealth of research on the colonizing process has shown, native peoples had only limited chances for cultural and physical survival. Viewing them either as a radical difference that had to be eliminated or subsumed, or as a sameness that needed to be assimilated and absorbed, the colonization process almost always worked to the benefit of the white conquerors and settlers. As James Axtell has argued, the problem was not that Europeans did not understand the Native American peoples. They understood all too well their attachment to land, knew their customs and often spoke their languages, or had a steady supply of reliable, if expensive, interpreters. In the end, however—and contrary to their initial promises and predominantly friendly encounters with the Indians—Europeans "chose . . . to ignore the natives' needs and wishes."[48] Axtell writes about the sizable number of whites who either married Native Americans or, for a variety of reasons, simply "went native" and lived among them. These people were attracted to, among other things, the integrity, honesty, and self-sufficiency of the native peoples. Some missionaries learned Indian languages and wrote about Indian customs accurately. Clearly, some whites were able to see common humanity in the native peoples despite obvious differences. Hamsun's attitude was quite different; he identified instead with the mainstream Caucasian discriminatory views of Native Americans.

Axtell's is only one of a number of recent texts that investigate the interaction between whites and indigenous peoples, including the way this interaction was represented. Susan Zantop, for example, has shown how the dispossession of the indigenous peoples was frequently presented using the seemingly benign metaphor of marriage between the European conqueror and the conquered native woman and her land.[49] In this union, the conquered people were assimilated and tamed; indeed Zantop shows how "what looked like the assimilation of the other into a partnership between equals turns out to be the other's erasure."[50] She describes how the use of the marriage metaphor traps the colonized by the promise of "eternal love," which both reinforces and veils the actual power relationship between the "marriage partners." The metaphor goes so far as to show the "union" producing a "child," the new colony, which ultimately becomes entirely the product of the conquering "father" race and does nothing to sustain the culture of the "mother."

Tzvetan Todorov describes the situation quite aptly when he writes: "Columbus has discovered America but not Americans."[51] He pinpoints two components in the perception of the Other that are found "in practice, down to our own day in every colonist in his relations to the colonized." First, assimilationism, or "the projection of [one's] own values on others," and second, the tendency to see first and foremost the Indians' difference, which is then "immediately translated into terms of superiority and inferiority."

According to Todorov, both these perceptions deny "the existence of a human substance truly Other, something capable of being not merely an imperfect state of oneself."[52] Even when their encounters with the native peoples in the "New World" were well intentioned, Columbus and other colonizers missed the mark. Todorov finds that even in the best scenarios the Spaniards might "speak well *of* the Indians, but with very few exceptions they do not speak *to* the Indians"—which reveals a consistent lack of equality in the perception of the native peoples.[53]

In "Fra en Indianerleir," Hamsun proceeds to rectify what he sees as a general lack of knowledge about Native Americans. He enumerates the American Indian language families, mentions their nomadic lifestyle, describes their oneness with nature, and discusses their hospitality, social rules, rituals, and so forth, all of which provides the reader with a fair amount of fairly accurate and interesting information. Nevertheless, he reverts to his basic biased viewpoint when he discusses, in a paragraph on archeology, the origin of Indian mounds.[54] His underlying premise here is consonant with the views of the white colonizers: the Indian peoples are too primitive and have too little culture and tradition to be responsible for the obviously highly developed culture that left behind these visible remnants. Mounds, earthworks, town settlements, and sacred paintings must belong to a now-extinct race, which was possibly exterminated by the vicious Indians. This myth of the "lost race," invented by whites during the most intense period of their settlement of Indian lands, presented the Indians as barbarians incapable of civilized achievement, as animals that should best be moved onto reservations. It was not until 1894, that is, after the Indian Wars in the West were largely over, that the myth of the lost race was abandoned and the link established between the Native Americans and their rich cultural heritage. "Native Americans could now be accepted as historical and sophisticated peoples with ancient and visible links to the land because, to white America, it simply did not matter any more," conclude Robert Birmingham and Leslie Eisenberg.[55] Hamsun repeats the idea of the "lost race" without disputing it or commenting on it.

Because the native peoples are incapable of cultural development, Hamsun asserts, they prefer to go under rather than bow. The inevitable conclusion is that they will die out: "But when they are driven down to the Pacific coast, to the outermost edge of land, then the last of the Indian race will see his sun for the last time."[56] Hamsun's deliberate use of repeated refrains and ideas shows that he was well aware of the importance of style in his writing. Clearly, he was just as concerned with *how* to write as *what* to tell, indicating that even at this early stage in his career, he was striving to be a writer first and a journalist only out of necessity. As a budding writer, he could not resist the idea of the proud natives, smoking their pipes and eating their buffalo meat, who would rather die than compromise.[57]

Hamsun's article derives from a visit that he and a friend who had connections with the Indians made to their village.[58] The final sections are laden with the kind of details often found in European narratives about encounters with other ethnic groups: noisy people and domestic animals, naked children with runny noses, mostly naked adults, and a pervasive stench. The chief's son, whom Hamsun's friend knew from hunting, invited them to enter the chief's wigwam. Hamsun describes the interior of the chief's tent, which might have come from an ethnographic museum: "there is a fire in the middle, around which women and children are reclining. Resting lazily on an elbow, Chief Yellow Thunder himself lies on a hide close to the wall of the tent, on an elk skin decorated with beads."

"Yellow Thunder was a large, solidly built Indian with a sharply chiseled head and with a gaze that burned in its hard brownness."[59] He was a "tame wildman" (*tam Vild*), who spoke a bit of English. Moreover, he "once" was the leader of a revolt, and the United States government had to yield to all his demands—another of Hamsun's "facts" that does not correspond to reality. "Such was Yellow Thunder" (Saadan var Yellow Thunder), the paragraph concludes, in a rhetorical refrain that will later be repeated.

The first installment of the article closes with Yellow Thunder telling the bitter story of an Indian girl, White River-Flower, who was the mother of Broad Shoulder: White River-Flower was raped by a Frenchman after a whiskey party, gave birth to Broad Shoulder nine months later, and died in childbirth. Here Hamsun is recounting the stereotypical story of the poor Indian maiden raped by a white frontiersman. Such tales were a staple of dime novels and feuilletons, counterbalanced by the commonplace image of the lustful Indian girl.[60]

The second installment of the article (published on May 4, 1885) comprised the following sections: "Broad Shoulder," "The Inside of the Tent and Its Inhabitants," "The Indian Women," "The Religion of Yellow Thunder's Tribe," and "Farewell to the Camp."[61] The longest section in this installment is the description of Broad Shoulder, a person of mixed blood who was raised by whites; this is essentially Hamsun's reflection on the issue of mixed races. After "twenty summers" with the white people, the text informs us, his Indian blood won the day and he ran away from civilization, back to the prairies and the buffalo. Although Hamsun begins by describing Broad Shoulder's appearance as "beautiful," he goes on to stress (in accordance with general European thought) that crossbreeding between primitive and civilized peoples is doomed to failure because the offspring will display the passionate wildness of the one race without the civilizing and restraining culture of the other.[62] In other cases, Hamsun writes, the mixed-blood child will show signs of physical degeneration and other deficiencies because of the influence of European culture: general infirmity, inferiority in the body, drooping shoulders, a flat chest, brittle bones, a low receding forehead, and a stubborn nose. Broad Shoulder, however, displayed no obvious physical deformities. On the contrary, he was well built, solid, and strong, with a nose, Hamsun writes, only slightly "Hebraic" (Hebraisk). Hamsun here elects to romanticize the Indians, following a well-established European literary tradition that idealizes the exotic as beautiful, vital, and vigorous while portraying civilized society as degenerate. But even as he praises Broad Shoulder's strength and beauty, Hamsun expresses, paradoxically, the belief that the Indians, unable to adjust to modern developments, will soon become extinct. It is noteworthy that Hamsun uses the word "race" only in reference to Indians, not to Europeans, while "Hebraic" features fall into the category of the exotic and primitive. What is more, Hamsun calls Broad Shoulder a "mulatto," following a long line of perplexed Europeans who blurred all other races and ethnicities together in a single category of foreignness.

Having fled the white community, and despite sometimes yearning for the comforts of civilization, Broad Shoulder now admits that it was only in the wild that he felt whole and happy:

> But out on these wild expanses, where the buffalo bellow in their herds, where the prairie wind blows like loosened avalanches of snow, and where the warrior storms an enemy tribe in order to avenge an injustice—here one forgets the tame whites. One forgets the white man's cultural artifacts and all of his knowledge and all of his achievements of the mind.[63]

Here more than anywhere else in the article, Hamsun is guilty of trafficking in stock Native American images and speech. Given that by the 1880s the prairies were no longer wide open and untouched and that the North American buffalo had been reduced to 1,019 head, we may consider this passage a good example of Hamsun's reliance on imagination and a mélange of stereotypes produced by European travelers, settlers, and writers. [64] Even at this early stage, Hamsun exhibits a propensity to write positively about intuition and criticize rational knowledge, a tendency that would later develop into a full-fledged rejection of the European Enlightenment and an approval of the Nazi revolution.

Similarly, Hamsun recycles stereotypes of Indian eloquence. If we accept Gayatri Spivak's well-known contention that the subaltern is rendered voiceless by his or her colonizer, then we must take issue with this singular voice, for as it speaks, the varied and genuine voices of the indigenous people are squelched and silenced. [65] Hamsun does not register the indigenous man's own voice. In the process of imagining and inventing the Other's speech, the Other's voice is rarely discernible from that of other participants, including the narrator's. Konstanze Streese has mapped pre-colonial to post-colonial representations in German writing as they mark changes in the representation and delivery of the Other's language. [66] By entirely—and patronizingly—appropriating the Other's voice, the voice of the imaginary Other is often made identical with that of the interlocutor, while any possibility of there actually being a message contained within this "chatter" is ignored.

Given the role of language in Norway's experience of national awareness, it may seem puzzling that Hamsun did not attempt to permit the Indians to have their own voice. By denying them their own authentic language, he fails to acknowledge them as speaking subjects and as a nation. Moreover, with their speech rendered as broken English, Hamsun's Indians appear childish and strange. In this way, Hamsun joined other writers in playing an important and influential role in the colonization process, influencing perceptions and actual decisions by the way they presented Native Americans through the use of controversial and ultimately unrealistic imagery.

One can imagine many reasons for presenting the Other in this way, immature writing skills being one of them, but the primary reason might well have been subconscious. As Fred R. Myers remarks, historically correct images were unpopular because they were a reminder of the resistance and adaptability of the native people. [67] Only after the Indians had been decimated and put away on reservations did they become acceptable as the continent's indigenous inhabitants, as romanticized images and as part of the colorful national heritage of the United States. Hamsun reflected on what, at the time, were frequently debated cultural topics: authenticity vs. alienation and nature vs. culture. His reflections take the form of a heated discussion between his American friend and Broad Shoulder. For Broad Shoulder, who argues fervently for nature, the pale, weak, and dried-up people in civilized society are an inferior species.

The discourse of drawing contrasts between the corrupt and decaying West (Europe) and the invigoratingly primitive and exotic East was a marker of cultural investigations of European artists that reached their peak around the turn of the nineteenth century. The Noble Savage, too, was frequently used by artists to represent vigorous, unspoiled, and exotic areas in contrast to the decadent white society of their own countries. Artists like Gauguin, Van Gogh, and Picasso were drawn to the depiction of primitive places, historically or geographically remote and unspoiled by development, where art was an integrated and authentic part of life. Whether responding to the strange beauty of African sculpture, the intense colors of the South Pacific islands, or the rugged shores of Brittany, art was perceived as inextricably linked to notions of authenticity and creativity. Part wishful thinking and part deliberate artistic construction, the strategy of primitivism relied heavily on the unspoiled environment as a backdrop.[68]

Lars Frode Larsen specifically commends Hamsun for portraying the Indians as individuals with names rather than as an undifferentiated crowd of natives, the stereotypical racist approach.[69] Be that as it may, Hamsun took great liberties with the truth. Although not always particularly careful about sources and data, Hamsun would never have dared to publish in Norway's main newspaper a fictitious interview with a white general ten years after the general's death. Indeed, the fact that Hamsun appropriated the name of a dead Indian chief as the focal point of his very romanticized account of a purportedly face-to-face interview places him firmly in the company of those writers who deal primarily in stereotypes.

Nevertheless, Olaf Øyslebø elaborates in detail on the fact that Hamsun owed more to the Indians' way of life than he was willing to admit, arguing that Hamsun's writing is "not unlike Whitman's Indian wild feelings."[70] In *Leaves of Grass*, for instance, Whitman recites in free verse the Indian names for regions and rivers, settlements and states. The exotic names are themselves poetry, Whitman implies, a sentiment that must have resonated with Hamsun's sense of language. In *From the Cultural Life of Modern America*, Hamsun devotes considerable space and effort, some thirteen pages, to a discussion of Whitman's poetry and of Whitman himself. He characterizes the American poet as a "primitive," an intense person who "is the sound of nature in a virgin, primordial land."[71] He quotes extensively from what he calls Whitman's catalogues of things and Indian place-names, gives examples of Whitman's unrestrained language, marvels at his descriptions of life on the open road, and wonders what it might mean to be the bard of democracy. There is something of the Indian about Whitman, Hamsun posits: he uses an Indian style, the uncultured Indian language. Both satirizing and admiring Whitman's fervor and his allegedly ponderous and unreadable language, Hamsun concludes by dismissing him as a writer whose works will not be remembered. Yet Hamsun also observes: "His words are ardent; they blaze. There is passion, power, fervor in his verse. You hear this desperate word-music and you feel his breast heaving. But you have no idea *why* he is so fervent."[72]

Hamsun admits that Whitman's style is seductive and appealing. He deplores the fact that Whitman has not been raised under more civilizing circumstances, for he might have become a little Wagner.[73] He also mentions Whitman's preferred choice of primitive reading material, the Bible. While Barbara Gordon Morgridge considers Hamsun's satirical and reductive evaluation of Whitman as proof that he ultimately failed to grasp the American poet's innovative voice,[74] Hamsun not only grasped but related intuitively to the music and chaotic logic of Whitman's verse all too well. In his attempt to be critical and satirical, he was masking his own attraction to Whitman's writing. Hamsun's true response was clearly heard in such statements as "You can feel the powerful beating of a heart in these pages."[75] This would morph, just a few years later, into the now-infamous lines, "the whisper of the blood, the pleading of the bone," which articulate the core belief in Hamsun's unofficial manifesto "Fra det ubevidste sjæleliv" (From the unconscious life of the soul; 1890). It is obvious, too, from Hamsun's numerous comments on his own writing, that he started to view the *why* of the literary endeavor as basically unanswerable. Moreover, he discarded sociological literature as uninteresting and decided instead to develop a subjective and intuitive investigation into the human condition, which he ultimately considered a mystery. It is at this level that he borrowed something from Whitman's "Indian wild feelings," productively transforming them in his fiction.

One needs to be careful, however, about drawing too many parallels between Hamsun's texts and those of his literary predecessors. Ultimately, Hamsun's complex and multilayered presentations and reflections are the result of his unique personality. But Hamsun explores primitivism in other works, too, such as the poem "Gravsted" (Grave site), where he writes: "I know the forest, I am its son" (*jeg kjender vel skogen, jeg er dens søn*).[76] *Pan*'s Glahn is also a son of the (Norwegian) forest, as is Nagel, although to a lesser degree. Øyslebø notes that Hamsun's cosmological system was not very well thought out and that, had Hamsun been more methodical about what he once wrote, "Jeg er fra jorden og skogen med alle mine røtter" (I am from the soil and forest with my entire roots), he would have written myths.[77] One might say that Hamsun flirted with, or even appropriated, the latent appeal of myth and primitivism, yet was unable to, or did not believe in, submitting to it fully. As a writer, he searched for those authentic moments of inspiration that would simultaneously confirm his writerly uniqueness and his connection to the universe.

In the next section of "Fra en Indianerleir," Hamsun represents native women. They sit "lethargically and brutishly" (*dorsk og dyrisk*) around the fire: "There was no sign of life in these meat-red filthy faces with blank, thoughtless eyes."[78] Hamsun even describes himself as lying down to look into the face of an old woman who has been staring at her knees, hoping in this way to coax some response from her, but when none comes, it serves only to confirm the dullness of these women. When a young Indian woman lying behind Yellow Thunder sits up, the blanket slides off her shoulders, but she remains there with her breasts exposed. She, too, stares into space with a lethargic, apathetic gaze: "her dead, passionless gaze, which could not be made attentive, gave her a fat animal's senseless expression. I once saw an injured buffalo lie down and lethargically bleed to death."[79] The woman is thus likened to an animal, a wounded, dying buffalo, and again the operative word is "lethargic."

In his way of gendering the primitive, Hamsun once more fits the general European model. Women, animals, and nature are all closely associated in one category, and all can be tamed and molded. Fin-de-siècle Europe, with its intense interest in primitivism, attempted to reinforce its own patriarchal values and the gender divisions in non-European areas. Nowhere is this more clearly expressed than in images of primitivism: the white male artist is confronted, tempted, and invigorated by the exotic female in primitive surroundings. This is abundantly evident in the visual documents, whether paintings or photographs, used to represent exotic travels and conquests. What we see through the lens of primitivism, then, is a gendering of modernism through the male gaze and the prominence of the female body.[80] Hamsun defines an evolutionary hierarchy in which Indian women are at the bottom, as a body, and enlightened, sophisticated white men like himself are at the top. According to Hamsun, Darwinian evolution progresses from monkeys hanging from trees to Indian women lying around. In his projection, it will take quite some time before women attain the evolutionary ranking of their male counter-parts. [81]

In the closing paragraphs of the article, Hamsun returns to his melancholy ponderings, as he reflects on the wasted beauty he has seen: first Broad Shoulder, the passionate and beautiful "mulatto," and now the beautiful woman in Yellow Thunder's tent. He had previously likened her to a buffalo, and now he calls her simply "this animal." He describes how the young woman at last looks at him, and he comments: "A glimmer of understanding seemed to move through the tepid marsh of her brain."[82] The women are, for Hamsun, nothing but exotic and abject objects to be observed and commented on—hardly speaking subjects who might express their own culture with its rich oratory tradition.[83]

What we see in Hamsun's descriptions of the Indian camp are his own projections of the Other, mixed, surely, with impressions about American Indians borrowed from earlier European writings. Hamsun reveals ample understanding in the beginning of his article about what constituted the Native Americans' cultural and physical genocide. Rather than presenting the Indians as half-apes, he might have argued that it was American federal policies that deprived Native Americans of any opportunity to develop their own prosperous and thriving permanent communities. Hamsun's logic implies that, while sad and deplorable, the decline of Native American societies was natural and logical given the Indians' animal-like nature and life style.

One cannot help noticing just how trite are some of Hamsun's ideas on display here. Perhaps his romanticized views of the exotic Other represented something new for the Norwegian daily press, yet they fit sadly into the dominant colonial discourse of the time. There is even the obligatory passage devoted to Native American spirituality. An overview of taboos is presented along with the consequences of their violation. Yellow Thunder answers the typically Western question regarding sacred writings with a reference to the invisible writing in the trees, on the cliffs, and at the sacred places in "Winnie Wony Forest" (Winnie Wony's *skoge*). Hamsun's visit to the Indian camp comes to an abrupt end when his friend bursts out laughing upon hearing that some American Indians worship a cowbell. The text closes by insisting that this is the last time that we will ever encounter Broad Shoulder.

But why is it worthwhile to examine "Fra en Indianerleir" in such detail? Why is it important to distinguish between "genuine" journalism and an article that started as investigative reporting but morphed into fiction? There are several reasons. First, the text can be viewed as a clear illustration of

Hamsun's idea of the primitive Other, in this case "the Indian." His idea represents a mixture of existing stereotypes about filthy, uncivilized natives and the Noble Savage, all set against a background of historical fact. Hamsun saw the Indians as an exotic and uncivilized phenomenon. True, as Hamsun scholars point out in his defense, such racist attitudes were not unlike those of the majority of white settlers, explorers, and writers. And yet, given his keen sensitivity to injustice, his radical political views, his condemnation of the elite classes and their materialism, and his writings against religious fundamentalism and hypocrisy, we might expect something better from Hamsun. He was fully aware of the broken land treaties, questionable missionary interventions, and cultural genocide. Instead, he exploited images of Native Americans for his own aesthetic purposes and in so doing contributed to a cultural environment that acquiesced to the eradication of the Indians and their culture. Second, his mixture of fact and fiction must be factored into our understanding of the genre of early reportage. Neither entirely fact nor pure fiction, the journalistic genre and its conventions need to be reexamined, especially since what comes across most clearly in Hamsun's article is his considerable attention to language and style. Third, the article reveals Hamsun's own interests and thoughts. Its contents were the result of artistic decisions and not the result of a journalistic attempt to present a faithful record of experience. What is obvious here, beyond Hamsun's interest in the exotic, is his awareness of the split within modern civilized man and of the possibility of spiritual healing by cleaving off the civilized part and returning to nature. Interesting though it might be to Hamsun, unity with nature is not really tempting as a life style, and Hamsun remains an ambiguous, detached observer of these "sons of the forest."

Roughly a decade later, Hamsun uses the same epithet, "son of the forest," to refer to *Pan*'s Glahn who decides to shed his civilized self for a summer in northern Norway. While the inspiration for *Pan* came from many sources, including Jean-Jacques Rousseau's call for a return to nature, it is tempting to conclude that Hamsun, after having seen the squalor of the Indian way of life, was only half-heartedly convinced that it was at all possible to be fully content living off the land and communing with nature.

In *Pan*'s epilogue Hamsun further undermines the illusion of a primitive paradise with the portrayal of another exotic location, India. The epilogue was first published as "Glahn's Death" in *Samtiden* in April 1894, and was only slightly revised for the novel. The alien environment of India, with its dark "Indians" and all the telling signs of being in a Third World country, provides a fitting background for Glahn's mental disintegration and subsequent death. The descriptions of filth and pervasive rain, along with the thick-lipped natives and degenerate half-breeds with whom Glahn freely and frequently congregates, create an apt metaphor for Glahn's mental state. Glahn's hunting companion, who has a sexual affair with a native girl, Maggie, narrates the epilogue and frequently mentions Glahn's animal attraction. Provoked by Glahn over Maggie, the hunting companion ends up shooting and killing him. "Glahn's Death" merits its interpretation as the Scandinavian precursor to Joseph Conrad's *Heart of Darkness*.[84] In an echo of the descriptions in "Fra en Indianerleir," the natives are described as dark, half-naked, and with dead, dark eyes. Sexuality is unregulated, exemplified by the tribal chief who has several wives, some as young as ten, but also by Maggie's promiscuous behavior. The two hunters stay in a run-down hotel owned by an old English half-breed woman. Glahn interacts freely with the local people as one of them, having gone native, so to speak, and that signals his downfall. Hamsun uses the exotic location to express a space absent of Western culture and its corresponding civilized behavior, resulting in the degeneration of whites in general and the death of Glahn in particular. Resolving a plot in the dark manner of *Pan*'s epilogue was very much in line with some of the prevailing popular and scientific racial thoughts of the time.

Hamsun further reflects on race in a two-page article, ostensibly about the Porcupine Creek Massacre, titled "Røde, sorte og hvide" (The red, black, and white), published in *Verdens Gang* in 1891. Hamsun again employs the practice of repeated refrains such as those he used in "Fra en Indianerleir," using similar wording to foretell the demise of the American Indian. The article opens with the melancholy statement: "Now he will die soon, the last red man" (*Saa dør han snart, den siste røde Mand*).[85] Hamsun here draws a number of contrasts between the red and black races and between the American East and the American South, emphasizing the powerful weapons of the whites. Unlike his largely negative presentation of Native Americans as primitives six years earlier, his 1891 article elevates them to the status of a people of "history, poetry, and ancient culture." They are also described as good diplomats and as smart and courageous hunters and warriors.[86] The distance in time and place since Hamsun's return from America three years earlier has intensified the myths and shifted the emphasis from "savage" to "noble."[87]

Taming the Exotic Woman: Teresita from *Livets spil*, Mariane from the *Segelfoss* books

DID HAMSUN'S RESPECT FOR THE NOBLE SAVAGE INCLUDE THE FEMALE? THE visit to the Wisconsin Indians, as we have seen, certainly punctured the myth of the Primitive in Hamsun's mind. But back in Norway, a little exoticism could spice up the dull everyday and provide for an interesting narrative. But what ending can a writer imagine for resolving conflicts emerging from a relationship with an exotic, strong woman? Teresita's fate illustrates one possibility: she is killed, accidentally we are told, by a character called Justice (Rettferdighet). In the Kareno trilogy's first play, *Ved rikets port* (At the gate of the kingdom; 1895), Kareno is a young non-conformist philosopher conceptualizing his great work and married to beautiful Elina. In its sequel, the play *Livets spil* (The game of life; 1897), Kareno is thirty-nine and actually producing his masterpiece. However, before it is finished he falls in love with the local beauty Teresita, with disastrous results for his emotional life and his manuscript. In the third play, *Aftenrøde* (Evening glow; 1898), Kareno is fifty, reunited with Elina, and a member of the conformist establishment that he had rejected in his youth.

With Teresita, Hamsun creates an interesting strong-woman protagonist who longs to be subdued by an even stronger man but fails to find him. Aside from other important narrative strains in the play, such as Hamsun's criticism of Kareno's abstract and inflexible convictions and old-age conformism, there is the gender power issue. The centrality of *Livets spil* within the Kareno trilogy, and the centrality of Teresita's role in the downfall of Kareno, warrants the evaluation of the play from this perspective. The erotic war between Kareno and Teresita continues Hamsun's reflection on the battle between a weak man and a vital woman, in this case one who detests the available and wants to submit to the unattainable. Kareno is seduced and rejected by the dangerous and passionate beauty, Teresita, whom Harald Næss describes as "the closest Hamsun ever came to drawing the biblical Salome, a favorite subject of the symbolists."[88]

The play in four acts is set in Nordland in contrast to the trilogy's other two plays set in the city. Nordland, traditionally perceived as an exotic location with endless creative and erotic options, was supposed to be the location of Kareno's rebirth. With a steady tutoring job and few external obligations, Kareno planned to complete his philosophical masterpiece. However, the Nordland of limitless possibilities turns out to be a deep black pit, principally because Kareno opts for a life of research in an isolated tower on the rugged coast.[89] Yet it is an appropriate location for Hamsun's investigation of the vital powers of love, greed, and jealousy that he believed govern our lives, as opposed to the academic setting of the first play or the social-establishment setting of the third play. As he fails to comprehend Teresita, Kareno also fails to grasp life's priorities in this vital test. His life of conformity in the final play is a logical extension of his emotional defeat by Teresita in Nordland.

Teresita, another of Hamsun's motherless protagonists with a hint of exotic blood, is the daughter of the local magnate, Oterman, whose two sons Kareno tutors. With a foreign name from a non-Scandinavian culture, Teresita is a mystery. Because of her family's wealth and their standing in society, she can step outside the social norms when she chooses, a fact reflected in her assertive speech. She flirts with Kareno, but Kareno only occasionally warms to her. He seemingly dominates conversations, with long passages that she interrupts with offbeat questions and remarks. Kareno's long outpourings achieve nothing, because Teresita keeps deliberately changing the topic. His efforts to seem erudite instead make him look ridiculous and pompous, self-centered and aloof. Kareno's behavior appears rational in light of his work and his responses are appropriate to the utterances addressed to him, but this makes no impression on Teresita. In keeping with the kind of person he is, he wants to rationally understand Teresita but fails. Her unpredictable nature and behavior and her skilled use of questions, remarks, and pauses make her unreadable. As Hamsun's "typical woman," she switches topics from one personal trifle to another, thus undermining Kareno's control of the conversation. As in other plays, Hamsun here uses transgression of the rules of communication as his creative technique. That it is a woman, Teresita, who transgresses the rules of normal conversation and ultimately of behavior is important. The way in which Hamsun fleshed out his protagonists' speaking styles illuminates Hamsun's understanding of men and women.[90] Stage instructions give us further insights into how Hamsun conceptualized his characters. While the stage instructions describe Kareno simply by his age and gray hair, Teresita is described in more detail. She is "slim, twenty-five years, dressed in black, even now in summer. She is very splay-footed."[91]

The erotic tension between Kareno and Teresita culminates in Act Three against the background of a deadly epidemic that reaches Oterman's place. The act ends with Teresita, delirious with pestilence, confessing to having looked for twenty years and finally having found her man.[92] This is meant as a moment of truth, as she acknowledges that she has found a master who can tame her and her erotic force. However, the last act reveals that the remarkably resilient Teresita survives the epidemic and finds a new lover, Brede. The tables now turned, an indifferent Teresita rejects a jealous Kareno with sympathetic yet aloof comments. She readily admits that he was not what she was looking for, that she is fickle and wants to be dominated. Finally, she is aware and accepting of the randomness and unpredictability of her own desire. Kareno, however, is left groping with the question of who she is.

Hamsun created Teresita as a player worthy of consideration, one who is determined to get what she wants at all cost. Kareno, perplexed and befuddled, merely wonders rather helplessly about Woman. While Teresita solves, or imagines to have solved, the "riddle" of Kareno and loses interest in him, he does not understand her ways. Hamsun portrays him as a verbose fool, incapable of making sense of the world, or of Woman. The stage instructions at one point call for Kareno to stare at her, speechless.

In Teresita, Hamsun depicts a mighty, impenetrable Woman and a dangerous opponent. She makes for a good story, but a woman like her is nevertheless a pathology, a Darwinian mistake, symbolically expressed in her deformity, splay footedness. Her father lovingly refers to her as a troll who should be put into an institution. Elina notices that Teresita has manly hands. Jens Spir, another protagonist, compares her to Ishtar, the Babylonian goddess of love, fertility, and war. The play ends with Teresita "accidentally" shot and killed by an old man (Thy) who goes by the nickname Justice, thereby conveying the message that her death is justified. The justification is reinforced by Hamsun's imagery of Teresita: her deadly and grotesque features, her splayed feet, her snake-like curl, and her strong neck. There is something inhuman and animal-like about her, which warrants her destruction. Simon Grabowski describes Teresita's emblems as "eminently suggestive of some powerful and crude primordial principle inhabiting the young girl."[93] Because of her strange nature and her transgressions, she deserves the end she gets.

Kareno, in the third play, is reunited with his now wealthy wife and is a good father to her illegitimate daughter, Sara. Elina, who was once naive, has become a calculating, corrupt, and conformist manipulator. "Hamsun's sexism is nowhere more evident than here," writes Næss about the portrayal of Elina.[94] In the Kristiania production of Ved rikets port, the part of Elina fell to Marie Andersen, an ominous sign, perhaps, for a young actress who would become Hamsun's second wife. The trilogy is, then, about a radical rebel and his eventual absorption into a conformist establishment after he has been tested and defeated by a woman and her sexuality. Kareno's logic, rational thinking, and academic achievements are of no help in the face of Woman. She leaves him speechless and befuddled, and had she not been shot, Teresita would have been a constant reminder of his defeat. The plot reflects Hamsun's solution to the problem of how to deal with a strong woman, all other options being exhausted.

Let us now turn to two novels Hamsun wrote in the second decade of the twentieth century, both of which feature the character Mariane Holmen-graa, the mixed-race daughter of a Mexican-Indian mother and a Norwegian father. All too often, *Børn av tiden* (Children of the age; 1913) and *Segelfoss by* (Segelfoss town; 1915) are characterized as almost sociological depictions of industrial change in modernity, but they represent much more than dry social analyses; indeed, they investigate, in rich novelistic form, the propagation and survival of a family.

In both novels, Mariane is described as sly and smart, dark and exotic, intelligent and wise. She knows instinctually the one person worthy of her love, namely Willatz Holmsen IV, the son of a cultured noble family now endangered by modernity's progress. It is Mariane who chooses Willatz, a gifted composer who adheres to his father's generous, aristocratic attitudes toward life and his community. Shallow-minded nouveaux riches deride both father and son as representatives of an antiquated, outdated century. Hamsun, in contrast, signals his support by giving Lieutenant Holmsen "arabic features," a reference to Oriental power and wisdom.[95] Because Mariane is half Indian—indeed, a noble savage—she can sense and understand issues that others in the materialistic environment can neither grasp nor appreciate.

The Holmsen family was able to avert bankruptcy by selling off its property piecemeal. The buyer was Mariane's father, Tobias Holmengraa, a successful local entrepreneur who had made a fortune in Mexico. After the death of his Mexican wife, he returned to Norway with his two children. This is one of the descriptions of Tobias's children from *Children of the Age*:

> There go Holmengraa's children, the girl is taller. . . . [B]oth look
> exotic, both have brownish skin and brown eyes. There is something
> across-the-ocean about them—something strong, something barbaric
> around the nose, and the mature lips make them alien. But they are
> diligent children; they came here to Segelfoss with only Spanish in
> their heads, now they've learned to speak Norwegian words in a short
> time; they are strong tall Norlendinger who play and work all day
> long. Look, here comes the girl running, Mariane, completely silly

and healthy, and the boy, Felix, behind her; both have their heads uncovered, with black hair and low foreheads; they're wild, hey.[96]

A bit further along, in a conversation among Holmengraa, a middle-class woman, and a doctor, we are told:

> Mr. Holmengraa is coming; he has his two children along, the two Indians, as he calls them.
> Oh my, are you going to call them Indians? says Madame.
> My small Indians, answers Holmengraa. They don't mind, really, because then they are descendants of Cuauhtémoc, which they actually are to a certain degree.
> How come?
> They have a bit of Indian blood in their veins, their mother was a quarter.
> Then they are quinterons, says the doctor. Very interesting.
> Yea, you are great kids! says Madame, and embraces both of them in her arms.[97]

Hamsun here makes fun of Madame's reluctance to call the Indians Indians, and he exposes the doctor as a boring scientist who, approaching the children as a scientific subject of sorts, tries to determine the amount of their pure blood. The novel contrasts such attitudes with a positive characterization of aristocratic and authentic foreigners. The passage that describes how Willatz falls in love with Mariane also captures her strange attraction:

> They were tall people, the small Indians now, and looked strange; their hair was so black, their skin so golden, and their brown eyes glimmered intensely. Truly, they looked even more Indian than their father had claimed, and there was something gliding in the way Mariane walked, as with the wild people, and she had lazy hands inherited from the idle tribe she came from. The young Willatz was perplexed by her and started after a while to fall in love.[98]

Both novels repeatedly tell us that Mariane has all the visual characteristics of her tribe: a low forehead, a big nose, brown skin, black hair, and the fluid and silent step of someone untamed. She both attracts and unsettles Willatz. Although her father has been unable to teach her the proper way to run a household—she is as lazy as her tribe—the two of them nevertheless display an intimate, warm relationship. The somewhat secretive education Mariane received in Christiania did not spoil her, and she retained her charm, her easy-going ways, and mysterious beauty. She is no average girl, the text explains at one point in *Segelfoss Town*, thus absolving her of household duties.[99] Her father jokingly but lovingly calls her "you little Indian troll." The text exposes the shallowness of one suitor, Dr. Muus, who is frightened away by Mariane's tall tale about her tribe's magic.[100] In another subplot, the implied narrator seems to enjoy describing how two shallow middle-class Norwegian girls bad-mouth Mariane because she has foreign blood, while Dr. Muus comments knowingly about race science.[101] Hamsun obviously explored and had fun with the issue of "Indianness" and its propensity to disconcert narrow-minded Norwegians. He repeatedly contrasts Mariane's different appearance with her complex, positive personality. The bottom line, however, is that Mariane has retained a primitive's pure heart and natural mind.

A mapping of Hamsun's usage of the word *race* in the two novels reveals an unstable meaning.[102] The word most often appears in connection with Mariane and her brother, yet it is also used in the sense of family or kin *(slægt)* when describing Willatz and his father. Toward the end of *Children of the Age*, the father, Willatz Holmsen III—once ridiculed and discarded by the community but now revered as a grand old man—has the following thoughts about his son:

> On the way he notices that he is strongly moved, his son has done him an honor, he is excited about him, his eyes moisten because of him. Young Willatz—well, he was the race's descendant, a Willatz Holmsen like his own grand and fine father had been.[103]

Finally, the word *race* is applied when discussing a social class or group and its symbolic standing. Holmengraa and others like him, modern self-made entrepreneurs, for instance, are grouped together as their own race. This pejorative use of *race* describes Holmengraa as a peasant who may have imitated and absorbed the manners, values, and language of the educated class but who nevertheless remains inferior. The narrator similarly uses *race* to describe the class of civil servants, doctors, and teachers in a most condescending way. The entire civil servant class, whose most distinct characteristics are diligence instead of creativity and narrow-mindedness instead of generosity, is portrayed as debilitated and yet possessing a sturdy ability to reproduce itself. If there is any evidence of degeneration in the novels, it is to be found in the character of Dr. Muus, who displays physical and mental symptoms of degeneration.[104]

In conclusion, then, although it may be tempting to see Mariane as merely a noble, exotic Other whose function is to invigorate banal Norwegian everyday life, Hamsun's emotional investment in Mariane leads us to a more complex understanding of her character. Here is a mixed-race protagonist who countervenes the generally accepted racist views of the day and who cannot be reduced to an interpretation based only on her origins.

At the end of the novel *Segelfoss Town*, the Holmsen and Holmengraa families, formerly adversaries, are to be joined in marriage: an old noble family with traditional values will be tied to an entrepreneurial, down-to-earth, and sturdy family. While Segelfoss has been transformed from a manor house into a modern small town, this is not a novel of degeneration but of survival. A man of persistence and quiet authority, Willatz IV is a survivor who has preserved his values and ethics in the modern world. Segelfoss has come full circle: the capitalist mentality and the foreign element that once endangered and transformed the town will now, through marriage, become an inherent, yet subdued, part of Norway's culture and people. The Holmsen dynasty has survived. The younger Willatz has a strong physique, a noble character, and has produced a musical masterpiece. His wife, the mixed-race Mariane, with her unspoiled instincts, quick mind, and selfless heart, bears no resemblance to the scarecrows that some eugenicists erected to frighten Norwegian audiences. In fact, she alone possesses the insight to appreciate Willatz's unique, exotic qualities, exotic at least against the background of an industrialized and modernized environment.

Still, one must wonder about the extent to which this story of marriage and its happy ending really challenges the stereotypes of the colonial era. As we have seen, colonial domination was often presented as an allegory of the civilized European male joined in matrimonial union with a wild exotic female—a union that erased *her* culture and language entirely. Such tales celebrated the victory of the dominant white culture as it either fully assimilated the foreign or accepted only token differences. Mariane's assimilation is symbolically expressed in her knowledge and use of languages. Using neither her mother tongue nor Spanish, she embarks on a new life employing Norwegian, the language of her father and her husband. She has, in effect, been silenced by marriage as surely as Teresita was silenced by a bullet.

4

IMAGINING BLACK AND WHITE

The Negroes are a people without a history, without traditions, without a brain, a slave people without pride and honor, a mob from ancient times, who let themselves be whipped for 75 cents and lied to for 25. . . . And the liberated black went out to street corners and sang from his wide hippopotamus jaws: America's weapon is shiny!

—Hamsun, "Røde, sorte og hvide," *Verdens Gang*, 1891

IN THE ABOVE QUOTE FROM AN 1891 ARTICLE, "RØDE, SORTE OG HVIDE" (THE red, black and white), Knut Hamsun renders his condescending judgment of former African slaves, now African Americans. His attitude was not unlike that of many of his contemporaries. More often than not, experts and lay people alike considered Africans the lowest of the low on the evolutionary scale. Hamsun could not muster a positive word about them. In his play *Livet ivold* (In the grip of life), Hamsun imagines a black protagonist, whom he uses as an image of primitivism and degeneration, as the sexual partner of a middle-aged white woman, Juliane. The play closes with Juliane and her black servant, "Boy," representing the victorious new erotic couple. Earlier in the play, she had sensed and predicted her own downfall when she uttered, "It'll probably all end up with a Negro."[1] The play had its premiere in November 1910 in Kristiania.

In the erotic union between the white Norwegian woman and the black "Boy," Hamsun portrays a patriarchal white society at its dusk, a society threatened by what Gayle Rubin has called, in a different context, Woman as Nigger.[2] It was the fracturing of the established order, the crisis in patriarchal society during the last decades of the nineteenth century that increased fear of the cultural Other, represented most often by women and sometimes by blacks or "Orientals." The twin fears of feminine power and blackness first appeared in Hamsun's cultural criticism in 1889, in *Fra det moderne Amerikas aandsliv*. *Livet ivold*, a text situated at the midpoint of Hamsun's career, manifests this particular alchemy in a fictional, dramatic form. Robert Ferguson comments dryly on Boy, remarking that to end up with a black person is "not quite the unthinkable tragedy today perhaps that it was in 1910."[3]

It is well known that Hamsun detested playwriting, preferring novels as his genre for mapping the psychological complexity of characters. Still, he wrote six plays, probably for financial reasons, perhaps in the hope of easy fame or to challenge Henrik Ibsen in his own territory. The Kristiania Theater produced Hamsun's Kareno plays rather successfully, as it did *Dronning Tamara* (Queen Tamara) and *Livet ivold*. Abroad, they were staged by Moscow's prestigious Stanislavsky's Theater and at several theaters in Germany.

Livet ivold centers on Juliane Gihle, a former cabaret singer, now middle-aged and married to a wealthy old man who adores her. They have no children. The play contrasts the present Mrs. Gihle, a respected woman of the community, and the Juliane of the past, a world-famous singer with many erotic liaisons behind her. Juliane's current lover, Alexander Blumenschøn, has just become engaged to a pretty young girl, Fanny, and is planning to emigrate to Argentina. His South American acquaintance Per Bast has returned to Norway for a quick visit. Bast, who was once Juliane's lover, is fatally bitten by the cobra he brought from Argentina, but before he dies he bequeaths his black servant, Boy, to Juliane. The end of the play implies that Juliane will spend much time with her new lover at the country estate that old Gihle has just bought for her. The action on stage is a settling of accounts between Bast and Juliane, whose love affair in Buenos Aires had ended on an unresolved note. It is Juliane who opens the cage that contains the snake and thereby causes Bast's death.

Juliane is portrayed as powerful and beautiful, but also manipulative, unreliable, shallow, desperate for attention, flirtatious, and jealous. On the one hand, she is a "typical woman" worried about her looks, her age, and the man in her life, while on the other, she often transgresses the rules of accepted behavior for a middle-class married woman. In spite of her assertiveness, she is afraid of a public scandal and has an acute sense of propriety. Although the play chronicles Juliane's downfall, the male characters circle around her: her wealthy, seventy-year old husband Gihle, whom she calls "Father"; her limping and unscrupulous lover, Blumenschøn, who leaves her only reluctantly; and her former lover, Bast. Juliane's ultimate end, the play implies, will have little effect on her wealth or security. Instead, at stake are her respect and honor in the community. It is Juliane's increasing age and her insatiable sexual appetite and past experiences, Hamsun suggests, that deliver her into the arms of a "Negro" as a form of existential punishment.[4]

Little scholarly attention has been paid to Boy, or to *Livet ivold*, for that matter.[5] The latest example of this blind spot was the omission of Boy from the list of characters in the National Theater's program for its 1989 stage production of the play.[6] Both racism and misogyny were commonplace in Europe and the United States during the nineteenth century, yet until recently Hamsun scholars have often argued that to investigate these issues was not only unworthy of attention in light of Hamsun's genius, but utterly reductive. However, Hamsun hardly typifies the kind of writer who would merely reflect such a commonplace. As a young radical, he specialized in the provocation of the establishment, be it literary, religious, or moral. Hamsun, having been a struggling artist himself, might be expected to be a bit more sympathetic to other marginalized individuals, differences among them notwithstanding. Though he loved to provoke the silent majority, he sided with it in this case. A closer look at *Livet ivold* and several other texts can shed some light on why and how.

Juliane describes herself as a successful former entertainer, frequently remembering how famous she used to be throughout the world and how men once lay at her feet. When Act One opens, however, she feels insecure and unfulfilled, and Blumenschøn's decision to leave for Argentina propels her further along the downward spiral we witness on stage. Per Bast represents the masculine world of colonial conquest and is, aside from old Gihle, the only positive male figure in the play. He is a successful rancher from Argentina, where he owns large tracts of land, thousands of head of cattle, and a surveying company. Like many other successful colonizers, he returned to Europe with artifacts for the local museum, such as pottery, axes, and a live cobra. And Boy. Boy and the cobra are often mentioned together as if they belong to the same animal world. Bast keeps him as a kind of brute bodyguard and bouncer, a "pet nigger" as evidenced by his name. "Boy" was a patronizing term used in the American South by racists when addressing black men. In the play, Boy is consistently discussed as an object of exchange, stereotypically assigned the qualities of sloppiness, stupidity, and animalistic sexuality.

Colonial Discourse and Sexuality

IN COLONIAL DISCOURSE, THE EXOTIC, THE DISTANT, THE INDIGENOUS, AND especially the black were, from the very start, infused with sexual potency. Foreign continents, along with foreign women, were portrayed as beautiful, voluptuous, and willing to be taken, while foreign men were portrayed as wild, even lascivious, and dangerous.[7] Foreign men were perceived as posing a direct threat to white men and consequently were to be watched closely. While the black woman's sexuality was portrayed as passive and available to the white man, the black man was presented as a potential rapist or seducer of the white woman. As the only races portrayed in *Livet ivold* are white and black, my discussion here will focus on their relationship. At different times, there were different manifestations of the white colonial enterprise around the globe, depending on location, and the colonizer's sense of politico-economic and personal vulnerability. In spite of the variations, blacks described in European texts, by authors from Ptolemy to Winthrop D. Jordan, are fundamentally marked by sexual pathology and promiscuity, prompting Anne McClintock to brand them as "porno-tropics."[8]

In many European descriptions of the settlement of the North American continent—letters, dairies, reports, articles, etc.—both Native Americans and African Americans are either absent or demonized. When they were present in descriptions, Native Americans were often represented sympathetically as "noble savages," whereas blacks were, with few exceptions, portrayed as lazy, sloppy, childlike, superstitious, sexually aggressive, and promiscuous—that is, their drives were completely uncivilized.[9] The representational hierarchy proceeded from white man/white woman to black woman/black man. And while sexual relations between a white man and a Native American or black woman were tolerated and even common in some circles, sex between a black man and a white woman was universally condemned and often ended in the killing or lynching of the man.[10] The fear of miscegenation was never far away.

Even scientists were affected by common assumptions about the races. Nancy Leys Stepan argues that scientists often explained scientific concepts with the help of common analogies and metaphors. She specifically addresses the analogy that links race to gender and its "strategic place in scientific theorizing about human variation in the nineteenth and twentieth centuries."[11] Stepan writes: "By analogy with the so-called lower races, women, the sexually deviate, the criminal, the urban poor, and the insane were in one way or another constructed as biological 'races apart' whose differences from the white male, and likenessess to each other 'explained' their different and lower position in the social hierarchy."[12]

In the nineteenth century, scientists' analogies regarding race, sex, and class were "widely accepted, partly because of their fundamental congruence with cultural expectations."[13] Thus subconsciously held cultural analogies were legitimized as theory by scientists. "Because interactive metaphors bring together a *system* of implications, other features previously associated with only one subject in the metaphor are brought to bear on the other," Stepan writes.[14] "In the metaphors and analogies joining women and the lower races, the scientist was led to 'see' points of similarity that before had gone unnoticed. . . . Metaphors, then, through their capacity to construct similarities, create new knowledge."[15] Such stretching of analogies ultimately suppressed knowledge and/or resulted in the neglect of new findings, while data contrary to the scientists' hypotheses were, inadvertently or not, disregarded. "For decades the Negro's similarity to apes on the basis of the shape of his jaw was asserted, while the white man's similarity to apes on the basis of his thin lips was ignored," writes Stepan. "Because a metaphor or analogy does not directly present a preexisting nature but instead helps 'construct' that nature, the metaphor generates data that conform to it, and accommodates data that are in apparent contradiction to it."[16] The growing acceptance of such metaphors in everyday language usage, and the societal respect given to science enabled analogous constructions linking race, gender, and class to reveal connections despite the comparison of apples and oranges.[17]

Olav Christensen and Anne Eriksen claim in *Hvite løgner* that the sexualized perception of blacks is the typical practice of white European men projecting their own fears and prejudices, political as well as personal, onto blacks.[18] They detail how the attitudes toward white women, black women, and black men come from the desires and fears of white men.[19] For example, while titillating European exhibits of black women (like the "Hottentot-Venus" of 1815) did not raise a moral eyebrow, the corresponding exhibits and caravans displaying black men were under constant attack by both the media and general public. Implied in this reaction is the notion that white women have less control over their own emotions and could easily fall prey to lustful black men, thereby displacing white men. It is helpful to keep this cultural background in mind when reflecting on Hamsun's Juliane and Boy.

In order to build narrative suspense, Hamsun allows his protagonists to talk about Boy but delays his appearance until Act Three. Just before he appears, he is defined as a potential rapist in the following dialogue between Bast and Juliane:

> *Mrs. Gihle:* What is the Boy here for?
> *Bast:* He can leave. You shouldn't despise him, though: he's quite a
> guy! His relatives were the same. His father was of the same kind,
> so he got hanged for it.
> *Mrs. Gihle:* For what?
> *Bast:* Oh, on a remote *estancia* he once got hold of one of our white
> women. She had no revolver. That was all. So we hanged him.
> *Mrs. Gihle:* And you had something to do with that? God help me,
> no! And you took that man's son into your service afterwards?
> Was this the Negro you offered to give me?
> *Bast:* Yes certainly. He's a relatively talented creature. He learned
> Norwegian from the maids at home in a few weeks. And he is a
> great coachman.[20]

Boy is discussed here as a gift, and a patronizing remark is added about his intelligence and ability to learn Norwegian. From subsequent conversations we also learn that he is eighteen years old and therefore sexually mature. Typical for the evolutionary thinking of the time, Bast implies that sex drive runs in families, and Juliane's astonishment also signals her understanding that Boy's sex drive is inherited.

When Boy enters, and stands silently and obediently at his master's side, Juliane has risen and stares in awe at Boy, perhaps in a state of sexual attraction, perhaps in doomsday apprehension, or perhaps both. Blumenschøn taunts her as being "zoological" (*zoologisk*) and complains about Negroes being everywhere. Hamsun expands on the attraction between Boy and Juliane by connecting blacks and the theater, which he detested, in the following utterance by Juliane: "Think, it was like an old acquaintance for me, we often had Negroes around the theatre (at which Blumenschøn laughs). I mean, around the cabarets."[21] Hamsun thus combines Woman, Negro, and Theater in one negative metaphor. In the German translation, the title of this play is "Vom Teufel geholt," meaning "taken by the devil," the devil being Boy.[22]

While information about Norwegian exposure to and attitudes toward blacks in the nineteenth century and at the beginning of the twentieth century is scarce, some books on the topic have appeared in recent years. The previously mentioned *Hvite løgner* (1992) offers fascinating data about the encounters between Scandinavians, mainly Norwegians, and blacks. Christensen and Eriksen demonstrate that there were only a handful of blacks living in Scandinavia prior to the mid-nineteenth century. Most of them came as servants of traders or soldiers working for government officials, sometimes as slaves captured by expeditions. In Scandinavian literature prior to 1910, when *Livet ivold* was published, there were only a few black or mixed-race protagonists. Hans Christian Andersen's eponymous protagonist from the play *Mulatten* (The mulatto; 1840) is one exception. This can be explained by the relative isolation of the Scandinavian countries and their limited participation in colonial expansion. Hamsun's Boy is primarily a titillating male fantasy of the sexualized Other. Hamsun lent a sympathetic ear to the white colonial enterprise, while at the same time articulating some of his own fears. Christensen and Eriksen write in their Preface:

> This is not a book about blacks, but about the "Negro"—a figure
> who in Western culture has been the very image of the foreign. "The
> Negro" is not a person, but a representation formulated by whites.
> He is the representation of the eternal other, the opposite, the deviant
> and the worthless. Over time the "Negro" has had many faces. He
> has been represented quite openly in a racist manner, at other times
> ostensibly humorously and innocently. But "the Negro" is always a
> negative figure. He is the primitive, dirty and ridiculous, who can
> be tricked, exploited and repressed. For whites he has been a tool to
> emphasize their own superiority.[23]

One of the more recent publications, *Nordmenn i Afrika—Afrikanere i Norge* (Norwegians in Africa—Africans in Norway; 2002) describes the mostly nineteenth-century entrepreneurial adventures of Norwegians in various African regions. It is a welcome mapping of journeys not following the usual immigration route to the United States, but rather to Africa.[24] Several chapters of the book describe how Africans have come to Norway: as slaves in order to enhance the reputation of their owners, as adoptees of Norwegian missionaries, as servants of ship owners, and as sailors.

Brita S. Brenna's chapter, "Negrer på Frogner" (Negroes in Frogner), discusses how the 1914 Norges Jubilæumsutstilling (Norway's anniversary exhibit) in Kristiania included an entire Congolese village, where approximately sixty Senegalese people were exhibited. It has not been documented that Hamsun saw this exhibit.

In his 1889 book of cultural criticism, *Fra det moderne Amerikas aandsliv*, Hamsun used the image of white woman/black man to epitomize the lack of culture in and degeneration of contemporary America. While Hamsun enumerates many reasons—materialism, shallowness, fear of foreigners, poor and uneducated immigrants—he singles out two groups as responsible for this poor state of affairs: first, women and/or feminists who refuse to bear children and instead participate in public life, dabble in art, and idle away time reading *Uncle Tom's Cabin*; and, second, blacks who "have all the rights of a white man and take all the liberties of a black."[25] Even though twenty years elapsed between *Fra det moderne Amerikas aandsliv* and *Livet ivold*, there are strong parallels between the representation of women and blacks in both works, which underline continuity in Hamsun's attitude to white-black relations.

The concluding chapter of *Fra det moderne Amerikas aandsliv* offers a distillation of stereotypes about black people, although disparaging remarks are not lacking in the preceding pages either.[26] These final pages start with the epigraph "Sort himmel" (Black sky) and conclude with the same two ominous words followed by an ellipsis. The threatening image of black skies thus frames the chapter, using the negative symbolism of the color black. Here Hamsun summarizes many of his previously articulated views and opinions, and outlines some of his most negative and repulsive descriptions of blacks, who are depicted as deficient, rudimentary, bodily lumps of clay. According to Hamsun, black people who were brought to America were "Negroes from Yum-Yum whose hands had never broken soil and whose brains had never conceived a thought."[27] Hamsun also lashes out against most newly arrived Americans, describing them as murderers, criminals, pastors, thieves, or barbarians. These white people of brawn could not think, but they could at least clear land, which redeemed them to a certain degree in Hamsun's view. Africans, however, could do neither.

Hamsun combines sexuality with these depictions, relating it to the absence of a cultural elite: "On the first of January 1863 they made the Negroes masters over the Southern landowners, took the muscle-animals from Yum-Yum into their families, gave them their sons and daughters to marry in order to breed a selection of cultured people."[28] From Hamsun's vantage point, American democracy was the political system that legitimized interracial unions and marriages. The regrettable lack of an elite was caused by institutions of political democracy extending too many rights to blacks. It may well be that Hamsun's later rejection of democratic institutions stemmed from his interpretation of American democracy. Elsewhere in *Fra det moderne Amerikas aandsliv*, Hamsun complains bitterly that women in the United States took advantage of new democratic principles and refused to play the traditional motherly role.

The negative references to black people are too numerous to be quoted in their entirety. It will suffice to quote one long paragraph in which Hamsun describes the decline of the once flourishing establishment in the Southern states, resulting in the absence of a cultural elite:

> In the fifties there were signs of an intellectual elite in two of the oldest Southern states, but the war came and uprooted it before it was established. Since then it has not shown itself. From that time on, the nation's blood was democratically mixed with that of the Negro, and intelligence sank rather than rose. Cohabitation with the blacks was foisted upon the people. Inhumanity stole them away from Africa where they belong, and democracy transformed them into civilized citizens against the entire order of nature. They have leaped over all the intermediate stages from voracious rat eater to Yankee. Now they are used as preachers, barbers, waiters, and sons-in-law. They have all the rights of a white man and take all the liberties of a black. A Negro is and will remain a Negro. If he shaves a man, he grabs him by the nose as his own blessed grandfather grabbed a crocodile leg along the Nile; if he serves a meal, he sticks his shiny thumb into the soup all the way up to his elbow. There is no use in rebuking him for his slightly uncivilized manner of doing things. If you are not rudely answered back, the African democrat will at least tell you in an insulted voice to "mind your own business!" And then you have to hold your tongue; the discussion is at an end. Still, if you are sitting there with two big fists, and right on your side, then you swallow your food with little appetite. Of course, it would be another matter if you had expressly ordered soup with thumbs.
>
> The Negroes are and will remain Negroes, a nascent human form from the tropics, creatures with entrails in their heads, rudimentary organs on the body of a white society. Instead of founding an intellectual elite, America has established a mulatto stud farm.[29]

Hamsun here laments the absence of an aristocratic elite and accuses Americans of being cultural barbarians for, among other things, giving too much freedom to blacks. One of the major problems with the United States, according to Hamsun, was the democratic mixing of the blood of whites and blacks. This is what destroyed the old civilization, the old order, the old family. In his lament, we can recognize the echoes of the evolutionary discourse in which blacks represented the lowest of the low. Moreover, it shows the normative European framework for conceptualizing Africans and, indeed, for conceptualizing the entire racial scale as the order of nature.

The strict observance by Hamsun of the "proper place" for blacks notwithstanding, there is a certain irony in Hamsun's position, since at the time he wrote these lines and for a period of time thereafter, he was an outsider relative to Norwegian and greater European cultural scenes. In fact, he was very much in opposition to the contemporary cultural establishment. His criticism of the already established writers, especially Henrik Ibsen, Alexander Kielland, Jonas Lie, and occasionally Bjørnstjerne Bjørnson, are well known, as are his attacks on other public figures such as the pietist leader Lars Oftedal. In *Fra det moderne Amerikas aandsliv,* he finds himself holding up as a model the elites that were the target of his attacks at home. What in all probability appealed most to him in the Old South was a social order described by Eugene Genovese and Elizabeth Fox-Genovese as not only paternalist but pre-capitalist, as opposed to a bourgeois capitalist order.[30] In one of Hamsun's comments about the American Civil War, he interprets the war as having been waged by "women from Boston" against the Southern aristocracy, not out of a sense of morality but because the move to emancipate the slaves resembled, to them, the feminist movement. He writes: "The war was a war against the aristocracy, waged with all the democrat's ferocious hatred of the plantation nobility in the South. The very same Northern states—the morally decent Northern states—that at the time wanted to crush the aristocracy in the South, were themselves speculating in slavery. This the women of Boston forget."[31]

Hamsun's representation of blacks is, of course, only one element in his portrayal of American cultural barbarism, yet it is integral to it and is clearly and very specifically connected to a system of political democracy. That he addresses "the women of Boston" is also significant, for Hamsun undoubtedly perceived these women as powerful and vocal, flaunting their newly established agency in the public sphere. To counter the degeneration, which he claims is the offspring of Negroes and white women, Hamsun advocates a kind of eugenic program in *Fra det moderne Amerikas aandsliv* that can be deduced from his complaint that healthy and good-looking white women refuse to have large families with their white husbands. Instead, they have affairs with blacks. He writes of a daughter of a wealthy Washingtonian, who runs off to Canada "with her father's irresistible stable Negro."[32] Hamsun sees the husbands of these white women either performing, or at least not opposing, abortions, implying that they have been tamed by their wives, a sign of the crisis of masculinity and the decline of "real men."[33] The final paragraph of *Fra det moderne Amerikas aandsliv* repeats the dark message: America is a mixture of "people from every zone, from the whites of the north to the apes and intellectual mulattoes of the tropics; a land with soft, fertile topsoil and preserved primordial spaces."[34]

Published in 1889, *Fra det moderne Amerikas aandsliv* occupies a curious and ambiguous position in Hamsun's œuvre. There seems to be a gentlemen's agreement among literary critics who study it to avoid the issue of racism. The tendency is either to dismiss the book as an adolescent prank, as Hamsun himself did later in his career, or to focus on its importance to the development of his writing style, usually through a discussion of writers like Ralph Waldo Emerson or Mark Twain.[35] The editor's introduction to the 1969 English edition, titled *The Cultural Life of Modern America*, while offering a well-researched and documented historical sketch, as well as a perceptive commentary on Hamsun's style, skirts the issue completely. It argues that the work was "less genuine social criticism than calculated self-advertisement."[36] It is indeed an exercise in style, as many other critics have confirmed, and an exercise in opposition, hyperbole, and provocation. Yet our question has to be: Is it not possible to be controversial without recourse to images of blacks as "creatures with entrails in their heads" or "rudimentary organs on the body of a white society"? Hamsun's most vulgar and physically repulsive depictions are reserved for the black population. Robert Ferguson is one of the few critics who actually discusses Hamsun and racism.[37] Harald Næss also deals with the issue of racism straightforwardly, situating Hamsun's anti-democratic and racist views in the broader social context of later Nazism. Næss writes:

> Freedom does not apply to all groups; there are some that Hamsun
> does not want to acknowledge—with them, one has to use discipline.
> In this there is possibly a seed of that social conviction Hamsun
> revered later in life, and if one should search for "Nazi" tendencies in

Hamsun's first adult book, it has to be in his harsh verdict over certain underprivileged groups in America, namely, women, the Indians and the Negroes.[38]

Hamsun's racist worldview is congruent with his decision to support the German occupation of Norway. Here it is helpful to keep in mind the scientific and evolutionary discourses of the time, which offered steady "evidence" of the deficiencies of non-white races. In addition, Hamsun's ideas on masculinity and its demise, and on women's rising powers, contributed to his discriminatory views. His harsh verdict should be understood as his own fear of so-called untamed groups becoming totally out of control, reaching for power, and destroying in the process the paternalistic social arrangement.

Models of Masculinity in *Livet ivold*

THERE IS A REMARKABLE ABSENCE OF MALE ROLE MODELS IN *LIVET IVOLD*. THE limping Blumenschøn is verbally abusive, arrogant, empty-headed, and, above all, irrelevant. He brags about his fine family and its great reputation, although nobody else in the play can remember what it is reputed to have accomplished. He is called "Blumen" (flower) by Lynum, surely a commentary on his masculinity, while his last name, Blumenschøn, can likewise be interpreted as an ironic comment on his manhood. He, in turn, refers to Boy as *negerdyret* ("the Negro animal") and to Bast as a *fæl indianer* ("a disgusting Indian").[39]

Lynum is another deficient, helpless, yet posturing male protagonist. He accuses Bast of flirting with Fanny and challenges him to a duel, explaining his sudden chivalry as an example of civilized behavior among white men. Hamsun reveals Lynum's notion of a white code of honor as empty rhetoric, lamenting the demise of the chivalric male tradition of by-gone years. Lynum believes that Bast, having been away from Europe for so long, has regressed into a sexually lax primitive. Bast, on the other hand, suggests that Lynum would enjoy being tamed by "his Negro" in a homosexual act.[40]

Juliane calls her husband "father," and he calls her "child," signifying the absence of a sexual relationship between them. Gihle has a number of redeeming values, yet in general, he is portrayed as the caricature of a fussy old man. He incessantly complains about the inattentiveness shown by youth toward the aged and constantly reminds his guests to keep off the grass. Gihle proudly thinks of himself as an old lion or an old fox. He considers himself a man of tradition, because he, like his grandfather and father before him, has refused to sell the family estate. Though wealthy, he is an aging, asexual, increasingly insignificant and ridiculous patriarch with a cheating wife. Having internalized the paternal values tied to land ownership, old Gihle has nevertheless produced no heirs, bringing the grandfather-father-son legacy to an end.

It is Juliane, the most developed character, who dominates the play. She possesses strength and the ability to make choices but also vulnerability and fickleness. In Act Three, set at a party at the Hotel Bristol, the audience gets a glimpse of Juliane's ambitions and nature. She basks in the music, enjoys the ambience and has several drinks, all as a nostalgic remembrance of her successful and famous past. At one point during the party, Juliane's friend Fredriksen evokes her "Negro doomsday prediction."[41] At Act Three's climax, Boy brings the snake into the room for the guests to view, but Juliane, in an impulsively jealous act, opens the lid to the cage and tries to push Miss Fanny's hand inside. This causes a general commotion, the snake escapes, and Bast, in an effort to capture it, is bitten and later dies. The Woman, the Negro, and the Snake are combined in a powerful image of destruction. Jealousy of her much younger acquaintance exposes Juliane's fear of becoming old and unattractive and reveals the absence of solidarity between women: Juliane and Fanny are rivals fighting for a man. Hamsun here reproduces one of the common themes from the turn of the century, that of the woman and the snake. Aside from the biblical evocation of Eve, this theme alluded to other portrayals of deadly and perverse women (Salome, Lilith, Ishtar, Medusa, the Snake-Queen) with the common denominator of Woman as a destructive and predatory sexual being.[42]

The configuration of protagonists in *Livet ivold* has to be viewed through a prism of frustrated male fantasy: first, through the negative representation of the Other, be it an independent and sexually assertive woman or an animalistic Boy; second, through the positive depiction of the old land-based paternalist society, now almost gone. Bast's Argentina is a metaphor for that part of the yet unspoiled New World, where gentlemen can still be gentlemen, undisturbed by rebellious women and blacks. On one level, the colonial and racist statements in the play serve to illustrate the protagonists' views: Blumenschøn's racist comments, for example, are his own and not automatically Hamsun's. Yet the positioning of the main protagonists, especially at the play's conclusion, suggests a parallel between the characters' racism and Hamsun's own. The harsh, if at times sympathetic, portrayal of Juliane and her attraction to the black protagonist portend societal punishment and must be viewed in connection with Hamsun's defense of patriarchal white masculinity, as illustrated in the remarkable reconfiguration of gender roles in this play.

Juliane and Boy are surrounded by male protagonists who are effeminate, posturing, loud-mouthed, indecisive, and plainly deficient. They are either limping, old, or feeble-minded, or, at best, mediocre. The old patriarch Gihle, who once had integrity and power, is almost out of the picture, and Bast, successful, manly, sexually active, and decisive, is dead. The remaining protagonist, the limping Blumenschøn, departs for Argentina. The real men are out, the "modern" men might still be going through the motions but they are merely hollow clowns. A similar gender configuration of weakling men and strong women is found in a number of Hamsun's texts. This portrayal of men and women, as well as of femininity and masculinity, reflects both the contemporary changes in gender roles and Hamsun's resistance to those changes.

How do we reconcile Hamsun's readiness to conform to the pseudo-scientific and quack medical discourses on race and sexuality with the fact that he provocatively broke numerous norms and conventions of accepted behavior? He attacked institutionalized religion, cultural elites, and even Norway's most manly and flashy hero, Fridtjof Nansen. Many factors must have contributed to Hamsun's willingness to conform to the pseudo-science about race and sexuality: cultural background, class, career, power, and so on. In this regard, Hamsun created a rather consistent worldview in which white patriarchs stand alone battling women and exotic others, a regressive worldview that has much in common with the tenets of what has been called primordial fascism.[43]

It is often argued in Hamsun's defense that he opened a window of opportunity for his modernist protagonists in his groundbreaking novels and that he redrew many boundaries. While true, only male artists/protagonists benefit from these new expanded boundaries. And while these artists often pay a heavy price, they are still usually successful in the end. However, women protagonists (and Juliane is a good example) are denied this outcome. Hamsun created male artists who appropriate traits traditionally associated with femininity, such as hysteric outbursts, intuitive thinking, and irrational behavior, to feed their creative projects, yet he dismissed female artists and their art by accusing them of precisely the same irrational traits. And he accused them of neglecting motherhood, the sin of all sins.

It is, then, perhaps no coincidence that the ideology of the Third Reich exercised such an attraction for Hamsun. With its goals of replacing the modern(ist) with an organic social order, the foreign with the home-grown, and idealizing Woman as the Family Mother Earth, the ideology fit Hamsun like a glove. Nazi propaganda before and during World War II constantly articulated the idea that cultural barbarism was the consequence of mixing the blood of whites with that of others. It is this kind of cultural barbarism that Hamsun describes in his book about America. Nazi propagandists divided their views of the *Untermensch* into several distinct categories, the most common being the Jewish Bolshevik, the degenerate Brit, and the barbaric American black man. Anthony R. E. Rhodes describes how "Goebbels singled out the black American G.I. as a symbol of cultural barbarism. This theme was often used later in the war when Allied planes were bombing German cities." One German cartoon cited by Rhodes depicts two befuddled black American soldiers. One of them says, "We're fighting for culture, Jimmy" and the other answers, "But what is culture?"[44] Another cartoon features a naked black man presenting a severed head to a white woman in a luxurious setting. The caption explains that the black man is the "Honorary Headhunter in the White House."[45] The fact that the woman occupies a leadership position is surely not a coincidence, nor is the pairing of a white woman and a black man, the twin looming dangers of modern America.

Livet ivold and *Fra det moderne Amerikas aandsliv* are filled with poetic paradoxes that reveal much about Hamsun the artist as well as Hamsun the man. Hamsun's visits to America were essentially a failure. He never became famous as a lecturer as Bjørnstjerne Bjørnson had done before him, never broke through as an author, and never became a wealthy merchant reminiscent of the fictitious Mack from *Pan*. Power, fame, and wealth eluded him. To make matters worse, the first time he returned from the U.S. he was diagnosed with tuberculosis, a disease that Susan Sontag describes as the metaphoric illness of women and artists. Hamsun was seriously ill, and he returned home a sick, effeminized, and deathly pale artist. But he recovered, and for a while thereafter cultivated the emaciated, hysterical protagonist, the most autobiographical of which is the hero in the short story "Et livsfragment" (1884). A bit later came the protagonist in *Hunger*.

Sontag pointedly writes, "Gradually, the tubercular look, which symbolized an appealing vulnerability, a superior sensitivity, became more and more the ideal look for women—while great men of the mid- and later nineteenth century grew fat, founded industrial empires, wrote hundreds of novels, made wars, and plundered continents."[46] Hamsun knew at the time that he did not belong to the category of men who conquered continents and built luxurious mansions, but more to the "other" alternative, the "feminine" one. As a consequence, he often portrayed men of the second type with deep understanding. In addition, Hamsun was acutely aware of the power of the new capitalist society, and its influence on art. This is convincingly articulated in his early short story, "Paa turnee" (On tour; 1886), in which the male artist is reduced to a kind of clown, yet—and this is the crucial difference between his female and male protagonists—he has discovered the power of ironic self-reflection. Hamsun is thus straddling, uneasily and ambivalently, two worlds: the old land-based paternalistic one and the new capitalistic one. He also straddles two gender worlds, at least in his fiction. His own manliness never in question, he nevertheless felt the power shift during his lifetime toward women who reached for and seized economic, cultural, and political power, while expressing their sexuality freely. In the case of men, the power shifted from aristocratic landowners to the entrepreneurs who "plundered continents" and also indulged in raw sexual freedom. Hamsun, in the creative world, could observe and comment on them.

In *Livet ivold,* Hamsun presents a multilayered story in which he validates the raw power of the Other, in this case Juliane and Boy. Yet, he laments the effect of their coupling: the unseating of "real white men" and the decline of patriarchal society. Juliane and Boy are strong, full of desire, and, in the absence of any white male counterweights, in charge. When Juliane's sexual drive is paired with "its own kind," she supposedly ends up with what she deserves. This is also indicated by the stage directions for the very last line of the play: first Juliane's head is bowed as if in punishment, and then a moment later she greets Boy with a welcome ("Velkommen"). In this final scene, with the sexually hungry woman and the irresistible black man, Hamsun recreates an image present in *Fra det moderne Amerikas aandsliv.* In Hamsun's cultural critique, a major reason for America's regrettable state of affairs is the sexual union of white women/feminists and potent Negroes, their drives unleashed in the new democracy. *Livet ivold* can be viewed as the artistic reinterpretation of the destruction of the old patriarchal way of life that Hamsun first thought he observed in America, and later believed he saw creeping into Europe.

Abel from *Ringen sluttet*

LIKE THE MALE PROTAGONISTS OF *LIVET IVOLD,* THE PROTAGONIST OF HAMsun's penultimate novel, Abel Brodersen, can also be interpreted as a superfluous man, who, in spite of his best intentions, cannot find his niche anywhere. Race manifests itself in numerous ways in *Ringen sluttet* (The ring is closed; 1936). Abel lives for a while in a black community in Kentucky, which serves as a central organizing trope of the novel. Back in Norway, the presence of black jazz musicians who perform in a Norwegian pub is also significant.[47] Because of Hamsun's black metaphors and Abel's life at the margins of society, Abel, an ethnic Norwegian, can be understood as a kind of white Negro.[48]

Ringen sluttet is a prime illustration of Hamsun's engagement in a reckoning with modernity that made the primitive attractive as its counter ideal. However, Hamsun's racism always contaminates his view of the primitive, giving rise to conflicted feelings about modernism and primitivism. In the first part of the novel, primitivism is represented positively, as a carefree way of life, but it soon devolves into random and pointless hopelessness. Much of the tension in the novel derives from counter positioning the attractive elements of primitivism against women's liberation, cultural globalization, shallow material values, and urbanization, all aspects of modernity that Hamsun abhorred and first depicted as American in *Fra det moderne Amerikas aandsliv*. Ultimately, Hamsun punctures the myth of primitivism by revealing the underbelly of the Kentucky life.

Ringen sluttet is a novel set in a small coastal town in Norway in the early decades of the twentieth century. It depicts Abel Brodersen's life from boyhood through adulthood and his gradual dissociation from any permanent commitments in life. The action takes place predominantly in his hometown, his world travels recounted primarily through reminiscences. His childhood relationship to the local beauty, Olga, mutates several times over their lifetime, with an early estrangement leading Abel to seek his fortunes abroad when he is but fourteen. His first long journey takes him around the world, and it is four years before he returns a somewhat cocky young man with adventures to tell. Nonetheless, Olga snubs him, as she has since becoming engaged to a rising young clergyman. It is only a matter of months before Abel sets out again to travel the world. His prolonged second visit to America is a crucial experience in his life, but the events there are only gradually exposed as the narrative progresses. While in Kentucky, he and his American wife, Angèle, live in a black village like content savages, away from modern, civilizing pressures.[49] Abel's colonial America is constructed as a contradictory paradise, where life unfolds in the manner of its primitive beginning, where language is barely used, and where sexuality is not reined in by civilized codes of conduct. Abel elaborates on his vision of the good life in a description that collapses facets of America into a narrative about the tropics, where the "natives" are proud and happy, beautiful, sexually free, and experience no societal pressures to compete and acquire material goods. The novel eventually reveals that Abel, having found his best friend Lawrence in bed with his wife, tried to kill him in a fit of jealousy but instead shot and killed Angèle. Abel returns to Norway, while Lawrence takes the blame for the killing and is eventually executed.

Back in Norway, Abel's life of poverty in Kentucky is idealized and remembered as simple, happy, and erotic. The local pub's band of black musicians invokes a link to the primitive lifestyle in Kentucky and simultaneously globalizes, somewhat anachronistically, Abel's otherwise typical Norwegian coastal community. Having inherited a sizable amount of money upon his father's death, Abel gradually gives his wealth away and lives modestly from day to day, trying to live the Kentucky life in Norway. Still, Abel succumbs to the pressures of the culture to "become somebody" and takes on several positions of responsibility. However, each foray into "becoming somebody" is followed by a period of shedding his accumulated material possessions in order to resume the life of a ne'er-do-well. As a metaphor for a primitive way of life, Kentucky regularly explains Abel's lack of ambition in Norway. Whenever his countrymen criticize his indolence, Abel invokes Kentucky as a viable alternative lifestyle and as justification for his desire to remain idle and to live simply.

Upon publication of *Ringet sluttet*, Hamsun wrote to Gyldendal publishing house director Harald Grieg that the title means "that the last link in the chain connects with the first."[50] Hamsun recast the central metaphor of degeneration in *Fra det moderne Amerikas aandsliv*, copulation between black men and white women, as a sexual liaison between the rootless Abel and the local "queen" Olga. *Ringen sluttet* would have the reader believe that aspects of modern American life styles had migrated to Norway. My proposition that the circle referenced in the title connects Hamsun's last novel to his first book, *Fra det moderne Amerikas aandsliv,* through its focus on America, is somewhat different from the contentions of several established critics.

Ståle A. Dingstad argues that the ring goes back to Hamsun's very first story, the 1877 *Den gaadefulle* (The enigmatic one).[51] Robert Ferguson and Harald Næss assert that the imagery of the circle in the title *The Ring Is Closed* alludes to Hamsun's breakthrough novel *Sult* (Hunger).[52] Atle Kittang implies the same. In spite of some common points connecting *Sult* and *Ringen sluttet*—such as the existence of two protagonists pared down to an absolute minimum, erotic middle-class seductresses, and similar resolutions—the *Sult* hero is an artist who hungers for success, while Abel is neither an artist nor driven. In fact, success is repellant to Abel.

There is a stronger topical link between the description of Abel's lifestyle in Kentucky, and to a certain extent in Norway, and Hamsun's criticism of modernity and progress in *Fra det moderne Amerikas aandsliv*. Its writing and publication pre-dated *Sult*, reinforcing the likelihood that Hamsun was referring to it as the "first" link. Additionally, the depictions of race and gender in both books must be considered relevant elements of an inclusive act of reading. The comparison is warranted by Abel's choice of a home in the United States, for he does not settle on the predominantly white and industrialized East Coast or in the rural Scandinavian Midwest but rather in the black culture of the American South. Abel refers to America as the place where he comes from.[53] He identifies with the black musicians who perform in the Norwegian wine pub.[54] His American identity reflects on his position at home in Norway, where he casts himself in the role of a white Negro at the margin of the community. He decides, for various reasons, not to be part of what is understood as modern progress and remains as primitive as possible. The black village in Kentucky serves as the ideal where Abel could lead an idyllic life with a beautiful wife, while neither working nor harboring ambitions for more in life than what was on offer for free.

In many ways, Hamsun is here problematizing primitivism, an idea which had most to do with the longings and fears of the Western world and as such constitutes an essential element of our conception of Western modernity. The primitivist dream conceptualized non-Western peoples as pure and simple, uncivilized, ritualistic, sexually unrestrained, and brutal and/or childlike, and Hamsun conferred many of these attributes on Abel. In this dream, the real geographical specificities were erased and the primitives envisioned, in Marianna Torgovnick's words, as "an inexact expressive whole."[55] The primitive stood for a social organization that was integral, cohesive, and wholesome, precisely as Abel's black community in Kentucky is first described. This in turn allows modern social organizations to be described as inauthentic and fragmented. Yet Hamsun simultaneously uses the black musicians as a metaphor for increasing cultural leveling and globalization. When he writes, "The Negroes were playing, and people were dancing on an oblong polished surface in the middle of the room—it was the same here as all over the world," he expresses resignation and despair over globalization.[56] By subverting Abel's attempts to transplant the Kentucky lifestyle to Norway, Hamsun not only points out cultural and geographic differences but also emphasizes the incompatibility of primitivism and modernity. In Abel, Hamsun created a white Norwegian infected and ultimately disillusioned by the primitive lifestyle in black America, thus collapsing the black and the white. The black-and-white metaphor is no coincidence, for Hamsun argued consistently that pathological sexual contact between whites and blacks was one source of the physical degeneration of Europeans. He claimed or implied that miscegenation either led to or was a sign of diminished biological fertility and weakened "life force" in individuals and nations. Such concerns about miscegenation and intermarriage became, as Patrizia Szobar explained in her essay on Germany between 1933 and 1945, "a central ideological obsession among National Socialists, who even before the demise of the Weimar Republic began to issue calls for measures to prevent the sexual contamination of Aryan women and the birth of 'mixed race' offspring."[57] This is not to imply that Hamsun was aware of the specifics of the new German laws, but rather that his fixation neatly fit the central ideological obsession of the new Germany.

Abel possesses a noble, old-fashioned character in the sense that he is reliable and trustworthy, yet he is modern in his restlessness and rootlessness. Abel is best defined by an absence of qualities; he has no ambitions and no obvious talents. Unlike characters in Hamsun's previous novels, Abel is neither an aspiring writer, a charismatic storyteller, nor a diligent farmer. Abel simply exists. He is an uprooted, modern everyman. If he has a battle to fight, he fights it for his right to remain idle and uncivilized. Abel's primitiveness is epitomized in his sexuality. He is sexually attractive and virile, impregnating three women in the course of the novel. His wife, Angèle, is pregnant when she is killed. His mistress, Lili, gives birth to two children by Abel and two by her husband Axel. The once unattainable, middle-class Olga, unable to conceive with either her first or second husbands, finally seduces Abel and becomes pregnant by him. As in Livet ivold, modernity is here depicted as having an adverse effect on fertility, while Abel's virility is the last remnant of an organic and fertile way of life.

While Hamsun's poetics is certainly unique and recognizably his own, Ringen sluttet reflects some of Konrad Simonsen's propositions in Den moderne Mennesketype (The modern human type; 1917), especially his critique of Western civilization's tendency to pressure people to "become somebody."[58] Hamsun puts Abel through repeated cycles of succumbing to the pressure to "be somebody" only to reject that path time and again. Hamsun first wrote about Simonsen's work in his 1917 story "Nabobyen" (The neighboring town), in which he describes a visit to a town in Nordland that has escaped modern development, except for the presence of a large factory. Hamsun reflects on his fear of the effect of industrialization on the town by bringing in the following reference to Simonsen:

> In this connection I have come to think of the most curious book
> I have read in this raw time, it is by Dr. Konrad Simonsen and is
> called *The Modern Human Type*. He is not one of the professors
> who read fifty or a hundred volumes in order to write one more, he
> travels around in the wide world and observes, he bows his head and
> reflects. What one and all may have felt about the mystery that is life,
> he calls forth into a deep and beautiful life's wisdom: away from our
> time's mechanization of people, back to a more spiritual existence! I
> owe this book such a big thank-you and recommend others the ben-
> efits of sinking into it.[59]

Hamsun, an extraordinarily complex man who yearned for simple answers, shared many of Simonsen's critical and reductive views of modern development, especially those relating to industrial capitalism and the soulless existence resulting from it. Abel's lack of ambition allows Hamsun to investigate a radical rejection of societal goals in modernity, for Abel consistently questions the imperatives of societal pressure to succeed at something. The above excerpt also reveals facets of Hamsun's philosophy of life: his distaste for academics and his anti-intellectualism on the one hand, and on the other, his admiration of "the mystery that is life." Both his anti-intellectualism and his reverence for the nebulous "mystery that is life" fit well into the Nazi party worldview and propaganda.

We recall how Simonsen's message in 1917 was essentially an appeal to reverse modernity's destructive advances. Hamsun's popular rural utopian novel *Markens grøde*, likewise from 1917, was a plea for Norwegians to colonize the North of Norway instead of immigrating to America. Nearly two decades later, *Ringen sluttet* represented an extraordinarily bleak and disillusioned artistic response to both Hamsun's own earlier work and Simonsen's call for spiritual renewal. To Hamsun's despair, the modern development he had observed in the United States had by then encroached upon Norway as well. Simonsen's book contains much the same racial imaginary that informs many of Hamsun's texts, an ambivalent imaginary that sees in primitive races both vigor and degeneration, fertility and promiscuity, and, above all, an absence of civilized restraint in general.

The stereotypes of promiscuous erotic blacks that Hamsun uses in *Fra det moderne Amerikas aandsliv, Livet ivold,* and eventually *Ringen sluttet,* fit into a broader Western tradition of expelling Others, including a vast array of various "white Negroes," be they the poor, criminals, revolutionaries, political radicals, Slavs, Gypsies, or Jews. The alignment of each of these disparate groups under the convenient label of "race," testifies to the fact that the label was used in unstable and shifting ways.[60] "Race," in addition to describing biological differences, could be used as synonymous with culture or nation, to define ethnicity or sub-groups within a majority population, or to invent and pinpoint distinctions between what we would now call social groups or classes. In Scandinavia, the Nordic race was traditionally pitted against the Sami and the Finns, who may or may not have looked different from the ethnic Nordic peoples. But the term "race" could indeed slide and encompass very different groups.

What complicates the definition of white Negroes in Scandinavia (as elsewhere in Euro-America) is the absence of the visual marker of a difference in skin color. As Simonsen writes (joining a long line of European apologists for imperial expansion and colonial domination), colonized peoples everywhere in the world were darker skinned than their white colonizers.[61] At "home," this presented a dilemma for pseudo-Darwinian discourse, since making distinctions based on differences of skin color was not possible. Consequently, Scandinavian racism had to invent other signs of degeneration. Barbaric language, sloppy hygiene, and general slothfulness constituted what Anne McClintock pointedly calls, although in a non-Scandinavian setting, "domestic barbarism."[62] With the narrative of imperial expansion having mostly come to an end, writes McClintock, the distinction between Europeans and Others was now displaced onto cultural values like cleanliness, polite behavior, and proper discourse, invoking the benefits of domestication.

As an artist who cherished independence and artistic intuition, and as a Norwegian critical of British imperialism and American consumerism, Hamsun writes in *Ringen sluttet* against the cult of domestication of the wild; thus his initial approval of Abel's lifestyle. Yet, artistically, he has nowhere to go. In a desperate attempt to add validity to Abel's life, he launches Abel into the imagined authenticity of a black American hand-to-mouth existence.

Jealousy, poverty, and crime destroy the idyll. Hamsun's portrayal of Abel complicates the us/them antagonism that essentially underlies the primitivist narrative. Abel ends up an outsider, a white Negro on both sides of the Atlantic, in Kentucky and in Norway.

The novel establishes a special connection between Olga and the black musicians, in whom she sees both sexual temptation and liberation. Attracted to their voices and music, their exotic and erotic appearance, she is an embodiment of Hamsun's sexist views of women; by her attraction to blacks she is, at a certain level, placed in the same category. What prevents her from realizing her vague dreams of sexual and social liberation are her (middle-)class pretensions, pretensions so often ridiculed in Hamsun's novels. Olga never departs from the socially accepted, clichéd talk about blacks: they have velvet skin; they stink; and they are musical, erotic, and promiscuous. In Olga's eyes, Abel, too, is an attractive outsider, a bit dirty and exotic, and virile.

Hamsun's depiction of the relationship between Olga and Abel also reveals how he genders modernity. The mismatched courting of Abel from a shanty and Olga from a villa shows the basic incompatibility of the two classes, lifestyles, and sexual sensibilities. Hamsun saw in modernity not the emancipatory possibilities for women, but shallow, crude, and barren lives. Olga, not unlike a number of Hamsun's women protagonists, represents a middle-class woman alienated from the authentic "natural" life of motherhood, who would rather read novels, smoke, and spend money. While insisting on material security and respectability, Olga is corrupt in her yearning for intimate sensations. Part of Olga's attraction to Abel is based on the rumor that he murdered his wife. Olga is described with a rather typical metaphor of modernity, an electric light without warmth, and her speech is characterized by disjointed sentences, snatches of thoughts, and restless shifts from topic to topic. Still, Hamsun sees Olga as in control. She maintains a constant emotional hold on Abel, and, after she becomes pregnant, she discards him as a human drone. At the novel's end, Abel, having realized that he has become superfluous, leaves for America one last time. It is unclear whether he will end up in the Kentucky black community again, in prison, or somewhere else entirely. The end vaguely proposes that Abel might face criminal charges in connection with Angèle's death.

How do we ultimately position this novel within Hamsun's oeuvre and in relation to his cultural politics? The novel has generated quite disparate opinions. Harald Næss calls Abel "lazy and optimistic" and elsewhere characterizes him as Hamsun's "most modern hero."[63] Atle Kittang defines Abel as the Hamsunian figure of a disillusioned artist.[64] Ståle Dingstad describes him as a cynic, in both the philosophical and everyday understanding of the word.[65] Far from being optimistic, cynical, or artistic, however, Abel stands out as somebody who simultaneously represents, rejects, and is unable to cope with modernity. Hamsun gives Abel's lifestyle certain logic and value, yet ultimately collapses it into a modern degenerate life, as is obvious from the metaphors of racial discourse. The narrative voice also degenerates, as Frederik Stjernfelt has shown, from an omniscient voice into a voice synonymous with small-town gossip.[66]

Throughout the book, Abel's opinions and attitudes are contrasted with those representing the Norwegian small-town community. Most of the judgmental opinions about Abel are attributable to characters in the story and are, at the beginning of the novel, explained, countered, and corrected by the narrator as a higher authority. The narrator's voice gradually changes, however, blending into a collective judgmental while maintaining its aura of authority. The comments become harsher. Abel is described as having a "mismanaged brain,"[67] or is depicted as a "loony, a human wreck from Kentucky's valley of lost souls,"[68] "a nameless one in a shed, a nothing, a loony."[69] Thus, while *Ringen sluttet* initially endorses Abel's indolent way of life as an attempt to recreate in Norway a worry-free and non-materialistic lifestyle, it ultimately concludes that such attempts, in modernity, are doomed to failure. In the process, the illusion of a primitivist escape is exposed as hollow. Even children, Hamsun's most cherished symbol of hope and resilience, are denied any redeeming features. Hamsun often "allows" protagonists who are social misfits or economic failures to be good parents, like Oliver the cripple in *Konerne ved vandposten* (Women at the pump; 1920). Avoiding moralistic judgments and appreciating vitality, Hamsun portrays children born of promiscuous affairs no differently from other children. Women who have been spoiled by education or modern cities are still sometimes given a last chance at redemption by having a child, like Ingeborg Torsen from Hamsun's novel *Siste Glede* (The last joy; 1912). Even Olga gets a chance, though she is not redeemed. Neither is Abel. Abel remains an anonymous sperm-donor to Olga's child and to Lili's children. Moreover, Abel terminates his own family line when he shoots and kills his pregnant wife Angèle in Kentucky. A man without successors, his biological children dispersed, Abel ends up absorbed, probably, into the vast American continent. What he leaves behind is equally unpalatable, a Norway forever changed by encroaching modernization symbolized by the black musicians from Kentucky. *Ringen sluttet* should be read as an expression of Hamsun's deepest cultural despair, for modernity has encroached from all sides and prevented Abel from finding a place of his own anywhere on the planet.

5

A TASTE OF THE ORIENT

The Orientals seem to me to possess a high ethical wisdom. They possessed, from time immemorial, satisfaction with life, they smiled at the Westerners' restless scurry and bowed their heads in contemplative tranquility, they were content with their own.

—Knut Hamsun, "Festina lente"

Dronning Tamara (1903), *I Æventyrland* (1903), and "Under halvmånen" (1905)

ALTHOUGH EUROPEAN ORIENTALISM CONTAINED A RANGE OF VARIED IMAGES, from those of wilderness to others of high intellectual achievement, for Hamsun the Orient meant primarily a place of contemplative tranquility uncluttered with material trifles. Many Western artists reacted to the perceived shallowness of Western materialism during the last decades of the nineteenth century by turning to Eastern philosophy, religion, and culture for redemption and consolation. They elevated the Orient to a place where authentic experience was far superior to the rational modernity of the West. Scandinavia, too, experienced this reaction, and Scandinavian writing on Oriental locations and topics flourished. Popular Orientalist texts fell into two genres: documentary and travel writing on the one hand, and fictional texts on the other, although the border between the two is often blurry. Of the two texts discussed in detail in this chapter, *I Æventyrland* (In wonderland) recounts Hamsun's 1899 trip through Russia and into the Ottoman Empire, and thus falls into the travel category. *Dronning Tamara* (Queen Tamara), Hamsun's 1903 play set in Georgia, is fictional but draws partially on Hamsun's impressions gathered during his trip to the Orient.

One of the protagonists in *Dronning Tamara* is the Muslim Khan of Tovin. In his description of the khan, Hamsun employs stereotypes of Oriental sensuality and fatalism that were widespread in European culture at the time. Hamsun neatly fits this Oriental sensuality into his perceived fears of changes taking place in Western culture: a deteriorating relationship between the sexes and a growing gender imbalance. The play does not explore the region's historical tensions between Muslims and Christians except insofar as it questions if such issues might come into play should the queen have an affair with the khan. Instead, the play focuses on the Christian Queen Tamara's marriage. The play attempts to show the impossibility of a healthy marriage between the queen and her husband, Prince Georgi. The crucial issue is the relationship between a woman and a man whose unequal power positions are quite literally reflected in their respective titles, queen and prince. Simultaneously, the play explores and recommends strategies for rectifying what in Hamsun's eyes is a deplorable situation. The khan appears in the play as an erotic third party of sorts, whose function is to awaken the queen's desires.

Dronning Tamara, a prose play in three acts, was first performed by the Kristiania National Theater in January 1904.[1] Hamsun expected it to be a success,[2] but, disappointingly, the play ran for only twelve performances. Hamsun blamed the ostensibly heavy-handed production for the failure rather than his own stage settings, instructions, and designs, all of which were overblown. The stage settings consisted of stereotypical props such as Oriental carpets and exotic instruments. Women wore veils and men kaftans. The script called for massive stagings, with musicians, veiled girls, and heavily armed soldiers.[3]

The play was a direct result of Hamsun's journey to the East with his first wife. After he and Bergljot Goepfert were married in 1898, they first stayed in Finland for almost a year. Their subsequent journey through Russia to the Caucasus and to the Caspian Sea ended in Constantinople. They returned to Norway via Serbia and Germany at the end of September 1899, having traveled in the Orient for approximately one month.[4] Hamsun later published a travel book about the journey, the underrated *I Æventyrland*.[5] Like many other Europeans of his own and earlier times, Hamsun sought to find in the Orient a fairytale paradise, and he actually imagined that he did. He writes at one point: "I have been to Petersburg and Moscow, have traveled through Russia and the Caucasus—I'll never experience a grander and more beautiful fairy tale, especially the journey from Vladikavkaz across the mountains to Tiblis . . . it is another world, more handsome people, redder wine, higher mountains. And I believe that God lives around Kazbek all year around."[6]

In Hamsun's account, the historical Georgian queen Tamar is a woman whose marriage has gone cold.[7] In the first act of the play, her husband Georgi hatches a convoluted plan to regain her affection. He tries to talk his Muslim opponents into joining him in an attack against the queen's forces, and hopes to regain her love through his show of strength. While he is away from the castle plotting the attack, the queen becomes enamored with a captive of an earlier battle, the handsome Khan of Tovin. After the queen's servant Fatimat realizes the attraction between Tamara and the khan, she helps him escape. However, he returns to see the queen one more time and is killed by Georgi's men. When this happens, Fatimat flees the castle, taking Tamara's first-born son with her. At first, Georgi offers himself to the Muslims if they will free his son, and then persuades them to attack the queen's soldiers, who succeed in defending the castle. Georgi, in desperation, attacks the castle one more time, butchers the majority of her soldiers, and enters the castle. The queen has, in the meantime, learned of his betrayal, but her love for him is reawakened because she believes he did it all because of his love for her. She greets him as a great warrior and a respected and loved husband. The khan's body is then returned to the Muslims, who become Tamara's subjects, while Georgi and Tamara experience renewed marital bliss.

Although Hamsun claimed that he followed history, the characters sound suspiciously like modern protagonists discussing their relationship problems.[8] It seems that Hamsun was simply not well versed enough about Georgia to write a convincing historical play about Queen Tamar. His use of Oriental stage props was superficial.[9] The religious aspects of the play are especially shallow: the Christians cross themselves; the Muslims touch their chests, mouths, and foreheads. Whenever the queen appears on stage she genuflects, while Fatimat is veiled and turns away from the cross. These are all simple mechanical devices with little intellectual depth. That a discussion of religious and political issues was not Hamsun's priority is clear from the overriding theme in the play: love is stronger than religion. For example, the queen at one point tells Fatimat that because the khan made her feel young again, she prayed to Allah so he would defeat her own God.[10] For the queen, the religious issues are not as important as personal feelings. Tamara refuses to listen to her own prior and chooses to act as a wife instead of as a Christian queen. As she herself puts it: "Be quiet, Prior. When he comes I will kiss him and show him my love in a thousand ways. In all conceivable ways and for my entire life. I don't care about you, Prior. I'm tired of looking coldly at prince Georgi whom I love. You won't make me do it any more."[11]

In a letter to Bergljot, Hamsun confirms his focus on the love theme by mentioning a poem about mandragora that introduces the play: "I'll write a tiny little poem in front of the book; it'll be called 'Mandragora.'. . . It will sort of give us the understanding of the play: that it is the damned love plant that is at stake here."[12]

Hamsun's *Dronning Tamara*, along with his travel texts, *I Æventyrland* and "Under halvmånen" (Under the crescent moon), can be productively approached through the lens of Edward Said's 1977 work, *Orientalism*, with certain modification, since Hamsun casts a critical eye on the role of the European powers in the areas which he visited. As a Western discourse on exotic locations east of the metropolises of Paris, London, and to a lesser degree Berlin, Orientalism glorifies these exotic locations at the same time that it colonizes and appropriates them.[13] Said's ideas, articulated in relation to the grand European empires that had direct contact with the areas in question, do not apply without mitigation to Scandinavian countries. They developed their own highly specific Orientalist discourse that both follows and deviates from Said's main thesis.

Orientalism encompasses activities ranging from philology to collecting and classifying manuscripts and art objects, to writing exhilarating travel books. It is a discourse that replicates itself in the West, despite minimal contact with the "Orient" on the part of those who participate in the discourse. The Orient was broadly understood to represent Islam, although it occasionally included regions such as China and India. Often, these areas were lumped together without regard to their specific cultural, economic, or political characteristics.[14] Orientalism had and has political implications. There are connections between the Orientalist academic discourse and the imperial project of conquering real places, subduing their inhabitants, and destroying or exporting their cultures. While being careful not to accuse every scholar of the Orient of collaboration with imperialist projects, Said points out that there is a "remarkable parallel between the rise of modern Orientalist scholarship and the acquisition of vast Eastern empires by Britain and France."[15]

The academic interest in, for example, philology, numismatics, and pyramids often went hand in hand with the political and martial colonization of vast areas of the East.

In this process, the East was treated as an object to be researched and categorized, even in those cases where scholars recognized that the natives themselves had long scholarly traditions. The bias rested on a system of opinions about the difference between "us" in the West and "them" in the East, between the scientific, rational West and the sensuous, eternal East, waiting, even gratefully, to be taken and led.[16] In that sense, it was a male idea of expansion, penetration, and submission that served as a means to acquire economic gain for the expanding powers and bolstered the expansionist's ideas of his own leadership and virility.

Travel and/or fiction writers were an important factor in the constitution of Orientalism. They, perhaps even to a greater degree than academics, were peddling projections, wishful thinking, dreams, and colonial appropriations. Often travel writers confirmed what the academics had already "discovered." Mostly, however, they sympathetically embraced the Orient, vehemently opposing the Occident, which for them represented shallow and destructive progress, modern consumerism, and dry scientific research.

Norway was neither a colonial nor an academic superpower. However, the Danish-Norwegian monarchy profited from colonial enterprises at the expense of non-European countries. Its trade companies were actively involved not only in transporting various exotic goods but also in the African slave trade. Hamsun detested the British, was not particularly fond of the French either, and wrote on several occasions against the British and French territorial expansions. He was neither a scholar nor an explorer. Indeed, in *I Æventyrland*, he argues explicitly against Western scientific projects in the East and ridicules the Western geographical societies' expeditions to the East. Said's reflections have to be approached with nuanced observations of the attitudes of writers from minor European countries like Norway. Hamsun displays an Orientalist's attitude, while simultaneously offering a critique of Western imperialism and the major European powers. This double-layered prism makes Hamsun and his fictional dreams about the Orient even more interesting and complex.

There were differences in the reception and creation of Oriental images among the individual Scandinavian countries, depending on a number of factors. Scandinavian Orientalism encompassed images ranging from China to Persia, from Egypt to Morocco, from the Middle East to the Caucasus, but was generally filtered through the prism of the continental powers and further influenced by domestic affairs. In other words, because of limited direct contact, images of the Orient were imported to Scandinavia through other European countries with their own agendas.

While Sweden for centuries was culturally tied predominantly to France, and thus to the trendsetting capital of Paris, Denmark had tighter connections with Germany. Norwegian intellectuals and artists often studied and published in Copenhagen, the natural place to do so because of the Danish-Norwegian monarchy. They continued to do so after the 1814 union of Sweden and Norway, although the relationship between Norwegians and Danes became more contentious. Hamsun spent prolonged periods of time in Copenhagen, most notably the period in 1888 after his second America visit.

German towns like Berlin, Dresden, and Munich were, concurrently, often the travel and work destinations for many Norwegians, especially painters. Toward the end of the nineteenth century, however, Paris established itself as the center of the Scandinavian expatriate community. The mediating countries for the importation of Orientalist images were thus France, Germany, and to a lesser degree England and Italy. The relationship between Norway and each of these European powers also played a role. Elisabeth Oxfeldt called this process of mediation triangular positioning. Some features of the eponymous protagonist of the romantic period's pivotal Danish work, Adam Oehlenschläger's *Aladdin eller den forundelige lampe* (Aladdin, or the magical lamp; 1805)—such as imagination, creativity, and opulence—were incorporated, Oxfeldt argues, into the construction of ideal Danishness to bolster Danish identity against Denmark's arch-enemy, Germany.[17]

Oxfeldt illuminates many puzzling elements of Danish literature and culture. She delineates three distinct periods in the appropriation of Orientalism. The first begins in the early nineteenth century with an "uncomplicated Aladdin model of incorporating the Orient into the Danish national image."[18] The second period, the mid-nineteenth century, was characterized by a more complex relationship between the national self and the global community. Here, Oxfeldt defines the 1867 Paris World's Fair as a crucial event that hailed the economic power and commodities of the participating countries, the core exhibits being those of France and England. There, many Europeans could view real objects and people from the Orient as opposed to the fictional images prevailing heretofore. Henrik Ibsen's play *Peer Gynt* (also from 1867), its fourth act set in North Africa, is in many ways a typical contemporary reflection of global identities. The third period, the 1890s, witnessed

Scandinavian Orientalist writing, mainly poetry, inspired by the experience of living in Paris, with its connections to the French colonies. In Oxfeldt's opinion, these poems can be read as "thwarted Scandinavian (especially Norwegian) efforts at evoking the Orient within Scandinavia's boundaries."[19]

Oxfeldt also explains how Tivoli—aside from the Mermaid, the most quintessentially Danish tourist attraction in Copenhagen—first appropriated such Orientalist elements as Chinese lanterns, a Chinese bazaar, opulent café furnishings, and sensual exotic dance revues. Driven by cosmopolitanism, this kind of appropriation did not function on a model of binary opposition between Occident and Orient but rather as a playful acknowledgment of the artifice of the foreign and domestic. Exemplified by Tivoli, it was incorporated skillfully into the modern Danish public space. As Oxfeldt writes: "With the opening of Tivoli in 1843, Orientalism was no longer limited to the literary realm, but was increasingly leaving an imprint on Danish social space, public as well as private, and affording Danes the opportunity to act out rather than imagine their participation in an Orientalized Copenhagen."[20] In its first season, Tivoli consisted of a Turkish-style concert hall, singing stages, pavilions, coffee and sweets shops, a Moorish-style theater, two cafés called Divan 1 and Divan 2, and a Chinese bazaar, which, among other things, included a restaurant.[21] Given Tivoli's popularity, then as now, facets of Orientalism were clearly perceived as positive and worthy of being incorporated into Danish everyday life. It was due to Georg Brandes's agenda for rationally addressing the problems of the day, beginning with his lectures in 1871, that the positive connotations associated with Oriental imagination and creativity started to shift toward perceptions of idleness, sluggishness, and promiscuity.

Cultural perceptions and events in Copenhagen certainly influenced those in Kristiania, long after 1814. However, Norwegian art and culture do not offer, for various reasons, the same riches or scope of Oriental materials that appeared in Danish art and culture. In general, the Norwegians were painfully aware of their own smallness and material poverty, which limited their attempts to create luxurious and colorful Orientalist settings. Hamsun was skeptical about the possiblity of importing Orientalist tropes to Scandinavia. He was even sceptical about experiencing them consistently in the Orient itself, as his travelogue *I Æventyrland* testifies. Still, his various texts display a certain admiration for an imagined Orient, a desire to absorb its moods and value system, and an old-fashioned romantic Orientalism. Statements such as the epigraph to this chapter can be read as recommendations of life values for Norway and Norwegians. There is also a fair amount of nostalgia for places removed in time and space in his texts, a nostalgia that complements his reactionary worldview.

The prevailing mood in Norway around 1900 was optimism in anticipation of the dissolution of the political union with Sweden, although anxiety of the unknown was also articulated. The positive sentiments changed as the twentieth century unfolded. Amidst increasing fears for the future, accompanied by a questioning of specific facets of modernity and development, real and fictitious exotic locations provided an escape from everyday pressures and an environment in which daydreams could be realized. Portions of Hamsun's Orientalist texts, primarily, "Under halvmånen" and *Dronning Tamara* are cases in point.

Temporarily disregarding Hamsun's ironic comments about Western idealization of the Orient, we can observe that the sympathetic and nostalgic attitude toward the Orient expressed by Hamsun was common in Europe at the time. There was a sense that the Orient, through its primitive, virile, and mystical powers, would regenerate an old and exhausted Europe. Hamsun joined a long line of European writers, of whom perhaps Goethe and Byron are the most representative, who wrote passionately about the exotic locales of the Orient and who expected to find there a force that would renew and revitalize them as writers and as men.

In *Dronning Tamara*, Hamsun translated his own understanding of the exhausted West into several narrative strands. The most obvious are his depictions of the two religions in question, Islam and Christianity. There is also the obvious juxtaposition of the khan and Georgi and their respective masculinities. In terms of religion, the positive connotations are ascribed to Islam and the negative ones to Christianity. The text equates Islam with sensuality and Christianity with asceticism. We learn, for example, that one of the reasons behind Tamara's cold behavior toward her husband is the prior's religious fervor. Muslims are portrayed as fatalistic, referring repeatedly to Allah's will, but Christians also speak in no unclear terms of God as the highest authority. Yet, while the former's fatalism is viewed as a stoic, worthwhile response to fate, the latter is a shrill act of aggression. Indeed, Christians represent intruders into foreign territories. They are also portrayed as stubborn fundamentalists unwilling to debate. To the Christian prior, the queen's advisor, Tamara is first a Christian and only secondarily a wife and mother. While the prior criticizes Queen Tamara for not being Christian enough, Georgi criticizes her for being too mild and forgiving because she shows mercy toward her Muslim prisoners and spares their lives. Georgi kills them on the spot and returns from the battlefield with only a few captives. In the course of the play, Tamara's *Bildung* consists of appearing crueler in her exterior actions—she does not even blink when her soldiers are killed—and milder in her sentiments toward her husband. In contrast to the unforgiving Christians, the Muslims embody wisdom and enjoyment of life. The Khan of Tovin gained his wisdom and powerful rhetoric at the caliph's court, a place of reflection, leisure, hunting, singing, and dancing, a utopia materialized.

In *I Æventyrland*, Hamsun mentions Queen Tamar three times, every time in connection with the ruins of her castle, thus creating a powerful image of a glorious past.[22] The third instance, with which Hamsun closes the text, leaves an image that lingers in the reader's mind long after the book has been put aside: "It's late in the afternoon. I'm sitting by the open window and see naked men ride horses through the waters of the Black Sea. Their bodies are dark against the blue sea. And the sun is still shining on the ruins of Queen Tamara's castle rising out of the fertile forest."[23] The image illustrates Hamsun's underlying fantasy of an Orient where naked men connect with nature directly. The description points to other instances in the work in which Orientals move elegantly, effortlessly, youthfully, and beautifully through their environment. Dignified masculinity resides in this paradise. Women, in contrast, are rarely seen. Sometimes they hide on the rooftops of their houses. When they are seen, they are mostly veiled. They do not ever seem to speak.

Yet in *Dronning Tamara*, in spite of his admiration for Oriental men, Hamsun cannot envision a permanent union between a Christian woman and a Muslim man. After all, the play could have ended with Tamara and the khan as a couple and Tamara's traitorous husband eliminated. Since the Muslim citizens ask Tamara to be their leader, why not cement this bond with a marriage? The role of the Muslim Khan of Tovin, however, is simply that of the third party in an erotic triangle, an exotic stimulator of sorts. He serves his purpose and is done away with, while the play continues to revolve around the two main Christian protagonists.

The khan's portrayal is interesting because it reveals why Hamsun was attracted to the Orient. He sees the Oriental male as magically attractive, virile and masculine and simultaneously noble and eloquent. This is most evident in the manner in which the kahn disarms the queen and transforms her into a "real" woman. In spite of his being the queen's prisoner, the khan dominates the encounter with her because of his manly youth, speech, and unusual attractiveness. When they meet, they are mesmerized by each other and repeatedly find excuses to be in each other's company.[24] The idea of irresistible love in this unevenly matched couple cannot be sustained for very long, much less consummated. Appropriately, then, the khan must be written out of the play.

After the khan is killed, even his opponents praise him for his courage and skill as a warrior, and they honor him with the respect that he is due. The tragedy is magnified by the fact that he produced no children, meaning that his noble family line will perish. The portrait of the khan and even the end of his family line fit nicely into the Orientalist idea of the noble yet doomed Oriental man. Demise seems almost a theme in Hamsun's treatment of primitives. Recall that he also believed that the American Indians would soon vanish.

The Battle of the Sexes

THE TWISTS AND TURNS OF THE PLOT OF *DRONNING TAMARA* ARE COMPLI-cated to the point of confusion. Yet its underlying theme—the battle between the sexes—is rather straightforward. The play opens with the disclosure of marital quarrels between Queen Tamara and Prince Georgi. While everyone at court is the queen's servant, Georgi suffers grievously from the fact that he is not a king, only a prince.[25] Moreover, he feels like a human drone: "I am not the king. I am only the father to her children, to her son and her daughter. . . . It is my lot to be the man in this house. I talk all the time to a son who is greater than me. I talk to my young daughter who might one day reign over me."[26] The prince complains that when he issues an order, everybody verifies that it is, indeed, what the queen wants.[27] And perhaps most important, he describes the recent years of his marriage as essentially a battle with his wife, who either never looks at him or looks at him coldly. He concludes: "This is how we fight."[28]

Prince Georgi, as the neglected husband, expresses his goal very clearly: to conquer the queen.[29] The prince, perhaps surprisingly, does not want to make himself king, he only wants to recapture control of his marriage. He sees this task as requiring that he tame the queen, which he plots to do by destroying her army.[30] To execute his project, Prince Georgi lays aside the religious differences between Christians and Muslims and strikes a deal with the Muslim Khan of Kars to attack and subdue the queen's soldiers. In this way, he hopes to upset the power imbalance between himself and his wife and force her to love him again. Georgi, who obviously equates force with love, eventually succeeds in his grand plan of recapturing his wife's love.

The play's development underscores the psychological change in the queen. At the beginning of Act Three, a letter from Prince Georgi to the Khan of Kars outlining Georgi's treasonous plan is given to the queen. In this crucial scene, the queen reads the letter of betrayal and forgives Georgi instantly.[31] After Georgi enters her castle with force, decimating her army, she accepts him with respect and love.

In the end, Hamsun was more than satisfied with his play, although in a letter to Bergljot, he expressed concern as to whether some ten pages preceding the end of the play would be *psykologisk rigtige*.[32] It is not completely clear what Hamsun meant by "psychologically correct," but it is certain that he paid a lot of attention to the plot's development. Given the play's focus and Hamsun's preoccupation during that period with the relationship between the sexes, he was probably referring to Tamara's change from a woman who treats her husband coldly to one who adoringly looks up to him. It may be a coincidence that in 1903, when the play was published, Otto Weininger's book *Geschlecht und Charakter* (Sex and character) also appeared. One of Weininger's main theses was that women, due to their carnal drive, are inferior in character to men. The strength and power in men is what women need to be happy—and tamed. The phenomenal success of Weininger's book testifies to the fact that it echoed the prevailing feelings about gender at the time, including those of Hamsun.[33]

Hamsun's biased views on women in his articles and in a more complex way in his novels are no secret. In his personal life, he enacted his imagined ideals with precision: his first marriage, which failed almost immediately, was to the upper-class, well-traveled, and experienced Bergljot, who resembled many of his fictional heroines. In *I Æventyrland*, which can be interpreted on one level as the description of the Hamsuns' honeymoon, Bergljot is consistently written out of the text, usually referred to simply as "my traveling companion" or "my escort" and only once as his wife. Hamsun's second wife, Marie Andersen, was more pliable in her role as Mrs. Hamsun, although the cost to her and her creative aspirations was enormous. Hamsun's life and his fiction in *Dronning Tamara* are similar to the extent that he could not conceive of the idea of both equality and love within a relationship. These were mutually exclusive. He viewed the normative patriarchal union as an extremely fragile institution in which women needed to be watched constantly, tricked, and tamed.

In his 1929 book on Hamsun, Trygve Braatøy deems the play an extremely important text, giving it an emphasis it has rarely received before or since and claiming that Tamara is one of the most telling of Hamsun's female protago-nists.[34] Braatøy includes a lengthy analysis of Weininger's *Geschlecht und Charakter*, calling it "a completely uninhibited attempt at creating an 'anti-feminist system'."[35] He concedes that it is possible to look at Weininger's book as confirmation of the newly achieved and publicly flaunted women's emanci-pation.[36] Braatøy suspects that the aggressive tone of the book veiled an inner uncertainty which even the scientific veneer could not hide.[37]

Indeed, in Hamsun's ironic portrayal of Georgi's aggressive actions, we can see both a veneer of strength, a performance of power, and an insecurity and awareness of a lost battle, or at best a constant battle perpetually in danger of being lost. Hamsun marks his awareness of and discontent with the recent shifts in gender relations with a strutting Georgi, who, for all his bravado, has little real power.

If the real and perceived advances of the growing women's movement in Norway and elsewhere in the West are the historical backdrop for *Dron-ning Tamara*, the imaginary Oriental setting reflects Hamsun's preference for a universe in which men are still men and women are silent, veiled, and humble creatures. With the exception of Tamara, that is. The situation of Tamara, Georgi, and the Khan of Tovin is Hamsun's representation of what happens when the patriarchal paradise has been lost or transgressed. Georgi has decided that his only hope for a satisfactory (to him) love relationship with Tamara is an assertion of power over her. His urge to control and sub-due Tamara is manifested in his attack on her castle and the resulting pile of corpses. His attack is effective, and thereafter the queen refers to herself as his wife.

"Is he coming . . . with force?" asks the queen, as the thick fog suddenly lifts and reveals the importance of this heroic scene.[38] Indeed, the play seems to be saying, on one level, that if anything works with women, it is brute power. Love, disguised as power, or vice versa, conquers all, even sound judg-ment. While Georgi is accomplishing his great plan, the queen's men die left and right. The queen, however, merely comments: "It is for my sake that he is doing this. He does not spare anything. You see, Prior, that he dared to do it."[39] She later comments admiringly, "He is like a mountain."[40] It is hard to believe that the prince's cruelty would earn him such admiration, but it does, and her love as well. After defeating the soldiers defending the castle, the prince enters victoriously, and Tamara looks at him respectfully and passion-ately, as in the days when they were first married.

Ironically, however, the queen had already realized on her own that she was a mother and a wife more than a queen and that Georgi's actions stemmed from his love for her, a development that renders Georgi's actions superfluous. She had already made up her mind to return the khan's body to his people in order to save her husband. She asks a simple yet crucial question: "Why now? It was not necessary."[41] In this statement is the realization that the prince is converting the converted, that his gestures are empty and, except for a collection of corpses, have attained nothing but that which had already been given. His reaction, as indicated by the stage instructions, is predictable: he is visibly disappointed, and his head bends as he hears this question and the answer.

At the conclusion of the play, the exchange between the prince and the queen attests to Hamsun's belief in the untamable essence of the woman, which sooner or later will destroy a very vulnerable and fragile balance between the spouses. The play ends as follows:

> *Queen* (stands up): Shall we go?
> *Prince Georgi* (likewise): Yes. (Remains standing)
> *Queen*: Now you are standing there and looking at me as to what you
>   should do. Georgi, you know I love you; I will go wherever you
>   go. (Puts her arm around him and leads him behind the curtain)[42]

The paradox that emerges out of the tension between the queen's words and the stage instructions articulates the open-endedness of the situation. The queen tells her husband that she would go wherever he goes, but the stage instructions reveal that she puts her arm around him and leads him out. Georgi's victory is a questionable one, especially in light of the fact that the Muslim warriors from Tovin have just asked the queen for protection. In the end, then, Tamara is even more powerful than at the beginning, yet tamed, albeit tenuously, by her love for her aggressive husband. The stage instructions reveal Hamsun's personal conviction about where the real power rests, with the formidable and attractive queen.

Tamara represents the period's fear of the loss of male power. Hamsun envisioned her as nature's deviation, a point clearly expressed in a crucial moment of the play. After her soldiers defeat the Khan of Kars's army, in a battle instigated by Georgi, the soldiers decide to honor the *queen* as their *king*, which the queen accepts.[43] The prince's reaction is telling, when he says: "Before I was the queen's husband, now I guess I am the king's wife."[44] The pages that follow are full of reminders of this gender bender: "You shall call the queen the king from now on, she is the king," we are told.[45] Surely Hamsun was trying to push her dominance so far into the grotesque that it would be perceived as unacceptable by the audience. The perplexing reality of fin-de-siècle gender roles and women's increasing visibility in economic and public life could not have been expressed more clearly than in the queen's acceptance of the title of king, with the prince being left, as he expresses it, as the king's wife. During the last quarter of the nineteenth century (and beyond) sexual identities were challenged, blurred, and redefined. Hamsun was one writer of the time who reacted immediately and critically to the desire of women to be more than mothers and homemakers. Queen Tamara can be read as an ambitious modern woman in a medieval costume. Hamsun pairs her with Georgi, not a king but only a prince. The relationship is between a vital, successful, and victorious woman and a man who is her subordinate in every respect.[46]

The power dynamic between the queen and the khan is, temporarily at least, a balanced one. Each is the leader of a people. However, in her contact with the khan, the queen loses her regal poise. She talks to him not as a queen who has power over him, but as a distracted woman worried about her looks and her dress, blushing and ready to flirt. Hamsun shows us Tamara as a wounded woman enraged over news that the khan wanted to flee with Fatimat, which was a lie on Fatimat's part. Concluding that the khan had betrayed her as a woman, she suddenly sees him as a Muslim traitor. Here, the gender issue is merged with the religious one, and the queen rejects the khan as an infidel.

Queen Tamara is also a woman who worries about her age. At one point she considers herself no longer young, and she realizes she is a mother first and a sexual being second. In Hamsun's universe, home is the most appropriate place for a woman. Significantly, Hamsun follows the scene in which the queen accepts the title of king with the scene in which she discovers that her son, having been kidnapped, is gone. This is the moment which articulates Tamara's difficult choice between motherhood and royal duties: one is either a mother and wife or a queen or king. Tamara realizes that being king means nothing if it means losing her son.[47]

Additionally, Tamara understands the kidnapping to be punishment for the "little joy" that she experienced in the presence of the khan. The queen, the queen with the title of king, realizes that the kidnapping is connected to her having overstepped her power, at the expense of her motherhood, and is at the same time a punishment for her desire for the khan. Tamara blames herself and accepts that she is guilty. In the eyes of others, she is also guilty. Georgi blames her for his own cruelty on the battlefield, where he kills rather than captures his enemies.[48] Fatimat blames her for the khan's death.[49] The accusations coincide with her own conclusion that she, having transgressed accepted gender roles, is responsible for the kidnapping.

With the exception of Trygve Braatøy's *Livets cirkel* (The circle of life), in which *Dronning Tamara* takes central place in the discussion of Hamsun's works, most considerations of Hamsun have either ignored the play or dismissed it as uninteresting at best and a clear failure at worst. Such omissions or dismissals illuminate reading practices and the process of canon formation. This play, perhaps an aesthetically mediocre one at best, is left out of the canon in spite of the rich insight it provides into Hamsun's universe, insight that should figure into analyses of his other texts, perhaps even the entire oeuvre.

For a better understanding of Hamsun, his failures as a playwright are immensely instructive. Whether he was simply an untalented playwright or was insufficiently interested in the craft of writing plays is beside the point. The fact is that in his "failed" plays messages come across clearly, if not crudely, and Hamsun's preoccupations are revealed with only a thin artistic veneer. The messages should be considered part of Hamsun's poetic and real worldviews, as Trygve Braatøy has claimed. [50] Braatøy argues that the failure of *Dronning Tamara* is due not only to Hamsun's lack of knowledge about the topic, but also to a deep-seated conflict which interested him at the time and which he did not really dare articulate.[51] The conflict manifested in the play is a power and gender disharmony between a queen and her husband-prince, a woman and a man. [52]

Hamsun's play *Livet ivold* was published seven years after *Dronning Tamara,* in 1910. It continues the investigation of powerful women, their legitimate yet insignificant husbands and exotic third parties. In the resolution of *Livet ivold*, Hamsun (erotically) pairs a middle-aged woman, Juliane, with a black Boy, proffering them as the new couple, while the white male characters are all old and feeble-minded, limping, or killed during the play. The central issue behind both plays is gender imbalance, which might well be the most crucial one in Hamsun's writing.

The resolutions of the two plays are simultaneously similar and yet different. The sensuous Muslim Khan of Tovin enters the relationship between Tamara and Georgi as a clear Other, in demonstrating the compatibility that exists between a powerful woman and an exotic Oriental. While the attraction between Tamara and the khan is powerful, it cannot be sustained, and in the overall design of the play its purpose is to strengthen the normative union of husband and wife. In *Livet ivold*, Juliane and Boy constitute the sexual couple remaining on stage at the end of the play, symbolizing that the Other has been victorious. If we consider the chronology of the plays, *Dronning Tamara* of 1903 and *Livet ivold* of 1910, along with the final power configuration of the two couples, we may conclude that, from the point of view of the white male, the gender situation was rapidly deteriorating.

I Æventyrland

WHEN THE HAMSUNS RETURNED FROM THEIR ORIENTAL JOURNEY, KNUT LEFT Bergljot in Kristiania and visited his parents in northern Norway, where he had not been for twenty years. His actions confirm the old adage that to travel is always an intimate experience, more about the traveler than the destination. Hamsun, spurred by his Oriental experience, attempted to "go native" in the place where he had spent his childhood, by living in a forest hut like a hermit. There, in 1899, he started to write the verse play *Munken Vendt* (Friar Vendt), which he did not finish until June 1902. Around 1900, Hamsun returned to Oslo and almost immediately left for Belgium. Although Bergljot was pregnant with Victoria at the time, Hamsun was, during this period, everywhere but home. Knut and Bergljot agreed to separate in 1906.

Hamsun's *I Æventyrland* was published in 1903 and can be read, on one level, as an unintentional illustration of the failure of the Hamsuns' marriage. The time the narrator (Hamsun) spends exploring exotic environments on his own is remarkable, and certainly the most exciting and amusing aspect of the text. The narrator's traveling companion (Bergljot Hamsun) incurs the narrator's wrath by being fresh, peeking into his diary, and uttering some critical remarks.[53]

I Æventyrland is both a tediously repetitive text—in the travel genre, it is typically difficult to avoid recurring descriptions of trains, coachmen, bedbugs, shabby hotels, swindlers, and so forth—and a delightful and funny commentary on a variety of issues: geography, commerce, multiethnic and multilingual misunderstandings, stereotypes of the Orient, and stereotypes of the Occident. Hamsun maneuvers skillfully between observing his environment and his own responses to it, while displaying his sense of humor and irony.[54] Hamsun added to the first edition the subtitle "Oplevet og drømt i Kaukasien" (Experienced and dreamed in the Caucasus), signaling that this was both a traditional documentary travel book and his own dreamlike, fairy-tale fiction.[55] He was a traveler observing magnificent nature and local customs, dreaming himself away into imaginary scenarios.

The text, divided into nineteen sections, follows Hamsun's travel itinerary from St. Petersburg to Batum on the Black Sea. The largest part of the book is devoted to the mountainous region of the Caucasus and the city of Tiblisi. It dutifully enumerates tourist attractions, quotes from travel guides, and reflects on economic development. One of its underlying themes is a broad comparison between the Orient and the West, especially the United States, as the two opposing poles of economic and cultural development. On the one hand, Hamsun observes with sympathy Oriental fatalism, wisdom, patience, and eternal values, and on the other reflects with a critical eye on the brutality of American technological progress. Still, this picture is forever problematized as the Orient becomes more and more complex, ultimately dissolving into a kaleidoscope of areas, ethnicities, and languages, and, most important, individuals who challenge the stereotypical presumptions of a typical Turk, a typical Russian, and so forth. Against a background of constant fleas, dirty cutlery, and general filth, Hamsun dismantles the romanticized perception, so common in the West, of an idealized Orient of luxurious harems and proud, wise warriors.

The Orient that Hamsun describes already contains within it an element of Europe almost everywhere he looks. Oriental wisdom is peppered with European rationality and logic. Batum, on the Black Sea, is described as South American (as if Hamsun knew that continent) and is populated with peoples from all around the world, from Japan to Austria. Hamsun also includes images of the Orient as backwards, lacking reflection, and in need of a strong leader. The way in which Orientals treat their horses and oxen is also painted in a critical light. Hamsun observes their sometimes cruel, sometimes indifferent treatment of animals, showing that they are a far cry from living in harmony with all living beings.

Nonetheless, the stoicism and fatalism of the Orient is several times described as eternal and wise. Further still, there exists a yearning in Hamsun's prose for the simple, uncluttered, unhurried, and contemplative way of life that he sporadically observes on his travels and finds in the Asiatic part of Tiblisi. The narrator writes: "And here everything was peaceful, no one was in a hurry, the calm of the Orient rested over people."[56] Finally, dignity (*værdighet*) and indifference (*likegyldighet*) are positive terms Hamsun associates with the Orient.

This calm and contemplative side of the Oriental life style is attractive to

Hamsun, not least because of the absence of superficial Western values. The text explains: "The closer one gets to the Orient, the less people speak. The ancient peoples have put behind them chatter and cackle, they keep quiet and smile. It is perhaps best this way. The Koran has shaped a view of life that one cannot hold meetings about or debate; its meaning is one only: happiness is to endure life, the afterlife will be better. Fatalism."[57] It is obvious that Hamsun equates life in the West with pretentiousness, while life in the Orient is secure in its eternal wisdom. Hamsun here collapses "Oriental" with "ancient," displaying what Anne McClintock terms "anachronistic time." One facet of Westerners' attitudes toward exotic primitive areas and their peoples, McClintock writes, is that such areas and groups are perceived as removed not only in geographic terms but also to some primeval era in time.

At the same time, Hamsun pokes fun at Western scientific expeditions, which had as their goal the mapping, measuring, and description of various facets of the Oriental way of life. This seemed an absurdity to Hamsun. When in the vicinity of Kasbek, he jokes that he would have liked to have been in the service of science.[58] At the end of his nighttime excursion to the Caucasian village of Kobi (whether the excursion was real or just a figment of his feverish mind is not specified), he writes with irony about his "scientific" research.[59] Similarly ironic is his reflection on fame and science in Tsjilkani.[60] The culmination of his "investigative" reporting comes during his visit to Nobel House in Baku, where, despite a prohibition against writing and taking notes, he scribbles behind his back, mixing up the scientific data on oil research that he was secretly recording.[61]

While the descriptions of America in *I Æventyrland* are not without nuance, they ultimately represent a negative symbol of modern life in conflict with a traditional way of life. This clash between the modern and the traditional is illustrated most dramatically in Hamsun's passage on oil drilling in Baku. It was American technology that enabled the extraction of oil and thus the development of an entirely new industry. However, the process of extracting the oil, writes Hamsun, sealed up the naturally occurring vents whose perpetual flames the locals thought of as eternally lit fires. Symbolically, Hamsun here contrasts scientific modernity with ancient times. Exploring further the difference between the traditional and the modern, Hamsun writes with irony about a harem and the lustful gazes of the local women,[62] poking fun at the Western idea of a harem's constantly available women. Yet he then immediately segues into a diatribe about Western women's suffrage and emancipation.[63] This in turn leads him to ridicule those who pursue their causes by writing letters to the editor, in essence disqualifying the idea of civil society and democratic discourse. In these pages Hamsun is very funny, but underneath his witticism targetting Western science and rational thinking is a deep resentment of all knowledge that is not based on intuition or direct experience. We can see these funny anti-intellectual jibes as merely brilliant entertainment, but they also express Hamsun's attitude toward what can broadly be understood as the process of enlightenment. It is worth remembering that decades later, Vidkun Quisling's party, with Hamsun's enthusiastic support, would run on a political platform of reversing the "damage" done by the Enlightenment.

The most interesting and humorous parts of the narrative underscore the impossibility of a European blending in seamlessly with the locals, the awareness of shifting identities, and the realization that the narrator has become the Other. This is illustrated most clearly by the episode in Baku in which the narrator, who has been taken for either a German or a Briton, decides to dress like the natives: "It is very hot and I get myself a ready-made yellow jacket in a shop. My appearance was now certainly a bit odd; but life became easier since I rid myself of my Nordic doublet. To top it off, I bought a hand fan."[64] One can imagine that for a man of Hamsun's appearance—tall and clearly European—a yellow silk jacket was not the perfect way to blend in. Even worse, at one point he is fooled by a Tartar who gives him a lesson in Oriental stereotypes by telling him a tall tale about a Bukhara khan's pilgrimage to Mecca.[65] Hamsun, at first perplexed, soon realizes that the Tartar is feeding this foreigner what he expects to hear. Aware that outsiders bring with them preconceived notions of Orientalism, the Tartar appropriates them and recycles them back to Hamsun.

That there is nothing specifically Oriental about the region is sometimes foregrounded with descriptions of geographical features that at times resemble those of Norway or remind Hamsun of America. About a watering spot in the Terek River valley, for instance, he writes, "this spot is completely Norwegian in its character."[66] At the foothills of the Caucuses, he observes a castle, which, in the trembling heat of the day, reminds him of the Soria Moria castle of Norwegian fairytales.[67] While on the surface adopting a critical attitude toward both the Orient and the Occident, the narrator ultimately endorses a languid lifestyle inspired by an Orient where the absence of deadlines and a calm attitude seem to be the main attractions. This Orient is part religion and part tradition, part environment and part biology. And in the majestic mountains he experiences, standing face to face with God, a perfect moment of nirvana that he had not experienced in other mountains, either at home in Jotunheimen, in the Alps, or in Colorado.[68] Here, in the Caucasus, he imagines that he could establish roots and never return to Europe.[69]

Crossing the Darjai Pass, the narrator senses that he could stay forever because of the favorable interplay between the environment and its people. He writes: "The people here have endured struggles that threatened to destroy them but they overcame everything; strong and sound and flourishing, today they are a people of ten million."[70] He admires the men of the Caucasus for their elastic movements, their posture, their sinewy bodies, and their endurance.[71] He does not see so much of the women, and judging from his ironic remarks about the women in the West, it is fine with him that women are neither seen nor heard.

The text concludes with the statement that the narrator will always long to return to the Caucasus because he drank from the river Kurt, an ending that reads like an audience-friendly advertisement for the romantic Orient. A similar image of drinking from the river also appeared earlier in the text, in the description of the Akstafa train station environment.[72] His romanticizing suggests the narrator's honest desire to find the "original" Orient, in spite of the reality he encountered on his travels. Ultimately, the text expresses the impossibility of discovering the romanticized Orient without relinquishing a belief in the existence of a perfect Orient. What Oxfeldt has termed "parodic Orientalism" is apt indeed, although it seems that Hamsun in the end sucumbs to the attractions of Orientalism and to the "essence of the Orient."[73]

Of all the descriptions in I Æventyrland, perhaps none has been quoted and challenged more often than the one about an officer with a Jewish face, whom the narrator meets on the train: "His face is unpleasant, Jewish."[74] The officer turns out to be a swindler and is eventually arrested. The unpalatable remark grows in importance as the plot surrounding this man develops further. The Jewish officer makes a "Jewish gesture" (den jødiske Gestus), one which signifies to the narrator that he is willing to be bribed. The negative connotation about the Jewish officer is reinforced with a subplot about two Armenian Jews, a fat old man and a fat young eunuch, who are also traveling on the train and making an uncanny noise.[75] Earlier, the narrator had been revolted at the sight of the eunuch being treated like a woman. This insinuation of homosexuality is later complemented by the description of a Jewish watch merchant, who opens a clock mechanism and shows the narrator an obscene picture inside. There is also a description of two Jewish women, a mother and daughter in a hotel restaurant in Batum, their fat fingers full of diamond rings.[76] There are negative descriptions of other nationalities in the text as well, of Tatars, Cossacks, and Russians, yet they are not connected specifically to either nationality or ethnicity. It is worth noting that the descriptions of Armenians are uniformly negative. The text reads: "We heard in the Orient that a Jew can swindle ten Greeks, but an Armenian swindles both Greeks and Jews."[77] Hamsun's other major Orientalist text, "Under halvmånen," written two years later, conflates the images of the Jews and the Armenians and creates one negative symbol of a bloodsucking people.

"Under halvmånen" (1905) continues Hamsun's investigation into many of the same issues he tackled in *I Æventyrland*. It describes the last leg of the Hamsuns' journey through the straits of Bosporus and into Constantinople. Again, the Eastern lifestyle is hailed and contrasted against the Western one, and Western stereotypes about wild, blood-thirsty, and man-eating Turks are ridiculed. There are regional differences, however. The Turks represent traditional wisdom recently under attack by Western forces and local Armenians, while the Greeks and the Jews are spiritually impoverished peoples who have sold themselves to Western materialism and tourism.

In addition to interesting observations on lifestyles, the text includes reflections on contemporary political events. One passage reflects on the Armenian genocide carried out by Turkish Sultan Abdul-Hamid II. The narrator clearly endorses the Turkish side, dismissing the Armenian genocide as Western propaganda. It is estimated that roughly three-quarters of a million Christian Armenians were killed between the 1890s and the 1920s, although figures are conflicting. Prior to Hamsun's visit to the Ottoman Empire in 1899, the number of Armenian victims might have been roughly 100,000 (various figures have been reported).[78] In order to explain—justify, really—the killings, Hamsun writes:

> The Armenians are the East's merchant Jews. They infiltrate themselves everywhere, from the Balkans to China, in all the cities one visits the Armenians are dominant. While the newspapers in the West are overflowing with tears shed over these people's ill fate, it isn't seldom one hears in the East that they deserve their fate, they are unanimously and strikingly presented as a people of rogues. In Turkey they push the country's own children out of work in one job after the other and take over their places. Trade comes into their hands, financial loans, and money. And bloodsucking.[79]

In his defense of the Ottoman Empire and Sultan Abdul-Hamid II, Hamsun steadily builds up accusations against the Armenians, who are allegedly backed by liberal European powers and their media. To Hamsun, it is the Turks who are the real victims of the Western press, with its propagandistic images of Turkish bloodthirstiness.[80] Hamsun sees the sultan as a hard-working and enlightened Muslim. The logic here, as it would be in 1930s Germany, was that a state has the right to defend itself from unwanted elements. The narrator then gives a rather unfortunate example: if the Jews in Norway exhibited hatred toward the state and staged an armed rebellion, they would be shot, and Jews all over the world would scream in protest.[81]

Just as he was haphazard in the 1880s about his sources for *Fra det moderne Amerikas aandsliv*, and selective in the 1930s regarding information about the Nazi Germany threat, in "Under halvmånen" Hamsun refers vaguely to a few sources to strengthen his argument, preferring instead to cite the "European press," "Christian Europe," "the newspapers," and so forth. The argument from *Harpers Monthly Magazine*, in essence, is that the most powerful men in Turkey are the Armenian Christians who occupy the most important positions and own three-fourths of the land in the Ottoman Empire.[82] From this "data," Hamsun concludes that the sultan is a rather forgiving man to law-abiding Christians. His conclusion nevertheless morphs into the conviction that Armenians are the blood-sucking Jews of the East who fleece the ethnic Turks. The justification of the sultan's genocide is only a short step away. Parallels to the construction of the "Jewish threat" come to mind. If one substitutes the Jews for the Armenians and Hitler for the sultan, Hamsun's rationale on behalf of the Turks could be mistaken for a rationale on behalf of the Nazis.

The section "Sultan's Visit to Church" opens with a description of a parade in front of the mosque before the sultan came to prayers. Hamsun describes with gusto the colorful peoples of different ethnic origins in the parade—Arabs, Albanians, Armenians, and Syrians among them. The Germans are defined as a "disharmonic element" (*disharmonisk element*) and the Yankees are "Chicago folk from the stock exchange" (*Chicagofolk, herrer fra børsen*), barely to be tolerated. The narrator expresses his doubts about the atrocities and his misgivings about Western newspapers' sensationalist reports on the sultan's lack of humanity. Eagerly wanting to balance these reports and quoting from sources he trusted, Hamsun claimed that the Armenians themselves staged the massacres in order to use them in their own propaganda. He supported the Turkish government's resistance to the call from Western powers for reforms that would have armed the Armenians. "A strong, master race cannot accept such a power adjustment," he writes.[83]

In the section "The Bazaar," there are again observations about the profit-oriented Greeks, who pester both tourists like himself and the dignified, wise Turks. About the Armenians and the Jews, we read: "Let the Armenian scream and the Jew bow and flatter and ingratiate himself for the foreign infidels—neither of them has the Turk's peace of mind and neither will get a spot in the prophet's eternal garden."[84] The Armenian and the Jew have now been conflated, they will do anything for money, and that is what makes them eternal outsiders. At the silk bazaar, the narrator, observing many Arabian noses, remarks that Jews stick to themselves in their own ghetto, where they can swindle each other to their hearts' content.[85]

When Hamsun and his companion arrive at the bazaar, an ingratiating Jew approaches them, but they demand a Turkish merchant instead. In his store, full of fairytale-like carpets and jewelry, they shop, drink coffee, smoke, and most importantly experience the dream of the Orient. The narrator, however, cannot avoid making a few ironic comments when he encounters some beautiful women: "I could take the two of you to Europe and give you instruction in piano, voting rights, and writing."[86] The threat of women's advances in Europe was obviously constantly on Hamsun's mind. The text concludes with a reflection on the history of the Ottoman Empire and its contemporary state, as well as a generous wish that Muslim culture will regain the relevance it once held.

Hamsun covers a lot of territory in his Orientalist texts, displaying sharp observations and witty self-reflections, admiring and undermining the relevant Orientalist tropes. In spite of his paradoxical attitudes toward the Orient he travels in, Hamsun the narrator ultimately succumbs to his desire to believe in the dream. He articulates many positive fantasies about the Orient: its overwhelming nature, authentic and organic life style, fatalism, simple existence uncluttered by material possessions, and, last but not least, its patriarchal gender relations. For Hamsun, that kind of Orientalism represented a powerful tool to critique Western modernity, and one that suited him temperamentally.[87] Often a dashing dandy, and certainly astute in financial matters, Hamsun nevertheless remained a thrifty if not parsimonious man. "To be content with one's own," was a personal motto, but also one with which he lobbied would-be Norwegian immigrants to settle in the often rugged North of Norway instead of in rich America. As he grew older, Hamsun frequently juxtaposed Oriental wisdom as he understood it with the real and perceived ills of modern life.

6

IMAGINING THE SLY MAGIC "LAPPS"

NORWEGIAN TRAVELERS TO THE UNITED STATES, PERMANENT IMMIGRANTS OR temporary visitors like Hamsun, carried with them certain mental models about other peoples. These models originated primarily in attitudes toward the Sami, the indigenous inhabitants of Scandinavia, and toward the Jews who settled in Scandinavia from the mid-nineteenth century onward. Those, in turn, were undergirded with attitudes toward the exotic peoples found in a range of colonial texts from various European countries. Hamsun, in his works, refers to the Sami as "Lapps," a word that has slowly been replaced by "Sami," the name the people use for themselves.[1] While not derogatory per se, the word "Lapp" acquired a derisive meaning during the period of nation-building in the North. Depending on the context and the speaker, it could be interpreted as either a definition of the indigenous people or an offensive term for the uncivilized Other. The Sami call the vast northern region that has been their home Sapmi, while outsiders refer to it as Finnmark or Lapland. Historically, the region and its people have been divided among, and exploited by, Norway, Sweden, Finland, and Russia.[2]

On January 15, 1911, the journal *Verdens Gang* published Hamsun's review of Johan Turi's *Muitalus samiid birra* (English edition, *Turi's Book of Lappland*), which was the first book in the Sami language about the Sami experience.[3] Today considered a literary classic,[4] it was published simultaneously in Sami and Danish in 1910. Johan Turi (1854–1936) was a Sami hunter and reindeer herder. Literary histories customarily mention that he was born on the Norwegian side of the border and later moved to Sweden, a piece of information reflecting the *realpolitik* of the Scandinavian national states. Emilie Demand Hatt, a Danish ethnologist and artist, edited the manuscript, translated it into Danish, and wrote the introductory and explanatory notes.[5]

Hamsun wrote a positive review of Turi's book as a whole and of Turi's style in particular. In his review, he somewhat condescendingly praises Turi for his knowledge of Sami social codes, customs, beliefs, and superstitions. Hamsun expresses appreciation for Sami resilience in coping with the harsh conditions of their lives. Above all, he lauds the book's unpretentious yet detailed and ultimately persuasive descriptions of nature. Hamsun associates "unpretentious" with being unsophisticated, and he interprets the text's precise descriptions of nature as representing the bond between the natives and nature.

Turi describes the everyday reality of Sami life in vivid detail, particularly their challenges in the face of ever-encroaching colonization by the Norwegian state. Turi stresses that the reindeer-herding Sami people were spread across large areas of Sweden and Norway before the expansion of settlements in the traditionally Sami regions began.[6] Commenting on the perplexing and frustrating process of colonization, Turi remarks: "Now the laws in Norway against the Lapps are like a veil through which the sharpest eye cannot see."[7] Later he writes: "Now it is no longer pleasant for a Lapp in Norway, now he is like a strange dog."[8] Under the heading, "Here I tell something more about Lapps, and this is almost the most important thing," Turi discusses the way in which the Crown has taken land from the Lapps and given it to colonizers. Cultivation resulted in reduced access to wild areas for the reindeer,[9] and access to pasture became the key issue in the Samis' daily struggle for survival.

Hamsun divides his review into three parts. The first deals with Turi's book as fiction, the second outlines the clash of values and political interests that Turi sees between the Sami and the Norwegian Crown, and the third is set up as a dialogue with Albert Engström, Hamsun's Swedish friend who sent him the book for review. When first giving his reasons for reviewing Turi's book, Hamsun writes:

But the book deserves it. It is definitely the most outstanding that has ever been created by a Lapp, about the Lapp life and environment. Here is good understanding of the Lapps and quiet mild sensibility. There is knowledge and superstition, moods, polemics, resignation; even the childish helplessness in the language is an additional charm.[10]

Hamsun continues by praising Demant's fine translation and gives her credit for collaborating on the book. Unaware of his patronizing attitude, he commends her skill in rendering into Danish Turi's grammatically incorrect sentences. He writes: "She has even imitated Turi's ungrammatical sentences so that I recognize them from Lapp speech in my childhood."[11] Hamsun points out that except for *Politiken*, newspapers and journals ignored Turi's book.

Hamsun gives examples of Turi's description of nature in the spring, of the creation of the *joik*,[12] and of the grounds on which the Sami set up their nomadic homes. Hamsun states that the text speaks with the compelling voice of nature and concludes that Johan Turi is an unaware artist.[13] Hamsun then quotes from a joik that expresses the Sami reverence for spring as the renewal of life. He rejoices in the Samis' appreciation of nature, love of life and sexuality, and gratitude to the earth that is going to be their temporary spring and summer home. It is tempting to conclude that he absorbed some of Turi's prose and some of the Sami reverence for nature while he reduced their complex worldview to an exotic background in his novels. Turi addresses some of the contemporary Sami stereotypes, describing a particular thief from his own district of Kautokeino, but he goes on to say, "And there have been many such Lapp thieves who were not Kautokeino folk . . . nor of that race. And he who will speak the truth must admit the truth of this that I write; and the above is proof that all thievery did not come with the Kautokeino folk."[14] Hamsun primarily represents the Sami in *Markens grøde* as thieves and beggars. Missing is a Sami protagonist of the caliber of the storyteller Turi.

In the second part of his review, Hamsun responds to what he views as Turi's underlying argument, which was that there was a gradual disappearance of good sustainable pasture for reindeer.[15] Hamsun frames the argument as a clash between Swedish nomadic Lapps and Norwegian settlers along the border. He imagines what Turi would say in this debate: that he, the Lapp, must be somewhere, preferably at his old grazing grounds which he had frequented from time immemorial. (Seasonal grazing rights were accepted as unwritten law.) Hamsun then rehearses the argument between the two parties, a reindeer herder and a settler, and concludes that since Sweden has colonized large tracts of land in Jämtland, thereby reducing the grazing areas for their Lapps, Norway cannot be responsible for the Swedish Lapps' welfare. Meanwhile, the Norwegian Lapps refrain from sending their reindeer over to Sweden.[16]

It is obvious that Hamsun frames his polemic within the discourse of national politics, the recent secession of Norway from Sweden in 1905, and the subsequent territorial division of the North. Marginalized in the debate among nation-states were the rights of the Sami, who regard themselves as one nation stretching from the Norwegian coast to the Siberian tundra. The Sami were squeezed between the strategic interests of individual states and the homesteaders who claimed increasingly more land as private property. Hamsun appreciates the Sami position yet continues the discussion of the topic as if it were an issue solely between Sweden and Norway. In the final analysis, he finds neither Norway nor the Norwegian settlers even partially responsible for the plight of the Sami.

In the third part of his review, in the imaginary conversation with Engström, Hamsun outlines his solution to the "Lapp Question."[17] He suggests "exchanging the Lapps" between the two countries, so that each country would be responsible for its "own." He would have Norway pay its obligations to Sweden and resolve the problem once and for all, overriding the spirit of the Karlstad Agreement between Sweden and Norway that established the grazing rights of the nomadic Sami.[18] Hamsun goes on to recommend Turi's "most outstanding" book as a document to be considered in the debate between Sweden and Norway. Thus he casts his focus on the Sami, yet he does not fundamentally think of them as partners in the debate, despite the fact that this was precisely the time when the Sami began to organize politically.

The review has all the characteristics of Hamsun's polemical style: his unrestrained praise for something he admires, in this case a text that he "enjoys blindly," coupled with provocative questions for the media and establishment. It testifies to Hamsun's tendency toward pragmatic and simplistic solutions; the formula for success is simply to resettle the Sami. In his 1926 article on the Jewish homeland, he suggests a similar solution: to resettle all of the European Jews to Palestine.[19] This approach illustrates Hamsun's inclination to support authoritarian solutions while ignoring some basic facts of human existence, and it shows his tendency to side with official authority to the detriment of its subjects, be they Jew or Sami. Still, it is commendable that Hamsun took Turi and his book seriously and did not reduce it to an ethnographic object. However, Hamsun supported the newly independent

Norwegian state and the politics of colonization. His reasoning was consistent with that of the majority of Scandinavians, including many progressive intellectuals and politicians. His conviction that Turi's writing embodied an admirable sensibility about nature was an outgrowth of the affinity he felt for the Sami life style, one which he tried to capture in his own writing. In this process, he gave full agency to Turi the writer and acknowledged the contribution of Emilie Demant Hatt.

It is interesting to observe how Demant Hatt describes Turi in the introduction to her translation of his book. While the general tenor of her text reveals her wish to portray herself as an enlightened European, she paints Turi as a secretive, animal-like person who disappears during hunting season. She writes: "Calmly does Turi lie down in the midst of mighty Nature, the terrors of the wild have no power over him; for all he is steeped in its mysticism. . . . Turi is naive and primitive in his manner of life and in his behavior toward Nature, as are most of his countrymen."[20] It is obvious from the introduction and notes that Demant Hatt, a gifted artist and translator, a capable ethnographer, and an astute business woman, harbored some mainstream patronizing feelings toward her collaborator. She was also catering to the expectations of the reading audience.

Most scholars agree that, historically, the Sami people's traditional way of life and nomadic movements were respected by their neighbors for many centuries, although corrupt traders, zealous missionaries, and relentless tax collectors did some serious damage. The general consensus is that prior to around 1800, the Sami retained both economic and cultural autonomy, although they were squeezed between Norwegian settlers coming in from the coastal regions and Kvens settling from Finland.[21] Many Sami along the coast settled permanently, supporting themselves by fishing and hunting and becoming somewhat integrated with other ethnic groups. The situation for the more nomadic Sami changed gradually during the first half of the nineteenth century, when the notion of distinct rights for the ethnically and racially different was replaced by equal rights for all. This paradigm shift was implemented with the strategic interests of the nation-states in mind.[22]

From the 1850s, Norwegian authorities aggressively pursued a new policy regarding the legal jurisdiction of unregistered land in Finnmark. It essentially declared all land not formally or legally claimed as private property to be the property of the state.[23] At that time, the Sami still represented approximately 50 percent of the population of Finnmark. They lived segregated lives, principally used the Sami language, and rarely made claims of land ownership.[24]

Norwegian was not widely spoken among the Sami. Culturally, they began to feel the pressure of the newly developed policy of Norwegianization (*fornorskningspolitikk*). The 1902 land-ownership law, for instance, stipulated that land could only be purchased by a person with a Norwegian name and Norwegian-language competency, thus excluding most Sami. The official and exclusive language in the schools became Norwegian. Such changes came in addition to more subtle cultural pressures that the majority population put on the minority. The State Lutheran Church considered Sami religious practices to be heathen. Strategic and security considerations, as well as the economic expansion of industrial enterprises, took a heavy toll on the traditional lifestyle of the Sami.

Moreover, publications like *Norsk folkepsykologi* (1899), by Andreas Martin Hansen, contributed noticeably to racist attitudes toward the Sami. Hansen divided and ranked Nordic inhabitants into progressive, smart "long-skulls" and underdeveloped "short-skulls," where most people would locate the Sami. Hansen also argued that the Sami were not the indigenous people of the North, providing more ammunition to the state in its expansionist project.[25] It has been claimed that the popular sentiments expressed in the media and among the general population toward the Sami, except in the North, were marked by benevolence. Advocates of this position cite as evidence the popularity of Matti Aikio's stories, Jens Andreas Friis' novel *Lajla* (1890) and its 1929 film adaptation, the availability of Sami national costumes in Oslo stores, and so forth.[26] But such benevolence was largely cosmetic, resembling the popular interest in Wild West Indian shows in the United States. The shows ignored the deplorable everyday reality of what settlement of the West was doing to Native Americans. It is true that during the thirties, the term "Sami" gradually replaced "Lapp." Furthermore, the influential Institutt for Sammenlignende Kulturforskning (Institute for Comparative Research of Cultures) published Konrad Nielsen's monumental *Lappisk ordbok* (Sami dictionary; 1932–38), among other academic publications on the Sami of high professional quality. But the Sami were losing their territories and way of life, with or without the dictionary. The clash between permanent settlers and nomadic reindeer herders, between ethnic Norwegians and the Sami, meant irreparable lifestyle changes for the indigenous Sami, even as the romanticized and exotic images of them flourished.[27]

In his 1937 book *The New Norway*, O. B. Grimley writes that "the grazing lands in the mountains are common lands (Almenning) with the property right vested in the state."[28] This book is typical of publications popularizing the

North during the interwar period. Grimley opens his section "Colonization of Home Soil" with the following sentences: "During the last generation, the Norwegians have become pioneers—homesteaders on their home soil. During this period they have cleared about 50,000 new homesteads, and this development is continuing with a scheme of about 20,000 new farms in the next ten years. . . . It is a realization in actual life of Knut Hamsun's book *The Growth of the Soil*—with its vision of the pioneer breaking virgin soil in his native land."[29]

Grimley explains that both private and public capital are used in this endeavor and that "the government aids colonization directly" by the parliament's diversion of liquor and lottery money to colonization funds. He further discusses the "state owned colonization bank" and "the colonist and his family."[30] While he warns the reader that this process is very difficult, he describes it in poetic terms, writing of those Norwegians who "set their shoulders to the wheel and their faces to the sun in a public-minded effort to develop the resources of their country."[31] The Sami are mentioned neither in this section nor in an earlier chapter on the people of Norway.[32] Grimley's book illustrates how Hamsun's contemporaries ignored the Sami and their aspirations. Hamsun, in spite of his knowledge of the Sami (as evidenced in his Turi book review), enthusiastically supported the colonization project in the North as a tool for stemming Norwegian emigration to the United States. In his letter, "Landets opdyrkning" (Cultivation of the country), he refers to "worthless high plateaus" (*verdiløse Vidder*) that need to be converted to useful areas, as if they had not sustained the Sami people for thousands of years. He does not mention the Sami.[33] In a related article, "Utvandrerne" (The emigrants), Hamsun laments the rootless emigrants who could have stayed at home and cultivated the soil.[34] The soil, again, is imagined as empty, and the Sami are not mentioned.

In popular conceptions and in fictional representations, the vast North has always been considered a borderland, a marginal space where dangerous, miraculous, and erotic things can happen. And so it is in several texts by Knut Hamsun, most notably *Pan*. However, Hamsun eventually punctures the myth in *Pan*, in *Friar Vendt*, and *Livets spil*, while he sustains it in *Markens grøde*. This mental distance is to a certain extent still in existence today. In one way this is not surprising; the driving distance between Oslo and Tromsø (1644 km) is roughly three-quarters of that between Oslo and Rome (2500 km). Nils Magne Knutsen has mapped the historical development of tensions between the North and the South, while Troy Storfjell has recently commented on the longevity of such tensions.[35]

In his œuvre, Hamsun depicts the Sami in contradictory terms. Magic-wielding shamans full of admirable wisdom, they are also irritating beggars, petty thieves, and evil gossipers who trespass onto private property and otherwise cause great distress. Hamsun's attitude toward the Sami echoes in general that of the majority of the population. Reimund Kvideland and Henning Sehmsdorf claim, for instance, that, "among the itinerant beggars were individuals who either could not or would not work, gypsies, Finns, and Lapps—all strangers in the eyes of the established community and therefore suspect."[36] More often than not, communities farther to the south viewed them with suspicion, accusing them of thievery, tricks, and deception. Hamsun then, in his depiction of the Sami, follows a well-established mainstream folk tradition wherein the Sami were considered outsiders, strangers, and petty criminals.

Kvideland and Sehmsdorf characterize Scandinavian societies as latecomers to the industrial revolution, in contrast to Great Britain or France. In spite of individual differences in the timing of industrial development among the Scandinavian countries, they collectively represented a less urban, less densely populated, and less developed area. Kvideland and Sehmsdorf illustrate that Scandinavia could still be considered a predominantly rural society with isolated pockets of industries in the late-nineteenth and early twentieth centuries. One of the consequences of such belated industrial development was that traditional folk beliefs remained a strong presence, and nature and its magic creatures remained part of Scandinavian everyday life; mythical and magical creatures co-existed with humans as benevolent helpers or malevolent adversaries. The mostly malevolent Sami were also part of this magical world.

John Lindow defines Scandinavia's perception of itself and of outside ethnic groups as relatively stable from Old Norse times to the beginning of the twentieth century, possibly even longer. This worldview was marked by "a breakdown of the distinction between ethnic and supernatural beings."[37] Mapping the relationship between the supernatural and the ethnic Other to show how "the supernatural is assigned to the ethnic others," Lindow suggests that even the earliest Scandinavians chose particular "emblems of contrast" to delineate between themselves and all others.[38] Some of these markers of otherness were shape-changing and magical powers, hyper sexuality, and/or non-Christian spiritual rituals. In this way, legends and folktales not only codified attitudes about ethnic minorities but also paved the way for later reincarnations of similar attitudes. As Lindow writes in his discussion of Old Norse–Icelandic literature, "'The Finns' are the outsiders and the dangerous ones. In fact, the 'Finns' imbued with magical powers are stock figures of Old Norse–Icelandic literature."[39] It needs to be clarified that in Norwegian, the word "Finn" is usually synonymous with "Lapp" or "Same," while the Finnish people are customarily referred to as "Kvens." In Knut Hamsun's worldview in *Markens grøde,* the ethnic Norwegians settled at the imaginary farm Sellanraa and the traveling Sami constitute two very different groups. The Sami, clearly outsiders, are described as sly and in possession of supernatural powers, as beggars and thieves, and as gossipers and messengers of the supernatural.

How the attitudes of ethnic Norwegians toward the Sami shifted over the years is well illustrated by the changing prominence of Sami collections in Oslo museums.[40] The original ethnographic collection from roughly the early nineteenth century at the University of Oslo, for instance, started out quite international, including both imported and domestic material. From the very beginning, the Sami material was treated as non-Norwegian and exotic.[41] When the University of Oslo Ethnographic Museum lost its preeminence to the newly established Folk Museum (opened in 1894), the university's Norwegian collection—excluding the Sami materials—was moved to the Folk Museum, while the Ethnographic Museum was essentially left to become the museum of foreign cultures.[42]

The Norwegian collection and the Folk Museum, especially its open-air architectural collection, were intended to contribute to Norway's sense of identity and, ultimately, to independence, by establishing and legitimizing traditional cultural roots. Within the context of the impending dissolution of the union between Norway and Sweden, it is not surprising that the fundamental thought behind this project was "we" against all the others. Some of the ideas of what constitutes Norwegianness at the beginning of the twenty-first century originated during the last decades of the nineteenth century and the first decades of the twentieth century.[43] Because the Sami material remained in the university collection, it was effectively excluded from the Norwegian materials until the 1950s, when it finally became part of the Folk Museum. It is fair to say that it was not really until the 1994 Olympic Games in Lillehammer, where joik was part of the opening ceremony, that Sami culture became an accepted and visible part of Norwegianness.

Displaying many similarities with the colonization of the North American continent, the process of Norwegian settlement of the North, as described in Turi's account, started with ethnic Norwegians claiming land for farms along the coast, thus driving the Sami inland. But later, as coastal land became scarce, the Norwegians intruded on the inland areas, squeezing the Sami out once again. In the end, the competition for land and resources between the Sami and the Norwegians became fierce, resulting in resentment, fights, even killings on both sides. The state subsequently intervened, and in many cases the Sami were made to pay large reparations.[44] It is difficult to understand how Hamsun and others could brush aside Sami complaints of the hardship created by the colonial settlement of the North. As acquainted as he was with the plight of the Sami, Hamsun nevertheless tends to present them as exotic. He rarely, if ever, depicts complex Sami protagonists. Instead, *Markens grøde* (1917) charts the development of the fictitious Northern colonial settlement of Sellanraa, painting an idyllic picture of the settlers' success, while demoting the indigenous inhabitants to stereotypical nomads. Amidst the mounting hardship of World War I and the disillusionment over progress and modernity, Hamsun describes a bucolic pioneer life in the unspoilt nature of Norway. It became a popular and critical success almost immediately and by 1920, when Hamsun was awarded the Nobel Prize for literature, it had undergone numerous printings in several European languages. Its success demonstrates that the attitudes it espoused found resonance among audiences throughout Europe. The Sami were the discounted victims of the colonists' success and the success of *Markens grøde*.

The novel's success can be explained by the attraction of the unpopulated wilderness and the process of its domestication. The opening passage of the book refers to a man and his endeavor to find a suitable homestead in northernmost Norway, to engage in the pioneering act of settling "a no-man's land." The oft-quoted opening of the book begins:

> The long, long path over the moors and up into the forests—who trod
> it into being? Man, a human being, the first who was here. There
> was no path before him. Afterward, some beast or other, following
> the faint tracks over marsh and moorland, wearing them deeper;
> after these again some Lapp gained scent of the path, and took that
> way from mountain to mountain, looking to his reindeer. Thus the
> path was created through the great Almenning—common land that
> nobody owned, no-man's land.[45]

In the words of Einar Niemi, these virgin lands described by Hamsun are rendered as if waiting for "the peasant's plough and scythe."[46] Indeed, value is placed on the cultivation of the wilderness by the main protagonist, the biblically named Isak, erasing ten thousand years of Sami habitation. The Sami way of life is illustrated with the image of a Sami as an animal, sniffing his way around the forest and following the man's tracks. The contrast between wild nature and cultivated farmland is the backbone of the novel's narrative; cultivation and growth of the settlement are praised as the countryside is tamed. Along with cultivation came the concept of private property, which greatly impacted the Sami's seasonal grazing patterns.

Although Hamsun knew of the practicalities of Sami life, as is evident from his Turi book review and his correspondence, ownership of land is simply not an issue in this novel. As Niemi points out, Hamsun's "great commons owned by nobody, the land without landlords . . . a no man's land" comes very close to the legal terms of *terra nullius* (the land of no one; territory not annexed to any nation) and *terra incognita* (an unknown land; an unexplored country).[47] The assumption that the land in question was empty made it easier for the state to annex it, and for the individual settlers to claim it. This legal stance, in addition to a host of regulations, taxation, and cultural prejudices, cemented the discriminatory policies of ethnic Norwegians toward the Sami. In fact, Roald Berg writes that elements of this pattern were repeated in other Scandinavian states during the period of the growth and consolidation of nation-states.[48] No longer a common property belonging to all, as its linguistic root implies, but clearly a property vested in the state, *Almenning* was suddenly off limits to the indigenous people who had been using the land for centuries. Hamsun, too, in *Markens grøde* touches on the role of the state. While at the beginning he refers to common lands, the description toward the end of the novel states specifically that the common lands are the property of the state. Hamsun does not problematize the state ownership.

It is quite possible that Hamsun conceptually conflated his own perception of homesteading with two vastly different areas: Norway's North that he knew from his childhood and the American prairies in the Midwest where he labored twice in the 1880s. In Norway, it was the social scientist Ottar Brox who applied the notion of the frontier when describing "the spatial and economic expansion in North Norway in the period 1800–1950."[49] In the United States, it was the historian Frederick Jackson Turner who articulated the idea of a *frontier* denoting a "moving, flexible border between the areas inhabited by the white settlers moving westward and the unconquered territories beyond."[50] Although Brox's theory has at times been contested, it is hard not to see parallels between the European colonial projects on other continents and the Scandinavian settlement in the North. The expansion northwards greatly accelerated during the last decades of the nineteenth century and first decades of the twentieth due to a combination of demographic pressures and improved technologies in the areas of mineral extraction and timber harvesting, both of which could now be carried out profitably in extremely cold conditions.

Most disputes, and wars, between new settlers or colonizers and indigenous peoples around the world have happened over issues of ownership of land and resources. The Sami, like most other indigenous peoples, perceived themselves as having the right to access and use land and resources, but they did not conceive of land as private property that was individually or collectively owned. It was precisely this attitude that was conveniently translated by Norwegian authorities into the notion that the land was empty, available, and ready to be taken and tilled. Once the colonizer established a certain area as his private property, he could also limit others' access to it. Note how Isak, once he has bought the land, can sell the mineral rights to corporations.

The first exchange between Isak and a nomadic Sami proceeds as follows: "You going to live here for good?" "Yap," said the man. "What's your name?" "Isak. You don't know of a woman who'd come and help?" "No. But I'll say a word of it to those I meet."[51] From this curt dialogue we learn a number of things about the settlers and how Hamsun imagined them: the settler's name, Isak; that he is looking for a woman, which indicates sexuality and family more than just domestic help; and that the Lapp who is helpful is not asked about his name, which signifies a hierarchy of positions.

After Isak has built himself a turf hut, just like the locals have, two more Sami come by one day. "Goddag," say the Lapps. "And here's fine folk come to live." "Lapps always talk that way, with flattering words," comments the narrator.[52] Yet they also accomplish that which Isak himself could not: find a woman! Inger simply shows up one day and stays, not merely as hired help but as Isak's intimate partner.

The most prominent and colorful Sami figure in *Markens grøde* is Os-Anders, the old Sami who schemes together with Oline, a temporary help, to cheat Isak out of his cheese. He begs, brings bad news to Isak's farm, is sneaky, and has shifty eyes. Os-Anders is initially a pleasant-spoken fellow, "like all the Lapps" as the text observes, suggesting obsequiousness rather than eloquence. In one particular exchange, his behavior makes Inger uncomfortable because he is *not* begging, inadvertently illustrating that the Sami can never do it right. Hamsun writes: "Inger wondered why he did not beg for anything; Os-Anders always begged, as do all Lapps. Os-Anders sits scraping at the bowl of his clay pipe, and lights up. What a pipe! He puffs and draws

at it till his wrinkled old face looks like a wizard's runes."[53] Os-Anders is
described as a wizard, and his face is compared to runes that in Scandinavia
have been connected with magic. The Sami are tied to black magic in the
novel with the recurring theme of a dead hare. When Inger, who has a cleft
palate, one day sees a dead hare in a Lapp's bag, she panics. Pregnant, she is
afraid that her child will also be marked with a cleft palate. This event develops into a local legend about spell-casting Lapps, although it is just as much
a comment on Ingrid's superstition.

Here, the older view of the Sami as mighty and often evil shamans became
conflated with late nineteenth-century impressions of the Sami as uncivilized
nomads who encroached upon homesteaders' farmland. The old and new
conceptions intertwined in Hamsun's text as they did in Norwegian mainstream culture. In the following excerpt, the Sami are described as invading
private property:

> Now a Lapp will beg as humbly as could be, but say no to him, and
> he turns vindictive, and threatens. A pair of Lapps with two children
> came past the place; the children were sent up to the house to beg,
> and came back and said there was nobody to be seen inside. The four
> of them stood there a while talking in their own tongue, then the
> man went up to see. He went inside and stayed. Then his wife fol-
> lowed, and the children after that; all of them stood inside the door-
> way, small-talking Lapp. The man sticks his head into the pantry;
> no one there either. The clock strikes the hour, and the whole family
> stand listening in wonder.[54]

Here, the Lapps act in accordance with the stereotypes of Lapp behavior.
They trespass into a private house, even if nobody is at home. They childishly
admire the clock, a symbol of Western technological development. And the
fact that they speak their own language is mentioned twice, as though they
should really be speaking another language when they are among each other.
Later they flatter and sweet-talk Inger, who comes running from a field; they
threaten and cajole food, wool, and shoes from her. When Inger is annoyed
at their continued begging and sends them out, they mention hares, which is
enough to intimidate her.

When the first part of *Markens grøde* ends, the taming of the wilderness
has been accomplished and modern progress firmly established, symbolized
by Isak's new mowing machine on which he sits like a majestic Margrave.

Part Two opens with: "Sellanraa is no longer a desolate spot; seven people live here, counting great and small."[55] The human beings consist of Isak and his family, who are populating the wild. The Sami have been erased. The Sami are, sadly and realistically, mentioned only once in Part Two, in a segment in which Sellanraa's size and growth is again admired. The quote underscores the fact that the Sami are not considered human beings:

The day is gone when wandering Lapps could come to the house
and get all they wanted for the asking; they come but rarely now,
seem rather to go a long way round and keep out of sight; none
are ever seen inside the house, but wait outside if they come at all.
Lapps always keep to the outlying spots, in dark spaces; light and
air distress them, they cannot thrive; 'tis with them as with maggots
and vermin. Now and again a calf or lamb disappears without a trace
from the outskirts of Sellanraa; from the farthest edge of the land—
there is no helping that.[56]

In this passage, by-gone days are portrayed as having been good for the nomadic Sami because they could get some handouts, but now they simply exist somewhere "out there." The centuries when the Sami were self-sufficient are not mentioned. There is no sympathy in the description of this development; on the contrary, they are described as resembling maggots or vermin. They could have been described as living in true communion with nature, or—arguably a stretch—as ecological guardians of nature, but instead the hard work of ethnic Norwegian settlers is praised.

Isak the Norwegian is the man who trod a new path into the wilderness on the first page of the novel, and he is the sower of the new harvest in its closing pages. He knows and respects the soil, with which he has an almost magical relationship, and he reveres nature. He is a strange sort of heroic character, however, an ugly giant, a simpleton who likes to be flattered, and he is easily fooled in quick conversations, especially with educated people. Full of traditional wisdom but lacking bookish knowledge, he is skeptical of village culture, let alone that of the city. He has only a rudimentary understanding of how a state works, an echo of Hamsun's conviction that legal and academic knowledge is dry and irrelevant. Isak childishly trusts the bailiff Geissler as his intermediary in matters of the state. Later, when he ages, his saving grace is the realization that he is the original pioneer, one of a chosen few who live in communion with nature: "And human beings are living there, moving and talking and thinking, being together with heaven and earth."[57] It is Hamsun's narrative mastery that leads us to believe that this mythical rural utopia is as close to paradise as possible. Perhaps, but what we witness is an early capitalist accumulation of wealth that soon enters its next phase, that of early industrial development, represented by the mining operation. Hamsun detested what we would call "progress" and in the novel lets the mine go bankrupt. At the end of *Markens grøde*, Isak is nine hundred years old and Inger is a Vestal in their home.

In spite of his portrayal as almost mythologically and mightily strong, Isak is both a man of modernity who uses contemporary technology and a man of tradition who remains superstitious. When he once meets the Evil One, he is frightened yet ultimately strengthened, a survivor who affirms his existence in a distinctly Scandinavian way, at the uneasy borderline of civilization. Lindow argues:

> By populating the mountains and forests, the rivers and streams, even the land under their farms and the days long ago with supernatural beings and by assigning to them the same emblems of contrast they assigned to the human groups and individual strangers they encountered, I submit that people *created* other social groups and categories and thought about them in the same terms they used to think about the other outside groups we would term ethnic groups. Let us make no mistake about this point: supernatural beings enjoyed an empirical existence and were probably—we can only guess about this—more real to many people than, say Hottentots or Bushmen or the King of England would have been.[58]

This would mean that the boundary between natural and supernatural, of human and supernatural, was at times permeable and flexible, and that the human and the supernatural were of equal importance. And so it is in Isak and Inger's world: their environment is a borderline area, where the family carves out its existence little by little, while the supernatural exists all around it. Lindow concludes that in traditional Scandinavian legend, "two of the major factors of intellectual discourse of the last century, class and gender, were apparently not much of an issue." He explains:

> I cannot see that the supernatural beings or ethnic others of Scandinavian rural legend tradition or folk belief highlighted their social

class or a class system or showed any particular interest in gender roles. This is not to say that these matters were not at issue. As Bangt Holbek verified (1987), they were probably central to fairy tales. How then could they be so absent from the emblems of identity? The reasoning followed here would suggest that crofters and peasants, day laborers and housewives, found in their situations more in common than in contrast. Only in the psychologically more expressive form of the fairy tale could they ventilate their differences.[59]

One can indeed argue that in the proximity of the overwhelming Norwegian natural world, perceived as being populated with supernatural beings, people of all classes united against the supernatural, willing to overlook their class and gender differences. Such a landscape must have had a soothing effect on Hamsun, who saw in contemporary class and gender struggles the source of personal and political tensions. On the other hand, much folkloric material depicts many sexual unions between humans and supernatural creatures. As Marte Hult writes in her examination of Norwegian legends:

> The boundary between the human and the Other is remarkably fluid in Norwegian legend tradition, due to the ability of the *underjordiske* (the sub-human) to shape-shift, even taking on the semblance of the human, and the corresponding ability of the human *trollkjerring* (troll witch) to change her shape as well. In addition, changelings and marriage with the *hulder* bring the Other into the inner realm, just as *bergtakning* (taking into the mountain) brings the human into the realm of the Other."[60]

In other words, national folk narratives underline the fact that "making the distinction between self and Other, the inner and outer realm, is fraught with complexity, and that things are never quite the way they may seem."[61] These commonly held beliefs created a paradox for the Norwegians, who wanted to believe that they were different from the Sami, while their folklore revealed shared supernatural ancestors and even relatives. So Isak might, in essence, be both similar to and different from Os-Anders. Still, Hamsun's "ranking" of the two groups in *Markens grøde* leaves no doubt that the ethnic Norwegian settlers have his blessing, while the Sami have been pushed back into the remaining wilderness and out of the novel.

Following Lindow's "advice" to examine more refined genres for significant gender markers as emblems of contrast, we can observe how Knut Hamsun, in his novels, uses sexuality to denote women as outsiders who have to be tamed. To practice sexuality in a restrained, "human" way was sanctioned behavior for those of the dominant group, Lindow writes. [62] Over and over, Hamsun regards women's sexuality as transgressing established norms and women as something to worry about. They easily fall prey to either their own excessive sexual desire or the temptations of the city in particular and modernity in general. So, while Inger's sexual abandonment with Isak is welcome because of the resulting offspring, Inger must be watched when in the company of other men. First brought to Isak by the Sami, she often dresses like them and flatters as they do, when, for instance, she clasps her hands and praises Isak. After the story of Sellanraa has been told, the steady tending of the land has been rewarded, industrial development has folded, the city has been relegated to the periphery, and those protagonists unwilling to be yoked by the land have been discarded. Inger has been yoked.

The book is situated within the long Scandinavian tradition of proximity to nature, where dependence on and reverence of nature intertwine, and where the natural and supernatural freely commingle. Because of this tradition, it is difficult to accept Leo Löwenthal's argument that Hamsun's depictions of bonding with nature signify Nazi tendencies.[63] If that were true, then a large portion of Scandinavian literature would repose in the same category. However, the message of the return to the idealized land, the return to traditional gender roles, the acceptance of one's social role, and ignorance of politics certainly overlap with those of the ideological propaganda of National Socialist parties.

Hamsun also includes stereotypical images of the Sami in his 1894 novel *Pan*. Here they constitute part of the background mystique of the far North.[64] He describes them as fatalistic and in possession of second sight, illustrated in a short tale, included in *Pan*, of an old blind Sami: "In the mountains I met an old blind Lapp. In fifty-eight years he had not seen anything, and he was over seventy. It seemed to him that he saw better and better as time went along, it got steadily better, he believed. If nothing got in the way, he would be able to get a glimpse of the sun in some years. . . . When we sat together in his hut and smoked, he told about everything he had seen before he became blind."[65] Given that Glahn's project is, at least on the surface, to live in harmony with nature and all beings, and temporarily forget his cultural side, the scarce presence of the self-sustaining Sami in the novel is remarkable. The absence of any complex Sami character emphasizes the fact that Hamsun only uses them as an exotic backdrop.

Hamsun has created some Sami protagonists who step beyond the stereo-typical portrayals and are fleshed out as individuals. The philosopher Ivar Kareno, the central protagonist of Hamsun's so-called Kareno trilogy, is one of them. Still, Kareno's stubbornness is rather simplistically attributable to his "Lapp" nature, and he is aware of his "Lapp" blood. He has lost the natural intuition with which the Sami would traditionally be equipped; instead, he is a bookish philosopher who has completely forgotten about the "blood instincts" and, as such, represents modern degeneration.[66] The trilogy traces Kareno's life aspirations and disillusionments over roughly two decades, and it is hard to avoid the conclusion that Hamsun uses him as a warning of what happens to "full-blooded" men when they leave their roots and get an education. Kareno loses his life's most important battle—for virility and authenticity—when he is discarded by his love interest, the exotic Teresita. In this struggle between two principles, the male and the female, he fails miserably and lives the remainder of his life as a contented yet essentially cuckolded husband.

The Omoinsa Lapp and his daughter Inger are two important protagonists in Hamsun's verse play in eight acts, *Munken Vendt* (Friar Vendt; 1902). *Munken Vendt* was to be part of a longer trilogy on faith, but Hamsun never returned to it. Considered too long to be performed, it has been staged or read in an abbreviated form only a few times. This verse drama, set in the far North in the eighteenth century, contrasts Vendt, an attractive yet calculating wanderer, with the traditional, yet settled Sami. Omoinsa Lapp and his daughter are both described as typical of their ethnicity. They live in a turf hut deep in a forest, eat reindeer meet, and dress in traditional clothes. Rounded characters and individuals, they are proud and wealthy, but still greedy and sly. They want to keep a treasure that they have found, but it really belongs to another man, Dyre Rein. Inger's infatuation with Vendt is greater proof of his animal attraction than of her sexual abandon. The Sami here are portrayed in a well-balanced way, with variety in their life styles and each having his own, distinctive personality.

Vendt is treated by the Sami families as an outsider, and is, in many ways, the Sami's Other. Hamsun started writing this play during his stay in Nordland, where he traveled to visit his parents whom he had not seen for twenty years. His Nordland trip occurred right after he had returned from the Caucasus, where he had realized the impossibility of melding with the locals. It is possible that this impossibility was reinforced during Hamsun's experience in Nordland, where he worked in a turf hut dug into a mountain. As Vendt rhymes after he had lived in a hut with the Sami: "Here I go, a fool, with a Lapp's attitude / and the whole day doing a Lapp's tasks / now I'm done with the poor performance / I played my role and did my time."[67] These lines articulate Hamsun's awareness of how difficult it is to cross cultural boundaries, change identity, and become the Other.

Gilbert the Lapp is Edvarda's irresistible and fearful lover in *Benoni og Rosa* (Benoni and Rosa; 1908). Gilbert prays to a powerful stone god in the wilderness and is widely feared in the village as a gossiper and a messenger of bad news. Rosa, at one point says: "The thing is: the Lapp was here today, Gilbert; he always makes me so afraid. He knows so much."[68] His erotic moments with Edvarda are described as ecstatic, and it is "unspeakable what they do" in the middle of the wild forest and in the presence of the pagan stone god.[69] With Gilbert, Hamsun has imagined a protagonist who is both an exotic outsider and an insider in the sense that he happens to be present at the most dramatic events in the text. Thus, his function is also that of a narrative tool. The 1912 novel *Den sidste glæde* (The last joy) also has Sami protagonists, described, for the most part, as uncivilized creatures. At the beginning of the novel, Hamsun sets its tenor, describing, not without humor, the events that are possible in a forest:

> One day I saw two Lapps meet. It was a boy and a girl. In the beginning they were behaving like humans. Boris! They said to each other and smiled. But right after that they fell in the snow and disappeared for quite a while. You should check on them, I thought after fifteen minutes were over; they could choke in the snow. Then they rose and went their separate ways. I've never in my down-and-out days seen such a greeting.[70]

Hamsun here follows popular perceptions about the Sami's unrestrained sexual behavior. The girl and boy are first referred to as humans, however, they soon turn into animals copulating in the snow and parting without words. More than a mere description of a passionate love affair, of which Hamsun created many, this is a comment on the uncivilized, animal-like behavior of Others. Later, we read a description of the narrator Pedersen spending time in a Sami hut, reminiscent of a passage in Hamsun's article "Fra en Indianerleir" of 1885. However, the most notable element of the passage is the way in which it undermines the reader's expectations about exotic locations. Pedersen's stay is simply boring, the Lapp himself a "boring nothing," for he cannot perform magic or cast spells.[71] His expectations of exoticism are not fulfilled. The Sami couple resemble idiots, and school has spoiled their daughter. To top this off, the entire family is characterized by "animalistic silence."[72] All they mumble is "mnei, mnja." When their daughter Olga arrives, she is just as silent; "mnja, mnei" is all the narrator can pull out of her.[73] They are rude, uncivilized, and standoffish. Since he can no longer bear to be with "these small creatures" and "these human grouts," he leaves, but not before he is supplied generously with food for the journey.[74] On the way, he is surprised by a storm, a reminder that he failed to pay heed to Olga's warning, and comments: "This could be the Lapp that does this magic! The Lapp? Oh, this human groat, the high mountain herring—and here I am! What do I have in common with this waste?"[75] Here Hamsun, through Pedersen, comments on how the shabbiness of the everyday makes it difficult to sustain any expectations of the magical, exotic Sami, much in the way that he dealt with perceptions of the Orient in "Under halvmånen." Instead, his racism emerges.

In *Men livet lever* (The road leads on; 1933), it is the proud Åse, allegedly part Sami and part gypsy/tinker, who has magical powers, or so the frightened villagers believe.[76] She is also a healer who is called upon when people or animals are hurt. No one knows where she sleeps at night and where she might show up during the day. It is bad luck if she spits when leaving someone's house. She can predict the future. She foretells that August's death will occur on a Friday. After August gives a horse to Cornelia, Åse casts an evil spell on the horse, which results in Cornelia's death. A woman with a strong erotic drive, Åse punishes those who reject her. Proud and independent, she does not flatter or ingratiate herself to anyone.

There is another drifter/tinker in *Men livet lever,* namely the handsome Otto-Alexander, who is the biological father of Gordon Tidemann, the powerful fish merchant at Segelfoss. Tall and skinny, always dirty, and with golden rings in his ears, Otto-Alexander is described as a small-time swindler but also as an outstandingly hard worker and skilled fisherman. Like Åse, he can heal animals and, like Åse, remains an outsider to the entire village. The widow Tidemann, called *gammelmoderen* (Grandmother), falls in love with him. Hamsun has given Otto-Alexander extraordinary erotic powers: "He was the devil, the Satan. The Oldie could not complain about him, he had his race's erotic greediness and held her in steady desire."[77] But Otto-Alexander is much more than a stereotype. Hamsun masterfully describes the complexity of a relationship that has a long time span, is passionate, full of love and gentleness, and results in a child.[78] When *gammelmoderen* finally wants to break off the relationship, he attacks and wounds her with a knife, leaving her wondering whether he is a human or an animal.[79]

In light of these characters, it is hard to accuse Hamsun of reducing the human dimension to ethnic formula. Yet there is no doubt that outsiders in Hamsun's novels, like Otto-Alexander, are endowed with special magical and erotic powers that partially stem from their primitiveness and race. Eventually Otto-Alexander simply disappears from the narrative. Hamsun searches for the moments when his characters can surrender to their passions, transgressing norms and rules. In his correspondence, he seems to wish the same for himself. His letter to Marie, in which he nostalgically wishes that they had been children of farmers so that they could have "gotten each other as often as we wanted," acknowledges and endorses a strong sexual bond between himself and Marie, a bond that he grants many of his protagonists. Still, in his life and in his literature, unbridled sexuality in women must ultimately be tamed, and when it is not, a price must be paid. No matter Hamsun's appreciation of such ecstatic moments personally and vicariously, "normative" behavior must eventually tame those who are unable to control themselves.

7

IMAGING DEGENERATION
AND REVOLUTION
The Interwar Period and the Occupation

> Why is it nothing less than a natural inevitability that Germany wins over
> England? The Germans have, as the healthy and budding nation they are, a
> huge demographic surplus. Germany needs colonial land, England and France
> have more colonial land than they need. . . . But regardless of how much he or
> I "know" about this issue, in the final analysis it is a question of intuition, and
> understanding. And even though Mr. Collin has read half a million more books
> than I, in a matter like this my understanding has a greater value for me than his.
> —Hamsun's letter to Professor Collin in *Tidens Tegn,* 1914

HAMSUN WROTE THIS STATEMENT IN 1914, IN A STRIDENT ARTICLE ADDRESSED
to Christen Collin, a professor of comparative literature at the University of
Kristiania. It was part of a rather lengthy exchange of opinions in a series of
newspaper polemics. At the beginning of World War I, Hamsun was firmly
on Germany's side. He framed this particular article, as well as the other
articles in the debate, in terms of a simplistic dichotomy between Germany
and England. In fact, he based many of his political opinions on the same
dichotomy and never wavered from that view. Moreover, he expressed his

conviction that inevitably Germany would win. Hamsun reasoned that, since the German population had increased by thirty million in forty short years Germany was justified in demanding more territory. This particular article is Hamsun at his most typical. It includes many references to historic events— such as the destruction of Louvain, the English colonization of the Transvaal, the alliance between the English and the Russians—all of which Hamsun interpreted, as he would have put it, intuitively. Such articles demonstrate that Hamsun read widely, but in his own selective way. The English and French colonial expansions were wrong, in Hamsun's opinion, but Germany's was justified.[1]

In 1914 Hamsun was in his mid-fifties, beginning seriously to fret over his own vitality as a man and as a writer. In 1926 he would undergo psychoanalysis with a medical doctor, Johannes Irgens Strømme, in order to revitalize his creativity. And in 1921, as Kolloen writes, Hamsun would visit a Copenhagen clinic for treatment to re-channel his sexual energy. In Hamsun's universe, health, sexuality, and creativity were connected. Similarly, in his universe, Germany was a vibrant young country.

Regardless of whether one sides with the critics who deem Hamsun's interwar poetics modernist (Kittang, Næss, Ferguson) or with those who define it as essentially realist (Dingstad), one can agree that, like Hamsun himself, his texts are considerably more pessimistic and resigned in their tenor during this period than his earlier works. One of the manifestations of Hamsun's pessimism is the intense exploration in his sizable novels of protagonists who are castrated (Oliver in *Konerne ved vandposten* [Women at the pump]; 1920), sterile (August in *Landstrykere* [Wayfarers trilogy]), virile but exploited as human drones (Abel in *Ringen sluttet*), or cuckolded (many). The crisis of patriarchal masculinity, as Hamsun saw and described it, demonstrates his deep disappointment with the modern world. His age, partial deafness, and several other health issues compounded his pessimistic outlook. *Konerne ved vandposten* and *Ringen sluttet* are perhaps the most relevant in this regard, because Oliver, for all his compensatory life-skills, is no more than a Darwinist survivalist, while Abel, decent yet uprooted, is representative of a life in modernity that is unappreciated and wasted.

By the time that Hamsun, at the age of seventy-seven, published *Ringen sluttet*, a novel he thought would be his last, he was a much-celebrated writer at home and abroad. He and his family, disillusioned over parliamentarism and fearful of organized labor and international Bolshevism, began supporting Vidkun Quisling and his Nasjonal Samling (National Union) party. NS, founded in 1933, was a party without much clout in the thirties. It is widely believed that if it were not for its later collaboration with the Germans, it would have remained rather insignificant.[2] The party, which was still split between various factions in 1933, had, by the end of 1934, developed a clear profile with race as one of its main ideological axes. Jon Alfred Mjøen was considered one of the spiritual fathers of the party.[3] Mjøen was the internationally acclaimed eugenicist and acquaintance of Hamsun who frequently lectured under the auspices of the Nordische Gesellschaft (Nordic Society) in Germany in the thirties. He lobbied for a "biological approach" to life in which decisions would be made based on considerations of parental hereditary makeup and racial hierarchy. While all political groups and parties at the time favored certain eugenics measures, they endorsed them for different reasons. Mjøen, in his numerous publications, ridiculed the liberals for promoting eugenics policies because they would bring about greater rationalization and efficiency, while his own motives were generated by concerns for the Norwegian (or sometimes Scandinavian) folk and its soul. Mjøen and Hamsun both agreed that modernity's rapid changes were the main cause of the decline of the healthy and authentic way of life, manifested most dramatically in the dissolution of the traditional family and in emigration. While the majority of Norwegian academic scientists who studied issues of heredity and race shunned Mjøen, he retained much of his international reputation and his connections, many of them with German scientists.

In Germany, anthropological/racial research became increasingly polarized toward the end of the twenties, partially due to the growing influence of National Socialism and its race-oriented program, and partially due to a generational change. As a sign of the times, Hans F. K. Günther, who was not an academic, was appointed professor of "racial science" at the University of Jena in 1930, an appointment that was deemed political by his professional opponents. Günther's 1929 book *Kleine Rassenkunde des deutschen Volkes* (Short ethnology of the German people) went through several editions between 1929 and 1943 and reinforced the concept of the Aryan with pure Nordic characteristics as the racial ideal. Ludwig Ferdinand Clauss's *Die nordische Seele* (The Nordic soul; 1932) focused on the connections linking environment, race, and mind. According to Clauss, the ideal Nordic man evolved and hardened within the natural geography of the North, resulting in harmony between his body and soul. Eugen Fischer, director of the Kaiser Wilhelm Institute for Anthropology, Human Heredity, and Eugenics, founded in 1927, did not join the Nazi Party, yet his ideas on eugenics, specifically those

on sterilization of the mentally, physically, or genetically unfit, were incorporated into Nazi Party policies. While it is correct to point out that many other
countries at the time had eugenics policies in place, and thus the early measures taken in Germany were not exceptional, this changed soon after 1933,
and certainly after the anti-Semitic Nürnberg laws were ratified in 1935.

During the twenties, there was frequent and sustained collaboration
among various Norwegian and German scientists: Mjøen and Halfdan Bryn,
and to a certain extent also the Schreiners, on the one hand, and Günther,
Fischer, and Rudolf Martin, on the other. They corresponded, attended the
same conferences, translated each other's articles, and extended invitations
to each other to lecture. Günther, whose wife was Norwegian, had professional and personal ties to Norway and some of its institutes and also lectured briefly at the race biology institute in Uppsala, Sweden. It is evident
from the correspondence between Günther and Bryn that the former was
well informed about those individuals in Norway sympathetic to the German
National Socialist cause and that he, especially after becoming a member of
the NSDAP (Nationalsozialistische Deutsche Arbeiterpartei) in 1932, urged
Bryn to join corresponding political organizations in Norway. It is also clear
that, while the two friends shared a belief in the Nordic ideal and Bryn never
challenged Günther's National Socialist allegiance, Bryn did not actively support the political developments in Germany.

Halfdan Bryn, perhaps the most internationally renowned Norwegian
anthropologist of the time, continued in important ways to promote and support the ideas of Andreas M. Hansen.[4] While mapping diseases in Norway
(he traced rickets and tuberculosis) and transposing his disease maps onto
the racial map of Norway, Bryn stressed the importance of both the environment and genetic heritage on health. Bryn considered urban areas breeding grounds for various diseases. However, during the twenties, his views
changed to embrace race- and culture-based explanations of health deficiencies (for instance, among the ethnic Norwegians and the Sami).[5] According
to Bryn, the individual races historically developed to their optimal potential
when there was no external interference from other races. Consequently, he
views race mixing as detrimental to the health and culture of all races, and
for individuals and society alike. He draws a parallel between a pure race and
a positive character, and a pure race and optimal cultural production. His
goal is the reestablishment of a state of harmony that supposedly once characterized races and their original environment and cultures, and which, once
reestablished, would be conducive to individual happiness and the survival

of society. Paradoxically, he also believed that it was the same harmonious state that resulted in cultural stagnation and eventual extinction, and that competition sharpened survival skills.[6] The Nordic race emerged as superior through social selection and the process of survival of the fittest.[7] Bryn's book *Der nordische Mensch* (The Nordic man) published in 1929 in Munich, cemented his reputation in certain professional circles in Germany.[8]

Bryn collaborated with many of the Danish and Swedish race researchers (for example, Hermann Lundborg, a Swede) and with the race biology institute in Uppsala. He became a member of Die deutsche Gesellschaft für physische Anthropologie in 1925, Die anthropologische Gesellschaft in Vienna in 1929, and Die deutsche Gesellschaft für Blutgruppenforschung, also in 1929.[9] His professional contacts demonstrate that eugenics and questions of race were widely researched in Europe, and that the relationships between Norwegian and German eugenicists had been established before 1933, the year that began the march toward the Holocaust. After Bryn's death in 1933, the Schreiners, a pair of Norwegian researchers, problematized his legacy. They criticized both his sloppy research methods and his belief in the superiority of the Nordic race. Kristian Emil Schreiner, in his *Zur Osteologie der Lappen* (The osteology of the Lapps),[10] and Alette Schreiner, in her numerous articles on the topic of eugenics, in no way refuted the notion of a fundamental racial hierarchy, nor did they dispute the racial superiority of ethnic Scandinavians over the Sami. However, they were convinced that there existed several equally superior races, and perhaps most importantly, that racial views ought not to be tied to ideological and political policies. Bryn's views were thus scrutinized in Norway, but his status was on the rise in Germany due to the increasing importance of the imaginary construct of the Nordic race, which some leading scientists there avidly advocated.

Ultimately, the fact that Norwegian racial research spread beyond strictly academic circles to broader audiences has to be viewed against an often ambiguous background of personal conviction, class status, and the growing tension between the established, both liberal and conservative, middle-class and the radical new working class. The situation must further be understood within the context of economic depression and the changing political situation in Europe and the Soviet Union. This complex background must be considered when we examine the case of the Hamsun family. The NS party evidently addressed some of the family's fears, clearly promising to rectify the worst of modernity's symptoms—symptoms that appeared to the Hamsuns to result in moral and cultural anarchy. Tore Hamsun became an NS party member in 1934, and Marie and Arild followed suit in the fall of 1940. Knut's membership has not been unequivocally established, though Marie paid the fee for both of them. In response to a questionnaire from *Fritt Folk* (Free folk), the NS party's main publication, Marie explained on November 27, 1940, why she was a member: "NS program's high idealism, during a time of materialism, slackness, and decadence, caused me to join, with my entire soul."[11] There is no reason why we should doubt her words; indeed, they in all probability express Knut Hamsun's position as well. It is reasonable to believe that Hamsun, disillusioned and resigned, turned to Quisling's party for its optimistic message promising a return to traditional roots and cultural renewal that would result in spiritual, gender, and ethnic purity.[12] NS was fundamentally concerned with overturning the principles and achievements of the Enlightenment and the French Revolution. As Quisling expressed in several of his speeches, the ideas of freedom, equality, and brotherhood have long been transformed into destructive principles, and it was the role of the NS to prevent further destruction. This would certainly have appealed to Hamsun, who, even during his visit to the United States, saw participatory democracy as granting too much power to marginal and undeserving groups.

Vidkun Quisling did not start his political career as a rabid anti-Semite, but rather adopted anti-Semitism into his program after the watershed year of 1933. The Norwegian NS party failed to attract votes in the national election of 1933, while the German National Socialist party was victorious. As Oddvar Høidal, the author of the highly respected *Quisling: A Study in Treason*, comments:

> For Quisling, the adoption of anti-Semitism, although originally
> motivated by opportunism, was not a radical departure. It served as
> an extension of his racial world view, already enunciated, in which
> he stressed Norwegian racial superiority: Norwegians during the
> Viking period, he maintained, had been part of the dominant Nordic
> race, which now was in the process of reasserting itself, with Norway
> destined to play a leading role in world affairs. Once anti-Semitism
> became part of his racial perspective, Quisling added the corollary
> that there were inferior races, first and foremost the Jews, who (in
> accord with Nazi belief), threatened the purity of the Nordic race
> through sexual defilement.[13]

In 1938 and 1939, Quisling gave a number of anti-Semitic lectures that tried to add fuel to the ongoing public debate about visas issued to Jewish refugees from Germany. Hamsun admired Quisling, followed his career closely, and considered himself a Quisling man. Hamsun announced in 1936 in *Fritt Folk* that if he had ten votes, Quisling would get all of them.

In the thirties, Hamsun considered Norwegian parliamentary politics void and corrupt. This is perhaps most obvious in his "Forord til 'Revolusjonspolitikk og Norsk lov'" (Preface to *Revolutionary Politics and Norwegian Law*; 1932), an introduction to Herman Harris Aall's book about the left in Norway. Aall, a lawyer and author of many legal treatises, branded leftist parties as revolutionary and thus in clear breach of the Norwegian constitution. In this preface, Hamsun considers the government and the parliament, the press and the courts, to be corrupt, and accuses them of falsifying facts, of enabling the importation of (the Russian) revolution, of not doing enough to curb labor strikes and general lawlessness, and of collectively opposing Quisling.[14]

Hitler appointed Josef Terboven as Reichskomissar of Norway on April 24, 1940, thus placing Norway directly under German authority. On September 25, all political parties except for the NS were dissolved. Subsequently, membership in the NS increased dramatically and peaked in late 1943, indicating, among other things, that it was affected by the victories and defeats on the war fronts. Still, after September 1940, NS, now the only legal political party, fed on dismissive attitudes toward representative democracy, such as those articulated by Hamsun, and translated them into political action. Its aim was to establish a model of the corporate state, as had been done in Germany. NS disbanded all popularly elected or appointed bodies, from parliamentary commissions to local community boards.[15] Socio-political organizations were to be replaced with older forms of leadership, organized through professional guilds (occupationally based "national councils").[16] Soon after the Germans assumed control of Norway, every aspect of Norwegian life was affected by the occupation. Mobility was restricted, jobs were supervised, selected books—especially by Jewish writers like Marx and Freud—were banned, newspapers and radio were heavily censored, in terms of both content and form, and the visual arts, as in Germany, were cleansed of abstract and modern style. NS-approved directors were appointed to head publishing houses; Gyldendal, for instance, was placed under the leadership of Tore Hamsun, Knut's oldest son.[17] Knut Hamsun, quick to comment on contemporary events, remained silent as these significant, indeed revolutionary, measures were incrementally introduced.

On April 14, 1940, only a few days after the April 9 German invasion of Norway, Hamsun wrote an article entitled "Et ord til os ved krigsutbruddet" (A word to us as war breaks out). He addresses his fellow Norwegians in order to convince them that Norway is neutral and not at war with Germany, and that Germany is, in actuality, Norway's protector. It is western European nations like England, Hamsun writes, who are at war with Germany and who now want to export war into others' territory. He accuses King Haakon VII and the Nygaardsvold government of being unpatriotic by leaving the country as the Germans entered and advanced. Hamsun, in his 1946 defense speech, repeats this accusation and claims that those who stayed in occupied Norway were the real patriots. In "Et ord til os ved krigsutbruddet," he also comments dismissively on Carl Joachim Hambro (1885–1964), the chairman of the Norwegian Parliament who fled to Stockholm immediately after the German invasion and was later in charge of the Norwegian branch of the BBC. Hambro was from an old Jewish family, well integrated into Norway's economic and cultural life, and belonged to the Høyre (Right) party. Hamsun writes:

> It was announced from Sweden that Carl Joachim Hambro would like to speak to the Norwegian people. Well, he is the right one! He is a son of a family that immigrated in its time and got to stay here in the country. A talker, a speaking machine. He, as others, surely has his merits, but to guide the Norwegian people right now; he is not the man for that. He lacks the basics: to be Norwegian in his soul. He has shown his lack of a Norwegian soul many times.
>
> Now he is proclaiming that Norway is at war with Germany. No, the speaking machine is wrong, but he cannot neglect spreading the blessed propaganda even after he has fled to a foreign country.[18]

Hamsun denies Hambro, a respected conservative politician, the right to speak because he belongs to a Jewish family that was merely allowed to stay in Norway, or so argues Hamsun. The first Hambro immigrated in 1810, that is, 130 years prior to Hamsun's statement. In Hamsun's eyes Carl Joachim (Hambro) is still a foreigner. Using vocabulary from Konrad Simonsen's description of mechanized modernity—a speaking machine—Hamsun criticizes Hambro for lacking the imaginary Norwegian soul. This soul is presumably found in ethnic Norwegians only.

After 1933, Hamsun must have learned of the German persecution of

Jews, if only from the many letters he had received from people fearing for their lives. He helped, for instance, his Jewish acquaintance Max Tau from Berlin and surely saved his life. It is in his correspondence with Artur Meyerfeld, however, that Hamsun reveals his fundamental attitude about Jews most clearly. In August of 1933 he writes to Meyerfeld:

> Your letter has touched me deeply, however, I cannot answer but what you already know from before. You, as a Jew, belong to a race that—of course because of your special attitude—dominates all cultural fields in all countries. In science, art, writing, industry—in everything the Jews reach the top. As far as I know this is disputed by nobody. That it is also Jews, who control the monetary arena, makes them a power in international politics and in world trade. You overpower the native population of the countries.[19]

This letter is but one example of several in which Hamsun refers to Jews as a separate race at odds with the "native" peoples, implying that the civilized Europeans must battle "intruders" who are so special. Artur Meyerfeld was a highly educated German Jew who managed a book store in Berlin until 1935, but Hamsun still views him primarily as a representative of his race.[20]

Meyerfeld lost his job following the passing of the Enabling Bill in the Reichstag on March 23, 1933, which conferred full power on Hitler. The Nazis' systematic assault on the Jews began just days later, on April 1, with a boycott of Jewish businesses. Soon afterward, Nazi authorities dismissed Jews from public service, limited their access to education, and excluded them from certain professions. May 10 was the day of the notorious burning of German books written by non-Aryans. As the assault escalated, Jews were dispossessed of their property, psychologically terrorized, and physically abused.[21] The initial policy of forcing the Jews to emigrate gradually became a policy of internment and extermination. Crucial to the legal legitimization of these abuses were the Nürnberg Laws of September 15, 1935, which stipulated the rights of "racial" Germans and established statutory discrimination against "racial" Jews. How Hamsun interpreted events in Germany in 1933 can be deduced from the second paragraph of his letter to Meyerfeld:

> I have not understood it as if Germany wants to eradicate the Jews from the country, but it is presented so by the Jewish politicians in England and France and by the Jewish press everywhere. I have

understood it that Germany only wants to curb the Jewish power inside the country so that it won't be the Jews but rather the Germans who would *rule* in Germany.[22]

This passage demonstrates that Hamsun refused to consider the reported consequences of the now-dominant racial ideology of the new Germany, but rather dismissed them as global political propaganda. Furthermore, Hamsun accepted the fundamentally anti-Semitic premise that Jews had extraordinary power in Germany—power which had to be curbed—and that Jews controlled the press in France and England. Finally, he gives the Germans the green light to rule as they see fit, as emphasized by his italicized verb "rule." As we know, Hamsun had access to Norwegian newspapers, such as *Dagbladet* and *Arbeiderbladet*, that accurately reported on the harassment of Jews in Germany, but he chose to ignore them. There were some general misgivings in Norway about the alleged Marxist leanings of the press (*Dagbladet* and *Arbeiderbladet* included) because, as the argument went, it had condoned violence in the Bolshevik Soviet Union and exaggerated events in Germany. The more conservative *Aftenposten* reported on the persecution of Jews with some doubt, sharing Hamsun's skepticism about the events in Germany. However, Hamsun was an avid reader of a number of Scandinavian newspapers and the post-1945 claim made by his apologists that he lived in "splendid isolation" does not hold up to critical scrutiny. Hamsun concludes his letter in the following manner:

> The misfortune is, that the Jews don't have a large enough country for themselves. Palestine cannot accept them, and in all five parts of the world it seems to be impossible to find their own land area large enough. It is dissatisfying for both parties, that the Jews are forced to be at home among foreign races. The Jews powerful in politics and money should not rest until a large new Jewish country will have been found.[23]

Hamsun's expression of sympathy with Mr. Meyerfeld's situation at the beginning of this letter ultimately becomes a statement of practical advice for establishing an independent Jewish state. While advocating an exclusive territory for the Jews, he is in actuality lobbying against the mixing of blood and culture. Many European Jews felt they were well integrated into their respective countries. There was a flourishing debate in Norway on biology and race at the time, which encompassed a range of opinions, including the view that racial divisions were insignificant in comparison to the commonalities among humans. If Hamsun was not ready to think through the "usual" contradiction between cherished and respected Jewish friends on the one hand and, on the other, their "unfortunate" inclusion in a dangerous and aggressive race, our conclusion must be that his racism was stronger than his empathy.

In sum, Hamsun sent three letters to Meyerfeld. The last one, dated November 24, 1935, in which he reiterates that the original tragedy lies in the fact that the Jews do not have their own state, concludes with the widespread German propaganda claim that the foreign "Jewish mass" is taking over. Hamsun writes: "But Germany has to be able to defend itself, when it is overwhelmed by the significant mass of this foreign race. The politicians and financiers should be able to *clear* space for the Jews in their own country, they have an older right to Palestine than the Arabs, they have *all* rights."[24]

Hamsun was, as his vast opus has demonstrated, capable of complex and nuanced thinking. That Norwegian scholars, some sixty years later, still whitewash his support for the Third Reich or tiptoe around uncomfortable conclusions is unscholarly, to say the least. Recent examples of such tiptoeing are works by Ingar Sletten Kolloen (2004) and Gunvald Hermundstad (1998).

Why Hermundstad added the content-accurate yet unfortunate title, *Om jødespørsmålet* (About the Jewish question), to Hamsun's letter published in *Nationalt Tidsskrift* (National journal), no. 11, in 1926, we can only speculate. The letter is dated December 1, 1925, and addressed to *Nationalt Tidsskrift* editor Mikael Sylten.[25] Sylten's publication, though its circulation was low, had been spreading a consistently anti-Semitic message since 1916, based on predominantly German sources.[26] Sylten was also the author of *Hvem er hvem i jødeverdenen* (Who is who in the Jewish world)—an anti-Semitic book about, in essence, whom to avoid and boycott in Norway. While Hans Fredrik Dahl doubts that Sylten's publications had any impact at all because they were "so far from acceptable,"[27] they obviously moved Hamsun to sit down and write this letter. The letter again endorses a long-term solution in the form of an independent Jewish state to resolve the alleged tensions between Jews and non-Jews. The problem was merely technical in Hamsun's opinion, namely, where and how to find the territory suitable for roughly twelve million people. Hamsun again explains how he likes his Jewish friends, adds how he dislikes the pushy and ambitious Jews, and closes by praising the Jews for their talents and skills in politics, literature, and art. Still, he concludes that they would best enrich the entire world by being brought together in one state. He writes:

> It would of course be desirable that the Jews be gathered in one country that they could call their own, so that the exclusively white race could avoid further blood mixing, and from where the Jews could still be productive with their best talents to the benefit of the entire world. But where is the country? . . . But as long as that does not happen the Jews have no home except others' homes. They have to continue to live and act in foreign societies, to the detriment of both parties.[28]

Hamsun's solution to this "problem" is essentially to resettle the Jews in a country where they could be safely contained. Projecting his own prejudices, he ignores the fact that the Jews did not necessarily feel the "detriment" of having to live in "foreign" societies. Whites—the unstated claim being that Jews are non-white—would be able to retain the purity of their own race. Hamsun's solution is congruent with his general racism.

From Hamsun's letter, and from Sylten's publications, it would seem that Norway was being overrun by a large numbers of Jews. Yet in actuality, the Jewish population was small. Oskar Mendelsohn writes that in 1866 there were 25 adherents of Judaism in Norway, which means that in the fifteen years since the constitutional prohibition against Jews settling in Norway was lifted in 1851, the Jewish population had grown by less than two people each year. There were 642 at the turn of the century, and in 1940 just over 1,800, many of whom were refugees.[29] Part of the explanation for the small size of the Jewish population lies in the Norwegian constitution of 1814. The original Article 2 specified the official religion of Norway, proclaimed certain religious groups unwelcome, and forbade Jews from entering the country:

> The Evangelical-Lutheran Religion shall be maintained and constitutes the established Church of the Kingdom. The inhabitants who profess the same religion are bound to educate their children in the same. Jesuits and Monastic orders shall not be tolerated. Jews are furthermore excluded from entering the Kingdom.[30]

It was the poet Henrik Wergeland (1808–1845) who fought tirelessly, primarily on moral Christian grounds, for an amendment to the constitution that would lift the restriction and allow Jews to settle in Norway. In 1851, the parliament finally passed the bill that opened the doors of Norway to Jews. In general, the Jews who came to Norway after being permitted to do so by the 1851 amendment, were left in peace. However, it is clear that they were not integrated. During the thirties, anti-Semitism would occasionally erupt, such as in discussions over kosher food and residence permits for refugees Wilhelm Reich and Leon Trotsky. In 1942, under Quisling's government, the constitution was re-amended with almost identical wording to that of the original Article 2, prohibiting once again the settlement of Jews in Norway.

During 1941–42, the Quisling government and its various departments prepared regulations to define the concept of "who is a Jew." The final determination was published in *Aftenposten* on January 22, 1942, its formulation quite similar to that of the Nuremberg Laws of 1935. Even before that, on January 10, an order was issued mandating that the identification cards of all Jews in Norway be stamped with a large "J." In February, "Questionnaires for the Jews of Norway" were sent out, which were later, in October, used as lists for rounding up, arresting, and eventually deporting many Jews to Auschwitz. Samuel Abrahamsen comments on the rounding up of the Jews and their deportation: "The arrests of Norwegian Jews reportedly came as a surprise to Berlin. The Quisling authorities had great difficulty in obtaining the ships necessary for deportation."[31] The Quisling government was apparently even more eager than that of Germany to go ahead with deportations. There was indeed close cooperation among the NS Hirden,[32] the police (which had an exceptionally high percentage of NS members), and the German authorities in Norway. The eagerness of the Norwegians—police, hirdsmen, and local collaborators—contributed significantly to the efficient roundup and deportation of the Jews. The well-planned arrests were swift, surprised large portions of the Jewish community, and did not trigger much protest from the general population.[33] Many church officials, however, protested loudly and read an open letter to Quisling protesting this treatment of the Jews from pulpits all over Norway. The divergent responses reveal both the courage of the churches and the intimidation of Norwegians facing the German authorities' escalating policies of repression during 1942.

After the arrests, Jewish property was first confiscated, and then was either auctioned off, kept in a special NS fund, or put at the disposal of individual NS members. It would have been encouraging to see more signs of civil disobedience, for instance, the police stalling the entire process, deceiving the German authorities by misplacing the lists. Boycotts of the auctions of

Jewish property and businesses never happened. As a result, and in contrast to Denmark, Norway lost more than half of its Jewish population. The first post-war census in November 1946 counted 559 Jews.[34] After the war, the government formally guaranteed the return of confiscated real estate, but few properties changed hands and many claims were not settled until the late 1990s.[35]

It has not been documented as to whether Hamsun read any of the announcements about the "Norwegian Jewish problem" or the "Norwegian Jewish solution" in the press (*Aftenposten, Fritt Folk, Hirdspeilet*). He does not seem to have commented in the media, favorably or otherwise, on the J-cards, arrests, property confiscations, or deportations. However, Hamsun knew of this widely publicized program of the government, as shown in a 1942 letter to his son, Tore, in which he comments on the questionnaires: "By the way, I don't think it is wrong that the Jews in Norway get the questionnaire. They won't get out of the country because of that, under no circumstances, at least not until after the war—and the war can drag on."[36] In another letter to Tore roughly a year later, Hamsun comments on literary critic Harald Beyer: "And the Jew Harald Beyer (the one with some sort of book about Kierkegaard), hasn't he been shot? He should have been."[37] Hamsun held a grudge against Beyer, who wrote a negative review of *Ringen sluttet*, yet his remarks express his anti-Semitism more than his hurt literary pride. In the 1942 article "Virkeliggjort kameratskap" (Realized camaraderie), published in German in the influential Berlin monthly *Berlin-Rom-Tokio*, Hamsun lashes out against Bolshevism and the American president Franklin Delano Roosevelt, expressing what Ferguson calls "the most explicit and sinister statements of Hamsun's anti-Semitism."[38] Roosevelt is branded as "a Jew in the pay of Jews, the leading figure in America's war for gold and for Jewish power."[39] The article wraps up with the statement that "Europe does not want either the Jews or their gold, neither the Americans nor their country."[40]

Hamsun regularly read *Fritt folk* and knew very well what Quisling's party stood for. If nothing else, in the questionnaire that Hamsun filled out on January 15, 1941, as part of the NS membership application, he answered "yes" to the question "Is your spouse free of Jewish strain in her family?" And he answered "no" to "Have you been married to a non-Arian before?"[41] The application was never sent, but it was public knowledge at the time, as it is today, that Hamsun considered himself a Quisling man. It is not possible to explain away Hamsun's anti-Semitism.

The often-debated "Ossietsky case" of 1935 can be seen as a missed opportunity for Hamsun to rethink his position. In actuality, he used it as the occasion to fully reveal his pro-German worldview. The case polarized opinions in Norway about the new German government, but Hamsun was the only major Norwegian writer who openly defended the right of the German state to confine dissident Carl von Ossietsky, and by implication, all opponents. Ossietsky was not a Jew but rather a critic of German domestic and foreign politics.[42] In a newspaper article, Hamsun blames Ossietzky for ending up in the Oldenburg concentration camp and insists that he could have emigrated either before or after 1933.[43] Hamsun sneered at the Norwegian writers' petition to protest Ossietsky's imprisonment and their lobby to award him the Nobel Prize. Published in *Aftenposten* on December 14, 1935, the petition was signed by more than thirty prominent writers, among them Nini Roll Anker, Johan Borgen, Olav Duun, Nordahl Grieg, Sigurd Hoel, Helge Krog, Sigrid Undset, and Arnulf Øverland. This petition alone undermines the comfortable apologia of some Hamsun defenders who argue that the situation in Germany was not really known in Norway. On the contrary, it is obvious that Hamsun understood the Nazi takeover as a cultural revolution and approved of it. Already in his short text from July 1934, "Vente og se" (Wait and see), he writes, "this is about how to reform *from the ground up* a society of 66 million people, and that is what Germany has struggled with for fifteen months."[44] He continues by favorably contrasting the new Germany with the old one. Hamsun's basic message to the Ossietzkys of Germany was: "If you don't like it, leave, but you've got no right to protest."

Hamsun's belief in the reformatory promise of the Third Reich is echoed in his eulogy to Hitler (May 1945), in which the dictator is praised as a radical reformer. Hamsun's appreciation of German heritage, culture, and art, and his gratitude to German audiences for their support are logical.[45] Yet from there to endorsing a repressive regime, and later welcoming Norway's integration into the Third Reich with all its consequences, is quite a leap.

His direct statements of support for the new Germany augmented his enthusiastic comments about the cultural change, indeed cultural revival, after 1933. In a short 1941 newspaper contribution "Knut Hamsun svarer på to spørsmål" (Knut Hamsun answers two questions), he expressed his conviction that Germanic cultural exchange and a new cultural field based on a Germanic worldview would bloom. [46] He asserted that this was not a prophecy but "healthy knowledge" (*sund viden*) and "historic intuition" (*historisk intuisjon*). That he uses vocabulary from biology in connection with knowledge and ties intuition to history reflects both his anti-intellectualism and an ideological conviction that mirrored that of Nazi Germany. He concluded: "This is a deep awareness of the known and of the secret, founded on family and blood. We are all Teutons."[47] In another newspaper piece, "Min mening om den norske legion" (My opinion of the Norwegian Legion), he approves of and praises those young Norwegians who joined the German SS volunteers on the Eastern Front.[48] Even Hamsun's son Arild later joined the volunteers.

In early June of 1943, Hamsun drafted a letter to Joseph Goebbels (Reichsminister für Volksaufklärung und Propaganda), and although no copy of the final letter has been found, a version of it must have been sent, as Goebbels sent Hamsun a response. The letter concerns Hamsun's Nobel Prize medal, which he received in 1920 for his novel *Markens grøde* and which he gave to Goebbels as a gift. Goebbels' response to Hamsun, dated June 23, 1943, said that he viewed the gift as "an expression of your commitment to our fight for a new Europe."[49]

That commitment was nowhere more in evidence than on the same June 23, when Hamsun gave a speech at the first plenary congress of the *Press Internationale* in Vienna (organized by Joseph Goebbels) to an audience of approximately five hundred journalists from forty countries. Actually, because Hamsun did not speak German, the speech was delivered by Arnt Rishovd, the main editor of *Fritt Folk*; Hamsun delivered a short introduction in his basic English. The speech was titled "England må i kne!" (England to her knees!) and was subsequently published in the main Austrian, German, and Norwegian newspapers. According to Gunvald Hermundstad, Hamsun's speech was the absolute high point of the congress.[50] In the speech, Hamsun first elaborates on how the power relations among European countries resulted in World War I, and then continues:

England always harvests the benefits of others' defeat. The German population has also, little by little, over the years been infiltrated by foreign elements that infected and weakened the Germanic spirit of the people: that was fine with England, Germany should be weakened. A spillover of non-Germanic peoples and races sprouted in the country and exploited the populace that had suffered after the war. Those were dark years for Germany that imposed a breathtaking billion burden in war reparations and left its fleet sunk, the colonies robbed, unemployment and shortages.[51]

The solution for Germany's problems was, Hamsun posits, National Socialism and its dynamic program. He concludes by imploring Germany, after defeating the Bolsheviks and the Yankees, to defeat England, for England is the cause of all the problems.[52] In this speech, Hamsun once again openly expresses a worldview consistent with the Nazi politics of the day, his racist rhetoric identical to that of the congress organizers, and his personal voice intertwined with the prevailing propaganda.

The speech aroused so much attention that a meeting with Adolf Hitler was organized in haste for June 26, 1943, according to Hermundstad.[53] However, Marie Hamsun, in her memoir, and Jan Troell, in his movie *Hamsun*, seem to suggest that a visit with Hitler had been planned earlier.[54] Marie's version is most likely a deliberate, post-1945 attempt to create the myth of Hamsun as patriot and to whitewash his contribution to the Vienna congress. The meeting between Hamsun and Hitler did not go well and resulted in Hitler's abruptly walking out. The discussion was secretly recorded by Hitler's translator, Ernst Edmund Züchner (1900–1975), who fled to Sweden after the war and wrote a report about the details of the meeting. The report became part of the evidence in Hamsun's postwar trial. The meeting is a profoundly tragic moment of truth for Hamsun that he nevertheless managed to repress. Deeply concerned about his home country, Hamsun complained to Hitler about Josef Terboven, Reichskomissar for Norway, and requested his removal; he begged for the reopening of international maritime routes for the Norwegian trading fleet; and he inquired about the role of Norway in the future. Still, he repeatedly expressed his support for the German occupation and for the Führer, even if he challenged him to the point that Züchner made the decision not to translate certain statements. The meeting left Hamsun in utter desperation, with suspicions about what had been translated and what had not, and with the full realization that Quisling's was a puppet government. The fact that Hamsun, after this meeting, continued to support Germany, shows the complexity of Hamsun's thoughts, feelings, and actions. His status as a literary figure failed to affect history in the way that he had perhaps envisioned; indeed, nowhere is it clearer than in the congress and the meeting with Hitler how blurred his private and political voices had become, and how they were implicated in the politics of the day.

Yet in addressing the question "Var Hamsun nazist?" (Was Hamsun a Nazi?), Hermundstad tiptoes around the issue.[55] He avoids it by redefining the term *Nazism* "in a narrow sense" (*i snever forstand*), though he does not specify what that actually means. Would it entail Hamsun's marching in NS uniform and active participation in the deportation of the Jews, or his displaying anti-Semitic posters in his window?

In order to better understand the logic behind Hermundstad's use of the phrase "narrow sense," we need to turn to another source. In Per Ole Johansen's discussion of the connection between the Norwegian state bureaucracy's anti-Semitic and xenophobic attitudes during the interwar years and the efficient Nazi-ordered deportation of Jews from Norway in 1942–43, he first draws parallels between latent anti-Semitism on the part of the Norwegian police and their failure to question Nazi orders. One way to defuse the charges of anti-Semitism after the war, Johansen writes—and it is here we can draw parallels to the logic of Hamsun's apologists—has been to confine it to the relatively small NS party and thereby conclude that it was rather insignificant.[56] Such logic may underlie Hermundstad's understanding of a "narrow sense." Membership in a political party is certainly one indicator of one's political views and cultural opinions, but everyday racism and prejudices affect the outcome of many political decisions. George Mosse's classic book, *Nazi Culture: Intellectual, Cultural and Social Life in the Third Reich*, pinpoints in an exemplary manner the way in which everyday attitudes and deep-seated beliefs were intertwined with the ideological premises of the Third Reich. These attitudes and beliefs worked similarly in Norway among certain segments of the population, although adapted to Norway's specific historical background and development.

Hermundstad answers the clearly stated question as to whether Hamsun was a Nazi by summarizing how others have addressed the very same issue (some a decisive yes, some a decisive no, and others "at the most 50%"), and he leaves it up to the reader. His conclusion represents a gentleman's way of evading the question:

> What the majority can agree on is that Hamsun, from his ivory
> tower, did not have the abilities to analyze Nazism's true being and
> made a series of fatal misjudgments. The problem has its source in
> that the Nazi ideology presented itself outwardly in finest robes,
> while the hard political realities were held secret. As so many others,
> Hamsun let himself be seduced and exploited by the Nazis' propa-
> ganda machine."[57]

Here we have Hermundstad, in 1998, using the tired old excuse of Hamsun's living in an ivory tower. Not only do Hamsun's Vienna speech and presence at the congress specifically endorse the NS program, his words include references to non-Germans as an infestation. Under the circumstances, this cannot be interpreted in any way other than as a reference to the Jews, or "Jews and others like that." The speech alone, given in occupied Vienna, answers the ubiquitous question, "Was Hamsun a Nazi?"

Finally, it is well documented that Hamsun read a variety of newspapers, journals, and periodicals, wrote articles and letters to the editors, and avidly corresponded with friends and acquaintances. The evidence from his letters and articles in numerous newspapers, from the Danish *Politiken*, the Swedish *Svenska Dagbladet,* and the Finnish press to journals such as *Tidens Tegn,* dismantles the well-entrenched argument that Hamsun was ignorant of international affairs.[58] Ingar Sletten Kolloen, one of the most recent Hamsun biographers, frequently refers to Hamsun's insistence on being well informed and well read, as well as to his having a map of Europe on his wall on which he followed the developments of the war.

Kolloen's two-volume biography, well researched and detailed, does not want to explicitly answer the question of Hamsun's Nazism either. Instead, Kolloen draws parallels between Hamsun's points of view and those of Nazi ideologists. He, too, devotes a section of his book to the question of whether or not Hamsun was a Nazi.[59] In the end, however, Kolloen equivocates. In his answer he suggests that we consider some "control questions," such as whether or not Hamsun was willing to undermine the existing social order by violent, undemocratic means. He then answers these control questions in the affirmative but avoids the big one.

In general, the strategy of Hamsun apologists is to isolate his statements and then explain them away, one by one, as insignificant. Yet the statements are frequent, unambiguous, and supported by Hamsun's actions, and they express a consistent worldview. The apologetic argumentation is a piecemeal refutation, as it does not consider how Hamsun's overall worldview accommodates such statements and fits them into a coherent whole. Jon Langdal calls this piecemeal logic "psychological atomism" in his dissection of the strategies of Hamsun apologists.[60] Langdal's is a rather isolated critique of the contemporary Norwegian literary establishment and its defense of Hamsun as a creative "enigma" and so on.

Both Marie and Knut Hamsun were extremely important for the NS propaganda that regularly featured articles and photos about the family. This was perhaps especially true of Marie, who toured Germany before and during the war as a kind of cultural ambassador, reading from Knut's and her own texts. She first did so in the spring of 1939 at the invitation of the Nordische Gesellschaft in Lübeck and continued until the late winter of 1943. Founded in 1921 during the Weimar Republic, the Nordische Gesellschaft had the goal of strengthening common Germanic, and especially Nordic, cultural interests. In the interwar period, there were many exchange visits made by artists and writers, resulting in numerous public readings and exhibitions. After Hitler's ascent to power in 1933, the Nordische Gesellschaft became an ideological tool of the new government and was supervised by the propaganda ministry. It was expanded to cover all of Germany's territories under the leadership of Alfred Rosenberg, the notorious race ideologue. The Norwegian Authors' Association eventually declined to participate in further cultural exchanges, but Marie agreed to go on lecture tours independently. Her last tour in 1943 took her from Vienna to Munich, Stettin, and Swinemünde, during which she performed readings in almost forty locations. After Knut's stroke in 1943, she decided to quit touring.

There were a variety of factions within NS at various stages and internal debates surrounding its program, because for a considerable length of time it struggled to create a definitive program. Most historians claim that it was ideologically divided into two large blocks, the "Germanic" and the "Norwegian."[61] After censorship was enforced in Norway, the NS party and its publications reflected the two-block division. This distinction is important because some later scholars have interpreted the "national/Norwegian" NS publications to be relatively innocent as opposed to the distinctly pro-Germanic ones.

The Germanic ideology was prevalent in *SS*-dominated groups, for instance among Eastern Front soldiers who were part of Waffen-*SS* formations, such as the regiments Nordland, Wiking, and the Norwegian Legion. The ideology was manifested in such publications as *Germanenen* (The Teuton), *SS-Hefte* (SS-Booklet), and *Germanske Budstikke* (Germanic Messenger).[62] These publications, perhaps especially *Germanske Budstikke*, are examples of the steady propaganda promoting the unity of Germanic blood and the Third Reich, the healthy Nordic family, and colonization of the East. They commemorate the Viking legacy and selected writers like Bjørnstjerne Bjørnson. The biology of the white race is discussed at length, as is sacrifice for the fatherland and future Nordic generations. They contain a relentless stream of articles against corrupt American businessmen, black jazz singers, Jewish merchants, Bolshevik revolutionaries, degenerated races, and the deficiencies of parliamentary democracy. Hamsun was either published or quoted often in these publications, although there were certainly other writers whose contributions appeared in almost every issue (Erling Winsnes, Hans S. Jacobsen). A long article by Hamsun, "Det amerikanske overmot" (The American arrogance),[63] dismisses the United States as the materialistic new continent lacking both spirituality and art. In "Et brev fra Knut Hamsun" (A letter from Knut Hamsun),[64] he writes that "little Hanna" ought to return from the city to the farm. An excerpt from his article "Realisert kameratskap" (Realized camaraderie) shows up as an epitaph for an anonymously written article titled "Jøden for årtusen tilbake den samme som idag" (The Jew from thousands of years ago is the same today).[65]

The "Norwegian" wing expressed its views mainly in *Fritt Folk* and *Hirdspeilet* (Hird's mirror), the publication of the NS's *Hirden*, as well as in minor local newspapers. While in general the articles are less rabid than those in the "Germanic" publications, and their focus is on seemingly neutral topics like folk costumes, camping, sports, and so forth, the contributions in *Hirdspeilet* still essentially advocate the Germanic brotherhood within the Third Reich. In the *Ideologisk Månedshefte for Hirden* (Ideological monthly for *Hirden*) Hamsun has a short text titled "Knut Hamsun om englenderne" (Knut Hamsun about the British) that is essentially a critique of British colonialism and the British character.[66] Particularly noteworthy is Hamsun's understanding of colonial expansionism as a sexual act of domination and emasculation, of colonized regions as castrated, and the local populations as castrates. He must have understood the German thrust to the East in a similarly sexual light; German masculine dominance would be a presumptive defense against those lewd others with uncivilized drives.

In "formally independent" publications like *Ragnarok* and *Nationalt Tidsskrift*, which clearly embraced the cause of the occupiers, Hamsun also published several texts. *Ragnarok* (which in Old Norse means the destruction of the gods and the world) printed Hamsun's article in defense of the Norwegian right to Greenland, in which he appeals to the Norwegian folk and their race to guard the colony.[67] In this case, Hamsun did not have a problem with colonial control.

Given Hamsun's trust in the German Reich, it is interesting to observe how the German occupiers perceived and presented Norway in publications during the occupation. A typical text is *Norwegen: Geschichte—Kultur—Wirtschaft—in Wort und Bild* (Norway: History—culture—economy—in word and image), published in 1943 by the Main Department for People's Education and Propaganda of the Reichskommissar for the occupied Norwegian

Territories.[68] The book, at times quite factual and detailed yet simultaneously misleading and full of omissions, reveals the official attitude of the Third Reich toward its Norwegian brothers. Dutifully reviewing the periods from earliest times up to the German occupation, the text highlights selected important dates and personalities. It interprets Norwegian independence in 1905 as England's attempt to draw Norway into its sphere of influence and a blow to "Scandinavianism." It understands immigration to the U.S as a draining of native "blood," and points out that the Norwegian representative to the League of Nations, Carl Joachim Hambro, is a "half-Jew." Also noted is the fact that American culture has weakened and replaced the Germanic culture in Norway. The editors accuse Norway of observing neutrality vis-à-vis Germany during World War I and cooperating with England. They claim that Germany is protecting Norway from an unavoidable English attack, which, as we recall, was also Hamsun's belief. Regrets about the failed Norwegian attempt to attain dominance over Greenland and the American occupation of this important strategic island are discussed. Further, it is argued that Vidkun Quisling's rise to power was logical because he alone would be capable of atoning for the sins of past liberal economic decisions, break the ties with the Western powers, and rejoin the Pan-Germanic community. The book is a clear example of German ideology as it was disseminated in various publications during the occupation.

The section entitled "Land und Leute" (Land and people) patronizingly depicts the Norwegians as primitives. The Norwegian language is not as nuanced as German, and the Norwegian (man) is difficult to understand because "he likes to combine the civilizing progress with a natural simplicity, which sometimes comes across as primitiveness."[69] A contrast is drawn between the hard-working and efficient German and the Norwegian who possesses less sense for production and usefulness. The German, furthermore, loves to transform nature to culture while the Norwegian adores wild nature, "the wilder the better for the Norwegian."[70] The Norwegians are further described as sloppy and somewhat lazy, in contrast to Germans who approach work with reverence. Nevertheless, the section concludes with the platitude that people need to have respect and understanding for each other. The section on the economy, however, shows that the German authorities understood very well the advantages of Norwegian timber, fish, minerals, and electric power industries.

In the section "Literatur," the text covers familiar territory starting with the sagas. The poet Henrik Wergeland is mentioned as having fought for the rights of Jews to settle in Norway, a battle, however, that only contributed to future political conflict. Those who worked quietly for the reestablishment of the old Norwegian cultural traditions of fairytales, folk songs, folk costumes, and rural architecture are praised. Ibsen is mentioned, not as a modernist playwright but rather as a writer of past generations, with *Peer Gynt* as his most performed play. Hamsun is pronounced a genius and Johan Bojer praised as a writer who dramatized the homesickness of Norwegian immigrants in North America. The major omission here is, of course, Sigrid Undset, the 1922 Nobel prize-winning novelist, omitted surely because of her anti-Nazi writing and lecturing. Also excluded is Aksel Sandemose, who warned of the dangers of fascism in general (as a mental makeup) and of Nazi Germany in particular. Not a word is said about Sigurd Hoel or Nini Roll Anker, popular writers whose novels were often set in modern urban areas. Modernist writers such as Cora Sandel, Claes Gill, and Rolf Jacobsen are missing as well. Selected works by Edvard Munch are mentioned and praised, yet not a word is wasted on his radical aesthetic philosophy. The decorative arts, stave churches, and traditional wooden architecture are all admired. The section ends with sports, described as having been formed by perpetual battles with nature and out of which a hardy people emerged.

The pictorial section opens with two portraits: that of a young blond man with a chiseled look, smilingly looking upwards, and that of an old man with a silver beard. The caption reads: "The Norwegian is a keeper of valuable Germanic blood-lines."[71] Several subsequent pages depict peasant women and children, mostly blond and in folk costumes. What follows are photos of rugged coast, ocean, forests, fjords, fishing, and harvesting. Oslo and marching German soldiers are allotted two pictures each, then various industries are shown, and finally a few photos of the Sami appear with the caption: "The Lapp and the reindeer belong together."[72] The section concludes with a picture of the grave of the unknown German soldier.

What conclusions can we draw from this presentation of Norway and its people? First, the German propaganda machine was a highly organized and sophisticated enterprise that obviously attracted specialists and experts. By stressing certain "obvious" beliefs and facts, omitting others, and skewing or falsifying yet others, it could create a believable and convincing product. Second, the propaganda machine stressed and exaggerated the importance of the Nordic race and common Germanic roots. Finally, it underlined the Nordic race's connection to wild nature, a bond that was interpreted as having contributed to its essential character and soul. Such "expert" texts could legitimize the German occupation and perhaps convince reluctant followers. That Hamsun lent his name to the Nazi project made a significant difference to the propaganda machinery.[73] It is therefore interesting that Hamsun, while proclaimed in this book to be a genius, is allotted a rather modest space. Perhaps the intention was to avoid overkill or to avoid praising a writer whose complexity could not be located unambiguously in the "blood and soil" ideology. Still, there is no doubt that the Norwegians are treated here with a patronizing attitude, while the occupation is portrayed as a fulfillment of the German mission to bring culture and civilization to Norway.

While Hamsun was not involved in the production of daily Nazi propaganda, the propagandists used him diligently. He never protested. While we might speculate about his reasons, we can see, by looking closely at a rather typical German propaganda article, how consonant it was with Hamsun's worldview. The article, "Norwegen und die Norweger" (Norway and the Norwegians),[74] focuses on the "state of affairs of racial and demographic politics of the Germanic peoples"[75] and conveys some of Hamsun's most firmly held views. In pseudo-scientific language, it explains how the new Europe depends on the preservation of Germanic blood and relates Scandinavian history from that point of view. Both the settlement of Iceland and emigration to America are described as a draining of good blood. The tone is condescending. Norwegians of the late nineteenth century were not able to think and act independently, and their actions were stalled in constant political bickering, while the state was unable to stem emigration. The article condemns the demographic decline that occurred among the wealthiest elites under the alleged influence of British and American cultural attitudes. The historical independence of the Norwegian farmer had degenerated into a form of extreme individualism that resulted in a new set of sexual mores. This new sexual reality, characterized by easily available contraception and abortion, was influenced by Soviet attitudes and supported by Oslo University research. The article specifically attacks the establishment of the Mütterhygienekontore (Mothers' health clinics) as the result of a pathological desire on the part of Norwegians to be modern. It attributes the increasing divorce rate and decreasing birth rate to spiritual degeneration. The closing sentence deserves to be quoted in full: "This development wouldn't have been possible if the Norwegian woman recognized and fulfilled her obligation as a true homemaker and mother—the Norwegian language knows the beautiful word 'husmor,' Hausmutter."[76]

The reason that Norwegian women are neglecting their motherly duties, it is explained, is because they socialize within Anglo-Saxon and salon-Bolshevik circles. They use alcohol and nicotine with abandon. The Germans who arrived in Norway on April 9, 1940, the text continues, were struck by how the Norwegian felt no responsibility to his own folk and the Germanic race. The article expresses regret that the University of Oslo allowed an African American band to entertain its students, who cheered "the niggers."[77] It is this university event, so the article states, that best illustrates the Norwegian attitude. All of this should sound very familiar to the serious Hamsun student. The text goes on to say that the Germans must now reeducate the Norwegian people to reject their elites because, as the condescending tone resurfaces again, "the race value and the hereditary health of the Norwegian folk are at least just as good as those of the German one."[78] From its conclusion, we learn that "education, especially of children and youth, will be able to make the Norwegians again into a 'Nordic' folk according to our concepts. That is our goal."[79]

Hamsun would no doubt agree with such a plan to reindoctrinate youth with the values of the past, an effort he would understand as a revival (*gjenreisning*), one of his oft-repeated words during these years.[80] The motif of revival or reform is one of the fundamental ideas in many of Hamsun's articles of the time, including his eulogy to Hitler, published on May 7, 1945, in *Aftenposten*. The entire text of the eulogy is as follows:

> I am not worthy of speaking loudly about Hitler, and neither his life nor his deeds invite any sort of sentimental feeling. He was a warrior, a warrior for humanity, and a prophet of the gospel of justice for all nations. He was a reformer of the highest order, and his historical fate was that he was active in a time of the most exemplary barbarism which in the end felled him. Thus might the average western European see Adolf Hitler. And we, his closest supporters, now bow our heads at his death.[81]

This text includes a kernel of Hamsun's worldview that had remained unchanged for decades: modern times were characterized by materialism and greed, increasing barbarism, and spiritual poverty. It endorses what Hamsun considered to be a much-needed revolution in Europe, a revolution promised by the holistic movement of Adolf Hitler's National Socialism. There is nothing innocent about Hamsun's May 1945 statement, despite what Ferguson writes in *Enigma*: "Probably nothing that he ever wrote shows more clearly the dreadful obstinacy of his mind, its frightening and finally catastrophic innocence."[82] Obstinacy, yes, but what actually comes across very clearly in this eulogy is Hamsun's fundamental conviction in Hitler's revolutionary cause. One certainly cannot speak of innocence here.

Markens grøde and Nazi Ideology

UMBERTO ECO AND GEORGE L. MOSSE ARE AMONG THOSE WHO HAVE PIN-pointed racism and traditionalism, insistence on "correct" genealogy, and a conservative ideal of womanhood as some of the crucial components of the pre-totalitarian worldview which nourished fascism and Nazism.[83] Among Hamsun's novels, none has been more debated as a "blood and soil" or "fascist" novel than *Markens grøde*. Isak's ability to communicate with nature, for instance, has often been interpreted as a "blood and soil" element. Isak's reverence for Nature, however, is a very traditional Scandinavian attitude, which has been shown to have survived up to as late as the twentieth century.[84] The ability to communicate with the natural, supernatural, and mythical worlds that Hamsun describes is common in native oral and literary traditions and is not necessarily an ideological stance. Nazi propaganda exploited and lauded the Nordic/Germanic link to Nature as a sign of primordial vitalism. Hamsun's descriptions of ecstatic moments in nature have been interpreted as having contributed to, and corresponded to, a mental predisposition in individuals who would be attracted to fascism. Yet, Norwegian critics noted as early as 1917 an ambivalence on Hamsun's part about such harmonious unity with nature.[85] Moreover, while idyllic, this bond with Nature is described as elusive and brief, as well as repetitive and boring, and Hamsun's prose exudes excitement over Geissler, his urban, educated, adventurous, unreliable, and creative protagonist.

However, there are other elements that do point to evidence of "blood and soil" ideology. Racism toward the Sami is manifest in *Markens grøde*, as is traditionalism, the importance of the family, and the prescribed role of women. While "correct" genealogy is a more questionable category here, there is no doubt that in his description of women, Hamsun is a patriarch if not an outright misogynist. But even here one must tread carefully. "Blood and soil" propaganda often depicted women as mothers and moral pillars of their families, with no extramarital affairs, limited intellectual activities, and no outside employment, unless her duty to the nation required otherwise. But propaganda functioned on one level, while daily practices were considerably less strict. Indeed, as Dagmar Herzog writes about sexuality and Nazi Germany:

> for much of the populace Nazism brought with it not only a redefinition but also a perpetuation, expansion, and intensification of pre-existing liberalizing trends. . . . But the liberalization of heterosexual mores was also, already before World War II, actively advanced as part of NSDAP policy. For the regime ultimately offered, to those broad sectors of the populace that it did not persecute, many inducements to pre- and extramarital heterosexuality—not only for the sake of reproduction but also for the sake of pleasure—and numerous celebrations of marital bliss."[86]

Thus, pure Nordic women ought to be natural and healthy, without make-up and fancy clothes yet sexual nevertheless. *Markens grøde* features erotic women who want their desires to be satisfied, often through illicit affairs, and as infanticidal mothers they certainly do not represent model motherhood. Moreover, by marrying Axel while pregnant with another man's child, Barbro transgresses the ideal of the pure family. These extra-marital affairs in the novel are fundamentally condemned, and, most important, by the novel's end the women are tamed and have become an essential part of the life cycle. It is the conversion of the sinners and their healthy offspring that redeem them as good citizens. It was not that sexuality was forbidden during the Third Reich, it was only certain practices that were not accepted. One can imagine that in order to produce as many Aryan children as the government had in its plan, women had to be willing to cooperate, the more often the better. As George Mosse also points out, although in general stressing the middle-class features of Nazism, the prescribed simplicity and naturalness of German women under the Third Reich could only be taken so far: "A shiny nose did not serve the Volk."[87]

When it comes to the men in the novel, Hamsun's apologists have pointed out that Isak is neither a hero nor a leader, but rather a towering mythic figure. And although that is certainly true, one can reply that Nazism was in need of precisely such mythic figures. He is also a perfect follower, one of those cogs that the fundamentalist machinery needed: a sturdy, patient, hard-working instinctual guy who does not ask questions and who trusts that things will work out in the end. In the meantime, he populates the soil with his tribe. As Nazi propaganda would constantly advertise, every individual's contribution counted: his hard work, his devotion, his trust, his family, his immediate environment, and perhaps most importantly, his ignorance of larger issues. Fundamentally, this novel praises the farm family as thrifty and simple, fertile and instinctual, nonintellectual and holistic in its belief in a larger, non-Christian scheme of life. It contests industrialization and urban life, women's issues, labor organizing, the state, and the law. Complex characters and alternative life choices are part of the novel, yet they are problematized, criticized, and ultimately discarded, or essentially tamed and shown to be irrelevant by "life." And then there is the novel's conclusion: most crucially, the end prohibits alternative interpretations as it sings a song of praise to Man and Woman as pioneers settling the soil and populating the wilderness. There is nothing ambiguous about its resolution, and Hamsun's ideology is clearly spelled out.

It is erroneous to presume that all Nazi books were simplistic propaganda without much depth and complexity, and infer that in order for Hamsun's text to qualify as "blood and soil" propaganda, his writing and his messages would have to be overtly ideological and didactic and his protagonists one-dimensional. In *Markens grøde*, "experiments" with modernity are dispatched into oblivion and superseded by a timeless tribe's hard work on the fertile soil. Isak and Inger can be read as perfect representatives of an instinctual hands-on approach to life, with no formal education and without any such aspirations. They are specimens of glorified vitalism, which was later appropriated as an essential part of Nazi propaganda about resilient Germanic settlers. It was no coincidence that *Markens grøde* was so heavily and successfully exploited by Nazi propaganda.

Hamsun's ideas about women in general, and about his women protagonists in *Markens grøde* in particular, certainly tapped into the Zeitgeist that hesitantly applauded and simultaneously contested women's liberation. His ideas are echoed in countless sociological, psychological, and fictional contemporary texts. They are also echoed in Adolf Hitler's writing on women's duties and in the population propaganda of the Third Reich, which masterfully captured the uneasiness of the general populace with regard to the Weimar liberalization reforms. The image of a stable family with a virtuous mother at its center, which Nazi propaganda incessantly reproduced and exploited, was often conflated with people's strong and real longing for stability, security, and happiness. The gap between National Socialist propaganda and everyday reality left many questions open, but it is indisputable that some of its core values were indeed cherished by wide audiences. Hence *Markens grøde*'s popularity.

The same gender ideology was contained in the NS program and was disseminated in Norway through various publications, activities, camps, and workshops. It is exemplified in the three-page article "Kvinnen i den nasjonal-sosialistiske stat" (Woman in the national-socialist state), published in *Ideologisk Månedshefte for Hirden*.[88] This publication was created as a manual for various *Hirden* workshops. In the new world, so the article claims, there is both a new ideal of beauty for the woman and a new goal. "In this connection, you've maybe thought of women standing behind the podium, or even more, talking and smoking in men's circles. That period is now forever behind us in history."[89] Why are there still women who fight for equality, the article asks, referring to Hitler's eloquent platitude that the man's battle is on the front and the woman's is in giving birth for her folk's existence or downfall.[90] The anonymous author claims that mothers with many children will never bring up the issue of equality. The National Socialist state has a place only for those women who are useful—that is, not the coffee drinking and gossiping women from better homes. Those German women and young girls who perform all the tasks that the men, now on the front, have left undone, are the role models in this new world. A long paragraph lobbies against the Hollywood beauty ideal with its outfit-matching fingernail polish, and for a healthy natural look hardened in nature and in sports competitions, and for women's simple fashion, preferably folk costume.[91] It ends with the admonition that a woman's first task is to keep her body healthy in order to participate fully in the folk mechanism. A 1942 issue of the *SS–Germanske Budstikke* includes an excerpt from Hitler's article on the German woman from April 5, 1933.[92] It is illustrated with a picture of a peasant woman wearing a modest scarf on her head, cutting grass with a scythe in an idyllic environment. Hitler proclaims the woman as the man's *arbeidskamerat* (comrade in labor), united in a battle. There are no men's rights and no women's rights. Both men and women have a right and a duty: the nation!

In occupied Norway, imposed or self-imposed censorship resulted in the recycling of predictable topics and aesthetics in the daily press and in literary publications. Hamsun did not write any new novels during the occupation, but published several articles and letters in various forums discussed in this chapter. One of them, actually a reprint, is his "Et brev fra Knut Hamsun" (A letter from Knut Hamsun) published in *SS-Hefte*.[93] It had first appeared as "Bonde-" (Farmer-) in *Aftenposten*, on March 9, 1918. It begins with a direct address to a farmer and urges him to take his daughter home from the city ("Ta din datter hjem fra byen"). Later, the narrator/Hamsun appeals to the daughter directly, "Back to the soil, little Hanna!" (Tilbake til jorden, lille Hanna!") He contrasts the empty life of the city with the domestic country life that benefits the spirit and the body; he compares a meager existence in a city shop with a rich and satisfying life among the folk and animals on a farm; in short, he offers a stark contrast between the *overflødig* (superfluous) and *nødvendig* (necessary, indispensable). He urges Hanna to return to the countryside where she will be indispensable. If need be, she can do men's work, and that is exactly as it should be, Hamsun writes. He illustrates his point with an example from the Red River Valley in the United States, where he often saw women driving tractors. One he remembers particularly well is a young woman, a former teacher, now married, living on a farm, and helping her husband with everyday chores. Hamsun here conveys fundamentally the same message of unequal partnership that he conveys in *Markens grøde*, in his other novels, and in his correspondence with Marie. Furthermore, he put it into practice in their marriage. In the case of women–men relationships, there is certainly a parallel between life and art, and this parallel goes a long way to explain Hamsun's intertwinement with Nazi ideology.

8

THE RHETORIC OF DEFENSE IN HAMSUN'S
PAA GJENGRODDE STIER

I have never sent any letter to Dr. Goebbels. But I should have. I should have
thanked him because Frau Goebbels once showed me her six little girls and one
boy, the most beautiful children I have ever seen.

—Knut Hamsun to Ragnar Thomassen,
assistant chief of police at Grimstad, January 25, 1946

IN A CIVIL TRIAL IN DECEMBER 1947, THE GRIMSTAD MUNICIPAL COURT CON-
victed Knut Hamsun for his membership in the NS party.[1] The charges had
been filed by Erstatningsdirektoratet (the Directorate for Compensations) to
claim compensation from Hamsun for his part in the damage done to the
country by the NS party. The three-judge jury passed its verdict on December
19, with a 2-to-1 vote. Though Hamsun was spared imprisonment, he was
fined the large sum of 425,000 kroner. In June of 1948, the Supreme Court
unanimously upheld the decision of the Grimstad court, although the fine was
substantially reduced.

The 1947 civil trial was preceded by an attempt to try Hamsun on criminal charges. On June 23, 1945, he was charged with treason against the state,
giving support to the enemy, and inciting others to commit criminal acts
against the state. Furthermore, there was suspicion that Hamsun had violated

an act passed on December 15, 1944, by the Norwegian government in exile, which made membership in NS after April 8, 1940, a criminal offense. The Norwegian authorities and the attorney general, Sven Artnzen, found themselves in a tricky position. They had to prosecute Norway's greatest living author, who, at the advanced age of eighty-six, was almost deaf and, as rumor had it, senile. The Norwegian public, exhausted and angry after five years of occupation, reacted on the basis of what Kierulf and Schiøtz call *den alminnelige rettsfølelse* ("common sense justice") and wanted him tried.[2] Hamsun's initial detention was twice extended. However, on October 15, 1945, he was transferred to the Vinderen Psychiatric Clinic for observation, from which he was released as *uhelbredelig* ("incurable") on February 11, 1946.[3] Based on the psychiatric report (which included an assertion that Hamsun was no longer of sound mind), on February 18, the attorney general dismissed the criminal charges, stating:

> After the findings of the experts, I have decided that the public good will not be served by proceeding with a case against the accused, who will soon be eighty-seven years old and is to all intents and purposes deaf. I thereby drop the charge against him by the authority vested in me.[4]

Hamsun was bitterly disappointed by the attorney general's dismissal of the charges. In his arrogance, he had convinced himself that he would be acquitted. He wanted to show publicly that he stood by his actions and prove that he was not mentally impaired. He carefully prepared his speech for the civil trial in December of 1947 and even performed a dry run at Nørholm. He decided to deliver his own defense speech, while Sigrid Stray represented him in other matters during the trial. His speech constitutes an integral part of his memoir *Paa gjengrodde stier* (On overgrown paths), demonstrating how he employed and appropriated legal and aesthetic discourses to serve his political agenda and artistic vision. What is most interesting is the difference between the fair verdict of 1947 and subsequent critical reassessments of the trial. The tendency of posterity has been to exonerate, minimize, and apologize for Hamsun's support of the Nazis. The extraordinary rhetorical skills and strategies Hamsun utilizes both in *Paa gjengrodde stier* and in the formulation of the speech itself may be credited with assisting in the rehabilitation of his image.

In their book *The Winning Edge*, Richard Lucas and K. Byron McCoy stress the decisive role of performance in court. They claim that "with the facts being even, it is control over performance that is the difference between winning and losing." They condense the features of the good, persuasive orator into (1) an ability to charm or establish credibility; (2) the competence to develop a sound, logical argument; and (3) the ability to move the audience with emotions.[5]

Precisely because Hamsun delivered his own defense speech, an examination of the legal rhetoric employed in his memoir is particularly revealing. Hamsun in his works writes with contempt about the legal profession. He distinguishes between art and science, between his own art with words and the mere verbal skills of trained lawyers, as he distinguishes between his own psychological intuition and the dry academic knowledge of Professor Langfeldt, one of the two psychiatrists who evaluated Hamsun's mental condition after the war. Nevertheless, the formulation of an argument is extremely important for both lawyers and writers. Some of the techniques of effective communication and persuasion are common to both professions, for the art of speaking, as much as the facts themselves, determines the outcome. Both depend on communication and persuasion, which involve, besides words, the knowledge of "how people behave, think, feel, choose, develop values, and are motivated or persuaded."[6] While delivering his defense speech, Hamsun elected to frame his artistic genius as superior to legal rhetoric. Yet, it was precisely the similarities in the two discourses that enabled Hamsun to so artfully intertwine them. Bettyruth Walter defines the genre of the closing argument as follows:

> Everything occurs through the spoken word. The "summation," a
> speech event embedded within the trial, which is the chronological
> and psychological culmination of it, is one of the few opportunities
> for the lawyer to communicate directly with jurors. But the speech
> genre summation involves preliminaries as well as the event itself;
> and it can affect the aftermath of the trial, for the decision of the
> jurors may be influenced by this discourse.[7]

When Hamsun addressed the court, he employed the fundamental strategy of audience persuasion, and at least one of the judges was influenced by the speech. Moreover, *Paa gjengrodde stier* has continuously created a sort of "aftermath" in Walter's sense of the term. No longer merely Hamsun's own account of the circumstances surrounding the trial, the memoir served as one of Thorkild Hansen's key sources of information for his 1978 publication, *Prosessen mod Hamsun* (The trial against Hamsun), which precipitated enormous debate because of its apologetic bent. P. O. Enquist's screenplay and Jan Troell's subsequent film *Hamsun* (1996), in turn, used *Prosessen mod Hamsun* as their point of departure. What comes across most powerfully in this film version, not surprisingly, is Hamsun's own version of the situation. While in the immediate aftermath of the trial, Norwegian public opinion was overwhelmingly on the side of the state, subsequent interpretations, predominantly by academics, of Hamsun's role during the occupation have been much more forgiving, if not outright exonerating. Although Norwegian authorities handled the case carefully and even-handedly, Hamsun's image as a victim seems to have become more pronounced with the passage of time. How is this possible? One explanation is, of course, that all literary texts automatically generate multiple interpretations. Hamsun provided a powerful impetus for pursuing such interpretive possibilities by deliberately leaving his text open and relatively free of facts.

We can gain better insight into the post-war assessment of Hamsun if we examine the role of audience(s). Chaim Perelman and L. Olbrechts-Tyteca argue that it is extremely difficult to establish what constitutes a speaker's audience using purely material criteria. They suggest instead that one define the audience as "the ensemble of those whom the speaker wishes to influence by his argumentation,"[8] and they provide the illustrative example of a government spokesperson in Parliament. Who is this individual's audience? Is it the Speaker of Parliament whom he/she formally addresses? Is it the opposition, the public in general, or his/her constituency? Perelman and Olbrechts-Tyteca touch upon the even greater difficulty in identifying a writer's audience. That is precisely the case with Hamsun's defense speech. Even as he, on one level, addressed the court in Grimstad, he also addressed an imaginary, later audience who would likely be more sympathetic to the artist's fate. Indeed, *Paa gjengrodde stier* appeals to an audience of select initiated readers who are familiar with Hamsun's earlier works, his wanderer protagonists, and his unique rhetorical style.

In the introduction, Hamsun addresses postwar generations by explicitly stating that he is not writing for himself but "for our grandchildren."[9] Considering that Europe in the 1990s experienced a genocidal war, in which intellectuals participated as eagerly as other citizens, the issue of the responsibility of artists and intellectuals during wartime is particularly worthy of examination. The American intervention in Iraq adds further relevance to an inquiry along these lines. It is difficult to look at Hamsun's last work as primarily an aesthetic text without reference to its specific historical context. Given the horrors of World War II, Hamsun was treated justly, perhaps even more leniently than other Nazi collaborators because of his age, physical health, and status. Many Norwegians were dissatisfied with the final verdict: they felt that Hamsun should have been convicted and sentenced to a prison term, like any other collaborator, and then perhaps pardoned because of his old age.[10]

Post-1950 perceptions of Hamsun's life and writing are very much colored by sympathy toward the old, partially deaf artist who had to undergo what he describes in his memoir as a cruel and rigid, and at times, indiscreet examination of his life. Most critics agree that one of the book's purposes was to depict Professor Langfeldt as an evil scientist. Indeed, Hamsun has constructed a narrative that has proven seductive to generations of subsequent scholars. The core of this narrative is as follows: Langfeldt evaluates Hamsun and in his psychiatric report pronounces him a person with "permanently impaired mental capabilities" (*varig svekkede sjælsevner*). In this way, Langfeldt, as the puppet of the state, intrudes gravely and humiliatingly into Hamsun's personal sphere. Sixty years later, Einar Kringlen, an internationally respected professor of psychiatry, defended the evaluation by commenting that "many other psychiatrists would have arrived at the same conclusion as Langfeldt and Ødegård. Besides, the conclusion would never have been in doubt had not Hamsun himself questioned the conclusion with his mocking final novel."[11]

The report was requested, Kringlen writes, by the Norwegian state in 1946 based on a law that mandated the mental evaluation of all defendants in order to establish their fitness to stand trial. One of the intentions behind the law was in fact the protection of mentally impaired defendants.[12] The evaluation was conducted and the final report signed by two psychiatrists, Gabriel Langfeldt and Ørnulv Ødegård, but Hamsun singled out Langfeldt as the villain. Robert Ferguson writes: "Thus began a war between Langfeldt and Hamsun which once again cast Hamsun in the role he was all along best equipped to play in life, that of the desperate but charming loser. It was to go a long way toward modifying the picture of the individual Knut Hamsun, unattractive to the point of irremediable, that would otherwise have been left to posterity."[13] The "war" between Hamsun and Langfeldt is Hamsun's perception, construct, and revenge, yet Ferguson seems to have found it irresistible himself, for he, too, is guilty of perpetuating this dramatic narrative. Hamsun was no loser—he and his family survived the war, their home intact—but rather an unrepentant collaborator.

The psychiatric report, however, contains much more than what has become a convenient sound-bite used to frame the "war" that Ferguson refers to. In their conclusion, Langfeldt and Ødegård express the opinion that "on the other hand, it must be stated that in relation to his age, his interests and his memory are not weaker than his age would indicate. On the contrary, it can even be stated that one seldom meets an eighty-six-year-old man who has such alert interests in current questions as the person mentioned above."[14] This observation conforms to Hamsun's characterization of himself in *Paa gjengrodde stier*, in which he presents himself as an alert old man whose brain is highly active, in both practical and aesthetic matters. He writes, not without a sense of humor: "Here I sit, sound and spry, and knowingly trick myself. It must be schizophrenia at least."[15] Asserting his health and robustness, Hamsun here mocks the medical discourse that labels schizophrenia a disease; for him, a mental imbalance has often been a source of artistic creativity.

Paa gjengrodde stier is not a book about "trifles," as Hamsun disingenuously states and as Carl Anderson, the English translator of the memoir, repeats.[16] Neither is it a book from "the other side of the author's life" as Kittang has called it,[17] nor merely a Taoist-like book of reflections as Ferguson has suggested.[18] Instead, it is a deliberate defense written for posterity, with the goal of persuading the reader that Hamsun's activities during the war were in fact patriotic acts. Many scholars have followed Hamsun's "instructions" on how to read the book and have concluded that his last work is "delightful." If nothing else, he effectively refutes professors Langfeldt and Ødegård's diagnosis.

The mostly positive reception of *Paa gjengrodde stier* demonstrates Hamsun's power of persuasion and urges us to revisit the original text with a critical eye. For, as Julia Kristeva reminds us in *Language the Unknown*, "the 'manner of speaking,' as is commonly said, is far from indifferent to the content of what is said, and every ideological content finds its specific form, its language, its rhetoric."[19] Kristeva argues that the most effective speakers have always paid particular attention to proofs (material content), style, and arrangement. However, in Hamsun's case, his defense speech demonstrates his avoidance of proofs and focuses instead on style and organization, thereby transforming a legal discourse into a literary one. Perhaps the following comment on Ol'Hansa, one of the minor protagonists in *Paa gjengrodde stier*, should have been chosen as the epigraph for the book: "What a shrewd dog I've been in all this! I have mixed together two journalists, Ol'Hansa and myself, so that neither of us has said anything."[20] Deliberately mixing two voices so that the content and the conventions of a particular utterance can be blamed on the other, Hamsun creates an intentionally ambiguous text, which either "condemns us to vacillate or allows us to oscillate, between referential and fictional readings," as Dorrit Cohn once put it.[21]

Hamsun states about his speech: "It has not been intended as any defense on my part."[22] But could, in fact, the opposite be true? The text seems to recycle a rhetorical strategy from his earlier texts, of which the most memorable example is Glahn's narration. While Glahn states repeatedly that he is writing to kill time, and that he has forgotten a certain girl, the documenting of his reflections on forgetting her results in an entire book, *Pan*, the story of Edvarda and Glahn.

With regard to the charges against him, Hamsun claims that he stands by what he has done: "From the first moment of the preliminary hearing held on June 23, I had assumed responsibility for what I had done and have maintained that standpoint unswervingly ever since."[23] The problem here is how to interpret the expression "what I had done." The vagueness of this statement parallels the lacunae in Hamsun's speech through which he avoids addressing the substance of the charges against him. Hamsun's faith in his own rhetorical skills was such that he expected to be acquitted of most of the charges. As he states in *Paa gjengrodde stier*: "I knew, you see, in my heart that if I could speak without hindrance, the wind would turn for me toward acquittal, or as close to acquittal as I would dare go and the court accept."[24] He continues: "I knew that I was innocent, deaf and innocent; I would do well during the examination by the prosecuting attorney solely by relating most of the truth."[25] Hamsun here builds upon his victim status. First, he is only "innocent," yet ultimately he is "deaf and innocent." Notice, too, modifiers such as "as close to" (acquittal) or "most of" (the truth). He does not offer "the truth, and nothing but the truth," but rather approximations and ambiguities. It is precisely this strategy that leaves the door open for later interpretive confusion and generous apologias.

Hamsun's rhetorical moves may be divided into four broad, at times overlapping strategies. He intends to: (1) discredit not only the legitimacy of the Norwegian judicial system but the entire Norwegian state and its representatives (e.g., the king, the government, the police, and, in a slightly different category, the press and the doctors); (2) minimize the weight of his political stance by employing textual ambiguity, misstating or avoiding facts, playing dumb, or lying outright; (3) discredit the possible verdict in advance by invoking the rather traditional image of the artist's immortality achieved through his art; and (4) evoke sympathies by presenting himself as an old, deaf, and modest man, a victim of conspiracy and a guinea pig for medical science. Hamsun's carefully planned strategies in his court speech are reproduced in the memoir as a whole. In this way, the speech becomes a sort of *mise-en-abime*.

A careful examination of the speech reveals that it contains almost nothing in the way of facts or evidence disputing the charges made by the Norwegian state against Hamsun. Indeed, its main characteristic is an avoidance of the facts. It is interesting to note that it is prefaced with the following cryptic remark: "What I spoke is recreated here based on the stenographer's report. (NB! From here on, it follows the officer's spelling and is not corrected by the author)."[26] This note about the stenographer's accountability slyly seeks to undermine the reliability of the legal system: if they can't take proper dictation, how can they make reliable judgments on more serious issues? Hamsun here makes a double move: he calls attention to the speech as speech, authenticating it as a truer, oral record as opposed to the rest of the book, and he alerts us to the fact that it is no longer his own speech, because it has been transcribed by a clerk. We are indeed caught between vacillation and oscillation. Let us now consider the speech paragraph by paragraph.

1   The first paragraph expresses Hamsun's humility and thus underlines his position as an outsider: "I do not intend to take up much of the honorable court's time."[27]

2   He immediately accuses the judicial system, which he had just called honorable, of colluding with the press in order to arouse suspicions about his culpability and *synderegister* (list of sins), and to create an atmosphere of scape-goating around him.

3   He describes the prosecutor's speeches as *flinkheter* (skills), implying that his own rhetoric is of a better kind. He then continues by saying that this is just fine, since the verdicts have mostly been in accordance with the prosecuting attorney's briefs anyway. As he puts it, "aktors påstann, den såkalte påstann." (Plaintiff's brief, the so-called brief).[28] In this important sentence, "*påstann*" is misspelled, something which Hamsun had already warned us about in his nota bene.[29]

4   Here he mentions his aphasia, which might cause his speech to be affected. This provides both mitigating legal circumstances and a warning to readers not to trust his words. Hamsun here reminds the audience of his agenda as a modernist writer: he has explored and doubted the meaning of words and identities.

5   He finally addresses his arrest. What does he say? Arrogantly, he claims: "Then there was the magistrate's hearing two, three, or five years ago. It's so long ago I don't remember, but I answered the questions."[30] Five years prior to the trial would bring him to 1941. He implies that he is not able to distinguish between the end and the beginning of the occupation, which, given the monumental nature of the event, is highly unlikely. He further questions the procedures he underwent in the mental hospital, suggesting the existence of a conspiracy between the judicial and medical systems by stating that perhaps the real reason behind his institutionalization was to establish that he was mentally ill.

6   He finally discusses his articles. He denies outright that he was a member of the NS, a crucial point disputed by the court and the majority of Norwegians.[31] In the sentences that follow, however, he uses conditional constructions such as: "It may well be that now and then I may have written in a Nazi spirit."[32] And further: "But it may well be that I did write in the Nazi spirit, that it might have filtered down a little to me from the newspapers I read."[33] Yet, he concludes generously that he stands by his articles and that everyone can read them. For those readers who won't have the time or ability to check his articles, Hamsun's "honorable" and "honest" invitation certainly makes an impression, while the undisputed support he expressed for the German forces gradually disappears into history. While many critics have expressed an admiration for Hamsun's unwavering attitudes—his personal code of honor, so to speak—it would have been preferable to see him stop his active support after his infamous meeting with Hitler, or even much later, if not change his allegiances in 1940. But he did not.

7   Hamsun emphasizes that he was writing in an occupied country, a fact for once, which, like all facts, lends credence to the whole.

8   He remarks that "we were told" about Norway's exclusive place in the Great Germanic Reich, "which we all believed in more or less—but all believed in it. I believed in it; therefore I wrote as I did."[34] This statement is not only perplexing, it is pure nonsense. The majority of Norwegians did not buy the Great Germanic Reich propaganda. Hamsun belonged to a tiny minority of Nazi collaborators. The misleading "we all" or "all" really consisted of Hamsun and roughly 40,000 other collaborators. The majority of Norwegians wanted an independent Norway free of German occupiers.

9   Here he makes the famous statement, *men aldri kom et lite vink til meg* ("but there never came a little hint to me"), one which has been disputed convincingly.[35] Hamsun presents himself as an utterly helpless and isolated man whose only connections to the outside world were the newspapers *Aftenposten* and *Fritt folk*, neither of which gave him any warning regarding his political beliefs. This is pure smokescreen, amply disputed by his own newspaper articles that reveal him to be an informed person who essentially supported the wrong side. Letters sent to Hamsun during the war by Odd Nansen and Ella Anker, who criticized Hamsun's articles, were presented in the court to refute his "splendid isolation" claim.[36]

10   This paragraph consists of a series of repetitions that are essentially statements, rather than explanations or information about his writing: "It wasn't wrong when I wrote it. It was right, and what I wrote was right."[37] Note Hamsun's rhetorical trick of sliding from "not wrong" to "right." But "not wrong" certainly does not necessarily denote "right."

11 and 12   Hamsun presents himself as a patriot who wanted to prevent loss of life among his fellow Norwegians. Several witnesses corroborated that he, on numerous occasions, intervened with German authorities on behalf of imprisoned Norwegians. As Johannes Andenæs states in his 1980 book, this was taken into account by the court. Yet it is an exaggeration for Hamsun to claim, "I sent telegraphs night and day when time was running short and it was a matter of life and death for my countrymen."[38] Hamsun pays close attention to style and repeats the "night and day" expression several

times in his speech. As if in passing, he mentions all those who fled to Sweden or England, implying that he, who stayed in Norway, was the real patriot. The "telegraph" argument actually works against him. Why did he not reflect on the fact that his beloved Germany found it necessary to continuously imprison and execute his fellow citizens? He reiterates that he was advocating for an independent Norway. He must have forgotten—and that is where aphasia comes in handy—that his meeting with Hitler at The Eagle's Nest in 1943 made it abundantly clear that Norway would be a mere province in the victorious Third Reich. Yet he continued writing pro-German articles.

13   He blames the king and the government for leaving the country, which left him "dangling between heaven and earth."[39] The expression "between heaven and earth" had also been used in Hamsun's letter to the attorney general. In that case, it was the latter's judicial actions which left him in that state of mind.

14   He admits that his actions were in contradiction to those of the majority of Norwegians. Yet he does not consider why this is so, why he would be out of sync with his fellow citizens under these special historic circumstances. Instead, he concludes that it does not matter, because time will erase all that. By mentioning time and the effect of the passage of time, he starts the process of addressing a different, later audience.

15   He repeats the expression "sent telegrams day and night," and raises himself above the role of a traitor by stating that he is at peace with himself.

16   He expresses an appreciation of his fellow men and of the court system, but concludes that "I am old enough to have a code of conduct for myself, and it is mine."[40] He concludes by repeating that he has always been a patriot, he thanks the honorable court, and he reiterates that his presentation is not intended as a defense. He claims that he has more material to present but will refrain from doing so. One may assume that he probably did not have any other material evidence, given that what he did present was so meager. He states that he has only presented some *kjensgjerninger* (facts). What facts?

His speech boils down to empty rhetoric and obfuscation. What if he had provided some facts, for instance, about his generous gift to Joseph Goebbels, about his visit aboard a German submarine, or his encouragement to young Norwegians to serve in the *SS*-units on the Eastern front?

The strategies of the speech are repeated in the memoir as a whole. Hamsun structured *Paa gjengrodde stier* by framing it between May 26, 1945 (the day when he was placed under house arrest) and June 24, 1948 (the day when the Supreme Court upheld the Grimstad municipal court's guilty verdict), thereby placing the text in a historical context. He opens with the following words: "The year is 1945. On May 26 the chief of police in Arendal came to Nørholm and served notice that my wife and I were under house arrest for thirty days. I had had no warning."[41] Here the rhetorical strategy is that the best defense is a good offense, and Hamsun immediately begins by discrediting Norwegian authorities. In what political system is the upcoming arrest of an alleged collaborator announced in advance? On a later page, Hamsun describes being called in for interrogation on September 22, too early in the morning, and again complains that nobody phoned him in advance. He could have reported that because of his age (he was eighty-six in 1945), he was actually treated quite leniently; he was put in a hospital rather than in jail or a camp. Another implicit accusation is suggested in his answer to the question of what his thoughts were on Germany's crimes against Norwegians. He answers that, since the police forbade him to read the newspapers, he knew nothing about it. These individual narrative elements cumulatively amount to a strong yet utterly deceptive defense. He consistently avoids questions and builds his own defense, for clearly strategic purposes. He ends the book with: "Saint John's Day, 1948. Today the Supreme Court has given its verdict, and I end my writing."[42] While the sentence can be read as a simple record of events, it is, within the framework of the accusations in the book, difficult to avoid a cause-and-effect insinuation; that is, he ends his writing because of the Supreme Court ruling. In other words, the judicial system has stifled his writing. The irony, of course, is that *Paa gjengrodde stier* is testimony that the opposite is true and that Hamsun's literary discourse has won out over the legal and psychiatric arguments.

The trope of state persecution of the artist is located at crucial places in the memoir. The sentence preceding Hamsun's letter to the attorney general dated July 23, 1946, for example, elaborates upon the adversarial connection between the attorney general's actions and Hamsun's "sixth sense" (*sjette Sans*). He complains bitterly: "What should I do now? I'm turned upside-down, that's the thing, I feel sorry for myself, have no desires, no interests, no joys. Four or five good senses in torpor, and the sixth sense bartered away. I can thank the attorney general for that."[43] Hamsun here complains about his usually creative universe being turned upside down by the imposition of the legal order. In the letter, he alleges a conspiracy between the judicial and the medical systems, and that the latter is using him as a guinea pig for its experiments.

The attorney general is described as a man who is not familiar with Knut Hamsun's name, hence as someone who does not read. Like Langfeldt, he is a dry scientific stick, in collusion with the doctors. Thus Hamsun suggests a contrast between his vibrant art and the tedious science of law and medicine. This contrast is extremely important, not only as a structuring device in *Paa gjengrodde stier* but also as an appeal to readers of subsequent generations. Dull scholars should not judge artists, is his message. Only other artists should do so, or at least sophisticated readers knowledgeable enough to place his memoir within the broader context of his entire body of work. This attack on the reader is significant, for who wants to be labeled a dry stick? Journalistic writing is disqualified as well. Hamsun claims that the attorney general takes orders from journalists and the press, making the serious charge that the press was not an independent fourth estate but rather an extension of the state.[44] The strategy of attacking the media runs throughout the book.[45]

Hamsun continuously plays dumb as to why he should be deemed a traitor and as to why people avoid him. But he offers the following "explanation" of his arrest: "We have acquired political prisoners in Norway. . . . the Thrane movement, Kristian Lofthus, Hans Nielsen Hauge do not count. But today we have one who does count; he is legion in the land of Norway and comes in forty, fifty, some say sixty thousand copies. And perhaps in many thousand more."[46] To compare himself and the NS political prisoners with Marcus Thrane, Kristian Lofthus, and Hans Nielsen Hauge is to make a specious argument, clearly meant to mislead. By equating himself with these three historical figures, Hamsun attempts to bask in their light. These three men were each systematically persecuted and imprisoned by the ruling authorities because they challenged the establishment and demanded, each in his own way, an expansion of democratic rights. Hamsun, politically an opponent of parliamentary democracy and what we customarily understand to be democratic rights, simply does not belong in the same category.

Hamsun is silent about the reasons behind his return to the nursing home in Landvik after his psychiatric evaluation, in February 1946. This results in an impression of a much longer "house arrest" at that institution, while Hamsun in fact paid to reside there and could have returned to his home Nørholm at any time. He most likely wanted to avoid his wife after almost two decades of a strained marital relationship, and because he now felt that Marie had irreparably betrayed him to Langfeldt.[47] He writes: "The year is 1946, February the 11th. I am out of the institution again. That does not mean that I am free, but I can breathe again."[48] Whether by "not free" he means that the trial still awaits him or that he is not free to go home is unclear. Yet it was probably precisely such ambiguity that misled subsequent readers. Carl Anderson, for example, writes in the introduction to his 1967 English translation of *Paa gjengrodde stier*: "This is Knut Hamsun's last book, a memoir written while he was interned from 1945 to 1948 on suspicion of treason."[49] Sverre Lyngstad's more recent translation of the book renewed interest in the work and led to a notion, widely expressed on various Internet sites, that Hamsun was imprisoned from 1945 to 1948. This erroneous impression continues to fuel the belief in the vindictiveness of the post-war Norwegian state against Hamsun.

Hamsun's speech did not result in an acquittal, although it was not a total failure. One of the Grimstad judges was persuaded of his innocence and his fine was reduced. All in all, it was neither his lack of eloquence nor his performance that decided the case, but rather the overwhelming facts in support of the charges against him that prevailed in the end. If we return to the definition of a persuasive orator by Lucas and McCoy, we can follow Hamsun's main strategies: he tries to charm, he tries to establish his credibility as a patriot, and he appeals to his readers' emotions. However, he sets aside a sound, logical argument in favor of an invitation to relate to him as a writer and person of honor, thereby asking us not to judge his deeds. By putting himself into the special category of artist, Hamsun refrains from using the so-called identification strategy, identification with the target audience being one of the avenues of successful persuasion. Yet he makes careful and strategic use of rhetoric. The book is not a delightful one. It is a calculated and coherent presentation of half-truths and ambiguities, as well as irrelevant arguments, spiced with appeals to emotion. Considering that Hamsun did not have the facts on his side, this was probably the safest way for him to proceed.

But time has been on his side. Hamsun's rhetorical skills have resulted in the generally positive reception of *Paa gjengrodde stier* and prevented many readers from seeing one of the book's crucial goals, namely an obfuscation of his role as a cultural persona who actively supported the Nazi occupation of Europe and Norway. Its influence is most obvious in the biased representations of Hamsun's case by Thorkild Hansen, P.O. Enquist, and Jan Troell, already discussed in this book. The long-lasting influence of Hamsun's rhetoric is also manifest in the analysis of American Hamsun scholar Harald Næss. In his biography *Knut Hamsun*, Næss compares *Paa gjengrodde stier* to *Hunger*:

> Its chief compositional device—the protagonist's gradual displacement, from the pleasures of the Palace Gardens to the slums behind the East Station—is also felt in the changing places and fortunes of the old author Knut Hamsun as he is being moved around as a political prisoner. In this sense the book is a documentary novel—like those many gripping accounts of imprisonment and deportation that appeared in the wake of World War II.[50]

The comparison of *Paa gjengrodde stier* with the accounts of victims of Nazism who suffered torture, deportation, hunger, displacement, or who lost family members is, to put it mildly, out of proportion. Hamsun's trials and tribulations as well as his complaints, while certainly real, are trivial in light of the collective human suffering caused by the war in Norway and in Europe. Yet, Næss's reading is precisely the kind that Hamsun had envisioned in 1949. With the passage of time, Hamsun is indeed winning his case, and there are plenty of apologists working on his behalf. In the never-ending debate about Hamsun's allegiances and culpability, the clearest voice comes from the legal expert Johannes Andenæs. Andenæs offers valuable legal expertise and a fine approach to putting Hamsun's trial into a historical context.[51] Næss's suggestion, to read *Paa gjengrodde stier* as a literary text worthy of comparison with *Hunger*, means that references to historical events lose their significance. But if we do take Næss's approach seriously and read the memoir in relation to other war documents, then we realize that Hamsun actually came out on top. He saved his life, kept his family home, Nørholm, and his Gyldendal shares, and published his last book. The fate of many other victims of World War II—if we are generous enough to refer to Hamsun as such—was very different. These are fates recorded in such texts as Lise Børsum's *Fange i Ravensbrück* (Prisoner in Ravensbrück), Petter Moen's *Dagbok* (Diary), or Johan Borgen's *Dager på Grini* (Days in Grini), and later, Kristian Ottosen's

I slik en natt (In such a night) and *Bak lås og slå* (Behind lock and bolt), and Vera Komissar's *Nådetid* (Time of mercy).[52]

THE MAIN FOCUS OF *PAA GJENGRODDE STIER* IS TO PRESERVE HAMSUN'S LEG-acy as a writer and minimize his role as a collaborator. Hamsun hoped that with time, the fictional truth would become *truth*. *Paa gjengrodde stier* ele-vates the value of literary discourse above legal and medical rhetoric and, by extension, places Hamsun the writer in an elite position vis-à-vis ordinary citizens and intellectuals alike. Throughout, the text emphasizes the differ-ences between the two worlds. Some examples: the repeated misunderstand-ings between Hamsun and the police ("We are talking about two different things," a policeman and Hamsun agree); the literacy gap between the attor-ney general and Hamsun ("I must assume that my name was unknown to the attorney general"); the completely different notions of the field of psychology and its terminology ("I was no stranger in the field of psychology," Hamsun says to Langfeldt); and most important, different attitudes to schizophrenia, aphasia, revelations, or divine madness. What doctors label as a medical condition, Hamsun considers the source of inspiration. The ordinary is con-sistently contrasted with the extraordinary. Martin from Hamarøy, Ham-sun's fictional alter ego, has meaningful things to say, as do literary texts and writers to which Hamsun refers: the Bible, Bunyan, Stevenson, or Topsøe. The psychiatrists and lawyers babble, their powerful acts encroaching upon Hamsun's universe and stifling his creativity. *Paa gjengrodde stier* can be interpreted as Hamsun's revenge on the medical and legal community and as the reestablishment of his poetic universe.

Throughout the text, Hamsun masterfully combines the everyday with the cosmic, as when he admires the "endlessly small in the middle of the end-lessly large in this magnificent world."[53] Or when he famously describes him-self as a faucet: "I am a faucet that goes on dripping, one, two, three, four," only to refer to stars in the next line.[54] Invoking the musings from *Markens grøde* about the "specks in the universe," Hamsun again invites those readers to his defense who are familiar with his opus. Within that landscape where "the mystery that is life" erases mundane "trifles," such as legal trials or acts of collaboration, all critical readers are reduced to dry sticks. "Trifles" such as the eulogy to Hitler or the present to Goebbels are likewise nonexistent in this beautiful poetic "life." The reception of the memoir ultimately confirms that readers, too, tend to dismiss these "trifles" and celebrate instead the Oriental-like nirvana that Hamsun seems to have attained.

Several portions of *Paa gjengrodde stier* talk about women and men. For instance, when the narrator retreats to a grotto in a forest where he composes a poem in praise of woman-as-primitive. Addressed to a "you," the poem celebrates broad hands and farming skills with corn and potatoes; it lauds the fact that the object of the poem neither reads books nor entertains dreams; that she is immersed in life's grandest miracle with all her senses; and that she is a mother who, even in old age, possesses a flaming smile.[55] Admitting that he is no Robert Burns, Hamsun nevertheless included the poem in his last book.

In a witty sketch a few pages later, Hamsun writes about the battle of the sexes, the battle that had occupied him during his most productive years. He gives us a bickering couple, Frode the painter and Olea the washer woman, who quarrel about everything—the crying baby, his art, her time, the money—yet they reconcile in the end. Hamsun's great insight into marital power relations is evident in his ironic wit, with which he targets both Olea and Frode. He lets Frode erase elements of a painting he is working on—St. John the Baptist's head on a platter and Herod's dancing daughter—and has him add some rather prosaic objects.[56] St. John the Baptist's head and Herod's daughter are certainly not randomly chosen objects but are in fact symbols of the great turn-of-twentieth-century battle of the sexes. Also important are the roles Hamsun assigns his characters (Frode as an artist and Olea as a homemaker and mother) and how masterfully he mixes reality and fiction. In real life, Hamsun imitates his fictional characters, reconciling with Marie who returned to Nørholm to nurse him during his final years. There is a whiff of fiction even in this as Marie's true feelings were revealed after her death: she did not want to be buried next to her husband.

It would seem that *Paa gjengrodde stier* is an ideal text to use to investigate the intertwinement of ideology and aesthetics, or the intertwinement of various discourses, in relation to Hamsun. It is therefore a puzzle as to why Atle Kittang leaves the work out of his study *Luft, vind, ingenting*. We can presume that Kittang excludes it because it ostensibly falls outside the scope of texts that undermine, through Hamsun's use of irony, "the novel's illusion."[57] But the reasoning behind Kittang's canon is circular at best and reductive at worst. Only ironic texts that undermine the "novel's illusion" are included, so it is easy to make the argument that ideology in Hamsun's texts is difficult to pinpoint and parallels between reality and fiction impossible to establish. *Paa gjengrodde stier* is a book in which Hamsun mixes discourses, and while the aesthetic prevails, the historical remains in place, pointing to Hamsun as a historical subject.[58]

Knut Hamsun supported the Nazi regime out of his convictions and based on his worldview, not because of his old-age feeble-mindedness, isolation, or even innocence. George Mosse's colorful metaphor describing how German men and women fell into the Reich's arms like ripe fruit from a tree fittingly describes Hamsun's willingness to collaborate.[59] Was Hamsun a Nazi? Yes. It is disappointing to see the discussion reignited within the humanities every so often, as if the legal indictment and Hamsun's actions and writings need additional clarification. He is no enigma, but it might well be that certain critics and readers crave a narrative about a mysterious genius. What Hamsun wrote and did leaves little doubt, and we should take him at his word when he insists, as he did in *Paa gjengrodde stier*, that he stands by his articles and his actions.

The Norwegian authorities, too, should have taken his articles and actions seriously and convicted him of the crimes with which he was charged. Whether or not he would then have served his term remains speculative. In a 1998 interview, Johs. Andenæs had the following comment regarding the criminal and civil charges against Hamsun:

> Seen in hindsight it would have been more orderly and better to go with criminal charges. Those might have shed better light on Hamsun's case than did the civil trial we eventually had, and in a criminal trial the discussion of Hamsun's membership in NS would not have been a decisive factor.[60]

How we approach and interpret the "case of Hamsun" is intricately connected to how we read and understand the role of writing and literature, and how we create canons. In their whitewashing, Hamsun apologists frequently claim that Hamsun's rich texts (often deemed ironic) deconstruct, refute, or undermine their own messages as well as Hamsun's basic reactionary worldview. This critique has to be countered on two fronts. First, not everything in Hamsun's texts is debunked.[61] While there are indeed many voices in Hamsun's texts, including those of implied narrators, they narrate, on a variety of levels and with varying intensity, contemporary social changes and reveal contemporary values. Second, Hamsun's protagonists are representatives of modernity who constantly juggle the issues of culture and nature. They are not necessarily at odds with the Nazi writing or Nazism itself, a movement often misunderstood as merely nostalgic instead of simultaneously and essentially modern. Recent research on sexuality and fascism by scholars such as

Dagmar Herzog refutes the myth that fascism is all about uniformity, obedience, and sexual repression. In part, it certainly was all that in relation to selected and targeted groups, but the average Aryan who conformed was encouraged to embrace what Hamsun would call "the mystery that is life" and celebrate joyful sexuality. In light of such findings, Ferguson's conclusion about the incompatibility of Hamsun and fascism is simply wrong.[62]

And then there are Hamsun's resolutions of his protagonists' fates, and his novels' conclusions. For example, Hamsun depicts Eselius from *Markens grøde* with depth, sympathy, understanding, and irony, but, ultimately, the fact that he remains a bachelor and is dispatched to America does express a view and a message on Hamsun's part. August, perhaps Hamsun's most beloved and Americanized protagonist, dies in an avalanche of his own entrepreneurial doing, and that is a message on Hamsun's part. The fact that Abel vanishes to America at the end of *Ringen sluttet* is not merely a random turn of events but rather an expression of despair. Another example is certainly Hamsun's depiction of women. There is not one positive portrayal of a creative, educated, ambitious, or single female protagonist in Hamsun's collected works who is depicted as happy and successful, and that, too, is a message. And finally, it is impossible to find a fully fleshed-out Hamsun protagonist who would opt for a job in a factory or defend democratic rights. Hamsun is far from being black-and-white about his values and is certainly aware of the complexities of life, yet he yearns and sometimes pushes for simple, reactionary resolutions.

The so-called "universalist" approach to reading Hamsun also needs to be mentioned. This type of reading waters down Hamsun's detailed and concrete (social) descriptions until they become nothing but a contrast between such broad concepts as illusion and reality, contrasts which ultimately do not convey much in relation to the richness of the text. Atle Kittang's 1994 "Knut Hamsun og nazismen" (Knut Hamsun and Nazism) is a typical text in this category.[63] Kittang considers it doubtful whether we can conclude from Hamsun's support for Hitler and Quisling that Hamsun was a Nazi in the political and ideological understanding of the term.[64] He probes the question of whether Hamsun's fictional oeuvre can in any way be called Nazi or fascist. Kittang is deeply skeptical, and, indeed, one has to agree that the relation between ideology and writing is an extremely complicated one.[65] Kittang's example is the postmaster from *Konerne ved vandposten* (Women at the pump) who is the moral voice in that novel yet becomes a tragic, dissonant figure caught between illusion and reality, learning and life.[66] Certainly, but why so lofty and exalted? The postmaster could be read more concretely as a tragic symbol of personal disappointment and family disintegration at a specific historical point in time. Given the importance of children and the generational continuity that they imply in Hamsun's later novels, we can read this novel in a more historical way, as a portrayal of the perceived loss of the organic Norwegian family.

Kittang's second argument is that Oliver, the castrate and symbol of degeneration as many critics have asserted, belongs to the company of so many other outsiders in Hamsun's oeuvre, just like Nagel or Glahn. Kittang writes, "but the castrate represents simultaneously the fantasy, the ability to imagine that which does not exist. . . . Precisely because he is castrated—empty, hollowed out—he has to build his own fantasy existence, and it is this that supports the life force in him."[67] Here, too, Kittang's universalist abstraction is problematic: Oliver is no outsider with creative imagination—an implied artist—but rather a survivor with a history of petty thefts and swindles who takes whatever his meager life apportions him. He is a sturdy and resistant individual who, in a Darwinian struggle of survival, manages to hang on. Moreover, there is a world of difference between Nagel, or even Glahn, on the one hand, and Oliver, on the other. The former two are 1890s protagonists who consciously reinvent themselves for new audiences, suddenly and rather inexplicably popping up, like apparitions from a fevered imagination. They harbor some artistic aspirations and have an agenda of sorts: Nagel as a musician and Glahn as a writer. Oliver lives, interacts, and survives among the people who have always known him and whom he cannot often cheat or dazzle with his occasional tales. He harbors no artistic aspirations, much less a plan or project. To read him as an outsider or an artist is to remove the focus from his everyday petty existence and lift him into a universal sphere where he does not belong.

That Oliver the castrate successfully raises his nonbiological children does not diminish the fact that Hamsun contrasts diverse families, biological and all others. By focusing on children fathered outside of marriage, the novel is essentially preoccupied with issues of fertility, erotic relationships, and a decrease in the expression of "appropriate" family values. Reporting on the social changes he observed or imagined, Hamsun depicts them in a complex way, yet essentially with a stamp of disapproval. Hamsun's overall framing of his novels and his charting of the dissolution of closely knit rural communities reflects his disillusioned worldview. The idealistic message that NS proclaimed about traditional values, natural women, and healthy children must have been appealing. The analysis of German scholar Ulrich Kriehn shows that Hamsun depicts children completely without irony.[68] The culture in which children are raised—women's sexual behavior, family, home, and heritage—was of utmost importance to Hamsun.

Hamsun's production includes not only his canonical novels in which many opposing voices form a rich tapestry, but also more uncomplicated works (*Ny jord*, *Redaktør Lynge*, perhaps even the *Segelfoss* books and, for the most part, his plays) in which his ideological stance is revealed, not utterly simplistically yet still rather unequivocally. Hamsun's articles offer insights into his reasoning over decades, although in these one has to consider that they comprise a different genre and are clearly referential. His correspondence constitutes yet another category displaying a variety of styles, depending on the addressee, Hamsun's reasons for writing, or simply his mood of the moment. Out of these rich sources, we can decode a set of values, an underlying ideology.

Hamsun's fiction is not fascist or Nazi per se, but it is not nonpolitical or nonideological, either. The world view expressed in fictional and aesthetically distinct form in his novels is articulated straightforwardly in his articles. The political views pointedly argued in his articles, in turn, spill over into his fiction. There is indeed an inner connection between the fundamental world view in Hamsun's oeuvre and his frame of mind before and during the war. Critical opinions have been overshadowed by enthusiastic supporters of Hamsun's literary genius for whom Hamsun's Nazism was easily relegated to the realm of politics.[69]

EPILOGUE

WHILE PUTTING THE FINISHING TOUCHES ON THIS MANUSCRIPT, I ENCOUN-
tered a Web site created by National Alliance and its *National Vanguard Magazine*, which featured "Knut Hamsun and the Cause of Europe," an article by Mark Deavin, a British historian of neo-Nazi leanings. I was struck by an odd sense of déjà vu. Deavin's is a well-researched, if brief, paper that uses much the same argument that I do, albeit to a radically different purpose. While I argue that many of Hamsun's views and actions were undemocratic and repressive and, since they supported the Nazi regime, also terribly wrong, Deavin defends and praises Hamsun for upholding the values of the New Europe. The article embraces Hamsun for his artistic and aristocratic vision, for his Germanic good looks, for his sense of racial identity, for his philosophy of nature, for supporting the rise of National Socialism in Germany, for sup-porting the cause and Hitler to the bitter end, and for never repenting. Deavin has no doubts, in other words, that Hamsun belongs to the Nazi world. In fact, he makes fun of Robert Ferguson and other "weak-kneed scribblers" and claims that the question "Was Hamsun a Nazi?" needs to be answered with a resounding "yes." He writes: "Not only was Knut Hamsun a dedicated supporter of Adolf Hitler and the National Socialist New Order in Europe, but his best writings—many written at the tail end of the nineteenth century—flow with the essence of the National Socialist spirit and life philosophy."[1]

Without giving too much legitimacy to Deavin's article, given its under-pinnings of racial hatred and dismissal of democracy, it is worth asking why such prominent scholars as Ferguson and, most recently, Hermundstad and Kolloen are so cautious about the question of whether or not Hamsun was a Nazi. It might be that in order to pronounce someone a Nazi, all facts and interpretations need to be carefully checked and checked again. My own checking provides a clear "yes."

Hamsun was always keenly interested in contemporary events and debates. We can discern a range of issues that preoccupied him during his long life and about which he expressed his opinion in a variety of texts belonging to dif-ferent genres. In order to develop a complete picture of what motivated him, I felt it necessary to examine a broad selection of his writing: from his earli-est articles and *Amerika* book to the necrology for Hitler, from his volumi-nous personal correspondence to letters to newspaper editors, from his plays and short stories to his novels. The following themes, drawn from Hamsun's work, reveal some of the preoccupations pertinent to a study of his character and the works he created: modern life and contemporary change, women's sexuality, children and families, racial or religious difference, and life in newly independent Norway. These themes are all connected insofar as they are tied to the question of national states and their borders, their inhabitants, and, inherently, to the question of identity.

Roughly in the middle of Hamsun's life, in 1905, Norway's union with Sweden was dissolved, which triggered reflection about Norwegian (and Swedish) identity. The redrawing of the national borders also contributed to tension over grazing areas for the Sami and the dispute over Greenland. Hamsun actively participated in the national conversations on all of these issues. In broader European terms, Hamsun considered the post–World War I Versailles Treaty, which changed Germany's borders and deprived it of its overseas colonies, extremely unfair to Germany. Finally and most tragically, he understood the Nazi takeover as a positive cultural revolution and Nazi Germany's imperial expansion into the fertile steppes of the East as a legiti-mate move to neutralize the Bolshevik threat and secure territory for future German generations.

Nazi expansionist policies mandated increasing birth rates for the master race and prohibited miscegenation. Women of the master race, as key ele-ments in this project, had to be persuaded, tamed, or coerced into cooperat-ing. Hamsun, as an advocate of natural fertility, consistently lobbied against women's rights in the modern enlightened sense. In his novels, he envisioned an erotic woman ultimately fulfilled only within a relatively simple and basic family life, as a mother. In his opinion, it was women who were the primary contributors to modern social disintegration, especially those who refused to have children, who fled the farms and found jobs in the cities, who became educated, who embraced modern fashion, or who deviated from the patriarchal norm in some other way. Of all his novels, *Markens grøde* articulates most clearly his normative vision of what a life ought to be. Braatøy's assessment that with *Markens grøde*, "Knut Hamsun in his art has come home" is a fitting one.[2]

In that ideal organic universe, every family member has an indispensable place and role. It was a universe that Hamsun also advocated in several of his articles. His novels can be read as portraits of the state of affairs after the collapse of the organic community. He considered women and their sexuality disruptive to traditional patriarchal arrangements and envisioned a variety of ways to tame them, although he also argued against Christian morality and in favor of natural and healthy fertility. The racial and cultural Others he invented brought to light and reinforced the raw disruptive force that women possess by virtue of being women. By coupling women with a variety of these Others, he exposed the danger that they allegedly posed to the balance of things. Simultaneously, Hamsun depicted his women as sexual and erotic beings. All of these feelings and opinions, including those on healthy sexuality, were axiomatic in Nazism. One can find these same sentiments expressed in Nazi-produced propaganda, which treated Hamsun's masterpiece *Markens grøde* as an integral part of the Nazi education campaign. These commonalities drew the Nazis to Hamsun and Hamsun to the Nazis.

Norway, as a sea-faring nation, has always had a certain amount of contact with non-Scandinavians, and images of difference and the primitive have been circulating in Scandinavian folklore and fiction for centuries. Knut Hamsun's ideas about difference coalesce with the traditional pattern up to a point. Beyond that point, Hamsun uses the primitive for his own projections: as a medium for his search for the source of creativity and erotic fulfillment, and for expressing his fears. Reading beyond the canonical novels has enabled me to consider previously marginalized protagonists and under-investigated aspects of Hamsun's work. Sometimes precisely because these works are not as accomplished as his canonical works, they reveal more about Hamsun personally and the angst within him. In addition, I have connected my investigation of the discourse of eugenics and race science to contemporary debates in cultural circles, situating eugenics within the politics of the day. While eugenics in the beginning of the twentieth century was a part of social planning in most European countries and the United States, it was the excesses of racial thoughts in the scientific debate over eugenics that later resulted in the pathological anti-Semitism of Nazism. Demonization and persecution of the Jews became the trademark of the Third Reich. And so it was in occupied Norway, where the homegrown NS party, in collaboration with the German occupiers, gathered up the Jews and sent them to concentration camps. Hamsun did not protest. Instead, he consistently wrote in support of the new Germany and in support of the German occupation of Norway.

My examination of a number of Hamsun's women protagonists reveals that Hamsun depicts them using a two-pronged strategy. On the one hand, the women needed to be interesting and sexual in order to whet the appetite of the author as well as the reader, yet on the other, that interesting uniqueness eventually had to be tamed, preferably by submission to motherhood. Hamsun's representation of the Native American primitive, which fits into the traditional Norwegian representation of the Other (from the Vinland Sagas to more contemporary emigration pamphlets), oscillates from "noble" myth to "savage" reality. Mariane Holmengrå, an interesting mixed-race character, is fleshed out as a complex protagonist but it might well be that it is her happy marriage to a Norwegian that tames her and provides for the happy ending. My analysis of Hamsun's writing about blacks confirms that American African male sexuality was powerfully attractive and terrifying to Hamsun at the beginning, middle, and end of his career.

I also expose Hamsun's exoticized fantasies of the Orient. Queen Tamara is essentially Hamsun's reflection on the pathology of modern marriage, her own marriage out of balance because of her power. At the same time, Hamsun's travel writings debunk Oriental fantasies, his self-conscious and ironic narrative expressing deep awareness of the Others.

The Sami are treated as local exotics, sometimes imbued with magic powers, while at other times the readers' expectations are mocked with descriptions of "boring" Sami who refuse to conform to readers' ideas. It is clear that throughout his life Hamsun insisted on upholding the idea of racial difference. However, this idea morphed into an attitude of exclusion and support for the politics of repression.

During the interwar and occupation periods, Hamsun reflected on some of his earlier attitudes, especially those related to sexuality and love. He saw in the New Germany a recipe for European revitalization, the cleansing of unwanted elements, and a return to a more traditional family. His belief that colonization was a kind of castration, as he described it when writing about Britons, corresponds with his understanding of the larger scheme of life. In the case of the British, he sympathizes with the native populations robbed of their sexual powers. In the case of the German expansion eastwards, he sees empowered German settlers battling Bolsheviks and barbarians from the East.

So where does all this lead us? If, with these insights in mind, one takes a fresh look at Hamsun's writings and actions, one must conclude that he wholeheartedly embraced "the whisper of the blood, the pleading of the bone." Thus, he responded to the beat of the German drum and the march of the Nazi boot. And he did so to the bitter end. I was stimulated to write this book when it became apparent that many movie viewers perceive Hamsun as a helpless victim of post–World War II circumstances and many readers shrug off his enthusiastic support of the Third Reich because of the seductive beauty of his prose. My study is offered as a corrective to studies that treat Hamsun's Nazi support as a peripheral and unimportant detail in an otherwise literary life of achievement.

NOTES

1 Introduction

1   Thorkild Hansen, *Prosessen mot Hamsun* (The trial against Hamsun) (Oslo: Gyldendal, 1978).

2   See Sten Sparre Nilson, *En ørn i uvær* (An eagle in storm) (Oslo: Gyldendal, 1960), and Thorkild Hansen, *Prosessen mot Hamsun.*

3   See Leo Löwenthal, "Knut Hamsun," in his *Literature and the Image of Man* (Boston: Beacon Press, 1956), 190–220. (This is a shortened version of Löwenthal's 1937 article, originally published in *Zeitschrift fur Sozialforschung* 6 [1937], 295–345.) Morten Giersing et al., *Det reaktionære oprør: Om fascismen i Hamsuns forfatterskap*, Skriftrække fra Institutt for Litteraturvidenskap 5 (Copenhagen: GMT, 1975); and Allen Simpson, "Knut Hamsun's Anti-Semitism," *Edda* 5 (1977): 273–93.

4   Atle Kittang's *Luft, vind, ingenting* (Oslo: Gyldendal, 1984). Other important sources are: Peter Kirkegaard, *Knut Hamsun som modernist* (Knut Hamsun as a modernist) (Copenhagen: Medusa, 1975); Mark Sandberg, "Writing on the Wall: The Language of Advertising in Knut Hamsun's *Sult*," *Scandinavian Studies* 71(3): 265–96; Jørgen Haugan, *Solgudens fall: Knut Hamsun, en litterær biografi* (The Sun God's fall: Knut Hamsun, a literary biography) (Oslo: Aschehoug, 2004); and Aasmund Brynildsen, *Svermeren og hans demon: Fire essays om Knut*

Hamsun, 1952–1972 (The dreamer and his demon: Four essays on Knut Hamsun) (Oslo: Dreyer, 1973).

5 Robert Ferguson, *Enigma: The Life of Knut Hamsun* (New York: Farrar, Straus and Giroux, 1987).

6 Žagar, "Hamsun's Black Man or Lament for a Paternalist Society: A Reading of Hamsun's Play *Livet ivold* through *Fra det moderne Amerikas aandsliv*," *Edda* 4 (1997): 364–79, and "Hamsun's *Dronning Tamara*," *Scandinavian Studies* 70 (1998): 337–58.

7 Ståle Dingstad, *Hamsuns strategier: Realisme, humor og kynisme* (Hamsun's strategies: Realism, humor, and cynicism) (Oslo: Gyldendal, 2003).

8 Petter Aaslestad, *Narratologi: En innføring i anvendt fortelleteori* (Narratology: An introduction to applied narrative theory) (Oslo: Cappelen, 1999), 97: "[J]eg vil hevde at jeg-fortelleren i Hamsuns noveller av og til ligger nærmere den faktiske Knut Hamsun enn det vi fremstiller det som, når vi vektlegger teksten som en autonom størrelse."

9 See Lars Frode Larsen, *Radikaleren. Hamsun ved gjennombruddet 1888–1891* (The radical: Hamsun at breakthrough, 1888–1891) (Oslo: Schibsted, 2001), 281–303.

10 Øystein Rottem, "Gåten Hamsun er en konstruksjon" (The enigma Hamsun is a construction), *Dagbladet*, July 24, 2000.

11 In "The Rhetoric of Defense in Hamsun's *Paa gjengrodde stier*," I argue that Hamsun employed and appropriated legal and aesthetic discourses to serve his political agenda and artistic vision. *Edda* 3 (1999): 252–61.

12 Gunvold Hermundstad, *Hamsun's polemiske skrifrer* (Hamsun's polemical writings) (Oslo: Gyldendal, 1998). Ingar Sletten Kolloen, *Hamsun Svermeren* (Hamsun, the dreamer) (Oslo: Gyldendal, 2003), and *Hamsun Erobreren* (Hamsun, the conqueror) (Oslo: Gyldendal, 2004).

13 Jørgen Haugan, *Solgudens fall: Knut Hamsun, en litterær biografi* (Oslo: Aschehoug, 2004).

14 Sverre Lyngstad, *Knut Hamsun, Novelist: A Critical Assessment* (New York: Peter Lang, 2005), xii.

15 "Ble ikke familien Hamsun svært hardt rammet? Ingen av dem hadde krummet et hår på noens hode. . . . Var ikke egentlig deres aktiviteter i 1940–45 mer innlegg i kulturdebatten enn ondsinnede bidrag til krig og vold?" Hans Fredrik Dahl, "Marie, Knut og de 55000 andre," September 2004 theater program for *Jeg kunne gråte blod*, *Riksteatret* (Oslo) 11–13, 12.

16 After Natasza P. Sandbu, a journalist for the main Oslo daily *Aften-posten*, wrote a critical article about the theater program (September 9, 2004), a debate flared up for a short time, a sign, in my opinion, that Hamsun still represents both a sore point and a blind spot for Norwegians. Sandbu has had only limited success in involving the cultural and academic elites in this debate, but silence is itself a kind of comment. See also Odd-Bjørn Fure's book, *Kampen mot glemselen: Kunnskapsvakuum i mediesamfunnet* (The battle against forgetting: Knowledge vacuum in the media community) (Oslo: Universitetsforlaget, 1997). Fure's book regrets the absence of an informed debate about recent history and its interpretations. Certainly Fure's comments are valid also in relation to a controversial figure like Hamsun.

17 Hans Fredrik Dahl, "Hamsun, Quisling og det norske rettsoppgjøret" (Hamsun, Quisling, and the Norwegian post-war trial), in *Hamsun i Tromsø: 11 foredrag fra Hamsun-konferansen i Tromsø, 1995*, ed. Nils M. Knutsen (Hamsun in Tromsø: Eleven lectures from the Hamsun conference in Tromsø, 1995) (Hamarøy: Hamsun-Selskapet, 1996), 9–26. See especially page 25.

18 "Det må i alle fall sies å være en alminnelig oppfatning nå, at vår store dikter fikk svi for sin brøde—hvis det da overhodet var noen brøde fra Hamsuns side at han holdt på det retten kalte 'sin særegne mening om politiske spørsmål' i en verden som pr. 1940 nok var blitt ham både for fjern og for komplisert." Ibid., 24.

19 Susanne Zantop, "Introduction" to *Colonial Fantasies: Conquest, Family, and Nation in Precolonial Germany, 1770–1870* (Durham, NC: Duke University Press, 1997), 5.

20 Edward Said, *Culture and Imperialism* (New York: Knopf, 1993), xii.

21 Anne McClintock, *Imperial Leather: Race, Gender, and Sexuality in the Colonial Context* (New York: Routledge, 1995), 5–7, 14.

22 Ibid., 7.

23 Elaine Showalter, *Sexual Anarchy: Gender and Culture at the Fin de Siècle* (New York: Viking, 1990); Rita Felski, *The Gender of Modernity* (Cambridge: Harvard University Press, 1995).

24 McClintock, *Imperial Leather*, 7.

25 Marshall Berman, *All That Is Solid Melts into Air* (New York: Penguin Books, 1988), 345–46.

26 Here, I will be using the term "race" as it was customarily and most broadly understood during Hamsun's time, namely, the late nineteenth

and early twentieth centuries. The concept of race emerged earlier, roughly toward the end of the 1700s, and referred to peoples with markedly different immutable physical characteristics. In Hamsun's time, races most often continued to be conceptualized in biological terms, but the view that racial differences were actually cultural differences also existed, resulting in a highly unstable concept. As I point out later, notably in chapter 1, there were widely differing views of what constituted a race, whether or to what extent physical traits could be automatically translated into mental capabilities, and so forth. Some researchers defended the view that there was only one race, and many agreed that there existed no pure races.

27   Zantop, *Colonial Fantasies,* 5.
28   Neil Kent, *The Soul of the North* (London: Reaktion Books, 2001).
29   Patricia Szobar, "Telling Sexual Stories in the Nazi Courts of Law: Race Defilement in Germany, 1933 to 1945," in *Sexuality and German Fascism,* ed. Dagmar Herzog (New York: Berghahn Books: 2005), 131–63.
30   "Blodets Hvisken, Benpibernes Bøn," reprinted in *Knut Hamsun Artikler,* ed. Francis Bull (Oslo: Gyldendal, 1939), 61.
31   McClintock, *Imperial Leather,* 36.
32   Here I use the word "Oriental" as it was generally understood in the nineteenth century, to refer to the peoples and cultures of the Near East (the Ottoman Empire, Persia, and the Caucasus), as well as, though less often, to India, China, and Japan.
33   Kwame Anthony Appiah, *"Race"* in *Critical Terms for Literary Study,* ed. Frank Lentricchia and Thomas McLaughlin (Chicago: University of Chicago Press, 1990), 276.
34   Fred R. Myers, "Introduction: Around and About Modernity, Some Comments on Themes of Primitivism and Modernism." In *Antimodernism and Artistic Experience: Policing the Boundaries of Modernity,* ed. Lynda Jessup (Toronto: University of Toronto Press, 2001), 14.
35   Ibid., 17.
36   Ibid., 13.
37   Ibid., 17.
38   Marianna Torgovnick, *Gone Primitive: Savage Intellects, Modern Lives* (Chicago: University of Chicago Press, 1990), 244.
39   Kathleen Stokker, *Folklore Fights the Nazis: Humor in Occupied Norway, 1940–1945* (Madison: University of Wisconsin Press, 1995); see especially pp. 147–48, 194, and 243 (notes 15, 16, and 17).

40 Ibid., 146.

41 Ibid., 147.

42 And then he lied about it. During a police visit to Nørholm on December 11, 1945, several of Hamsun's letters were confiscated and Hamsun was later asked about the letter and gift to Goebbels. Hamsun flatly denied having written any letters to Goebbels. See his letter dated January 25, 1946, to Asst. Chief of Police at Grimstad, Ragnar Thomassen. For the English translation of the letter, and further comments, see *Knut Hamsun: Selected Letters,* vol. 2, ed. Harald Næss and James McFarlane (Norwich, UK: Norvik Press, 1998), 237.

1 Discourses of Race and Primitivism in Scandinavia

Chapter epigraphs: (1) Letter from Hamsun to Terboven cited in Gunvald Hermundstad, ed., *Hamsuns polemiske skrifter* (Olso: Gyldendal, 1998), 243. (2) "August Strindberg," *Dagbladet,* December 10–11, 1883, in *Hamsuns polemiske skrifter,* 100.

1 Nancy Stepan, "Biological Degeneration: Races and Proper Places," in *Degeneration: The Dark Side of Progress,* ed. J. Edward, J. Chamberlin, and Sander L. Gilman (New York: Columbia University Press, 1985), 112.

2 Ibid., 116.

3 See the essays in Chamberlin and Gilman, eds., *Degeneration.* In his contribution to the collection, "Sociology and Degeneration: The Irony of Progress," Robert A. Nye examines the perception of Europe's decline and argues that "two binary oppositions dominated sociological discourse in the nineteenth century: progress/decline and social/individual" (49). He focuses on how the ideas of the individual, heredity, phrenology, and eugenics were all intertwined with this perceived decline. In his wide-ranging essay "Sexology, Psychoanalysis, and Degeneration: From a Theory of Race to A Race to Theory," Sander L. Gilman discusses the linkage of history, sexuality, and degeneracy in nineteenth-century thought; the sexuality of the adult European male was considered to be the most advanced, and the norm, while the sexuality of all others (the child, the primitive, the cretin, the deviant, the Jew, as well as women and blacks) was seen as retrogressive (87). In Freud's view, the term "degenerate" should not be used interchangeably with the term

deviant, since degeneracy was "an illness of civilization" (85); Freud's view was a departure from previous theories, however, as it was based on character rather than biological structures (82). Moreover, "Freud, like his great contemporary adversary Karl Kraus, repudiated the model of degeneracy because both saw within themselves the qualities ascribed to the Other" (89). Compare also Stepan's introduction to her book *The Hour of Eugenics: Race, Gender, and Nation in Latin America* (Ithaca, NY: Cornell University Press, 1991).

4 Stepan, "Biological Degeneration," 100.

5 I will discuss this book, as well as Hamsun's views on African Americans, in more detail in chapter 4.

6 Here I follow Nils Roll-Hansen's concise explanation, as presented in his article "Eugenic Sterilization: A Preliminary Comparison of the Scandinavian Experience to That of Germany," *Genome* 31 (1989): 890–95.

7 Ibid., 891.

8 Important resources with a special focus on Scandinavia include: Sonja Pollan, *Vi selv og de andre: Raseteorier i Norge for hundre år siden* (We and the others: Race theories one hundred years ago) (Oslo: Universitetsforlaget, 1978), and Andreas Martin Hansen's *Norsk folkepsykologi* (Norwegian folk psychology) (Kristiania: Jacob Dybwads Forlag, 1899). For more recent sources, see Olav Christensen and Anne Ericksen, *Hvite løgner: Stereotype forestillinger om svarte* (White lies: Stereotypical ideas about blacks) (Oslo: Aschehoug, 1992); Neil Kent's *The Soul of the North* (London: Reaktion Books, 2001)—especially the chapters "Germans, Xenophobia, and the Growth of National Identities" and "A Peculiar Institution: Slavery, the Tropics and Scandinavian Colonial Expansion"; Jon Røyne Kyllingstad, *Kortskaller og longskaller: Fysisk antropologi i Norge og striden om det nordiske herremennesket* (Short skulls and long skulls: Physical anthropology in Norway and the battle about the Nordic master man) (Oslo: Scandinavian Academic Press/ Spartacus Forlag, 2004).

9 Jon Alfred Mjøen, a trained pharmacist, is today known primarily for his idea to tax liquor based on its alcohol content and his warnings about environmental poisons, e.g., lead. He advocated many social support measures for mothers and was an early proponent of implementing a eugenics program in Norway. Although he was internationally respected as a eugenicist, he was an outcast from the Norwegian scientific establishment for several reasons: his unscientific and dilettantish approach

to the issues; his unreliable policy proposals, and his restrictive views on, among other things, birth control, abortion, and the right to procreate for some socially marginal groups. From 1919 to 1932, Mjøen published the journal *Den Nordiske Race* (The Nordic race). His book *Racehygiene* first appeared in 1914 (Kristiania: Jacob Dybwads Forlag) and was reissued in 1938.

10 He made this statement years later, reflecting on his earlier work. See Jon Alfred Mjøen, "Harmonic and Disharmonic Racecrossings," in *Eugenics in Race and State: Scientific Papers of the Second International Congress of Eugenics* (New York: Garland, 1922), 2:59.

11 Nils Roll-Hansen, "Norwegian Eugenics: Sterilization as a Social Reform," in *Eugenics and the Welfare State: Sterilization Policy in Denmark, Sweden, Norway and Finland*, ed. Gunnar Broberg and Nils Roll-Hansen (East Lansing: Michigan State University Press, 1996), 160. Here Roll-Hansen maps the historical development of eugenics in Norway, charts attitudes toward science, and discusses the interaction of science with politics. He defines two ways of viewing science. The instrumental view is an inherently amoral or "value-free" application of science rooted in Max Weber's philosophy, while the classical liberal view sees science as a fundamental cultural activity "aiming to gain knowledge of the world" and absorbing common sense into its analysis (152). Roll-Hansen focuses here on the problematic situation in the early twentieth century created by scientists who dabbled in politics, specifically in Norway, but also elsewhere in the world (e.g., Germany and the United States).

12 Ibid., 187.

13 Rune Slagstad, *De nasjonale strateger* (Oslo: Pax Forlag, 1998), 167: "[s]osialøkonomer, samfunnshygienikere og ingeniørarkiteker som ideologisk avantgarde."

14 During the German occupation of Norway, the conditions for sterilization were expanded to allow a doctor, or the head of a school, prison, or hospital, to initiate an order for sterilization. The new law also permitted the use of force (see Roll-Hansen, "Norwegian Eugenics: Sterilization as a Social Reform," 179). A sharp increase in the number of sterilizations occurred as a result. Initially less than 100 per year, this number jumped to 280 per year under Nazi rule. "Apparently, there was also little or no sabotage of the law by Norwegian doctors," Roll-Hansen observes (180).

15 Johan Scharffenberg, *Hovedpunkter i Arvelæren* (Main points of hereditary teaching) (Oslo: Der Norske Arbeiderpartis Forlag, 1932). Slagstad labels Scharffenberg a "mainstream" left-radical ideologue (*De nasjonale strateger*), 173.

16 Roll-Hansen, "Norwegian Eugenics: Sterilization as Social Reform," 157.

17 Carl Schiøtz, *Lærebok i hygiene* (Oslo, 1937).

18 Kristiania was the pre-1925 name of Oslo; before 1877, it was spelled Christiania.

19 See Roll-Hansen, "Norwegian Eugenics," 158–61.

20 Otto Lous Mohr, *Arvelærens grundtrek* (Kristiania: Norli, 1923), 62: "Vi har intet videnskabelig holdepunkt for at saa er tilfælde."

21 Otto Lous Mohr, "Menneskeavlen under kultur," *Samtiden* 37 (1926): 22–48.

22 Introduction (unpaginated): "Rasehygienikerne forlanger store barne-flokker. Kapitalistiske system gir meget liten plass for barn," Karl Evang, *Rasepolitik og reaksjon: Tillegg: Det norske forslag til sterilisasjonslov* (Race politics and the reaction: Supplement: The Norwegian proposal for a sterilization law) (Oslo: Fram Forlag, 1934).

23 See, for instance, ibid., 17: "Innenfor de fleste land står der her til tjen-este for de politisk reaksjonære krefter retninger innenfor rasehygienen som mere eller mindre fullstending stiller sig på det samme grunnlag. De mest fremtredende representater for disse rasehygienikere i Skandinavia er Jon Alfred Mjøen i Norge, og Herman Lundborg i Sverige." (In the majority of countries, factions within eugenics are willing to serve the politically reactionary forces by more or less fully supporting the same arguments. The most prominent representatives for these eugenicists in Scandinavia are Jon Alfred Mjøen in Norway and Herman Lundborg in Sweden.)

24 "Påstanden om at befolkningen i sin alminnelighet stadig blir av dår-ligere kvalitet, at den "degenererer" i det moderne samfund, går igjen hos praktisk talt alle moderne rasehygienikere, og danner et centralt punkt i hele deres tankegang . . . Noget bevis for denne påstand er de dog ikke i stand til å føre." Ibid., 82.

25 Evang quotes Dr. Hans Michael Frank, a German lawyer who was instrumental in defining post-1933 law in Germany. In October 1933, Dr. Frank proclaimed: "Tysk rett vil i fremtiden være raserett" (German law will be race law in the future). Ibid., 104.

26 I continue this discussion in more detail in chapter 7.

27 Nils Roll-Hansen, "Den norske debaten om rasehygiene," 283.

28 I discuss the Sami and the Jews separately in other chapters. Here, let me say only that both groups were subject to intense suspicion and persecution, although at different times.

29 Jenny Jochens, "Race and Ethnicity in the Old Norse World," *Viator* 30 (1999): 79–103, 81.

30 Ibid., 103.

31 Ibid., 102–3.

32 Ibid., 87.

33 For Jochens's detailed discussion of names and nicknames derived from the adjectives "black" and "ugly," see ibid., 97–99.

34 Ibid., 92.

35 See "Vikings Westward to Vínland: The Problem of Women," in *Cold Counsel: Women in Old Norse Literature and Myth*, ed. Sarah May Anderson and Karen Swenson (New York and London: Routledge, 2002).

36 Ibid., 131–32.

37 Ibid., 147.

38 Ibid., 147.

39 John Lindow, "Supernatural Others and Ethnic Others: A Millennium of World View," *Scandinavian Studies* 67 (Winter 1995): 8–31.

40 The Dakota Uprising of 1862—also referred to as the Minnesota Sioux Uprising, the Dakota Conflict, and the Little Crow War of 1862—was a series of battles between the Dakotas and the white settlers and took place from August to September of 1862 in the vicinity of New Ulm, Minnesota. The Dakotas, frustrated over broken promises stemming from the treaties with the U.S. government and the relentless encroachment of white settlers into areas traditionally theirs, wanted to defend their territories and way of life. In the October 1862 trial, more than 300 Dakotas were sentenced to death for their involvement in the uprising. After President Lincoln pardoned most of those involved, 38 Dakotas were hanged in Mankato on December 26, 1862.

41 See Betty Ann Bergland, "Indigenous Peoples and Norwegian Immigrants: Imagining *Vesterheimen* after the Dakota Conflict," presented at the Western History Association, 42nd Annual Conference, "Western Roots and Migration," Colorado Springs, Colorado, in 2002. Bergland concludes that the Dakota Conflict represents a turning point in

interethnic relations: while at least some of the pre-conflict stories told by the white settlers portrayed Native Americans with empathy, the situation changed drastically after 1862. The whites were harsher and crueler in their portrayal of Indians, thereby constructing a rationale for the landtaking. Other relevant articles by Betty Bergland include: "Norwegian Immigrants and 'Indianerne' in the Landtaking, 1838–1862," *Norwegian-American Studies* 35 (2000), 319–50); and "Norwegian Immigrants and the Dakota Conflict," presented at the 93rd Annual Meeting of the Society for Advancement of Scandinavian Studies, Minneapolis, Minnesota, 2003.

42 The Church remained a strong presence in the lives of the Scandinavian immigrants, with missionary outposts and church activities providing an important link between America and Scandinavia, as well as a crucial social network within the United States.

43 See Bergland, "Norwegian Immigrants and 'Indianerne' in the Landtaking, 1838–1862," 319–50.

44 See Sven H. Rossel, "The Image of the United States in Danish Literature: A Survey with Scandinavian Perspectives," in *Images of America in Scandinavia*, ed. Poul Houe and Sven Rossel (Amsterdam: Rodopi Press, 1998), 4.

45 Those by the Danes Vilhelm Topsøe (1872) and Henrik Cavling, the editor of *Politiken* (1897), were perhaps the most widely read.

46 Wilhelm Dinesen's memoirs of America originally appeared in 1889 as *Jagtbreve* (translated into English by Lise Lange Striar and Myles Striar as *Boganis, Letters from the Hunt* [Boston: Rowan Tree Press, 1987]), followed in 1892 by *Nye Jagtbreve* (New letters from the hunt). Dinesen's memoirs were republished in 1935 as *Boganis jagtbreve* (Copenhagen: Gyldendal).

47 It should be stressed that Hamsun's relationship to America was rather ambivalent, going beyond the mere equating of America with the darker side of modernity. Hamsun's writing effuses with the vitality of American journalism, which he praised on several occasions, and resonates with the rhythms of Walt Whitman's poetry. Hamsun himself displayed a certain mannerism that prompted the Norwegian writer Arne Garborg to call him a "Yankee type." (Quoted in Harald Næss's *Knut Hamsun og Amerika* [Knut Hamsun and America] [Oslo: Gyldendal, 1969], 224).

48 Sonja Mjøen, *Da mor var ung: Samtaler og minner* (When mother was

young: Conversations and memories) (Oslo: Cappelen, 1975), 188.

49 Ibid, 65–66.

50 Sigurd Ibsen, son of the playwright Henrik Ibsen, was a writer and politician. His wife Bergljot, the daughter of Bjørnstjerne Bjørnson, was an actress who performed with Max Reinhardt's theater in Berlin in 1916.

51 Sonja Mjøen, *Da mor var ung*, 20 and 27.

52 "Når det kom folk på besøk, eller ved festlige anledninger, måtte gjestene først forsamles i det store laboratorium som han hadde oppført som tilbygg til villaen. Før de gikk til bords, holdt han et foredrag om arvelighetsforskning for dem og forklarte sine fremtidsperspektiver, sine nye ideer. . . . Det var dessuten almengyldige problemer, populærvitenskapelige ideer som var lærerike for de fleste." Ibid., 61.

53 See Jon Alfred Mjøen, "Harmonic and Disharmonic Racecrossings," 41–61, in *Eugenics in Race and State: Scientific Papers of the Second International Congress of Eugenics*, vol. 2 (New York: Garland, 1922).

54 Ibid., 51.

55 Ibid., 60.

56 Ibid., 60 (Mjøen's emphasis).

57 Dag O. Bruknapp, "Idéene splitter partiet: Rasespørsmålets betydning i NSs utvikling" (The ideas split the party: The importance of the race question in the development of NS), in *Fra idé til dom* (From idea to judgment), ed. Rolf Danielsen and Stein Ugelvik Larsen (Bergen: Universitetsforlaget, 1976), 26.

58 Mjøen, "Harmonic and Disharmonic Racecrossings," 49.

59 Ibid., 59.

60 Konrad Simonsen, *Den moderne mennesktype* (Kristiania: Aschehoug, 1917).

61 In the early thirties, after controversy about some of the inflammatory statements in the book, Aschehoug publishing house took it off the market. Hamsun then urged Aschehoug to reprint it—see Hamsun's letters to the publishing house dated October 12 and October 27, 1932, in *Hamsuns brev*, vol. 5, p. 460, letter no. 2261, and p. 465, letter 2267). In the former, Hamsun refers to his own "lines of writing" (*noen linjer*) on Simonsen's book from the time when the book first appeared, which, he claims, "I still support" (*som jeg ennu står ved*). He adds that the book is "just as current as before" (*like aktuel som før*). Several days later, on October 31, 1932, he writes to Harald Grieg, Gyldendal's director, to ask him to either publish the book or engage Simonsen to write a new

one. On November 5, he writes to Grieg that he is himself willing to lend financial support to the publication of Simonsen's book (*Hamsuns brev*, vol. 5, 465–67).

62 See Konrad Simonsen, *Georg Brandes: Jødisk aand i Danmark* (Georg Brandes: The Jewish spirit in Denmark) (Copenhagen: Nationale forfatterres forlag, 1913).

63 Simonsen's inspiration came to a large extent from Walther Rathenau's works, *Zur Kritik der Zeit* (Criticism of the age; 1912), and *Zur Mechanik des Geistes; oder vom Reich der Seele* (On the mechanism of the mind; or, concerning the realm of the soul; 1913). See also Jeffrey Herf's discussion of Rathenau's ideas in *Reactionary Modernism* (Cambridge, UK: Cambridge University Press, 1984).

64 *Den moderne mennesketype*, 25. Simonsen writes: "Almost anybody can devote time to his private interests. . . . Machines reproduce artworks in limitless editions and at cheap prices, so that everyone can own them, and the same applies to books. Most people . . . are educated in bright school palaces, get educated in free libraries, museums, art collections and lectures." (Omtrent Enhver kan faa Tid til at dyrke sine private Interesser. . . . Ved Maskiner reproduceres Kunstværker i talløse Eksemplarer og til billige Priser, saa de kan blive hver Mands Eje, og det samme gælder Bøger. De fleste . . . opdrages i lyse Skolepaladser, udvikles ved gratis Biblioteker, Museer, Kunstsamlinger og Foredrag.)

65 "undersætsig, tætbygget, har bredt Ansigt, korte Lemmer, lav Pande, smaa øjne . . . og oftest havde mørkt Haar og dunklere Hud." Ibid., 41.

66 See chapter 7 for a fuller discussion of anti-Semitism.

67 "Gud skabte hvid Mand, og Gud skabte sort Mand, men Satan skabte Eurasieren." Ibid., 36.

68 "Ad videnskabelig Vej vil vi endvidere ved Racestudium og Iagttagelse af Menneskets Ydre, hvorved vi saa overordentlig let kan faa Besked om hans Evner og Begrændsning, udvikle vor hidtil saa primitive Menneskekundskab." Ibid., 112.

69 Jon Røyne Kyllingstad's *Kortskaller og langskaller: Fysisk antropologi i Norge og striden om det nordiske herremennesket* (Round skulls and long skulls: Physical anthropology in Norway and the battle over the Nordic master man) (2004) offers by far the best discussion of the theories and research on the physical appearance of Scandinavians and their corresponding mental makeups. I have already discussed briefly Andreas Martin Hansen's 1899 book *Norsk folkepsykologi*. See also

Sonja Pollan's 1978 discussion of Hansen's book, *Vi selv og de andre: Raseteorier i Norge for hundre år siden* (and note 9, this chapter).

70 Allen Simpson, "Hamsun's Anti-Semitism," *Edda* 5 (1977): 283.

71 I will discuss both novels in more details in chapter 3.

72 At the turn of the twentieth century, Scandinavia's population was about 14 million, compared with 40 million in France and 35 million in Britain. Population growth was strong and while about a quarter of the Scandinavian population emigrated to the United States, internal immigration to cities was also on the rise. Copenhagen was the largest of the Nordic capitals at this time with almost 500,000 inhabitants, followed by Stockholm (400,000), Kristiania (almost 230,000), and Helsinki (130,000), while Reykjavik was the smallest with 12,000 inhabitants. Kristiania's population more than doubled between 1878, when it was around 112,000, and 1900, when it reached 227,000.

73 Michelle Facos, *Nationalism and the Nordic Imagination* (Berkeley: University of California Press, 1980). Facos describes how the "relationship between a landscape and its inhabitants [as depicted by 1890s artists] was both historical and biomystical" (4). She links this with the notion, developed by Pierre Bourdieu, of *habitus* as the pervasive force that reinforces correct thoughts and practices within a culture, stronger than formal rules or norms.

74 Nina Witoszek, *Norske naturmytologier: Fra Edda til økofilosofi* (Norwegian mythologies about nature: From Edda to eco-philosophy) (Oslo: Pax Forlag, 1998). In an earlier article, "Der Kultur møter Natur: Tilfellet Norge" (Where culture meets nature: The case of Norway), *Samtiden* 4 (1991): 11–19, Witoszek argued persuasively that the typical Nature vs. Culture contrast does not apply to Norway, where Nature is equivalent to Culture.

75 Knut Hamsun, "Nabobyen," in *Knut Hamsun: Artikler, 1889–1928*, ed. Francis Bull (Oslo: Gyldendal, 1965), 120.

76 See T. K. Derry, *A History of Scandinavia: Norway, Sweden, Denmark, Finland, and Iceland* (Minneapolis: University of Minnesota Press, 1979).

77 For a discussion of the growing role of nature and travel in constituting the Norwegian national identity, see Marte Hvam Hult's *Framing a National Narrative: The Legend Collections of Peter Christen Asbjørnsen* (Detroit: Wayne State University Press, 2003). In early travel writing by Norwegians, we can discern what Hult calls "total disregard for

what today is called 'scenery'" (60). Hult detects a shift of perception toward landscape and scenery in the late eighteenth century (59).

78 See especially page 57. For more on this idea, see Hult's chapter 3, "A National Identity Built on Nature," in *Framing a National Narrative*.

79 Ibid., 85–86.

80 For a good discussion of Scandinavian colonial efforts in the New World, see the relevant chapters in Neil Kent's *The Soul of the North*. Kent examines the Nordic social, architectural, and cultural themes in the eighteenth and nineteenth centuries along two chronologies: political and cultural/scientific.

81 Ibid., 369.

82 Ibid., 367.

83 The painting is by Abraham Wuchters, circa 1650, and reproduced in Kent.

84 Kent, *Soul of the North*, 374.

85 In her book *Det nordiske i arkitektur og design: Sett utenfra* (The Nordic in architecture and design: Seen from outside) (Oslo: Arkitektens Forlag og Norsk Arkitekursforlag, 1997), Ingeborg Glambek explores the reception of the idea of "the Nordic" by examining the individual Nordic countries' participation in nineteenth-century world exhibitions. She notes, for instance, that the Nordic countries stood out from the bulk of the participants at the 1900 Paris world's fair. Though not on a par with more distant participants, they were nevertheless perceived as "special and a bit exotically exciting" (*som spesielle og litt eksotisk spennende*, 42). This was especially true for Norway, Sweden, and Finland, while Denmark was seen as a smaller and sweeter version of Germany (42). The Scandinavian countries were viewed both in terms of a homogenous Nordic whole and as individual states. Glambek points out that most reviewers saw Nordic art as both modern and anchored in national traditions, although their rhetoric went little beyond mentioning magnificent nature, dramatic weather, and so forth. The French reviewers were more critical, while the more positive Germans emphasized the unity of a mutual Germanic cultural tradition. According to Glambek, the Germans wanted to see their own idealized image in the North (43).

86 For a good overview, see, for instance, Roald Nasgaard, *The Mystic North: Symbolist Landscape Painting in Northern Europe and North America 1890–1940* (Toronto: Art Gallery of Ontario and University of Toronto Press, 1984).

87 Werenskiold, one of the most technically accomplished Scandinavian painters of his time, achieved his greatest fame with his illustrations of Norwegian fairy tales. In these pictures, now classics for children and adults alike, *trolls, nisse, huldre,* and other magical creatures populate nature.

88 Roald Nasgaard, *The Mystic North,* 6.

89 See Yrjö Hirn, "Kalevalaromantiken och Axel Gallen-Kallela" (Kalevala romanticism and Axel Gallen-Kallela), in *Lärt folk och landstrykare i det finska Finlands kulturliv* (Educated people and vagabonds in the Finnish-Language cultural life of Finland) (Helsinki: Wahlström and Widstrand, 1939), 205.

90 See Per Arneberg, "Brekkesaga," in *Norsk skrivekunst: En essay-antologi* (Norwegian art of writing: An essay anthology), ed. Erling Nielsen (Copenhagen: Hans Reitzel Publishing House, 1958). Arneberg writes about Per Christian Asbjørnsen's texts as "having opened a view into a 'closed world, a kind of Scandinavian Tibet.'" (292).

91 Writers, too, contributed to the popularity of the Nordic image on the continent. Bjørnstjerne Bjørnson's short tales set in an idealized Norwegian countryside were widely translated in Europe. The life portrayed in these tales is a far cry from that revealed in the data collected by the sociologist Eilert Sundt who studied the health, work, and family habits of Norwegians and found a rural population that was unhygienic, alcoholic, promiscuous, and idle. Still, Bjørnson was an early representative of what was seen as a vigorous and balanced life close to nature. Several decades later, Jonas Lie was in vogue in Europe with his tales of the supernatural North. And, of course, there was Henrik Ibsen, whose early radical plays focusing on social issues caused scandals across Europe; his later plays, however, shifted the focus to an examination of the irrational primeval forces of life.

92 Fridtjof Nansen was active in several areas. Among his activities as a polar explorer, his skiing trip across Greenland (1888–89) and his North Pole expedition with the ship *Fram* (1893–1896) became legendary. Two of his books, *Paa ski over Grønland* (The first crossing of Greenland; 1890) and *Eskimoliv* (Eskimo life; 1892) describe in detail, among other topics, the culture of the Inuits and how they coped with harsh living conditions. In the interwar period, when Norway and Denmark both claimed Greenland, Nansen positioned himself on the side of the Inuits. As a diplomat at the beginning of the twentieth century,

Nansen contributed significantly to the acceptance by the Western powers of the idea of Norwegian independence. Nansen later worked for the United Nations on humanitarian and refugee projects.

93 Riksmål, the language of the realm, was the official language during the union of Denmark and Norway (1380–1814), essentially Danish. Landsmål, the language of the countryside, was created as a written language by the scholar Ivar Aasen during the mid-nineteenth century, primarily from the dialects of the western and central rural districts of Norway. In 1929, *landsmål* became *nynorsk*. As Derry writes, "In Norway, where the ardent nationalists had regarded the University of Oslo as the citadel of the conservative bureaucracy, their triumph found expression in democratic changes in the curriculum: in 1896 Norwegian educationists pioneered the removal of Latin from its traditional place as an essential requirement of university entrance, and in 1907 they introduced a unique stumbling-block for urban and upper-class opponents of *landsmål* by elevating the artificial language of a rural minority into a compulsory matriculation subject" (*A History of Scandinavia*, 268).

2   Hamsun's Women as Scapegoats for Modernity's Sins

Chapter epigraph: Letter to Marie in *Knut Hamsuns brev 1908–1914*, vol. 3, p. 163, letter no. 919.

1 The Constitution of 1814 prohibited women from owning a business, property, or money, and assigned them to the guardianship, first, of their father, and later of a brother or husband. For specifics on the incremental improvements in all aspects of women's lives between 1814 and 1913 and beyond, see the brochure, "Milestones in Norwegian Women's History," published by the Norwegian Centre for Gender Equality (Likestillingsenteret, no date). I would add that sociologists and historians generally agree that women in rural and coastal areas had always been actively involved in the household and were therefore more or less equal partners with their husbands in decision-making regardless of what the law said. The long fishing and hunting seasons, which took the men away from home, left women in charge of the farm during their husbands' absence and thus in the position of being responsible for many short- and long-term financial dealings.

2 Of the numerous books and articles on the 1890s in Scandinavia, these

were the most informative to me: *100 år etter: om det litterære livet i Norge i 1890-åra*, ed. Harald Bache-Wiig and Astrid Sæther (Oslo: Aschehoug, 1993); Per Thomas Andersen, *Dekadanse i nordisk litteratur, 1880–1900* (Oslo: Aschehoug, 1992); *Fin(s) de Siècle in Scandinavian Perspective: Studies in Honor of Harald S. Næss*, ed. Faith Ingwersen and Mary Kay Norseng (Columbia, SC: Camden House, 1993); George C. Schoolfield, *A Baedeker of Decadence: Charting a Literary Fashion, 1884–1927* (New Haven: Yale University Press, 2003). Finally, Stefanie von Schnurbein's *Krisen der Männlichkeit: Schreiben und Geschlechterdiskurs in skandinavischen Romanen seit 1890* (Göttingen, Wallstein Verlag, 2001) offered many intriguing insights.

3 See Susan Groag Bell and Karen M. Offen, eds., *Women, the Family, and Freedom: The Debate in Documents, Volume Two, 1880–1950* (Stanford, CA: Stanford University Press, 1983), which includes a section on the new Woman of the North, 18–32.

4 Of these artists, Hans Jæger (1854–1910) is perhaps the least known today. His *Fra Kristiania-bohêmen* aroused such a scandal that it was impounded and Jæger imprisoned. In this and his trilogy of *Syk kjærlihet* (Sick love; 1893), *Bekjendelser* (Confessions) (1902), and *Fængsel og fortvilelse* (Prison and despair; 1903), all of which were banned in Norway, Jæger advocated the Bohemian lifestyle in subversion of the establishment and traditional culture. His promotion of "free love" and frank discussions of sexuality caused the otherwise weak text to be banned. Jæger, hopeful that the Bohemian lifestyle would eventually prevail, can be likened to Oscar Wilde and other continental bohemians. Hamsun was a reluctant participant in the Bohemian culture, and only to a point. He always was a hard worker himself, and he had a decidedly ambivalent view of artists and was disdainful of those whom he perceived to be merely discussing issues in cafés.

5 Neil Kent, *The Soul of the North*, 80.

6 Ibid., 89.

7 In Part 3 of *Sult* (Hunger), in the well-known meeting between the Hunger-man and Ylajali in her home, Hamsun displays a deep knowledge of the social roles men and women were expected to play.

8 See *Sexual Anarchy* (London: Viking Penguin, 1990). Showalter discusses in detail an anonymous satire published in 1882 in England, *The Revolt of Man*, as representative of this backlash. The book depicts a utopian, matriarchal England in which women are judges, doctors, and

the like, while men are relegated to manual jobs and forced to marry older women. The primary message of this book is that women cannot create, compose, write books or be creative in general. After a male rebellion, women are put into their proper places as home-keepers.

9   See Dijkstra, *Idols of Perversity: Fantasies of Feminine Evil in Fin-de-Siècle Culture* (New York: Oxford University Press, 1986).

10 Ibid., "Introduction" and, for instance, page 209.

11 Rita Felski, *The Gender of Modernity* (Cambridge: Harvard University Press, 1995), 92.

12 Pil Dahlerup, *De moderne gennembruds kvinder* (Copenhagen: Gyldendal, 1983). "Modern Breakthrough" was a movement in Scandinavian literature, culminating in the 1870s and 1880s, that debated burning contemporary social issues.

13 Jørgen Lorentzen, *Mannlighetens muligheter* (Masculinity's possibilities) (Oslo: Aschehoug, 1998).

14 Birgitta Holm, "Den manliga läsningens mysterier: Knut Hamsuns roman 100 år efteråt" (The mysteries of the male reading: Knut Hamsun's novel a hundred years later), *Edda* 3 (1992): 261–70.

15 "Att bereda kvinnor plats i en värld där mannen var norm, där manlig rationalitet härskar, intresserade honom inte. 'Store mænd' är inte efterföljansvärda i hans värld. . . . Men feminist var han, i *Mysterier*. Feminist ungefär som Irigaray. Det Hamsun vill röja plats for är det som går emot en patriarkal logik: 'Modsigelserne,' 'Inkonsekvensen' det som är förträngt av manlig rationalitet och fallisk logik." Holm, "Den manliga läsningens mysterier," 270.

16 See Patricia Berman, *Munch and Women: Image and Myth* (Alexandria, VA: Art Services International, 1997).

17 J. W. McFarlane, "The Whisper of the Blood: A Study of Knut Hamsun's Early Novels" in Modern Languages Association Papers 1956, vol. 71. See also Harald Næss, who in *Knut Hamsun* repeatedly refers to Hamsun as a misogynist, while Robert Ferguson, in *Enigma: The Life of Knut Hamsun*, is more forgiving, although extremely observant regarding Hamsun's treatment and description of women.

18 Ibid., 591.

19 Monika Žagar, "How Knut Hamsun Imagines Juliane and Her Speech: Hamsun's Play *Livet Ivold*," in *Gender-Power-Text: Nordic Culture in the Twentieth Century*, ed. Helena Forsås-Scott (Norwich, England: Norvik Press, 2004).

20 Rita Felski, "Tragic Women." Address to the conference "After the Decline of the 'Master Narrative': Rethinking Modernism, Art, and Politics in Germany and Scandinavia, 1850–1950," held at the University of Minnesota, Twin Cities, April 25–27, 2002; with the permission of the author.

21 Pål Bjørby, "Eros and Subjectivity: Knut Hamsun's *Pan* and Ragnhild Jølsen's *Rikka Gan*," in *Fin(s) de Siècle in Scandinavian Perspective*, 123–40.

22 Robert Ferguson, *Enigma*, 206.

23 *Knut Hamsuns brev*, vol. 3, p. 181, letter no. 924.

24 "Herregud Marie om du og jeg havde truffet hverandre da og der ikke havde været saa forfærdelig en Forskel i Alderen og vi havde blit glad i hverandre og giftet oss! Og faat hverandre saa ofte vi vilde. Og arbejdet ude i fri Natur og jeg ikke været nervøs og blit slem mod dig og grint. For jeg skulde lissom været Søn paa Nabogaarden og ikke havde med sligt Tull som Bøger og Skrivning at gøre. Og din og min højeste Ærgærrighed skulde blit at grejes godt med Gaarden og faa vakre stærke Børn." Ibid., p. 195, letter no. 929.

25 "Du gik her og var et prægtig Østerdalsbarn, der er ikke Skidt og Sludder og Konster her, og det ved du inderst inde for du har søgt tilbage til din oprindelige Natur . . . Derfor vilde jeg ogsaa saa gærne at vi ikke skulde være længe i Byen, men komme os hid hvor du før har lært at leve et godt og trofast og rensligt Liv." Ibid., p. 198, letter no. 930.

26 The play is examined in more detail in chapter 4.

27 "Jeg vilde gjerne forsøke i boken min å gi en antydning av hvordan hans mening, hans vilje gjaldt i alle ting. Hvordan han tyranniserte mig og drev mig fra skanse til skanse i ungdommen, fordi jeg på alle vis var avhengig av ham, noe han jo sørget for at jeg blev. . . . men jeg vil jo heller ikke gi det bildet av ham, at han med vilje tråkket mig utover under skosålene sine, holdt mig i evig angst for hvad han kunde finde på, aldri trygghet, i alle år et liv med hjertet i halsen." Birgit Gjernes, *Marie Hamsun: Et livsbilde* (Marie Hamsun: A life portrait) (Oslo: Aschehoug, 1994), 142.

28 "Jeg husker min Knut gav mig sine Feberdigte en gang i forlovelsestiden. Det som bet sig fast hos mig var linjene: Da er det jeg som kommer, det er jeg som er til hest, og du som løper hund ved min side. Hvor ofte fikk jeg ikke leilighet til å minnes de ord. Og tross alt, jeg angrer ikke på noget." Ibid., 150.

29 Encouraged by Bjørnstjerne Bjørnson, Ellen Key published the contro-
    versial books *Love and Marriage* and *The Century of the Child*, both
    of which gained her considerable world fame. Two of her documents are
    included in the important anthology *Women, the Family, and Freedom*:
    The Debate in Documents, vol. 2: *1880–1950*, ed. Susan Groag Bell and
    Karen M. Offen (Stanford: Stanford University Press, 1983).

30 See Ellen Key's "A New Marriage Law" in *Women, the Family, and
    Freedom*, 196–200. Originally published in Swedish in 1904, as the
    opening text of Key's *Lifslinjer*.

31 Ibid., 197.

32 Ibid., 200.

33 See, for instance, Sølvi Sogner's essay "Fra flerbarns-til fåbarnsfamilier"
    (From multi-child to few-child families), in *Kvinnenens kulturhistorie:
    Fra år 1800 til vår tid* (Women's cultural history: From year 1800 to
    our own time) (Oslo, Bergen, Stavanger, Tromsø: Universitetsforlaget
    AS, 1985), vol. 2, 160–64. Sogner writes that "children born outside
    marriage constituted only 2–7% of all births before the demographic
    decrease" (Barn født utenfor ekteskap utgjorde bare fra 2–7% av alle
    fødsler før fruktbarhetsfallet), 161.

34 "Kvinnehistorikere har hevdet at fruktbarhetsfallet fra slutten av
    1800-tallet var et viktigere og mer meningsfylt periodeskille i kvinners
    historie enn mer tradisjonelle vendepunkt ut fra politisk utvikling. Da
    seksualitet og reproduksjon ble atskilt, endret kvinnenes situasjon seg på
    grunnleggende vis." Ibid., 160.

35 "Omkring århudreskiftet kan vi således spore en ung generasjon av
    kvinner med et annet syn på ekteskapet enn det deres mødre hadde
    akseptert. Blant de faktorer som de unge så annerledes på var spørsmålet
    om barnetallet. . . . Fra 1900 til 1910 ble fødselstallet på vestkanten av
    Kristiania redusert med 36%." Ida Blom *Barnebegrensning: Synd eller
    sunn fornuft* (Childbirth control: Sin or common sense) (Oslo: Univer-
    sitetsforlaget, 1984), 122.

36 "i et klima hvor omtale og bruk av prevensjon snarere ble frarådet enn
    tilrådet." Ida Blom, *Barnebegrensning: Synd eller sunn fornuft*, 52.

37 "Andre studier av fødselshyppigheten i ekteskap har vist at fallet tok til
    også i agrare distrikter på Vestlandet og i Nord-Norge allerede i 1890-
    årene." Ibid., 40.

38 "Selv i en saa afsidesliggende Del af Landet som Nordland, kan jeg
    oplyse at Kjendskab til den Slags Ting (preventive midler) slet ikke er

sjelden." Ibid., 48.

39 "Tvertimot kan det være naturlig å tenke seg at 'beherskelse' og 'forstand'—i form av avbrutt samleie eller seksuell avholdenhet—har vært et meget brukt middel til å begrense antallet svangerskap innenfor rammen av familien." Ibid., 53.

40 "[N]oen avgjørende faktor bak fallet i fødselshyppigheten kan kvinnenes yrkesaktivitet ikke ha vært." Ibid., 113.

41 "mikroskopiske." Ibid., 116.

42 "[A]t for alle de kvinner som fortsatt bodde på landsbygda, førte det dobbelte arbeid med barn og hjem på den ene siden, med fjøs, fjærkre, vannbæring, bærplukking, osv. på den annen, ikke til de samme praktiske og ideologiske konflikter som tilfellet var for deres medsøstre i de voksende byene. På landsbygda fortsatte ennå lenge den gamle samfunnsformen, hvor kjønnenes ulike arbeidsoppgaver hadde mindre betydning. Men også for disse kvinnene gjaldt det selvsagt at deres formelle rettigheter var beskåret av lovens bokstav." Ida Blom, "Kvinnen—et likeverdig menneske?" (Woman—an equal person?), *Norges Kulturhistorie*, vol. 5: *Brytningsår: Blomstringstid* (Norway's cultural history: Time of change, time of flourishing) (Oslo: H. Aschehoug, 1980), 56.

43 "Noen av de som var opptatt av spørsmålet, oppfattet utviklingen, så sped den enn var, som en trusel mot kvinnens traditionelle funksjoner som hustru og mor." Ida Blom, *Barnebegrensning-synd eller sunn fornuft*, 116.

44 Reprinted in *Hamsuns polemiske skrifter*, 116–19.

45 "Når de kvindeeksemplarer dør, der skjød op i syttiårene . . . så er vi kommet ind i et nyt århundrede, der anlægger andre moder. Da bliver det kanske ikke længer sa "kjekt" for kvinden at være karslig." Ibid., 118–19.

46 See *Hamsuns polemiske skrifter*, 95–111.

47 "Kvindeseier" (Woman's victory), in the collection *Stridende liv* (Struggling life), 1905. "Macabre" is Næss's choice of adjectives (see Næss, *Knut Hamsun*, 82).

48 See Elisabeth Oxfeldt, "Orientalism on the Periphery: The Cosmopolitan Imagination in Nineteenth-Century Danish and Norwegian Literature and Culture," Ph.D. diss., University of California, Berkeley, 2002, 192.

49 "Meget af Snærperiet i Amerikas Kunst kan forklares deraf, at et stort Flertal af dem, som sysler med Kunst er *Kvinder*. Denne Omstændighed

har Betydning, den er en vejvisende Forklaring af et helt Folks Kunstanskuelse. Kvinderne i Amerika leder Kunst i deres Land, ligesom Tysklands Kvinder nu leder *deres* Literatur—og lægger den øde ved deres Penneførhed. Enten er det Døttre af Rigmænd, som har lært sin Kunst i et af de 88 amerikanske Akademier, eller ogsaa er det gifte Koner, some af egen Drift, af Kedsomhed og af god Tone har givet sig til at kunste hjemme. At gøre Malerier er i Amerika simpelthen et kvindeligt Haandarbejde; for at blive oppmærksom herpaa, behøver man ikke at besøge ret mange Familjer derover. Det synes næsten, som om de amerikanske Kvinder tror at skylde sig selv at sætte et Par Høns ind in verden. Den feminine Indflydelse, som igen er dannet af Aanden fra Boston, virker ved sin rige Mængde ind paa al Landets Kunst. Og ikke blot de bildende Kunstnere, men ogsaa Digterne og Skuespillerne skatter under den. I Amerika siger Kvinden, hvor Skabet skal staa." Hamsun, *Fra det moderne Amerikas aandsliv*, 78. Excerpts are from the Barbara Gordon Morgridge translation, which appeared as *The Cultural Life of Modern America* (Cambridge: Harvard University Press, 1969), 86.

50 Hamsun, *The Cultural Life of Modern America*, 128. "Ægte Amerikanerinder har intet Hus at bestyre, ingen Mand at hjælpe, ingen Børn at opdrage; i de to første Aar af deres Ægteskab hænder det maaske, at de faar indtil to Børn—ved Uforsigtighed; saa faar de ingen flér. Som de nu sidder i Kirkerne i den unge 30–35 Aars Alder, har de ingen børn at stræve med længer. De har absolut intet at stræve med, de er arbejdsløse Mennesker. Hvad de har at ivaretage er om Formidaggen at pleje deres Nerver, til Klokken to at male Kunstværker, til Klokken seks at læse "Onkel Tome Hytte," til Klokken otte at spadsere. Timeplanen for deres daglige Virksomhed er imidlertid skiftende. Tre eller fire Gange i Ugen sér de sig maaske nødt til—trods den Kunstnedlæssethed, som tynger dem—at stjæle fattige otte a elleve Timer hver Dag til Deltagelse i Kvindekongresser . . . Amerikanerindene sér sig altsaa istand til følgende Livsgærning i denne Verden: At have Nerver, male Kunstverker, nyde Negerpoesi, spadsere og være i Kongresser. Derimod sér de sig ikke Tid til at føde Børn." *Fra det moderne Amerikas aandsliv*, 115–16.

51 See Monika Žagar, "Hamsun's Black Man, or Lament for Paternalist Society: A Reading of Hamsun's Play *Livet ivold* through *Fra det moderne Amerikas aandsliv*," *Edda* 4: 364–79.

52 See Hamsun, *The Cultural Life of Modern America*, 128. "[De sér] sig ikke Tid til at føde Børn. Ved at sætte to Papirhøns ind i Verden, mener

de at have opfyldt sin Modermissjon. De vil paa Sæt og Vis undgaa at faa Børn; de gider ikke at amme Børn, de vil ikke have den Plage. Følgen er, at Yankeernes hele Opfindelsestalent sættes i Sving, forat hitte paa Midler, der kan forebygge Børnefødsler. Disse Midler kendes lige sa nøje af Amerikas Kvinder, som Luthers Katekismus kendes af vore. Gaar det, trods disse Midler alligevel galt—ved Uforsigtighed, saa er der dog en Raad: I det samme Land, hvor en Mand i Moralens Navn dømmes til Fængsel for en Teori om fri Kærlighed, dér averterer Lægerne aabenlyst sin Specialitet i Fosterfordrivelser. . . . Amerikanerkvinderne besøker dem. Hænder der nu, at det allikevel ikke gaar efter Ønske—man kan jo komme en Bagatel af fire, fem Maaneder *for sent* til Lægen—saa maa altsaa Ulykken ske. Der kommer et veritabelt Barn til Verden, rent ud sagt et uforskammet faktisk Barn. Og det er en Ulykke. Der følger ingen Formandsplads i Kvindekongressen med et saadant Barn. Og det ruer Moderen." *Fra det moderne Amerikas aandsliv,* 116.

53 Around the turn of the century, the topic of sexuality was still mainly taboo, but the question of birth control was debated in most Norwegian womens' magazines, especially in *Urd, Nylænde* and *Husmoderen.* It was during an exchange of opinions in Nylænde in 1901 and 1902 that Katti Anker Møller used this rather notorious expression. Quoted in Blom, *Barnebegrensning-synd eller sunn fornuft,* 119.

54 See *Knut Hamsuns brev,* vol. 4, p. 205, letter no. 1472.

55 "Nu hadde vesle Sølvhorn kalvet, gjeiterne kidet og sauerne lammet, det vrimlet av småfæ i bumarken. Og hva med menneskene? Eleseus gik alt på sine ben hvor han vilde og lille Sivert var kristnent. Inger? Hun laget sig visst til med barn igjen, hun var så frodig. Hvad var endda en gang et barn for hende? Ingenting- [. . .]-nu var det hendes tid, hun utfoldet sig, hun stod idelig i flor og gik med barn." *Samlede verker* (Oslo: Gyldendal norsk forlag, 1963), vol. 7, 167; the translations are mine, yet based on W. W. Worster's 1921 English translation, *Growth of the Soil.*

56 "den muskelsterke og utholdende kvinnen var ute av motebilde," Brit Berggreen writes in "Fra kvinnebonde til bondekvinne" (From woman farmer to farming woman), in *Kvinnenes Kulturhistorie,* 107–13, 113.

57 Compare the unfavorable portrayal of Barbro and Inger with the attitude Hamsun displayed in his article "Barnet" (The child), published in *Morgenbladet* on January 16, 1915. Hamsun lobbied for the death penalty by hanging for infanticidal mothers (and fathers); he simultaneously challenged liberals and moderates who had supported more liberal

criminal law for such offenses and introduced welfare support for single mothers. "Murderous mothers should pay dearly," he insisted. "We need to be able to afford living, well-built children" (Her maa være Dyrtid paa Mordersker. Vi maa ha god Raad paa levende, velskapde Børn). After protests by prominent politicians and intellectuals, and numerous letters to the editor of every major newspaper in Norway, Hamsun published six more articles defending his position. He would not budge. Quote is from Harmundstad, *Hamsuns polemiske skrifter*, 202.

58 "Da sa Inger: Hvad kan det gjøre om han kommer? Han kan ikke skade mig mere. —Oline reiste ører: Nå har du lært et råd for det? —Jeg får ikke barn mere, sa Inger . . . Hvorfor skulde ikke Inger få flere børn? Hun var ikke uvenner med sin mand, de var ikke hund og kat, så langtfra. . . . Hun kunde ha været over femti år og fåt børn, men som hun stod og gik var hun kanske ikke engang firti. Alt hadde hun lært på anstalten—hadde hun også lært nogen kunster med sig selv? Hun kom so opstuderet og velundervist hjem fra omgangen med de andre mordersker, hun hadde kanske også hørt et og annet av herrerne, av vagten, lægerne. Hun fortalte Isak en gang hvad en ung medicinmand hadde sagt om hele hendes udåd: Hvorfor skulde det være straf for å dræpe børn, ja endog sunde børn, endog velskapte børn? De var ikke andet end som kjøtklumper." *Markens grøde*, 235.

59 "å det var en god tid, han hugget favnved og Inger så på, det var hans bedste tid. Og når mars og april kom så blev han og Inger gale efter hverandre, akkurat som fugler og dyr i skogen, og når mai kom så sådde han kornet og satte poteten og trivedes døgnet rundt. Det var arbeide og søvn, kjærlighet og drømmeri, han var som den første storoksen, og den var et vidunder, stor og blank som en konge når den kom. Ibid., 367.

60 "mangel på fristelser." Ibid., 318.

61 "Inger? Hun var i bærmarken, hadde været i bærmarken helt siden Isak gik tilfjelds, hun og Gustaf, svensken. Det gamle menneske, hun var blit så tullet og forelsket. . . . Kom og vis mig hvor det er multer, sa Gustaf, hjortron! sa han. Hvem kunde stå for slikt! Hun løp ind i kammerset og var både alvorlig og religiøs i flere minutter, men der stod han utenfor og ventet, verden var hende like i hælene, det blev til at hun ordnet håret og speilet sig omhyggelig og gik ut igjen. Hvad så, hvem vilde ikke ha gjort det samme? Kvindfolk kjender ikke det ene mandfolk fra det andre, ikke altid, ikke ofte." Ibid., 322.

62 "liten ynkelig negerhjærne." Ibid., 301.

63 "måtte ha et bånd på hende." Ibid., 271.

64 "At stillingen var blit løsere, Barbro fandt sig ikke mere hjemme på Måneland end en anden taus vilde ha gjort, heller ikke mere bundet, hans tak i hende hadde raknet da barnet døde. Han hadde tænkt så stort at bare vent til barnet kommer! Men barnet kom og gik." Ibid., 293.

65 "Et barnemord var jo for hende uten ide, uten overordentlighet, det var bare al den moralske skittenfærdighet og løshet som kunde ventes av en tjenestepike." Ibid., 298.

66 "End alt det som gifte folk i byerne gjorde? De dræpte børnene før de fødtes, det var doktorer til det. De vilde ikke ha mere end som et barn eller i høiden to børn, og så åpnet doktoren ørlite på morslivet." Ibid., 300.

67 See Berggreen, "Fra kvinnebonde til bondekvinne," 110.

68 "Et bilde av mannen som åkerbruker, februker og hagebruker har lagt seg over det tidligere bildet av norsk bondekultur, hvor kvinnene var virksomme i disse rollene." Ibid., 113.

69 " I flere hundrede år hadde vel hans forfædre sådd korn, det var en handling i andagt en stille og mild kvæld uten vind. . . . Poteten det var en ny frugt, det var intet mystisk ved den, intet religiøst, kvindfolk og børn kunde være med og få den sat, disse jordeplerne som kom fra fremmed land likesom kaffen, stor og herlig mat, men i slægt med næpen. Korn det var brødet, korn eller ikke korn det var liv eller død." *Markens grøde*, 161.

70 "det var en klar oppfatning om hva som var mannsarbeid og hva som var kvinnearbeid." Ibid., 110.

71 "En rar mand i marken, en herre med tynde skriverhænder og et kvindfolks sans for stas og paraply og stok og galoscher. Borttufset, forbyttet, en uforståelig ungkar. Det vil ikke vokse et videre brutalt skjæg ut på hans overmund heller." Ibid., 383.

72 "Lensmand Heyerdahl var blit gift ifjor. Hans kone vilde ikke være mor og skulde ingen børn ha, tak. Hun hadde heller ingen." *Samlede verker*, 189.

73 "Men lensmandsfruen hadde fåt barn—hun som altid i kvindeforeningen hadde talt imot de overhåndtakende børnefødsler i fattigstuerne: lat kvinden heller få stemmeret og indflytelse på sin egen skjæbne! sa hun. Nu var hun fanget. Ja hadde prestefruen sagt, hun har nok brukt sin indflytelse, hahaha, men allikevel undgik hun ikke sin skjæbne! Dette vittige ord om fru Heyerdahl gik bygden rundt og blev forståt av nokså

mange; Inger forstod det kanske også, bare Isak forstod ingenting." Ibid., 275.

74 "Da hendes tur kom stod hun der ved skranken og var meget til dame, hun optok spørsmålet om barnemord i hele sin bredde og gav retten et numer, det var som hun hadde utvirket tillatelse hertil på forhånd. Man kunde ha hvad for mening man vilde om lensmandsfruen, men tale kunde hun og lærd i politik og samfundsspørsmål det var hun. Det var et under hvor hun fik ordene ifra. Nu og da syntes lagmanden å ville føre hende litt tilbake til saken, men han hadde vel ikke hjærte til å forstyrre hende, han lot hende holde på." Ibid., 341.

75 Amy van Marken, review of Bolckman's dissertation, *Edda* 56 (1969): 63.

76 Næss, *Knut Hamsun*, 63.

77 *Ny jord* (Oslo: Gyldendal, 1992), 146.

78 "Denne uutholdelige velsignelse med et barn hvert år to år i træk gjorde hende også virkelig fortvilet; Herregud, man var blot og bart barn selv, fuld av blod og ufornuft, man hadde sin ungdom foran sig. Hun tvang sig en tidlang, det gik tilslut så vidt at den unge frue lå og gråt om nætterne. Men efter den forståelse ægteparet endelig kom til ifjor behøvet ikke fru Hanka å ægge noen tvang på sig mere." Ibid., 146.

79 "Hanka er ikke hjemme, der er ingen mat, jeg ser ikke et menneske i stuerne. Ved venskapelig overenskomst har vi ophævet vor husholdning." Ibid., 150.

80 "Hun bor nu og da der jeg bor, vi ser til børnene, går ind og ut av dørene og skilles igjen." Ibid., 152.

81 "Så blev Aagots lille gåsehodet rørt." Ibid. 194.

82 Ibid., 208–9.

83 Ibid., 231.

84 Ibid., 295–96.

85 "Hvor de har fordærvet hende, hvor de hadde fordærvet hende." Ibid., 320.

3 Imagining the Indians

Chapter epigraph: *Knut Hamsuns brev 1879–1895*, p. 105, letter no. 60. Hamsun is probably referring to Drude Janson's book *Ensomhed* (Loneliness), a tragedy about life on the Minnesota prairie, published in Minneapolis in 1888.

1 Philip Deloria, *Playing Indian* (New Haven: Yale University Press, 1994), 4.

2 Deloria dissects the contradictory notion of "noble savagery" as "a term that both juxtaposes and conflates an urge to idealize and desire Indians and a need to despise and dispossess them." He continues, "Two interlocked traditions: one of self-criticism, the other of conquest. They balance perfectly, forming one of the foundations underpinning the equally intertwined history of European colonialism and European Enlightenment." Ibid., 4.

3 The identification of such social boundaries and of an inside group and an outside group has become commonplace, the ideas harkening back to the influential *Ethnic Groups and Boundaries* (Boston: Little, Brown, 1969), edited by Fredrik Barth.

4 "Fra en Indianerleir" is the fourth article Hamsun wrote about America. All were published under the pseudonym "Ego." I refer to the article "Fra Amerika," as reprinted in Knut Hamsun, *Hamsuns polemiske skrifter*, ed. Gunvald Hermundstad (Oslo: Gyldendal, 1998), 35–45.

5 Hamsun describes them as members of the Shawnee tribe, but he is most probably writing about the Ho-Chunk people, better known to Anglo-Americans as the Winnebago.

6 See Žagar, "Imagining the Red-Skinned Other: Hamsun's Article 'Fra en Indianerleir' (1885)," *Edda* 4 (2001): 385–95. I show that there is, in fact, no historical record of the Shawnee having had a leader named Yellow Thunder, as Hamsun claims. Hamsun's noble Shawnee warrior chief was most probably based on the historical Ho-Chunk (Winnebago) leader, Yellow Thunder, who in 1837 was forced to sign a humiliating treaty in Washington that ceded large portions of Wisconsin to the United States government. The Ho-Chunk Yellow Thunder, who according to historical records lived from 1774 to 1874, was a famous chief who resided in the same general area of Wisconsin that Hamsun visited in 1883, that is, nearly ten years after Yellow Thunder's death.

7 Larsen, *Den unge Hamsun*, 380: "Virkelighetstroskap er idealet."

8 Barbara Gordon Morgridge, who edited and translated into English Hamsun's 1889 cultural history *Fra det moderne Amerikas aandsliv*, carried out painstaking research on Hamsun's sources; she demonstrates that he often quoted from articles that cannot be found, misquoted from others, or simply borrowed at random from a variety of sources. See also Petter Aaslestad's comments about Hamsun's short texts in *Narratologi:*

En innføring i anvendt fortelleteori (Oslo: LNU Cappelen, 1999), 97.

9   See Will T. Ager, "Fra Hamsuns Amerika-Ophold" (From Hamsun's stay in America), *Kvartalskrift* (January 1916), 1–7.

10 The greater area around Lake Mason, where Ager's family had a home, includes the Wisconsin (River) Dells, an area associated with and often photographed by H. H. Bennett. As a photographer, Bennett primarily focused on three themes: nature, and especially the Wisconsin River in the rapidly developing tourist area of Wisconsin Dells; urban scenes from Milwaukee, Chicago, Saint Paul, and Minneapolis; and images of Indian life in Wisconsin. The native peoples, and primarily the Ho-Chunk Indians, considered the Wisconsin River area their homeland and often camped there in spite of repeated evictions by the U.S. government.

11 The H. H. Bennett Studio and History Center in Wisconsin Dells has an extensive collection of Bennett's photographs of Ho-Chunk Indians.

12 See *Bennett, Steichen, Metzker: The Wisconsin Heritage in Photography*, exhibition catalogue (Milwaukee: Milwaukee Art Center, 1970).

13 Larsen, *Den unge Hamsun*, 116–17.

14 Atle Kittang, "Jeger, elskar, forteljar: Moderniteten in Knut Hamsun's *Pan*" (Hunter, lover, storyteller: Modernity in Knut Hamsun's *Pan*), in *Hamsun i Tromsø: 11 foredrag fra Hamsun-konferansen i Tromsø 1995* (Hamsun in Tromsø: 11 lectures from the Hamsun conference in Tromsø in 1995) (Hamarøy: Hamsun-Selskapet, 1996), 58.

15 See Sven H. Rossel, "The Image of the United States in Danish Literature: A Survey with Scandinavian Perspectives," in *Images of America in Scandinavia*, ed. Poul Houe and Sven Hakon Rossel (Amsterdam: Rodopi, 1998), 13.

16 See Wilhelm Dinesen, *Boganis jagtbreve* (Copenhagen: Gyldendal, 1935). Originally published as *Jagtbreve* (1889) and *Nye jagtbreve* (1892).

17 Richard B. Vowles, "Boganis, Father of Osceola; or Wilhelm Dinesen in America 1872–1874," *Scandinavian Studies* (1976): 369–83.

18 For an interesting discussion on Norwegian literacy, see Marte Hult, *Framing a National Narrative: The Legend Collections of Peter Christen Asbjørnsen* (Detroit: Wayne State University Press, 2003), 206n9. Michelle Facos writes in her *Nationalism and the Nordic Imagination* (Berkeley: University of California Press, 1998) that there was nearly universal literacy in Sweden in the 1890s (5).

19 See Deloria, *Playing Indian*, 5. Deloria identifies the Boston Tea Party of

1773 "as a generative moment of American political and cultural identity" in American history. His claim is based on the fact that the participants disguised themselves as Mohawk Indians, demonstrating how the Indian had become part of the American national identity (9).

20 Ibid., 5.

21 "[T]he practice of playing Indians," Deloria says, "has clustered around two paradigmatic moments—the Revolution, which rested on the creation of a national identity, and modernity, which has used Indian play to encounter the authentic amidst the anxiety of urban industrial and postindustrial life." Ibid., 7.

22 For instance, Hamsun gave a speech at a Minneapolis fundraiser in support of Harald Sverdrup's moderate–left government in Norway.

23 Betty Bergland, "Norwegian Immigrants and 'Indianerne' in the Landtaking, 1838–1862," *Norwegian-American Studies* 35 (2000): 322.

24 Odd Lovoll, *The Promise Fulfilled: A Portrait of Norwegian Americans Today* (Minneapolis: University of Minnesota Press, 1998), 14.

25 Lovoll, *The Promise of America*, 153.

26 Hamsun claims that Broad Shoulder is a person of mixed Indian-French descent, also known as Louis Newman, and is Yellow Thunder's son-in-law. Newman graduated from the Boise City High School and was subsequently enrolled in the Boise City Seminary. While at seminary he wrote for the local newspapers and gave public lectures. The Wisconsin Historical Society and the Idaho Historical Society, on my behalf, kindly conducted an extensive search to confirm Hamsun's information but came up empty-handed. The only seminary that existed in Boise during the pertinent time period folded in its first year of operation, 1867. A search through the main local newspaper of the time, *The Idaho Statesman*, turned up nothing about or by any Louis Newman, or anyone else with a similar name. In addition to the newspaper, the Idaho Historical Society consulted the following sources: Oscar Nelson, *History of the Schools: Boise, Idaho* (1990); Harold Farley, "An Unpublished History of Idaho Education" (1974); Frank Pierce Baird, *A History of Education in Idaho through Territorial Days* (1928); and Grace Ritchie, *The Way We Were: The Early Schools of Idaho* (1976). My investigation thus turned up no evidence whatsoever of this Mr. Newman, much less any record of the activities Hamsun attributes to him.

27 "det blev en Deling mellem min vaneløse, oprindelige Natur og Ritualerne, Schemaerne, Liturgierne." Hamsun, "Fra en Indianerleir," 41.

28 "Og jeg henrykkes af Jubel og Lyst paa de veiløse Vidder og i den Natur, som jeg selv er en levende Part af. Og jeg vasker min Spyd i Bjergbjørnens Bryst og jeg æder Bisonens ristede, rygende Yver. Og jeg lægger mig i Duggens Kjølighed, naar Natten dæmrer og Fuglen tier i Trærne, og jeg vaagner naar Vagtens Signalhyl melder en Fare nær. Der er *dette* jeg kalder det 'egentlige' Liv; thi det er det naturlige." Ibid., 42.

29 A convenient introduction to this genre is *Great Speeches by Native Americans*, ed. Robert Blaisdell (Mineola, NY: Dover Thrift Editions, 2000).

30 "Thi jeg var Indianer og havde min Races hede Sind og Længsler. Jeg udstod ikke Virkningen af den Masseviden." Hamsun, "Fra en Indianerleir," 41.

31 "Kulturlivets tæmmende Tugt." Ibid.

32 Nancy Stepan, "Biology and Degeneration: Races and Proper Places," 97–120.

33 Ibid., 97.

34 "Indianernes gradvise Undergang," "Deres daglige Liv," "Sociale Tilstande," "Ankomst til Leiren," "Høvdingen og hans squaw," "The white river-flower."

35 "Kanoer flyder ikke længere spidse og lydløse henover Østens Sjøer og Floder . . . og deres græsrige, umaadelige Sletter og vide Skogegne ligger nu oprodet af Plougfurer eller overbygget af Kolonisternes Byer og Farme."

36 "snart vil det sidste kobberbrune Menneske staa paa sin sidste Plet af Jord nede ved Stillehavskysten og se sin Sol synke for sidste Gang." Hamsun, "Fra en Indianerleir," 35.

37 "men medens raa, barbariske Stammer nede i Nordafrika florerer og formeres, er Indianeren ude af Stand til at leve i Civilisationen og ude af Stand til at leve *ved siden af* den. Han gaar daglig sin egen Opløsning imøde." Ibid.

38 Bergland, "Norwegian Immigrants and 'Indianerne' in the Landtaking, 1838–1862," 336, 338.

39 Robert A. Birmingham and Leslie E. Eisenberg, *Indian Mounds of Wisconsin* (Madison: University of Wisconsin Press, 2000).

40 Ole Rynning, *Sandfærdig beretning om Amerika: Til oplysning og nytte for bonde og menigmand* (True account of America: Information and help for peasant and commoner) (Christiania, 1838).

41 For more information about the reception and impact of Rynning's *True*

Account of America, see Frank G. Nelson, "Translator's Foreword," in Johan Reinert Reiersen, *Pathfinder for Norwegian Emigrants to the United States of America and Texas* (Northfield, MN: The Norwegian-American Historical Association, 1981), vii–xi. (This is a translation of Reiersen's *Veiviser for norske emigranter til De forenede nordamerikanske stater og Texas,* published in Christiania in 1844.)

42 Ole Rynning, *True Account of America,* trans. and ed. Theodore C. Blegen (Minneapolis: The Norwegian-American Historical Association, 1926), 90–91.

43 Ibid., 70.

44 Bergland, "Norwegian Immigrants and 'Indianerne' in the Landtaking, 1838–1862," 319–20.

45 Reiersen, *Pathfinder for Norwegian Emigrants,* 183.

46 These letters were later translated and edited by Gunnar J. Malmin as *America in the Forties: The Letters of Ole Munch Ræder* (Minneapolis: University of Minnesota Press, 1929).

47 Bergland, "Norwegian Immigrants and 'Indianerne' in the Landtaking, 1838–1862," 331–33.

48 James Axtell, *Natives and Newcomers: The Cultural Origins of North America* (Oxford: Oxford University Press, 2001), 75. Axtell's book is one of the most comprehensive studies on the attitudes, practices, and interactions between Native Americans and Europeans during the settlement of the North American continent. Especially during the early stages of European settlement, there was trading and bartering, peaceful coexistence, and intermarriage, all of which, Axtell claims, was to the benefit of both groups.

49 Susanne Zantop, "Domesticating the Other: European Colonial Fantasies 1770–1830," in Gisela Brinker-Gabler, ed., *Encountering the Other(s): Studies in Literature, History, and Culture* (New York: State University of New York Press, 1995), 269–83.

50 Ibid., 271. According to Zantop, the Native American people are "erased from and subsumed by the . . . evocation of an erotic union between European man and American continent." Thus, the subdued peoples are really nothing more than a part of the natural landscape the Europeans conquer and transform. This is an extension of the longstanding conflation of land and woman, which Annette Kolodny has called "America's oldest and most cherished fantasy" (quoted by Zantop, 271–72; also see Kolodny, *The Lay of the Land: Metaphor as Experience and History*

in American Life and Letters [Chapel Hill: University of North Carolina Press, 1975]). The land/woman is then allegorized as a "yielding virgin or as threatening amazon," which creates the "dual femininity of the other that dominates the imagination of actual and would-be colonizers" (272–73). This fantasy—the presentation of violent colonial encounters as love-and-marriage stories between a European male and an indigenous female—survives well into the nineteenth century.

51 Tzvetan Todorov, *The Conquest of America: The Question of the Other,* trans. Richard Howard (New York: Harper Perennial, 1992), 49.

52 Ibid., 42–43.

53 Ibid., 132.

54 Hamsun, "Fra en Indianerleir," 35.

55 Birmingham and Eisenberg, *Indian Mounds of Wisconsin,* 33.

56 "Men naar de ere drevne til den yderste Linje af Land nede med Stille-Havs Kysten, da vil Indianerracens sidste Bærer se sin Sol den sidste Gang." Hamsun, "Fra en Indianerleir," 37.

57 As the many recorded speeches by famous Ho-Chunk (and indeed, most Native American) orators show, the natives were initially ready to compromise and share land with the whites. Later they reluctantly agreed, often under coercion, to sign land treaties. They also agreed to establish permanent settlements, contrary to their customs, and to farm in the European manner. Nevertheless, the white settlers' appetite for more and more land caused the native peoples to be displaced again and again. Native American speeches addressed to Indian agents or United States government officials contain constant and polite reminders of broken promises regarding such essential items as blankets, shoes, and basic food staples, let alone promised annuities. See Mark Diedrich, ed., *Winnebago Oratory: Great Moments in the Recorded Speech of the Hochungra, 1742–1887* (Rochester, MN: Coyote Books, 1991). When interpreting Native American speeches, readers need to be aware that many printed in the nineteenth century were composed by whites for consumption by a white audience (see, e.g., A. Furtwangler, *Answering Chief Seattle* [Seattle: University of Washington Press, 1997] and David Murray, *Forked Tongues* [Bloomington: Indiana University Press, 1991]).

58 In all likelihood, Hamsun is referring to his American friend and roommate Will T. Ager. See especially Harald Næss, *Knut Hamsun og America,* 28–41, for a description of Hamsun's stay in Wisconsin. Neither

Ager, in his reminiscence, nor Næss mentions anything about Hamsun visiting American Indians.

59 "Yellow thunder (Gul Torden) var en stor, bredbygget Indianer med skarpt skaaret Hoved og med et Blik, som brændte i sin haarde Brunhed." Hamsun, "Fra en Indianerleir," 38.

60 Even as early as 1781, Knud Lyne Rahbek's heroic epistolary poem "Hanna til Vilhelm" (Hanna to William) shows the era's moralizing trend with its love-story warning, "But watch out, my dear, for Indian girls!" See Rossel, "The Image of the United States in Danish Literature," 6.

61 "Bred-Skulder," "Teltets Indre og dets Beboere," "Indianerkvinderne," "Yellow Thunders Stammes Religion," "Afsked med Leiren."

62 "primitivt, vildt, kobberbrunt med civilisered, blegt, tæmmet er et Misforhold" (the primitive, wild copper-brown with the civilized, pale, tamed is a disparity). Hamsun, "Fra en Indianerleir," 39.

63 "Men ude paa disse vilde Vider, hvor Bisonen brøler i sine Horder, hvor Prairievinden suser som løsnede Snelaviner og hvor Krigeren stormer en fiendtlig Stamme for at hævne en lidt Uret—her glemmer en de tamme Hvide. Man glemmer den hvide Mands Kulturparagrafer, og al hans Viden og alt hans Hjernebrud." Ibid., 40.

64 "By 1850," the American Indian scholar George E. Tinker writes, "the immigrant invasion was rolling unabated over the plains to both Oregon and California. . . . Highways filled with wagon trains suddenly divided what had been undisputed tribal lands. Game began to disappear; Indian hunting patterns and lifeways were thoroughly disrupted." Tinker, *Missionary Conquest: The Gospel and Native American Cultural Genocide* (Minneapolis: Augsburg Fortress Press, 1993), 97–98. For buffalo hunters, see http//www.americanbisonsocietyonline.org.

65 See Gayatri Chakravorty Spivak, "Can the Subaltern Speak?" in *Marxism and the Interpretation of Culture*, ed. Cary Nelson and Lawrence Grossberg (Urbana: University of Illinois Press, 1988).

66 See Konstanze Streese, "Writing the Other's Language: Modes of Linguistic Representation in German Colonial and Anti-Colonial Literature" in *Encountering the Other(s): Studies in Literature, History, and Culture* (New York: State University of New York Press, 1995). Streese examines representations in eighteenth- and nineteenth-century German literature—by Gillert, Wieland, Claudius, Herder, Tieck, Seume, Lenau, Chamisso, and Keller—all of whom described themselves as "critical

observers of the practices of colonialism" (286).

67 Fred R. Myers, "Introduction to Part One: Around and About Modernity: Some Comments on Themes of Primitivism and Modernism," in *Antimodernism and Artistic Experience: Policing the Boundaries of Modernity*, ed. Lynda Jessup (Toronto: University of Toronto Press, 2001), 17–19. In a section pointedly titled "Performing Primitivism," Myers stresses "the larger frame of intercultural exchange and transaction," which is partly a discourse of cultural appropriations and partly a charged social field. Myers focuses on the values and images imposed by the majority discourse onto the minority, thus creating "binding doctrines of authenticity and cultural purity." (18) Myers salutes the recognition in recent scholarship that the Other actually often embraced primitivist representations as allowing them a space for recognition (17–18). Still, it is hard to ignore the magnitude of disruption in most indigenous people's lives. In his text, Hamsun acknowledges the woeful displacement of the native peoples in the first part of the article, yet in the second half, where he portrays them as proud and free, he is clearly unable, or unwilling, to take account of the historical facts. The Indians are made to correspond to Hamsun's ideal of the purity of the Other and are thus deprived of the ability to determine their own representation.

68 They are marked by *"udlevet aktivitet,"* he claims. Here Hamsun, presumably relating Broad Shoulder's exact words, provides the "original" English term in brackets, "decayed activness [sic]," referring to contemporary debates about race and degeneration. In Broad Shoulder's opinion, whites resemble "flies in autumn" (*fluer om høsten*), their entire knowledge is merely "the brain's roe spawn" (*hjernens rognegyd*), and the authentic person is the nature-man (*Naturmenneske*), rather than the decadent Westerner.

Robert J. Goldwater, in his influential book *Primitivism in Modern Painting* (New York: Harper and Bros., 1938), was perhaps one of the first art historians who rigorously separated the primitive from the primitivist. Goldwater maps the life and art of artists in the primitivist movement. For more on this topic, see Colin Rhodes, *Primitivism and Modern Art* (London: Thames and Hudson, 1994).

69 "Han behandler dem respektfullt som selvstendige individer (i hvert fall mennene)" (He treats them respectfully as autonomous individuals [at least the men]). Larsen, *Den unge Hamsun*, 382.

70 "Ikke så ulikt Whitmans 'indianervilde følelse.'" Olaf Øyslebø, *Hamsun*

gjennom stilen (Hamsun through style) (Oslo: Gyldendal, 1964), 202. Øyslebø devotes considerable attention to Hamsun's presentation of the American writers Walt Whitman, Ralph Waldo Emerson, and Mark Twain, and concludes that Hamsun absorbed more in style from these writers than he was willing to acknowledge openly. He writes about the similarity between Hamsun's and Whitman's primitivist relation to nature and the magic of words (68). Further, he notes that in America, Hamsun must have learned, or had reconfirmed, his belief in the importance of man's respect for nature's laws. Øyslebø is obviously referring solely to *The Cultural Life of Modern America*, since in 1964 "From an Indian Camp" had not yet been attributed to Hamsun.

71 Hamsun, *The Cultural Life of Modern America*, 40 (English edition of *Fra det moderne Amerikas aandsliv*).

72 Ibid., 45.

73 Ibid., 47.

74 Barbara Gordon Morgridge, "Editor's Introduction" to Hamsun, *The Cultural Life of Modern America*, xxviii.

75 Hamsun, *The Cultural Life of Modern America*, 52–53.

76 Hamsun, *Det vilde kor* (The wild choir) (Oslo: Gyldendal, 1904), 35.

77 Øyslebø, *Hamsun gjennom stilen*, 204–12.

78 "Der var ikke Spor af Liv i disse kjødrøde, smudsige Ansigter med de stive tankeløse Øine." Hamsun, "Fra en Indianerleir," 42.

79 "Men hendes døde, lidenskabsløse Blik, som intet kunde gjøre opmærksomt, gav hende et fedt Dyrs sanseløse Udtryk. Jeg har engang set en saaret Bøffel lægge sig ned og bløde sig dorsk tildøde." Ibid., 43.

80 Fred Myers, for instance, writes that it is impossible not to notice "the gendered and sexualized positioning of the Primitive." He goes on to say, quite aptly, "The anxiety of the modern artist is also arguably an anxiety of sexuality." Myers, "Introduction to Part One," 20.

81 "Da maatte jeg mindes Darwin og de 17 Generalgrader. Hvorlaenge skulde Indianerpigen ligge paa Bugen og tygge paa sin Tunge, forend hun vlev et erkjendende og afklarnet Vaesen som vi? Og hvorlaenge havde hun ligget saa fra den Tid hun hang i Traeerne som Abehun? — Thi Forholdet er ikke det samme for Indianernes Kvinder som for deres Maend; disse er Generationer forud for hine" (Then I was reminded of Darwin and the seventeen evolutionary levels. How long would the Indian girl lie on her belly and chew on her tongue before she would become a thoughtful and enlightened being like us. And how long has

she lain there since the time she had hung as a monkey in the trees? — Because the circumstances are not the same for Indian women as for their men; the latter are generations ahead of the former). Hamsun, "Fra en Indianerleir," 43. With gratitude to Jole Schackelford.

82 "Der rodede sig vist et Slags Forstaaelse gjennem Hjernens lunkne Myr." Ibid., 45.

83 Earlier in the article, Hamsun had written admiringly about the Indians' hospitality, the Indian women's labor and skills, and the amazing variety of Indian languages, yet none of this figures into his judgment about his hosts in general, and about the women in particular. It is worth noting that historical sources inform us that Yellow Thunder's wife was given the name "Washington Woman" because she had been part of the Ho-Chunk delegation to Washington in 1837.

84 See Britt Andersen's "Det hjemlige og det fremmede i Hamsuns *Pan* (The domestic and the foreign in Hamsun's *Pan*), in *Hamsun 2000: 8 foredrag fra Hamsun-dagene på Hamarøy* (Hamsun 2000: Eight lectures from the Hamsun days at Hamarøy) (Hamarøy: Hamsun-Selskapet, 2000), 28.

85 Hamsun, "Røde, sorte og hvide," in *Hamsuns polemiske skrifter*, 115.

86 Ibid., 115–16.

87 See also Lars Frode Larsen, *Over havet* (Across the ocean) (Oslo: Gyldendal, 1990), 132.

88 Næss, *Knut Hamsun*, 67.

89 In his article about the relevance of *Livets spil* for interpreting the Kareno trilogy, Simon Grabowski comments on the fact that Kareno is a Lapp and writes: "one would have expected him to look to the great nature of the place for new strength; but he is only interested in the seclusion which it offers." Simon Grabowski, "Kareno in Nordland: A Study of *Livets Spil*," *Edda* 21 (1969): 297–321, 317.

90 Since we have no recorded speech from that sliver of Hamsun's time, and all collected stories and folklore interviews might be more reflective of the folklorist himself than of folklore, we do not know with certainty how people used to speak. We can make an educated guess based on analyses of the daily and weekly press from Hamsun's time. Moreover, we can look at books and pedagogical manuals and try to establish what the normative guidelines for various kinds of speech and behavior were at church, school, Parliament, receptions, funerals, and so forth. We can discern the norms of appropriate feminine behavior in various manuals for middle-class women, advice columns in women's weeklies and

other publications. In addition, we know that in Hamsun's time there was a marked division between public male and private female domains. Public discourse was information-driven and adversarial in style, while private discourse was more cooperative. One can well imagine instances of cooperative public discourse and of adversarial private discourse, but it is well documented that merely assertive public speech by women was regarded as scandalous.

91 Hamsun, *Livets spil, Samlede verker*, vol. 14 (Oslo: Gyldendal Forlag, 1964), 74. "Slank, 25 år, sortklædt, skjønt det er sommer. Hun går med stærkt utadvendte føtter."

92 She explains to a Læstedian preacher who admonishes her to stop sinning: "Don't sin any more? Oh, you God's slave, I don't sin, I obey somebody" (Synd ikke mere? O, du Guds slave, jeg synder ikke, jeg adlyder nogen). Ibid., 112.

93 Simon Grabowski, "Kareno in Nordland: A Study of *Livets spil*," *Edda* 21 (1969): 297–321, 306.

94 Næss, *Knut Hamsun*, 67.

95 Harald Næss also interprets the use of the adjective "Arabic" as Hamsun's way of defining the Lieutenant as a Norwegian version of the kind of omnipotent Oriental lord Hamsun imagined and admired: wealthy, free, noble, and cultured, in command of his subjects, including, of course, his women. Næss, *Knut Hamsun*, 101–2.

96 Knut Hamsun, *Børn av tiden* (Kristiania and Copenhagen: Gyldendalske Boghandel Nordisk Forlag, 1913), 213–14: "Det er Holmengraas Børn, Piken er størst. . . . begge ser eksotiske ut, begge er brunlige i Huden og har brune Øine. Der er noget oversjøisk ved dem: noget kraftig, noget barbarisk ved Næsen og de modne Læber gjør dem fremmedartede. Men de er flinke Børn, de kom hit til Segelfoss med bare Spansk i Hodet, nu har de i kort Tid lært at tale norske Ord, de er store lange Nordlændinger som trives og sjauer Dagen lang. Se der kommer nu Piken springende foran, Mariane, aldeles gal og frisk, og Gutten Felix efterpaa, begge barhodet og med sort Haar og lav Pande, stormende frem, ho."

97 "Hr. Holmengraa kommer, han har sine to Børn med, de to Indianere, som han kalder dem.

Stakkar, skal De kalde dem Indianere? sier Fruen.

Mine små Indianere, svarer Holmengraa. Aa det er ikke dem imot, må De tro, for saa blir De Efterkommere av Kuohtemoc, hvad de virkelig ogsaa til en viss Grad er.

Hvorledes det?

De har litt indiansk Blod i Aarene, deres Mor var Kvart.

Så er de Quinteroner, sier Doktoren. Meget interessant.

Ja dere er pragtfulde Børn! sier Fruen, og samler dem begge i sine Armer." Ibid., 245.

98 "De var lange Mennesker de smaa Indianere nu og saa mærkelig ut, de var saa sorthaarede og gule og deres brune Øine var sterk glinsende. Sandelig, de syntes at være endda mere indianske end Farn hadde opgit, ogsaa ved Marianes Gang var det noget glidende som hos en Vild og hun hadde late Hænder som slægtet på det Lediggjængerfolk hun var kommet av. Ung Willatz blev forbauset over hende og begynte efter kort tid å bli forelsket." Ibid., 303.

99 Hamsun, *Segelfoss by* (Oslo: Gyldendal, 1995), 56.

100 Ibid., 44–45.

101 Ibid., 171.

102 In Norwegian: *rase*; also spelled *race* in the early twentieth century.

103 "Paa Veien mærker han at han er stærkt bevæget, hans Søn har gjort ham Ære, han er begeistret over ham, gaar der og faar dunkle Øine over ham. Ung Willatz—jo han var Racens Ætling, en Willatz Holmsen som hans egen store og fine Far hadde været." Hamsun, *Børn av tiden,* 418.

104 "Så skulde denne lærer fra en eller annen bygd gå om i stuerne på Segelfoss og spise ved bordet og høre til inde; holdt han skole om dagen sat han om nætterne og studerte videre til præst eller prokurator. Løitnanten kjente *racen,* han kunde ikke tale med slike folk, deres tankegang var en anden, intet var dem medfødt, de hadde bare lært skolekundskap." Ibid., 46.

4 Imagining Black and White

Chapter epigraph: *Hamsuns polemiske skrifter* (Oslo: Gyldendal, 1998), 116.

1 "(d)et ender vel med en neger." *Livet ivold,* in *Samlede verker,* vol. 15, 85. English translations are my own. There is an authorized English edition, titled *In the Grip of Life,* translated by Graham and Tristan Rawson (New York: Alfred A. Knopf, 1924).

2 Rubin's article from 1969 establishes clear parallels in the treatment of women and blacks by the white patriarchal society in the USA. Reprinted in *Masculine/Feminine:Readings in Sexual Mythology and*

the *Liberation of Women*, ed. Betty Roszak and Theodore Roszak (New York, Harper Colophon Books, 1969).

3   See Ferguson, *Enigma*, 217.

4   Both Harald Næss and Robert Ferguson took this play to be a warning from Hamsun to his much younger wife, the actress Marie Andersen, who lived with an actor prior to meeting Hamsun.

5   Carla Waal, in her article, "The Plays of Knut Hamsun," reads the unfavorable portrait of Juliane as Hamsun's conviction that "the way of life of professional theater artists leads to degradation," but does not comment on either the misogynist or racist underpinnings of the plot. *The Quarterly Journal of Speech* 57 (Feb. 1971): 75–82. Jørgen E. Tiemroth in *Illusionens vej: Knut Hamsuns forfatterskab* (Illusion's way: Knut Hamsun's oeuvre) (Copenhagen: Gyldendal, 1974), devotes some space to Boy (214–18). Ronald G. Popperwell treats Boy as just another minor protagonist. See Popperwell, "Knut Hamsun's *Livet ivold*," in *20th Century Drama in Scandinavia: Proceedings of the 12th IASS Study Conference* (Helsinki: University of Helsinki, 1979), 211–18. Allen Simpson discusses Boy briefly in connection to Hamsun's anti-Semitism. See his 1977 article "Knut Hamsun's Anti-Semitism."

6   My own 1997 article focused on the racial aspect of the relationship between Boy and Juliane. See Žagar, "Hamsun's Black Man, or Lament for a Paternalist Society: A Reading of Hamsun's Play *Livet ivold* through *Fra det moderne Amerikas aandsliv*," *Edda* 4 (1997): 364–79.

7   Among the vast literature on this matter see, for instance, Winthrop D. Jordan's *White over Black: American Attitudes toward the Negro, 1550–1812* (Chapel Hill: University of North Carolina Press, 1968). See especially section 1, "First Impressions: Initial English Confrontation with Africans," and section 4, "Fruits of Passion: The Dynamics of Interracial Sex." See my footnotes in chapters 1 and 2 for more sources.

8   Anne McClintock. *Imperial Leather: Race, Gender, and Sexuality in the Colonia Contest* (New York: Routledge, 1995), 22.

9   See, for example, William Hannibal Thomas, *The American Negro: What He Was, What He Is, and What He May Become* (New York: Macmillan Company, 1901). See especially his chapter "Moral Lapses."

10 This is a basic pattern with many exceptions and variations. For a detailed discussion of discrepancies in laws and attitudes concerning biracial relations and relations between freemen and slaves, see Jordan, *White over Black*. For further discussion of gender relations in the slave

South, see *Society and Culture in the Slave South,* ed. J. William Harris (London: Routledge, 1992). "The Fruits of Merchant Capital: The Slave South as a Paternalist Society," by Eugene Genovese and Elizabeth Fox-Genovese, about the slave South as a "paternalist society" is especially relevant.

11 See Stepan, "Race and Gender: The Role of Analogy in Science," in *Anatomy of Racism,* ed. David Theo Goldberg (Minneapolis: University of Minnesota Press, 1990), esp. 38–39.

12 Ibid., 40–41.

13 Ibid., 42.

14 Ibid., 47.

15 Ibid., 48.

16 Ibid., 51.

17 "As metaphors in science become familiar or commonplace, they tend to lose their metaphorical nature and to be taken literally . . . due to the identification of the language of science with the language of objectivity and reality." Ibid., 52.

18 Christensen and Eriksen, Preface to *Hvite løgner.*

19 See "Erotikk i svart og hvitt" (Eroticism in black and white). Ibid.

20 "*Fruen*: Nei hvad skal den boy her?
Bast: Så kan han gå igjen. Forresten skal De ikke foragte Boy, frue, han er nemlig svært til kar. Ja han har godt å slægte på også, hans far var av samme slag, så han blev hængt.
Fruen: Hvad for?
Bast: Å han fik fat på en av vore hvite fruer engang, på en avsides estancia. Og hun hadde ikke revolver. Det var alt. Så hængte vi ham.
Fruen: Var De med på det? (*slår hænderne ihop*) Nei Gud bevare mig! Og så tok De sønnen til Dem efterpå? Var det negeren De vilde gi mig isted?
Bast: Ja gjærne det, sa jeg. Han er et forholdsvis begavet væsen, nu lærte han norsk av pikerne derhjemme på nogen få uker. Og han er en storartet kusk." Hamsun, *Livet ivold,* 125.

21 "Tænk, det var som et gammelt bekjendtskap for mig, vi hadde ofte negere ved scenen (*da Blumenschøn ler*). Jeg mener ved varietéerne." Ibid., 126.

22 See Tore Hamsun's *Knut Hamsun: Lebensbericht in Bildern* (München: Deutscher Kunstverlag, 1956), 26.

23 "Dette er ikke en bok om svarte, men om 'negeren' —en figur som i

vestlig kultur har vært selve bildet på den fremmede. 'Negeren' er ikke et menneske, men en forestilling, skapt av hvite. Han er forestillingen om den evige andre, den motsatte, den avvikende og mindreverdige. Gjennom tidene har "negeren" hatt mange ansikter. Han er blitt fremstilt åpenlyst rasistisk, andre ganger tilsynelatede morsomt og uskyldig. Men 'negeren' er alltid en negativ skikkelse. Han er den primitive, skitne og latterlige som kan lures, utnyttes og undertrykkes. For hvite har han vært et middel til å framheve egen overlegenhet." Christensen and Eriksen, *Hvite løgner,* vii.

24 Kirsten Alsaker Kjerland and Anne K. Bang, eds., *Nordmenn i Afrika— Afrikanere i Norge* (Bergen: Vigmostad & Bjørke, 2002).

25 Hamsun, *Fra det moderne Amerikas aandsliv:* "alle et hvidt Menneskes Rettigheder og tager sig alle en sort Negers Friheder," 130.

26 Look for the phrases "a few thousand African half-apes" and/or "black half-ape with glasses" sprinkled in the text. This is probably an echo of the so-called scientific or/and medical discourse in which blacks were often portrayed as the "missing link" between apes and people, or an echo of denigrating remarks about "half-apes" striving to appear intelligent and resemble whites.

27 "Negre fra Niam-Niam hvis Næver aldrig havde ryddet Jord og hvis Hjerner aldrig havde tænkt." Hamsun, *Fra det moderne Amerikas aandsliv,* 128–29.

28 "Den 1. Januar 1863 gjorde de Negrene til Herrer over Syddens Selvejere, tok Muskeldyrene fra Niam-Niam ind i sine Familjer, gav dem sine Sønner og Døttre tilægte—forat avle et Udvalg af Aandsmennesker!" Ibid., 129.

29 "Der tegned sig til en Aandselite i to af Sydens ældste Stater i 50-Aarene; men Krigen kom og opsled den førend den var grundlagt. Siden har den ikke yttret sig. Folks Blod blev fra den Tid demokratisk blandet med Negres, og Intelligensen sank istedetfor at stige. Man paanødedes disse Sortes Samliv. Umenneskeligheden raned dem bort fra Afrika, hvor de hører hjemme, og Demokratiet gjorde dem til civiliserede Borgere stik imod al Naturens Orden. De har sprunget over alle mellemliggende Udviklingstrin fra Rotteslugere til Yankeer. Nu bruges de til Præster, Barberere, Opvartere og Svigersønner. De har alle et hvidt Menneskes Rettigheder og tager sig alle en sort Negers Friheder. En Neger er og bliver Neger. Barberer han en Mand, griber han om Ens Næse, som hans salig Bestefader greb efter Krokodilleben ved Nilen; bringer han

En et Maaltid Mad, holder han sin glinsende Tommelfinger helt op til Anklen i Suppen. Det nytter ikke at bebrejde ham det lidt negerske i denne Handlemaade; faar man ikke et grovere Svar, vil den afrikanske Demokrat ialfald yttre fornærmet: *Mind your own business!* ('Pas deres egne sager') Og da maa man tie, Forhandlingen er tilende. Men sidder man med to store Næver og Retten paa sin Side, saa svælger man Maden med ringe Appetit. Det var jo en anden Sag, om man udtrykkelig forlangte Suppe med Tommelfingre.

"Negrene er og blir Negre, en Menneskebegyndelse fra Tropen, Væsner med Tarmer i Hovedet, rudimentære Organer paa et hvidt Samfundslegeme.

"Istedetfor at danne en Aandselite, har man i Amerika grundlagt et Mulatstutteri." Ibid., 130. Translation is from *The Cultural Life of Modern America*, ed. and trans. Barbara Gordon Morgridge (Cambridge: Harvard University Press, 1969), 144.

30 See Eugene Genovese and Elizabeth Fox-Genovese, "The Fruits of Merchant Capital: The Slave South as a Paternalist Society," and Elizabeth Fox-Genovese, "Within the Plantation Household: Women in a Paternalist System," in *Society and Culture in the Slave South*, ed. J. William Harris (London: Routledge, 1992). Hamsun fleshes out his own Nordic version of the paternalist, early capitalist social order in *Markens grøde*.

31 "Krigen var en Krig mod Aristokratiet og ble ført med demokratiske Menneskers hele rasende Had til Sydens Plantageadel. De samme Nordstater—de sædelige Nordstater—som dengang vilde knække Sydens Aristokrati, spekulered selv i Slaveholdet. Dette glemmer de Kvinder fra Boston." Hamsun, *Fra det moderne Amerikas aandsliv*, 119 (p. 132 of translated edition).

32 "med sin Faders uimodstaaeligste Staldneger" Ibid., 117.

33 "De vil paa Sæt og Vis undgaa at faa Børn; de gider ikke at amme Børn, de vil ikki have den Plage. Følgen er, at Yankeernes hele Opfindelsestalent sættes i Swing, forat hitte paa Midler, der kan forebygge Børne fodsler." Ibid., 116. (In a way, they want to avoid having children; they don't want the bother of nursing them; it is too much trouble. As a result, all the Yankee's ingenuity is set in motion, looking for means of preventing childbirth). B. G. Morgridge, trans., *The Cultural Life*, 123.

34 "Folk fra alle Zoner, fra Nordens Hvide til Tropens Aber og Aandsmulatter; et Land med blød, gødet Madjord og fredede Urmarker." Ibid., 131.

35 See, for instance, Edvard Beyer, ed., *Norges litteraturhistorie*, vol. 4 (Oslo: J. W. Cappelens forlag, 1975), which states that *Amerikas aandsliv* is a "frekt og voldsomt polemisk panorama over kultur- og samfunnsforholdene i USA" (audacious and violently polemical panorama of cultural and social relations in the USA) (140). Rolf Nyboe Nettum's *Konflikt og visjon: Hovedtemaer i Knut Hamsuns forfatterskap, 1890–1912* (Conflict and vision: Main themes in Knut Hamsun's authorship, 1890–1912) characterizes it as "lynende vittige og polemisk knivskarpe" (witty as lightning and polemically as sharp as a knife), and proceeds by focusing on the book as "en eksponent for Hamsuns nye litterære program" (a platform for Hamsun's new literary program) (46). Nettum shows parallels between *Amerikas aandsliv*, Hamsun's upcoming essay "Fra det ubevidste Sjæleliv" (From the unconscious life of the soul) and his subsequent work. He briefly discusses Darwinism, but avoids mentioning either "negro," "black," "apes," or "mulattoes" even a single time. Tore Hamsun's states in the introduction to the 1962 edition: "Det er også mulig at Hamsun, om han hadde oppholdt seg i Amerikas sydstater istedenfor blant nordstatenes yankee'er, hadde sett anderledes på Amerika" (It is also possible that Hamsun, if he had spent time in the American Southern states instead of among the Northern Yankees, would have perceived America differently). It is particularly telling that Hamsun had such a high opinion of the South never having been there.

36 Hamsun, *The Cultural Life of Modern America* (1969), xx.

37 See Ferguson, *Enigma*, 104–6 and 344–45.

38 "Friheten skal ikke gjelde alle grupper; der er noen Hamsun ikke vil anerkjenne - overfor dem må man anvendes disiplin. I dette ligger vel en spire til det samfunnssyn Hamsun hyllet senere i livet, og om en skal søke etter "nazistiske" tendenser i Hamsuns første voksne bok må det bli i hans hårde dom over visse underpriviligerte grupper i Amerika, nemlig kvinnene, indianerne og negrene." Næss, *Knut Hamsun og Amerika* (Oslo: Gyldendal, 1969), 146.

39 Hamsun, *Livet ivold,* 158, 161.

40 Hamsun, *Livet ivold,* 100.

41 Fredriksen, a musician, reminds her: "Det går nedover, Fredriksen! sa De til meg for nogen år siden, ja det kommer til å ende med en neger, sa De. Det var nu Deres ordsprog" (I'm going downhill, Fredriksen, you said to me some years ago. Indeed, it'll end up with a Negro. That's what your expression was). Ibid., 172.

42 See Dijkstra, *Idols of Perversity*, 305–13; Showalter, *Sexual Anarchy*, 149.

43 See chapter 7. See for instance, Umberto Eco, "Tåkete totalitarisme og urfascisme" (Foggy totalitarianism and primordial fascism), *Samtiden* 5 (1995): 49–59, trans. Siri Nergaard. In English, "Ur-Fascism" (*The New York Review of Books*, vol, 42, no. 11, June 22, 1995).

44 Anthony R. E. Rhodes, *Propaganda, the Art of Persuasion: A World War II Allied and Axis Visual Record, 1933–1945* (Secaucus, NJ: Wellfleet Press, 1987), 32.

45 Ibid., 35. The white woman is clearly a caricature of Eleanor Roosevelt.

46 Susan Sontag, *Illness as Metaphor* (New York: Farrar, Straus and Giroux, 1978), 30.

47 Two of Hamsun's other texts include depictions of blacks. The novel *Landstrykere* (The wayfarers) describes the gang-rape of a black girl, in which August, the main protagonist, participates. Although the memory of the rape can perhaps be considered insignificant in the overall scheme of the novel, it marks August and erupts at crucial points in his life. In the novel *Segelfoss by,* there is a reference to a local girl who gives birth to a "mulatto" child after foreign ships that bear foreign sailors visit the local fjords. Hamsun uses the episode to expose the promiscuity of local girls.

48 See, for instance, the section "'White Negroes' and 'Celtic Calibans'" in Anne McClintock, *Imperial Leather: Race, Gender, and Sexuality in the Colonial Contest* (New York: Routledge, 1995), 52–56.

49 Hamsun's original Norwegian text has the events in America taking place in Kentucky, while the English translation portrays them as having taken place in Texas.

50 "at siste Led i Lænken føier sig til første Led." *Knut Hamsuns brev: 1934–1950*, vol. 6, p. 152, letter no. 2517.

51 Dingstad, *Hamsuns strategier: realisme, humor og kynisme.* (Oslo: Gyldendal, 2003), 177. Dingstad's argument is based primarily on the similarities the two texts display regarding the genre of *Bildungsroman.*

52 See Ferguson, *Enigma*, 318; and Næss, *Knut Hamsun*, 153.

53 "Vi gik i skjorte, bukse og revolver der jeg kommer fra" (We had a shirt, pants and a revolver where I come from). Knut Hamsun, *Ringen sluttet*, in *Samlede verker,* vol. 13, 1964, 46. Translation mine.

54 "Ja de er fra Kentucky, sa Abel. Mine landsmænd. Vi sat om kveldene og hørte negrene synge hist og her" (Yes, they are from Kentucky, said

Abel. My countrymen. We would sit around in the evenings and listen to the Negroes sing here and there). Ibid., 57.

55   See Marianna Torgovnick, *Gone Primitive: Savage Intellects, Modern Lives* (Chicago: University of Chicago Press, 1990), 20.

56   "Negrene spilte og menneskene danset på et avlangt gulvbræt, det var det samme her som over hele verden." Hamsun, *Ringen sluttet*, 44.

57   See Patricia Szobar, "Telling Sexual Stories in the Nazi Courts of Law: Race Defilement in Germany, 1933 to 1945," in *Sexuality and German Fascism*, ed. Dagmar Herzog (New York: Berghahn Books, 2005), 131–63, 131.

58   Discussed in detail in chapter 1.

59   "Jeg kommer i denne Forbindelse til at tænke paa den mærkeligste Bok jeg har lest i denne raae Tid, den er av Dr. Konrad Simonsen og heter 'Den moderne Mennesketype.' Han er ikke av de Professorer som læser femti eller hundrede Bind for at skrive sammen endda et, han reiser omkring i den vide Verden og iagttar, han sænker Hodet og grubler. Hvad nogen hver kan ha følt overfor det Mysterium som Livet er, det utløser han til en dyp og skjøn Livslære: bort fra vor Tids Mekanisering av Mennesket, tilbake til en mere sjælelig Tilværelse! Jeg skylder denne Bok saa stor Tak og jeg under andre den Berikelse at dukke ned i den." "Nabobyen," quoted from a reprint in *Knut Hamsun—Artikler i utvalg*, ed. Frances Bull (Oslo: Gyldendal, 1939), 189–90.

60   See McClintock, *Imperial Leather*, 52–56.

61   Konrad Simonsen, *Den modern mennesketype*, 1918, 35–6.

62   McClintock, *Imperial Leather*, 53.

63   Næss, *Knut Hamsun*, 148; and "*Ringen sluttet*: In Defence of Abel Brodersen," in *Facets of European Modernism: Essays in Honor of James McFarlane*, ed. Janet Garton (Norwich: University of East Anglia, 1985), 320.

64   Kittang, *Luft, vind, ingenting*, 298.

65   Dingstad, *Hamsuns strategier*, 233.

66   See Frederik Stjernfelt, "Hvad blir vi som ikke blir noget? Anerkendelsens strukturer in Hamsuns *Ringen sluttet*" (What becomes of us who don't become anything? Structures of acknowledgement in Hamsun's *The Ring Is Closed*), *Norskrift* 57 (1989): 20–60 (op. cit. 549).

67   "forkvaklede hjerne." Hamsun, *Ringen sluttet*, 62.

68   "denne tomsing, dette vrak fra Kentuckys jammersverden," Ibid., 108.

69   "En navnløs i et skur, en ingenting, en tomsing." Ibid., 114.

5 A Taste of the Orient

Chapter epigraph: *Hamsuns polemiske skrifter* (Oslo: Gyldendal, 1998), 226.

1   The play was published in Germany in the same year, but was not staged there until 1920 in Darmstadt.

2   In a letter to his wife Bergljot, he writes: "Sikker paa det skal blive en vakker Succes og en god Skilling af "Tamara" (I am sure that "Tamara" is going to be a fine success and bring a good penny). See *Knut Hamsuns brev 1896–1907*, vol. 2, p. 237, letter no. 637.

3   Hamsun wrote to his friend Wentzel Hagelstam: "Her i Kristiania sattes Stykket op med formeget Guld og Glitter og Trommer og Kommers, alt druknet i Larm. . . . 'Tamara' maa slet ikke sættes op med altfor meget Udstyr, det er en Fejltagelse. Men her i Kristiania kunde jeg ikke hindre det; Bjørn Bjørnson tror ikke paa stort andet end Udstyr og Larm" (Here in Kristiania the play was staged with too much gold and glitter and drums and hubbub, it was drowned in noise. . . . "Tamara" should not be staged with too many props, that is a misunderstanding. But here in Kristiania I could not prevent it; Bjørn Bjørnson does not believe in much other than props and noise). Ibid., p. 256, letter no. 656.

4   Hamsun himself referred to his journey as "min Rejse i Kaukasien og Orienten" (my travels in the Caucasus and the Orient), see *Knut Hamsuns brev, 1896–1907*, vol. 2, p. 133, letter no. 528, to Klara Johanson. See also his letter no. 542, p. 144, to A. Langen, where he calls it "min Orientfærd" (my Oriental journey).

    In another letter to Hagelstam, Hamsun repeats his admiration for the Orient: "Og saa Kaukasus! Jeg har ikke i min vildeste Fantasi tænkt mig noget saa vældigt. Det virked saa voldsomt paa mig iblant, at jeg begyndte at græde.—Men at sidde her og skrive Bøger, det er for gement" (And then the Caucasus! In my wildest dreams I have not imagined anything so awesome. Sometimes it had such a powerful effect on me that I started to cry. But to sit here and write books, that is just ordinary). See *Knut Hamsuns brev, 1896–1907*, vol. 2, pp. 138–39, letter no. 536.

5   See *I Æventyrland, Samlede verker*, vol. 4 (Kristiania: Gyldendalske boghandel-nordisk forlag, 1916).

6   "Jeg har været i Petersburg og Moskwa, har rejst gennem Rusland og Kaukasien, —et veldigere og skønnere Æventyr oplever jeg aldrig, specielt Rejsen fra Wladikaukas over Bjærgene til Tiflis. . . . Det er

en anden Klode, vakkrere Mennesker, rødere Vin, højere Bjærge. Og omkring Kasbæk tror jeg, at Gud bor hele Aaret." See *Knut Hamsuns brev, 1896–1907*, vol. 2, p. 165, letter no. 559, to Dagny Kristensen. Dagny's brother Brede was a known philologist, historian of religion, and Egyptologist. He briefly became professor of Oriental studies in Kristiania before getting a position in Leiden. He and Hamsun knew each other from Paris, and he was probably a source of some information about the Orient.

7   The historical Tamar, the legendary Georgian queen (1165–1213), ascended to the throne in 1184. Under her reign, the monarchy bloomed, expanded its boundaries, and attained what is usually considered its golden era. Throughout its history, the monarchy waged battles with neighboring Arabs, Turks, Persians, and finally Russians, with religion one of the main points of contention. The Georgian monarchy converted to Christianity in the early fourth century, whereas the kingdom's eastern parts later converted to Islam.

8   In a letter to Hagelstam, Hamsun writes: "Jeg vidste ikke at Lermontov har skrevet Tamaradigte. Jeg har hele Vejen holdt mig til Historien" (I did not know that Lermontov has written poems about Tamara. I kept to history the whole time). See *Knut Hamsuns brev 1896–1907*, vol. 2, p. 240, letter no. 639.

9   Marija Pavlovna Blagovesjtsjenskaja, the Russian translator of Hamsun's texts, has this to say regarding *Dronning Tamara* and *I Æventyrland*, also set in the Caucasus: "For oss russere har de ingen interesse. Under sitt kortvarige opphold i Russland kunne Hamsun vanskelig gjøre seg kjent med et folks ånd og skikker som var ham fullstendig fremmed" (For us Russians they are of no interest. During his short stay in Russia it would have been difficult for Hamsun to become acquainted with a people's spirit and customs that were totally foreign to him). See *Knut Hamsuns brev 1896–1907*, p. 331, letter 744a, footnote 3.

10   "Jeg bad til Allah for ham at han vilde beseire min egen Gud." *Dronning Tamara*, 42. All quotes are taken from *Dronning Tamara*, in *Samlede verker*, vol. 15 (Gyldendal, 1955). Translations are mine.

11   "Ti stille, Prior, når han kommer vil jeg kysse ham og vise ham min kjærlighet på tusen måter. På alle optænkelige måter og hele mit liv. Jeg bryr mig ikke om dig, Prior, jeg er træt av å se koldt til prins Giorgi som jeg elsker, du får mig ikke mere til det." Ibid., 58.

12 "Jeg skal skrive et bitte lidet Digt i Fronten af Bogen, det skal hedde 'Alrunen' . . . Det skal ligesom angive Forstaaelsen af Stykket: at det er den Pokkers Kærlighedsurt som er paa Spil." *Knut Hamsuns brev, 1896–1907*, vol. 2, p. 237. Hamsun wrote three more poems about the magic mandragora. All four of them were printed in *Det vilde kor* in April 1904.

13 Said writes, for instance: "Orientalism is the generic term that I have been employing to describe the Western approach to the Orient; Orientalism is the discipline by which the Orient was (and is) approached systematically, as a topic of learning, discovery and practice. But in addition I have been using the word to designate that collection of dreams, images, and vocabularies available to anyone who has tried to talk about what lies east of the dividing line." Said, *Orientalism* (Vintage Books, 1994), 73.

14 That the Orient was defined rather broadly in Hamsun's imagination as well is shown by his interest in *Sakuntala*, an Indian play from the fifth century that was translated into Danish in 1841. Just before embarking on *Dronning Tamara*, Hamsun asked Lauritz Christian Nielsen, the Gyldendal editor, for a copy of this book. See *Knut Hamsuns brev 1896–1907*, vol. 2, p. 208, letter no. 611.

15 Said, *Orientalism*, 343.

16 Toward the end of his play, Hamsun has the Muslims begging the Christian queen for protection and leadership.

17 See Elisabeth Oxfeldt, "Orientalism on the Periphery: The Cosmopolitan Imagination in Nineteenth-Century Danish and Norwegian Literature and Culture" (Ph.D. diss., University of California at Berkeley, 2002), 44. Oehlenschläger, however, was not the only writer preoccupied with the national self. N. F. S. Gruntvig (1783–1872) had his own vision of how to mold a homogeneous nation through education. His highly successful nation-building project focused on the Danish peasant as the bearer of Danishness, and Gruntvig's *højskole* system was established in opposition to the Copenhagen university.

18 Oxfeldt, "Orientalism," 211.

19 Ibid., 213.

20 Ibid., 58.

21 Ibid., 61; quoting from Alfred Jeppesen, *Kjøbenhavns sommer-Tivoli, 1843–1968* (Copenhagen's summer-Tivoli, 1843–1968) (Copenhagen: Aschehoug, 1968).

22 For the first two instances, see *I Æventyrland*, 59 and 111–12, respectively.

23 "Det er ut paa Eftermiddagen. Jeg sitter her ved det aapne Vindu og ser nakne Mænd som rider Hester tilvands i Sortehavet. Deres Kropper er mørke mot den blaa Sjø. Og Solen skinner endnu paa Ruinene av Tamaras Borg som reiser sig op av den lodne Skog." Ibid., 166.

24 In the queen's description of the Khan as a man *med slikt et blik*! ("with such a gaze!"), we recognize Hamsun's earlier protagonist, Lieutenant Glahn from *Pan*, who is irresistible to women, at least for a while, because of his animal-like eyes. Hamsun, *Dronning Tamara*, 23.

25 As Harald Næss so aptly puts it, this play "argues the impossibility of a situation in which a husband is not master of his household." Næss, *Knut Hamsun*, 71.

26 "Jeg er ikke kongen. Jeg er blot far til hendes børn, til hendes søn og hendes datter. . . . Det er min lodd å være mand i dette hus. Jeg taler hele tiden til en søn som er større end mig. Jeg taler til min lille datter som kanske engang skal regjere over mig." Hamsun, *Dronning Tamara*, 11.

27 Ibid., 12.

28 "Således kjæmper vi." Ibid., 15.

29 "Jeg vil erobre dronningen." Ibid., 14.

30 "Jeg vil tukte dronningen, hun skal ingenlunde tænke ringe om mig. Står jeg foran hende med khanens hær tar jeg ikke luen av, men sier: Tamara, dette er din husbond; ser du mig tydelig?" (I want to chasten the queen; she shall never think me insignificant. When I stand in front of her with the Khan's army I won't take my cap off, but will say: Tamara, this is your husband, do you see me clearly?) Ibid., 15.

31 Hamsun has the queen utter the following lines: "Prins Giorgi har kanske gjort noget galt, ærværdige fader, men jeg takker ham for det allikevel, han har gjort det for min skyld fordi han elsker mig" (Prince Georgi has perhaps done something wrong, venerable Father, but I thank him nonetheless. He did it for my sake because he loves me). And a bit later: "Han vilde tukte mig og ikke tigge mig om nogen gunst i verden, hvem kan fortænke ham deri?" (He wanted to chasten me and not beg me for any favor in this world, who can blame him for this?) After the prior reminds her of Georgi's destruction of her army, she says: "En stor plan, en vældig plan, ingen har hat så stor en plan for min skyld" (A grand plan, an awesome plan, nobody has had such a grand plan for my sake). Ibid., p. 53.

32   See *Knut Hamsuns brev 1896–1907*, vol. 2, letter no. 632, p. 233.

33   Harald Næss writes: "Hulda Garborg var (som også Hamsun) inspirert av Otto Weiningers bok *Geschlecht und Charakter* (1903) og av "anti-feminister" som Ellen Key og Laura Marholm." (Hulda Garborg was [as was Hamsun] inspired by Otto Weininger's book *Geschlecht und Charakter* [1903)] and by "anti-feminists" like Ellen Key and Laura Marholm.) See *Knut Hamsuns brev 1896–1907*, vol. 2, p. 268, note 4 to letter no. 667. Næss also writes: "Marie Hamsun har fortalt at hennes mann beundret Weininger" (Marie Hamsun has said that her husband admired Weininger). Næss here comments on Hamsun's statement from the letter to Sigrid Stray: "Weininger har Ret: Kvinden kan endog lyve for sig selv" (Weininger is right: Woman can indeed lie for herself). See *Knut Hamsuns brev, 1934–1950*, vol. 6, p. 105, note 2 to letter no. 2457. Hamsun's statement is on the same page. With gratitude to Harald Næss.

34   Trygve Braatøy, *Livets cirkel: Bidrag til analyse av Knut Hamsuns diktning* (Oslo: Fabritius & Sønners, 1929), 32.

35   "et eneste ubehersket forsøk på å danne et 'antifeministisk' system." Ibid., 195.

36   As he explores reasons why young intellectual women of the time accepted Weininger's book as enthusiastically as they did, he writes: "Underbevisst opfattet de at den var et symptom på kvinneemancipasjonens seiergang: En ung genial filosof samler sammen alt det materiale som samtidens videnskap synes å by på, for å vise at kvinnen er inferiør. Et sikrere bevis på at hun begynte å bli farlig i konkurransen på mannens egne områder hadde kvinnen ennu ikke fått" (Subconsciously they understood that it was a symptom of the success of women's emancipation: a brilliant young philosopher collects all the material which contemporary science seems to offer in order to prove that woman is inferior. Woman had not received more conclusive proof that she was beginning to become a dangerous competitor on man's own turf). Ibid., 195–96.

37   Ibid., 198.

38   "Kommer han . . . med magt?" Hamsun, *Dronning Tamara*, 64.

39   "Det er for min skyld han gjør det. Han skjøtter om intet. Ser du, abbed, at han våget det!" Ibid., 65.

40   "Han er som et berg." Ibid.

41   "Hvorfor nu? Det var jo ikke nødvendig." Ibid., 64.

42   Dronningen (reiser sig): Skal vi gå?

Prins Giorgi (likeså): Ja (blir stående).

Dronningen: Nu står du der og ser på mig hvad du skal gjøre. Giorgi, jeg elsker dig jo, jeg går hvor du går (lægger armen om ham og fører ham ind første forhæng)." Ibid., 71.

43 Ibid., 45.

44 "Før var jeg dronningens mand, nu er jeg vel kongens kone." Ibid., 46.

45 "du skal kalde dronningen for konge herefter, hun er konge." Ibid., 47.

46 It is interesting to consider the parallels between Tamara and Georgi and Queen Victoria and Prince Albert of Great Britain, a country Hamsun detested. I thank Kaaren Grimstad for this observation.

47 Tamara says: "Og jeg er ikke konge, det er Giorgi som skal være konge. Hvad har jeg gjort, at ulykken skal komme så stærk? Jeg var litt glad i morges, en liten glæde flakket gjennem mig, men den varte ikke længe" (Queen: And I am not the king. It is Georgi who shall be the king. What have I done, that misfortune has hit me so strongly? I was a bit happy this morning, a little joy flickered through me, but it did not last long). Ibid., 48.

48 The text is as follows:

Prins Giorgi (ser på hende): Tamara, skal vi dele skylden for dette?

Dronning: Dele den? Nei. Befalte jeg dig din blodtørst?

Prins Giorgi: Befalte? Du drev og jog mig ind in den, slik befalte du mig . . .

Prince Georgi (looks at her): Tamara, shall we share the blame for this?

Queen: Share it? No. Did I command your bloodthirstiness?

Prins Georgi: Commanded? You forced and urged me into it, that is how you commanded me. Ibid., 30.

49 See the conversation between Fatimat and Tamara after the khan's death. Ibid., 42.

50 "Efter disse betraktninger over Dronning Tamara, 'Trilogien' m.m. er det kanskje lett å forstå hvorfor det er hensiktsmessig å gå ut fra det ufullkomne for å forstå det kunstverk som lever. Hvor kunstnerens motiv ikke er blitt levendegjort i stoffet der kan man lett se komponentene, man ser symbolet og betydningen" (After these observations about Queen Tamara, "The Trilogy," and more, it is perhaps easy to understand why it makes sense to start from the imperfect to understand the artwork that is alive. Where the artist's subject has not been elucidated in the material, one easily sees the components; one sees the symbol and meaning). Braatøy, Livets cirkel, 187.

51 "I 'Dronning Tamara' er skildringen uten interesse og symbolene uforståelige for den almindelige leser. Begge ting henger sammen og bevirker at stykket som kunst faller helt til jorden. Det kan gjettes på at skildringen er så blodfattig fordi det symbolske innhold, motivet, på det tidspunkt bandt Hamsuns evne til realistisk utarbeidelse; levendegjørelsen var hemmet fordi materialet var så dypt fortrengt" (In 'Droning Tamara,' the portrayal is uninteresting and the symbols are not transparent to the average reader. The two are connected and the result is that the play as an artistic creation is a disappointment. One can guess that the portrayal is so anemic because the symbolic content, the theme, restricted Hamsun's ability at the time to render a realistic execution; the personification was inhibited because the material was repressed so deeply). Ibid., 184–85.

52 Braatøy, however, views the play through the lens of the Oedipal competition for the mother. Ibid., 33.

53 Hamsun, *I Æventyrland*, 114–15.

54 A precursor to *I Æventyrland*, Hamsun's short story "Dronningen av Saba" (The Queen of Sheba; 1892) imparts an equally ironic attitude, and its main message proclaims the impossibility of adopting Orientalism in the materially and culturally different environment of Scandinavia, even at the simplest level of escapism. The text ironically juxtaposes the Orient with Scandinavia, Norway with Sweden, history with modernity, a femme fatale with a local Swedish girl, deconstructing as many as four referents in the process. While importing the popular French, indeed European, decadent trope of the predatory woman into the Scandinavian context, Hamsun contrasts the Oriental fantasy and the rather shabby Scandinavian reality as two worlds apart, achieving a rather comic effect. For an inspiring and detailed recent reading of this text, see Oxfeldt, "Orientalism," 185–203.

55 Hamsun claims that his travel experiences reminded him of the distant Arabian Nights, as well as the homegrown Soria Moria tale. Hamsun, *I Æventyrland*, 30.

56 "Og her var alt fredelig, ingen hadde Hast, Østerlandens Ro hvilte over Menneskene. " Ibid., 125–26.

57 "Jo længer man kommer mot Østen des mindre taler Menneskene. De gamle Folkeslag har overvundet Pratets og Skrattets Standpunkt, de tier og smiler. Der er kanske det bedste slik. Koranen har skapt en Livsbetragtning som det ikke kan holdes møter om og debatteres om, dens

Mening er én: Lykken er at holde Livet ut, siden blir det bedre. Fatalismen. " Ibid., 38.

58 Ibid., 54–55.

59 Ibid., 69, 76.

60 Ibid., 104.

61 Ibid., 137–39.

62 Ibid., 70–71, 74.

63 Ibid., 72, 74.

64 "Det er en stor Hete og jeg faar mig en færdigsydd gul Silketrøie i en Bod. Nu blev mit Utseende vistnok litt rart; men Livet blev mig let at leve da jeg blev kvit min nordiske Vams. Jeg fik mig atpaa Kjøpet en vifte i Haanden." Ibid., 139.

65 Ibid., 151–53.

66 "Denne Plet er fuldkommen norsk i sin Karakter." Ibid., 48.

67 Ibid., 30.

68 Ibid., 51.

69 Ibid., 92.

70 "Folket her har utholdt Kampe som truet med at lægge det øde, men alt har det overvundet, det er stærkt og sundt, det florerer, det er idag et Folk paa ti Millioner ialt." Ibid., 94.

71 For instance, Ibid., 97.

72 Ibid., 134.

73 Oxfeldt, "Orientalism," 203–8.

74 Hamsun, I Æventyrland, 16. "Hans ansigt er ubehagelig, jødisk."

75 Ibid., 25–26.

76 Ibid., 161.

77 "En Jøde kan svindle ti Grækere, men Armenieren svindler baade Grækerne og Jøden, hørte vi i Orienten." Ibid., 131.

78 See the Center for Holocaust and Genocide Studies at the University of Minnesota Online: chgs.umn.edu/histories/armenian/theArmenians/shadow.html. See also Encyclopedia Britannica Online: Lib/hmn/eb.article–44274 (Armenia), and article–9117457 (Armenian massacres). As Taner Akçam writes: "Various figures have been given for the total number of dead resulting from the different incidents between 1894 and 1896. Kaiser Wilhelm II claimed, on the basis of reports he had received, that by 20 December 1895, some eighty thousand Armenians had been killed. The figures, given in French and English reports, are two hundred thousand and one hundred thousand, respectively. Johannes Lepsius, the

German pastor and Armenian advocate, puts the total figure at eighty-eight thousand, while the Armenian partirachate argued that the real number was in the area of three hundred thousand." Akçam, *A Shameful Act: The Armenian Genocide and the Question of Turkish Responsibility*, trans. Paul Bessemer (New York: Metropolitan Books, 2006), 42.

79   "Armenierne er Østens Handelsjøder. De borer sig ind overalt, fra Balkan til Kina, i alle byer hvor man kommer er Armenierne paafærde. Mens Vestens Aviser flommer over av Taarer over dette Folks Vanskjæbne, er det ikke vanskelig at høre i Østen at deres Skjæbne er fortjent, de fremstilles paafaldende enstemmig som et folk av kjæltringer. I selve Tyrkiet arbeider de landets egne Børn ut av den ene stilling efter den andre og indtar selv deres Plasser. Handelen kommer i deres Hænder, Pantelaanervirksomheten og Pengene. Og Utsugelsen." "Under halvmånen," *Stridende liv* (Kristiania: Gyldendahl, 1905), 266.

80   Ibid., 265.

81   "Sæt nu at jøderne i Norge begyndte å vise åpenbart eller hemmelig fiendskap imot staten og endog gav efter for en kronisk lyst til å gjøre væbnet motstand mot den—hvad så? Så dæmpet vi motstanden, skjøt opprørerne ned. Men dermed var ikke saken endt. Nu begynder jøderne over hele verden å hyle. Og de får med sig det kristne Europa til å hyle." Ibid., 266.

82   Ibid., 266. Articles from *Contemporary Review* and *Harpers Monthly Magazine* are mentioned, but authors' names, essay titles, and dates of publication are missing.

83   "En slik magtflytning finder ikke en stærk og herskende race sig i." Ibid., 293.

84   "Lat armenieren hyle og jøden krumme sig og hviske og smiske for den fremmede vantro,-ingen av dem har tyrkernes fred og ingen av dem får plass i profetens evige haver." Ibid., 298.

85   Ibid., 298.

86   "Jeg kunde ha tat jær med til Europa og lært jær op i pianospil og stemmeret og forfatterskap." Ibid., 302.

87   As Kittang observes, "Etterkvart som Hamsuns kulturkritiske holdningar skjerpar seg både i diktning og polemikk, blir motsetnaden mellom det orientalske og det oksidentalske eit stadig viktigare tema." (As Hamsun's cultural criticism becomes sharper, both in his fiction and polemical articles, the opposition between the Oriental and the Occidental becomes an increasingly important theme). *Luft, vind, ingenting*, 134.

6 Imagining the Sly Magic "Lapps"

1   The term "Lapp" was originally used both for the geographic regions in the North-East of Scandinavia and for their nomadic inhabitants: fishermen, hunters, and trappers. It appears to have first been used in the Russian region as "lop," later established as "lopaŕ." The earliest written appearance in Norse sources is in Saxo Grammaticus's *Gesta Danorum* (The deeds of the Danes) from about 1200. It soon appeared in Swedish, and eventually in Norwegian. Lars Ivar Hansen and Bjørnar Olsen discuss the historical usage of the terms "Finner"/"skridfinner" (Finns/skiing Finns), the customary Old Norse designation for the Sami, and "Lapper" (Lapps). See Hansen and Olsen, "Navngivningen av samene" (The naming of the Sami), in *Samenes historie fram til 1750* (History of the Sami up to 1750) (Oslo: Cappelen Akademisk Forlag, 2004), 45–51. See also Friedrich Kluge, *An Etymological Dictionary of the German Language* (London: George Bell and Sons, 1891), 203.

2   Several publications that approach Hamsun's texts from a post-colonialist framework have appeared recently. To mention just a few: Marit Elin Skrødal, "Samene i Knut Hamsuns diktning: En gjennomgang av samene og noen tatere i Hamsuns litterære verker" (Ph.D. diss., University of Tromsø, 1995); Troy Storfjell, "Samene i *Markens grøde*— kartlegging av en (umulig) idyll," in *Hamsun i Tromsø III*, ed. Even Arntzen and Henning H. Wærp (Hamarøy: Hamsun-Selskapet, 2003); Kristin Jernsletten, "Det samiske i *Markens grøde*: Erfaringer formidlet og fornektet i teksten," *Nordlit:Arbeidstidsskrift i litteratur* 12 (2003): 41–57.

3   The review is reprinted as "En bok om Lappernes liv" in *Hamsuns polemiske skrifter*, 193–97.

4   Harald Gaski, ed., *In the Shadow of the Midnight Sun: Contemporary Sami Prose and Poetry* (Kárásjohka: Davvi Girji, 1996) 43.

5   For an analysis of the collaboration between Turi and Demand Hatt, see Kristin Kuutma, "Collaborative Ethnography Before Its Time: Johan Turi and Emilie Demand Hatt," *Scandinavian Studies* 75(2) (2003): 165–80.

6   References and quotes are from the E. Gee Nash translation of Turi's book that appeared as *Turi's Book of Lappland* (New York: Harper & Brothers, 1931), 20–23.

7   Ibid., 107.

8   Ibid.

9   Ibid., 107–8.

10 "Men Boken fortjener det. Den er sikkert det mærkeligste skrift som nogensinde er frembrakt av en Lap om lappisk Liv og Miljø. Her er god Lappeforstand og stille, vek Følsomhet, her er Kundskap og Overtro, Lune, Polemik, Resignation; selve den barnlige Hjælpeløshet i Sproget er en Ynde mere." *Hamsuns polemiske skrifter*, 193.

11 "Selv Turis ugrammatikalske Sætninger har hun eftergjort saa jeg kjender dem igjen fra Lappens Tale i mine unge Dage." Ibid., 193.

12 *Joik* is traditional Sami singing, alluding to a person, place, or animal. Sometimes accompanied by drumming, joik can be reminiscent of Native American chanting.

13 "Johan Turi er en ubevidst Kunstner." *Hamsuns polemiske skrifter*, 194.

14 *Turi's Book of Lappland*, 45

15 *Hamsuns polemiske skrifter*, 194.

16 Ibid.

17 "Lappespørsmaalet." Ibid., 197.

18 The Karlstad Agreement, signed October 26, 1905, was the result of negotiations between Sweden and Norway about issues pertaining to the dissolution of the union. The two sides agreed on, among other issues, the grazing rights of the nomadic Sami on both sides of the border.

19 "Om Jødespørsmålet," in *Hamsuns polemiske skrifter*, 222. (The title was not Hamsun's but was added by Hermundstad.)

20 *Turi's Book of Lappland*, 10.

21 Einar Niemi, "Sami History and the Frontier Myth," in *Sami Culture in a New Era: The Norwegian Sami Experience*, ed. Harald Gaski (Kárásjohlea: Davvi Girji, 1997), 68.

22 Ibid., 70.

23 Ibid., 71.

24 Ibid., 73.

25 Kyllingsrad, *Kortskaller og longskaller*, 56–58.

26 Hans Fredrik Dahl, "Fascistisk fare for Norge?" (The Fascist danger in Norway?), in *De store ideologienes tid. Norsk idéhistorie, Bind V*, ed. Trond Berg Eriksen and Øystein Sørensen (Oslo: Aschehoug, 2001), 195.

27 In the 1950s there were still strong pressures on the Sami to Norwegianize, to adopt Norwegian as their primary language, abandon traditional customs, and settle permanently, although this was a period

of renewed Sami awakening and increased recognition of Sami rights. It was not until the 1960s, however, that popular attitudes toward the indigenous population shifted in significant ways, resulting in, among other things, increased interest in Sami languages, the establishment of Sami radio, graduate Sami Studies programs, and the Sami Parliament.

28 Grimley, *The New Norway: A People with the Spirit of Cooperation* (Oslo: Griff-Forlaget, 1937), 32.

29 Ibid., 35.

30 Ibid., 37–38.

31 Ibid., 38–39.

32 Ibid., 16–30.

33 First published in the newspaper *Vestoplændingen*, June 11, 1918. Reprinted in *Hamsuns polemiske skrifter*, 220.

34 First published in the newspaper *Grimstad Adressetidende*, December 1, 1927. Reprinted in *Hamsuns polemiske skrifter*, 223.

35 See Nils M. Knutsen, *Knut Hamsun og Nordland: Den lange veien hjem* (Tromsø: Angelica Forlag, 2006); Troy Storfjell, "Mapping a Space for Sámi Studies in North America," *Scandinavian Studies* 75(2) (2003): 153–64.

36 See Reimund Kvideland and Henning K. Sehmsdorf, *Scandinavian Folk Belief and Legend* (Minneapolis: University of Minnesota Press, 1988), 8.

37 Lindow, "Supernatural Others and Ethnic Others," 21.

38 "The earliest outsiders, the blámenn and skrælinger, and the later ones, the Samis and Finns, Gypsies and tinkers, were all marked with similar attributes or emblems of contrast." Ibid., 22.

39 Ibid., 11.

40 Per Bjørn Rekdal, *Norsk museumsformidling og den flerkulturelle utfordringen* (Norwegian Museum Stewardship and the Multicultural Challenge) (Oslo: Norsk museumsutvikling 7, 1999). Rekdal includes a valuable overview of how ethnographic collections in Norway came to be, illuminating the attitudes of Scandinavians toward non-Scandinavian peoples in the process.

41 See Rekdal's chapter, "Fra nasjonal ensidighet til inkludering av urfolk og nasjonale minoriteter" (From national one-sidedness to inclusion of indigenous peoples and national minorities), ibid., 29.

42 Mary Bouquet's study of the University Ethnographic Museum, *Sans og samling/Bringing It All Back Home* (Oslo: Universitetsforlag,

Universitetets Etnografiske Museum, 1996), illustrates this shift well.

43 The passionate public discussion (winter 2005) in connection with the reorganization of the exhibits in the National Gallery in Oslo within the parameters of European artistic movements rather than within the framework of the Norwegian state-building project, shows how deeply ingrained nineteenth century ideas about Norwegianness still are. See, for instance, Lars Roar Langslet's "Nasjonalgalleriets undergang" (The National Gallery's destruction), *Dagbladet*, March 31, 2005; also online at http//www.dagbladet.no/kultur/2005/3/31/427532.html.

44 *Turi's Book of Lappland*, 23–27.

45 "Den lange, lange sti over myrene og ind i skogene hvem har trakket op den? Manden, mennesket, den første som var her. Det var ingen sti før ham. Siden fulgte et og andet dyr de svake spor over moer og myrer og gjorde dem tydeligere, og siden igjen begyndte en og anden lap å snuse stien op og gå den når han skulde fra fjæld til fjæld og se til sin ren. Slik blev stien til gjennem den store almenning som ingen eiet, det herreløse land." Hamsun, *Markens grøde, in Samlede verker*, vol. 7 (Oslo: Gyldendal, 1992), 145. Translation is mine, although it is based on Hamsun, *Growth of the Soil*, trans. W. W. Worster (New York: Vintage, 1972 [original c. 1921]).

46 Niemi, "Sami History and the Frontier Myth," 62.

47 Ibid., 62.

48 Roald Berg, "Nation-Building, State Structure, and Ethnic Groups: The Scandinavian Sámis, 1905–1919," *Scandinavian Journal of History* 20: 61–69. See also Helge Salversen's chapter "Sami Ædnan: Four States— One Nation? Nordic Minority Policy and the History of the Sami," in *Ethnicity and Nation Building in the Nordic World*, ed. Sven Tägil (Carbondale: Southern Illinois University Press, 1995).

49 Niemi, "Sami History and the Frontier Myth," 62.

50 As quoted by Niemi, ibid., 62.

51 "Skal du bo her for godt? —Ja, svarte manden. —Hvad du heter? —Isak. Du vet ikke av en kvindfolkhæjlp til mig? Nei. Men jeg skal orde det der jeg farer." *Samlede verker*, vol. 7, 146.

52 "Ja goddag sier de, og at her er kommet gromt folk i marken!—Lapperne de slesker altid." Ibid., 147.

53 "Inger forundret sig over at han ikke tagg om noget, det gjorde Os-Anders ellers altid, det gjør alle lapper, de tigger. Os-Anders sitter og karver i sin kridtpipestubb og tænder. Å for en pipe, han røker og drager

så hele hans gamle rynkede ansigt står som en rune." Ibid., 168.

54 "Men en lap han tigger ydmygt, men får han nei så blir han hævngjær-
rig og truer. Et Lappepar med to børn kom forbi nybygget, børnene
blev sendt ind i stuen for å tigge, de kom tilbake og mældte at det var
ingen i stuen. Familjen stod en stund og talte det over på lappisk, så gik
manden ind for å se. Han blev borte. Konen gik efter, derpå børnene, de
blev alle stående i stuen og småpratet lappisk. Manden stikker hodet ind
i kammerset, det var heller ingen der. Stueklokken slår, familjen lytter
forundret og blir stående." Ibid., 184–85.

55 "Sellanrå er ikke længer et øde sted, her er syv mennesker med småt og
stort." Ibid., 283.

56 "Lapperne kommer ikke længer forbi og gjør sig til herrer på nybygget,
det er for længe siden ophørt. Lapperne de kommer ikke ofte forbi, de
gjør helst en stor bue utenom gården, men de kommer ialfald ikke ind
i stuen mere, de stanser ute, hvis de i det hele tat stanser. Lapperne de
vanker i utkanterne, i det skumle, sæt lys og luft på dem, og de vantrives
som utøi og makk. Nu og da blir en kalv eller et lam tvært borte i Sellan-
rås utmark, langt borti en utkant. Det er intet å gjøre ved." Ibid., 312.

57 "Og der går menneskene og snakker og tænker og er sammen med himmel og jord." Ibid., 369.

58 Lindow, "Supernatural Others and Ethnic Others," 20–21.

59 Ibid., 27–28.

60 Marte Hvam Hult, *Framing a National Narrative: The Legend Collection of Peter Christen Asbjørnsen* (Detroit: Wayne State University
Press, 2003), 156. Here I follow Hult's translation of Norwegian terms.

61 Ibid., 156.

62 In terms of sexuality, Lindow argues, the marker that divided the two
groups was an ability to control one's sexual impulses (for insiders), in
contrast to the animalistic, immediate satisfaction of one's impulses (for
outsiders). Lindow, "Supernatural Others and Ethnic Others," 27.

63 Leo Löwenthal, "Knut Hamsun," in *Literature and the Image of Man*
(Boston: Beacon Press, 1957).

64 Hamsun first mentions his novel set in the region of the Lapps in a letter
to Albert Langen from July 22, 1894. *Knut Hamsuns brev*, vol. 1, pp.
418–20, letter no. 332.

65 "Jeg lærte å kjende en gammel blind lap tilfjælds. I otte og femti år
hadde han intet set og nu var han over sytti. Det forekom ham at han
så bedre og bedre tid for tid, det gik jævnt fremover, syntes han. Kom

ikke noget iveien vilde han kunde skimte solen om nogen år. . . . Når vi sat sammen i hans gamme og røkte fortalte han om alt han hadde set før han blev blind." *Pan*, in *Samlede verker*, vol. 2 (Oslo: Gyldendal, 1963).

66 The trilogy is discussed in greater detail in chapter 2.

67 "Her går jeg til nar i en laps mundering/og driver al dagen en laps håndtering,/nu slutter jeg op med den dårlige flid,/jeg spilte mit spil og tjente min tid." *Munken Vendt*, in *Samlede verker*, vol. 14 (Oslo: Gyldendal, 1964), 247.

68 "Men saken er: lappen har været her idag, Gilbert; han gjør mig altid så angst. Han vet så meget." *Rosa*, in *Samlede verker*, vol. 5 (Oslo: Gyldendal, 1963), 227.

69 "Det er unævnelig hvad de gjør. " Ibid., 205.

70 "En dag så jeg to lapper møtes. Det var en gut og en pike. Til å begynde med bar de sig ad som mennesker gjør. *Boris!* sa de til hverandre og smilte. Men straks efter faldt de overende i sneen og blev borte for mig en god stund. Du får se efter dem, tænkte jeg da et kvarter var gåt, de kunde kvæles in sneen. Da reiste de sig op og gik bort hver sin vei./Jeg har aldrig i mine luvslitte dager set maken til hilsen." *Den siste glæde*, in *Samlede verker*, vol. 7 (Oslo: Gyldendal, 1992), 7–8.

71 "Et kjedelig ingenting." Ibid., 20.

72 "Dyrisk taushet." Ibid.

73 Ibid., 21.

74 "Disse små væsener; disse menneskegryn." Ibid.

75 "Det er vel gjærne lappen som troller dette! Lappen? Å den menneske-grynen, den høifjældssilden—og her er jeg! Hvad har jeg med alle disse skral å skaffe?" Ibid., 23.

76 "Åse var høy og mørk, hendes far skulde være tater og morn lap" (Åse was tall and dark, her father was rumored to be gypsy and her mother a Lapp). *Men livet lever*, in *Samlede verker*, vol. 12 (Oslo: Gyldendal, 1992), 19.

77 "Han var fanten, farken. Gammelmoderen kunde ikke klage på ham, han hadde sin races erotiske grådighet og holdt henne i stadig hiken." Ibid., 85.

78 Ibid., 83–86.

79 "Er han et dyr eller et menneske?" Ibid., 143.

7 Imagining Degeneration and Revolution

Tidens Tegn, December 6, 1914; reprinted in *Hamsuns polemiske skrifter* (Oslo: Gyndendal, 1998), 200.

1   In another contribution to the debate with Professor Collin, Hamsun referred to English women as being on a "forward march toward sterility" (here quoted from Ferguson, *Enigma*, 235), the implication being that German women had much higher reproductive rates than degenerating England had.

2   Hans Fredrik Dahl writes that there never was a realistic chance for radical nationalism to take over without the support of German troops. The Norwegians' patriotic feelings had been channeled into constituting their own state in 1905, while the period between the wars concluded the Norwegianization process. For instance, there were a number of writing and spelling reforms to cleanse the language of Danish, some cities were renamed, the Norwegian Gyldendal publishing house (of which Hamsun was a major shareholder) was established, and so forth. Minority questions were essentially insignificant. In other words, there were no major frustrations or repressed patriotic feelings that Nazi Germany could exploit. See Hans Fredrik Dahl, "Fascistisk fare for Norge?" (Fascist danger for Norway?), in *Norsk idéhistorie*, vol. 5 (Oslo: Aschehoug, 2001), 189–228. For a good source of information in English, see Oddvar K. Høidal, *Quisling: A Study in Treason* (Oslo: Universitetsforlaget, 1989).

3   His ideas are discussed in detail in chapter 1.

4   For instance, in *Trøndelagens antropologi*. See Kyllingstad, *Kortskaller og langskaller*, 94.

5   Among his numerous publications, several stand out as milestones in his development. *Bidrag til belysning av det norske folks anthropologi i begyndelsen av det 20de aarhundrede: Trøndelagens antropologi* (Contribution to the illumination of the Norwegian folk's anthropology in the beginning of the twentieth century: The anthropology of Trøndelag; 1917) is considered his breakthrough study. *Menneskerasene og deres utviklingshistorie* (Human races and their developmental history; 1925) and two articles published in the German journal *Anthropos* in 1926 explain in detail his views on the interconnections between human hereditary traits, geographic environment, and cultural development.

6   Kyllingstad, *Kortskaller og langskaller,* 128.

7   Ibid., 92–111.

8   As Kyllingstad shows, Bryn also corresponded with German scientists who were extremely critical of the idea of the Nordic race, for instance, Karl Saller and Walter Scheidt, who viewed the idea as a political, nationalistic, and dangerous construction. Ibid., 172–74.

9   Ibid., 93.

10 Kristian Emil Schreiner, *Zur Osteologie der Lappen,* vols. 1 and 2 (Oslo: Aschehoug, 1931–35).

11 "NS programs høye idealitet midt i en tid av materialisme, slapphet og dekadense gjorde at jeg av hele min sjel sluttet meg til," as quoted in Birgit Gjernes, *Marie Hamsun: Et livsbilde* (Marie Hamsun: A life portrait) (Oslo: Aschehoug, 1994), 94.

12 Heming Gujord's article "Norske forfattere i historiens tjeneste" (Norwegian writers in the service of history), charts how the German National Socialist party, after it came to power in 1933, started an intense program of nation re-building which was not just German but Nordic. It promoted the idea of the common Nordic spirit and race, and established, or expanded, a number of exchange programs between the new Germany and the individual Scandinavian countries. *Edda* 2 (2000): 158–70.

13 Oddvar K. Høidal, "Vidkun Quisling and the Deportation of Norway's Jews." Manuscript. The article will be part of the "Norway, World War II, and the Holocaust" conference proceedings. The conference itself took place on April 21, 2007, at the University of Minnesota.

14 Quisling had, in a speech, accused the leaders of the labor parties of being agents of the USSR. See *Hamsuns polemiske skrifter,* 230.

15 Dahl, *Norsk idéhistorie,* 295.

16 Dyrik Danielsen et al., *A History of Norway: From the Vikings to Our Own Time* (Oslo: Universitetsforlaget, 1995).

17 The fact, however, that many writers could write undisturbed during the war, as evidenced by the immense output of publications in the years 1945–46, is remarkable. In no way should the harshness of war circumstances in Norway be minimized, but it would be hard to imagine that writers of stature would be left alone this way in Poland or Yugoslavia. This "benevolent" treatment on the part of German authorities in Norway was, of course, based on the idea of the Pan-Germanic racial brotherhood.

18 "Det meldtes fra Sverige at Carl Joachim Hambro vilde tale til det norske folk. Ja, han var den rette! Han er sønn av en i sin tid innvandret
familie som har fått være her i landet. En prater, en talemaskin. Han har
vel sine fortjenester han og, men det å rettlede det norske folk just nu,
det er han ikke mann for. Han mangler grunnlaget: det å være norsk i
sin sjel. Denne mangel på norsk sjel har han vist flere ganger.

"Her forkynner han nu at Norge er i krig med Tyskland. Nei, tale-
maskinen har uret, men den velsignede propaganda må han jo ikke
forsømme selv efter at han er rømt til et fremmed land." *Hamsuns polemiske skrifter,* 239.

19 "Ihr Brief hat mich tief gerührt, ich kann aber nichts anders antworten
als was Sie vorher wissen. Sie gehören als Jude einer Rasse, die—natürlich
wegen ihrer eigenartigen Einstellung—auf allen Kulturgebieten in allen
Ländern überlegen ist. In Wissenschaft, Kunst, Dichtung, Industrie—in
allem sind die Juden auf dem Gipfel. Das wird soviel ich weiss von nie-
mand verweigert. Dass es auch die Juden sind, die von dem Geldgewalt
im Besitz sind, macht sie zu einer Macht in der internazionalen Politik
und im Welthandel. Sie überwältigen die eigene Bevölkerung der Län-
der." Hamsun to Artur Meyerfeld, August 22, 1933, in *Hamsuns brev,
1925–1933,* vol. 5, 503. Knut Hamsun, for all his admiration of Germany and German culture never learned the German language. It was
his wife, Marie, who translated his correspondence into German.

20 Meyerfeld fled to the United States where, after a variety of jobs, he held
a position at the Stanford University Library. See Allen Simpson, "Knut
Hamsun's Anti-Semitism," *Edda* 5 (1977): 273–93.

21 Nazi ideology appropriated facets of an anti-Semitic and racist worldview that had circulated around Europe long before the 1930s, and
transformed these common prejudices and latent attitudes into a political program. Originally based on religion, and later compounded by eco-
nomics, anti-Semitism entered the political sphere and converged with
racial anti-Semitism resulting in Jews being labeled as *Untermenschen*
(subhumans). It also had a strong sexual component. Intellectuals were
not immune to anti-Semitism. Many of the ideas, later appropriated by
the Nazis, were first articulated, probed, contested, and advanced in
intellectual circles.

22 "Ich habe es nicht so verstanden, dass Deutschland die Juden aus dem
Lande rotten will, so wird es aber allerdings von den jüdischen Poli-
tikern Englands und Frankreichs und von der jüdischen Presse überall

dargestellt. Ich habe es so verstanden, dass Deutschland nur die jüdische Macht innerhalb des Landes hemmen will, so dass es nicht die Juden sind, sondern die Deutschen, die in Deutschland *herschen* sollen." *Hamsuns brev,* vol. 5, 503.

23 "Das Unglück ist, dass die Juden kein grosses Land für sich allein haben. Palästina kann sie nicht fassen, und in allen fünf Weltteilen scheint es unmöglich ein eigenes Landgebiet, gross genug für sie zu finden. Es ist für beide Parteien unbefriedigend, dass die Juden dazu gezwungen sind unter fremden Rassen zu Hause zu sein. Die in Politik und Geld mächtigen Juden sollten nicht ruhen, ehe ein grosses neues Judeland gefunden war." Ibid.

24 "Aber Deutschland muss sich wehren können, wenn es in grosser Mass von dieser fremden Rasse überwältigt wird. Politiker und Finanzmänner sollten für die Juden Raum *roden* können (sic!) in ihrem eigenen Land, sie haben zu Palästina älteres Recht als die Araber, sie haben *all* Recht." *Knut Hamsuns brev,* vol. 6, p. 104, letter no. 2456 (November 24, 1935).

25 Reprinted in *Hamsuns polemiske skrifter,* 222–23.

26 See Hans Fredrik Dahl, "Fascistisk fare for Norge?" 200.

27 Ibid., 200.

28 "Det ønskelige var vel at Jøderne blev samlet i et Land som de kunde kalde deres eget, saa den eksklusivt hvite Race slap for videre Blodblanding og hvorfra Jøderne allikevel kunde virke med sin beste Egenskaper til Fordel for hele Verden. Men hvor er det Land? . . . Men saa længe ikke dette sker har Jøderne intet andet Hjem end andres Hjem. De maa da fremdeles leve og virke i de fremmede Samfund, til Ulykke for begge Parter." Hamsun, "Om jødespørsmålet." *Hamsuns polemiske skrifter,* 223.

29 Oskar Mendelsohn, "Jødene i Norge," in *Judiskt liv i Norden,* 39–51. The summary in English, titled "History of the Jews in Norway" is on p. 51. The summary reveals that 1880 was a watershed year; prior to this date most new Jewish settlers came from Germany, Austria, or Denmark, after that date from Eastern Europe. After Norway was occupied by Germany in 1940, more than 900 of the 1,800 Norwegian Jews escaped to Sweden, while only 25 of the approximately 760 who were deported in 1942 survived.

30 As quoted in Samuel Abrahamsen, *Norway's Response to the Holocaust* (New York: Holocaust Library, 1991), 25.

31 Ibid., 102.

32 "Hirden," a name taken from the medieval Norwegian warriors whose main task was to protect the king, identified the militant core of the NS party. Though unarmed, members wore uniforms and were placed in charge of security issues.

33 Abrahamsen, *Norway's Response to the Holocaust*, 112.

34 Ibid., 153.

35 Bjørn Westlie, "Still No Peace for the Jews of Norway: The Unresolved Restitution Claims," Institute of the World Jewish Congress, Policy Forum no. 12, Jerusalem 1996. See also Westlie's book, *Oppgjør i skyggen av Holocaust* (Settling of accounts in the shadow of Holocaust) (Oslo: Aschehoug, 2002).

36 "Jeg synes forresten ikke det er galt at Jøderne i Norge faar det Skjema. De kommer ikke ut av Landet for det, under alle Omst., ikke før efter Krigen—og Krigen kan dra ut." Knut Hamsun to Tore Hamsun, March 15, 1942. *Knut Hamsuns brev*, vol. 6, p. 310, letter no. 2699.

37 "Og Jøden Harald Beyer (han med en Slags Bok om Kierkegaard) er ikke han skutt? Skulde vært det." Knut Hamsun to Tore Hamsun, February 14, 1943. *Knut Hamsuns brev*, vol. 6, p. 337, letter no. 2733. The issue of Beyer's book on Kierkegaard had occupied Hamsun for a while; in an earlier letter he commented: "As if a Jew can write about Kierkegaard!" (Som om en Jøde kan skrive om Kierkegaard!). Knut Hamsun to Tore Hamsun, April 12, 1942. *Knut Hamsuns brev*, vol. 6, p. 314, letter no. 2703.

38 Ferguson, *Enigma*, 365.

39 "en jøde i jødisk tjeneste, den førende ånd i Amerikas krig for gullet og jødemakten." "Virkeliggjort kameratskap," in *Berlin-Rom-Tokio*, no. 2, 1942. Reprinted in *Hamsuns polemiske skrifter*, 259.

40 "Europa ønsker seg hverken jødene eller gullet deres, hverken amerikanerne eller landet deres." *Hamsuns polemiske skrifter*, 260.

41 Quote from Jørgen Haugan, *Solgudens fall*, 316–17.

42 Hamsun defended Germany's right to rearm, which went counter to the Versailles Treaty of 1919. While he attacked Great Britain for its imperialist appetites, he supported Germany's desire for colonial expansion on the basis that Germany was a young country in need of more territory.

43 "Ossietzky," in *Tidens Tegn*, November 22, 1935; quoted in *Hamsuns polemiske skrifter*, 235.

44 "Det her gjaldt at omdanne *fra Grunden* et Samfund paa 66 Millioner

Mennesker, og at dette har nu Tyskland strævet med i femten Maanader," *Aftenposten*, July 10, 1934; quoted in *Hamsuns polemiske skrifter*, 233. The text is actually Hamsun's response to Johan Fredrik Paasche's comments of three days earlier, "'Vente og se' og norsk nasjonal samling."

45 The early acceptance of Hamsun's works in Germany and his successful collaboration with Alfred Langen Publishing house in Munich surely has much to do with his German sympathies. But underneath the more tangible causes is, I believe, an essential compatibility of *weltanschauung*.

46 *Grimstad Adressetidende*, January 30, 1941; quoted in *Hamsuns polemiske skrifter*, 250.

47 "Det er en dyp bevissthet om det kjente og det hemmelige, grunnet på slektskap og blod. Vi er alle germanere." Ibid., 250.

48 First published under "Ærer de Unge" in *Aftenposten*, December 15, 1941; quoted in *Hamsuns polemiske skrifter*, 252.

49 *Knut Hamsun, Selected Letters*, vol. 2: *1898–1952*, ed. Harald Næss and James McFarlane (Norwich: Norvik Press, 1998), 331.

50 *Hamsuns polemiske skifter*, 264.

51 "England høster alltid fordel av andres nederlag. Den tyske befolkning hadde også litt etter litt i årenes løp fått innsig av fremmede elementer som infiserte og svekket den germanske ånd i folket—det passet England godt, Tyskland skulde svekkes. Et overdrev av ugermanske folkeslag og raser grasserte i landet og utbyttet befolkningen som no var utpint etter krigen. Det var mørke år for Tyskland, pålagt en eventyrlig milliardbyrde i krigsskadeerstatning, flåten senket, koloniene røvet, arbeidsløshet og nød." *Hamsuns polemiske skrifter*, 266.

52 Ibid., 267.

53 Ibid. Ferguson also shares this opinion, see *Enigma*, 373.

54 Gjernes, *Marie Hamsun*, 101.

55 Hermundstad, *Hamsuns polemiske skrifter*, 13.

56 Per Ole Johansen, "Norsk Embedsverk og jødiske innvandrere og flyktninger 1914–1940," in *Judiskt liv i Norden* (Jewish life in Scandinavia), ed. Gunnar Broberg, Harald Runblom, and Mattias Tyden (Uppsala: Acta Universitatis Upsaliensis, 1988), 287.

57 "Det de fleste kan være enige om, er at Hamsun fra sitt elfenbenstårn ikke hadde evnen til å analysere nazismens virkelige vesen og gjorde en rekke fatale feilvurderinger. Problemet bunner i at den nazistiske ideologien utad presenterte seg i finklærne, mens de harde politiske realiteter ble holdt skjult. Som så mange andre lot Hamsun seg forføre og utnytte

av nazistenes propagandamaskineri." Hermundstad, *Polemiske skrifter,* 13.

58 See also Hamsun's article "Virkeliggjort kameratskap" (Realized camaraderie), published in the German monthly *Berlin-Rom-Tokio,* Nr. 2, 1942. Here Hamsun displays broad yet biased knowledge of the international state of affairs and writes of the Bolsheviks, the British, and their "Friendship" against Germany, of the Eastern front and of Roosevelt's actions. It is interesting that Hamsun distinguishes between the Russians and the Bolsheviks, but does not make the same distinction between the Germans and the Nazis. Reprinted in *Hamsuns polemiske skrifter,* 255–260.

In his article "Hilsningstelegram til Presseklubbens Finnlandskveld," published in *Aftenposten* on February 23, 1944, Hamsun refers to Finnish newspapers he reads and mentions that he follows the developments on the front and uses a map on his wall. Reprinted in *Hamsuns polemiske skrifter,* 272.

59 Kolloen, *Hamsun Erobreren,* 457.

60 Jon Langdal, "Hvordan trylle bort det ubehaglige?" (How to conjure away the uncomfortable?), *Agora* 1–2 (1999): 232–64. "Psykologisk atomisme" is on p. 234.

61 Hans Fredrik Dahl, "Huset i mørkret," *Norsk idéhistorie,* vol. 5, 283–84.

62 Ibid., 284.

63 *Germanske Budstikke,* 5–7 (1943): 211–16.

64 *Heftet* 1 (1944): 42–43.

65 *Germanske Budstikke* 2(5) (1942): 246.

66 *Ideologisk Månedshefte for Hirden* 2 (May 1941), 30.

67 *Ragnarok* 9–10 (1944): 413.

68 *Norwegen: Geschichte—Kultur—Wirtschaft—in Wort and Bild,* ed. Wilhelm Arppe et al. (Oslo: Kamban forlag), and *Das bibliographische Institut A. G. Leipzig* (The Bibliographical Institute in Leipzig), 1943.

69 "Er den zivilisatorischen Fortschritt mit natürlicher Einfachkeit, die manchmal wie Primitivität erscheint, zu verbinden liebt." *Norwegen,* 35

70 "Die namenlose Natur je ungebändigter, desto lieber für den Norweger." Ibid., 36

71 "Der norwegische Mensch ist ein Erhalter wertvoller germanischer Blutsgüter." Ibid., 130.

72 "Lappe und Renntier gehören zusammen." Ibid., 238.

73 See, for instance, Bjørn Westlie, *Oppgjør i skyggen av Holocaust,* which mentions Hamsun's fame as an influence on peoples' political decisions (45).

74 "Norwegen und die Norweger" was published in Oslo in *Für ein Gross-germanien, Schwert und Wiege* (For a Great Germania, sword and cradle), ed. Wilhelm Rediess (Oslo: Aasj Wahls boktrykkeri, 1943), 7–19.

75 "Rassen- und bevölkerungspolitische Lage der germanischen Völker," *Norwegen und die Norweger,* 7.

76 "Diese Entwicklung wäre nicht möglich gewesen, wenn die norwegische Frau ihre Pflicht als wahre Hausfrau und Mutter—die norwegische Sprache kennt dafür das schöne Wort 'husmor,' Hausmutter—erkannt und erfüllt hätte." Ibid., 17–18.

77 "Die norwegische akademische Jugend aber jubelte den Niggern zu!" Ibid., 19.

78 "Denn die rassischen Werte und die Erbgesundheit des norwegischen Volkes sind zumindest ebenso gut wie die des deutschen." Ibid.

79 "Eine Erziehung besonders der Jugend und der Kinder wird auch die Norweger wieder zu einem 'nordischen' Volk nach unseren Begriffen machen können. Das ist unser Ziel." Ibid.

80 See, for example, his article "Jeg bier paa at vaare studenter skal storme frem og være med" (I am waiting for my students to rush forward and join), where Hamsun urges the students to do what is necessary for Norway to become "et frit og gjenreist Folk i Europas Nyordning" (a free and restored people in Europe's New Order). First published in *Bergens Tidende,* March 30, 1942. Reprinted in *Hamsuns polemiske skrifter,* 261.

81 "Jeg er ikke verdig til at tale høirøstet om Hitler, og til nogen sentimental Rørelse indbyder hans Liv og Gjerning ikke. Han var en Kriger, en Kriger for Mennskeheden og en Forkynder av Evangeliet om Ret for alle Nasjoner. Han var en reformatorisk Skikkelse av høieste Rang, og hans historiske Skjebne var den, at han virket i en Tid av den eksempelløseste Raahet, som tilslut fældte ham. Slik tør den almindelige Vesteuropæer se paa Adolf Hitler. Og vi, hans nære Tilhængere, bøier nu vaare Hoder ved hans Død." *Aftenposten,* May 7, 1945; quoted in *Hamsuns polemiske skrifter,* 274.

82 Ferguson, *Enigma,* 386.

83 Umberto Eco, "Ur-Fascism," *The New York Review of Books* 42 (June 22, 1995); George L. Mosse, *Nazi Culture: Intellectual, Cultural and*

Social Life in the Third Reich (Madison: University of Wisconsin Press, 2003; originally published in 1966).

84 See my earlier discussions of research by John Lindow in chapter 1, and of research by Reimund Kvideland and Henning Sehmsdorf in chapter 6.

85 In his 1917 book *Norsk naturfølelse i det nittende aarhundrede* (Norwegian feelings for nature in the nineteenth century) (Kristiania: Aschehoug, 1917), Theodor Caspari maps the Norwegian writers' appreciation for the native landscape, from earlier writers like Ludvik Holberg and Peter Dass to Hans E. Kinck and Knut Hamsun at the beginning of the twentieth century. Caspari, writing in the same year that Hamsun published his *Markens grøde*, positions Hamsun's appreciation for nature in a wider, native literary tradition. In Hamsun's worldview, he posits, culture and nature coexist ambivalently and contradictorily, while God is only *en aesthetisk Pynt* ("an aesthetic decoration," 184). A Hamsun contemporary here makes important observations of Hamsun's modernity in the same year when his novel was hailed as the colonization-as-salvation book of the decade.

86 Dagmar Herzog, *Sex after Fascism: Memory and Morality in Twentieth-Century Germany* (Princeton: Princeton University Press, 2005), 15–16.

87 Mosse, *Nazi Culture*, 21.

88 *Ideologisk Månedshefte for Hirden* 1 (July 1941): 9–12.

89 "I denne forbindelse har de kanskje tenkt seg kvinnen stående bak talerstolen, eller til og med snakkende og røkende i mennenes krets. . . . Denne tidsepoke er for alltid et tilbakelagt stadium." Ibid., 9.

90 Ibid., 10.

91 Ibid, 10–12.

92 "Adolf Hitler om den tyske kvinne," *SS–Germanske Budstikke* 1 (1942): 48.

93 "Et brev fra Knut Hamsun," *SS-Hefte* 1 (1944): 42–43.

8 The Rhetoric of Defense in Hamsun's *Paa gjengrodde stier*

Harald Ness and James McFarlane, eds., *Knut Hamsun: Selected Letters*, vol. 2 (Norwich, UK: Norvik Press, 1998), 237.

1 Johannes Andenæs points out that Hamsun's beliefs were not at issue but rather his articles and actions. *Det vanskelige oppgjøret: Rettsoppgjøret*

etter okkupasjonen (Oslo: Tanum-Norli, 1980), 265.

2   Anine Kierulf and Cato Schiøtz, *Høyesterett og Knut Hamsun* (The Supreme Court and Knut Hamsun) (Oslo: Gyldendal, 2004), 16.

3   Ibid., 41.

4   Quoted from Ferguson, *Enigma*, 402.

5   Richard H. Lucas and K. Byron McCoy, *The Winning Edge: Effective Communication and Persuasion Techniques for Lawyers* (New York: Wiley Law Publications, 1993), xi and chapter 1.

6   Ibid., xi.

7   Bettyruth Walter, *The Jury Summation as Speech Genre* (Amsterdam/ Philadelphia: John Benjamins Publishing Company, 1988). Abstract.

8   Chaim Perelman and L. Olbrechts-Tyteca, *The New Rhetoric: A Treatise on Argumentation* (Notre Dame, IN: University of Notre Dame Press, 1969), 19.

9   "For vaare Børnebørn." Hamsun, *Paa gjengrodde stier,* 60. All quotes are from the 1949 edition (Oslo: Gyldendal). Translations are mine. There are several English translations, the first being *On Overgrown Paths,* trans. Carl L. Anderson (New York: Paul S. Eriksson, Inc., 1967).

10   As recently as 2004, Norwegians have expressed their loathing for Hamsun's support of the occupiers. In a letter to the editor, a resistance veteran from Romsdal, Olaf Johan Hartmann-Johnsen, wrote that those who fought the Germans could not understand why Hamsun was not convicted of a crime and his property confiscated. The psychiatric report was a pathetic attempt by the authorities to save Hamsun from a prison term, he said. While Hamsun enjoyed himself at Nørholm, many survivors of the war suffered greatly. "A shame for Norway," Hartmann-Johnsen concluded the letter. Olaf Johan Hartmann-Johnsen, "Knut Hamsun fortjente vår avsky" (Knut Hamsun deserved our loathing), *Aftenposten,* October 30, 2004.

11   "Jeg tror mange andre psykiatere ville ha landet på samme konklusjon som Langfeldt og Ødegård. Denne konklusjonen ville vel for øvrig neppe ha blitt bestridt hvis ikke Hamsun selv hadde stilt spørsmål ved konklusjonen med sin harselerende sluttroman." Einar Kringlen, "Knut Hamsuns personlighet," *Nytt norsk tidskrift* 1 (2005): 18–29, 28.

12   Ibid., 28.

13   Ferguson, *Enigma*, 390.

14   "Derimot må det sies at i forhold til alderen er hans interesser og hans hukommelse ikke ringere enn hans alder tilsier. Det kan vel tvertimot

sies at det er sjelden å treffe på en 86 årig mann som har såpass våkne interesser for aktuelle spørsmål som obs." Gabriel Langfeldt and Ørnulv Ødegård, *Den rettspsykiatriske erklæring om Knut Hamsun* (Oslo: Gyldendal, 1978), 100.

15 "Jeg sitter her frisk og sund og jukser mig selv med Vilje. Det maa mindst være Schizofreni." Hamsun, *Paa gjengrodde stier*, 74.

16 Hamsun, *On Overgrown Paths*, x.

17 "frå hi sida av diktarlivet." Atle Kittang, *Luft, vind, ingenting*, 13, note 3.

18 Ferguson, *Enigma*, 417.

19 See Kristeva's chapter on "The Practice of Language," in *Language the Unknown: An Initiation into Linguistics*, trans. Anne M. Menke (New York: Columbia University Press, 1989), 278–94. The quote is on p. 282.

20 "Her har jeg nu vært vittig Hund. Jeg har blandet godt sammen Blad-skriverne, Ol'Hansa og mig selv. Saa ingen av os skal faa noget at si." Hamsun, *Paa gjengrodde stier*, 144.

21 Dorrit Cohn, *The Distinction of Fiction* (Baltimore: Johns Hopkins University Press, 1999), 34.

22 "Det har ikke vært ment som noe forsvar fra min side." Hamsun, *Paa gjengrodde stier*, 155.

23 "Jeg hadde allerede fra første Stund i Forhørsretten den 23. Juni paatat mig Ansvaret for det jeg har gjort og siden hele Tiden hevdet dette Stand-punkt uavkortet." Ibid., 61.

24 "Jeg visste jo nemlig med mig selv at dersom jeg kunde tale ubundet, vilde Været vende sig til Frifindelse for mig, eller saa nær Frifindelse som jeg selv turde gaa og Retten akseptere." Ibid., 61–62.

25 "Jeg visste jeg var uskyldig, døv og uskyldig, jeg skulde ha klaret mig godt i en Eksaminasjon av Statsadvokaten bare ved at fortelle det meste av Sandheten." Ibid., 62.

26 "Det jeg talte følger her efter det stenografiske Referat. (NB! Herfra efter Referentens Retskrivning og er ikke rettet av Forfatteren)." Ibid., 147. The NB is not in the English translation.

27 "Jeg skal ikke oppta så svært lang tid for den ærede rett." Ibid., 147.

28 Ibid.

29 Hamsun would have spelled it "Påstand" with an 'nd', just as he would have written "Undskyld" instead of "unnskyld," and he would have used capital letters for nouns.

30 "Så var det forhørsretten for 2, 3 eller 5 år siden. Det er så lenge siden at jeg intet husker, men jeg svarte på spørsmålene." Hamsun, *Paa gjengrodde stier*, 148.

31 For a succinct summary of the argumentation on the part of the court, see Johs. Andenæs's article "Knut Hamsun og landssvikoppgjøret," reprinted in *Det uskyldige geni? Fra debatten om "Prosessen mot Hamsun,"* ed. Simen Skjønsberg (1979), 138–63, 149.

32 "Det kan godt være at jeg nå og da kan ha skrevet i NS' ånd." Hamsun, *Paa gjengrodde stier*, 148.

33 "Men det kan godt hende at jeg har skrevet i NS' ånd, at det altså kan ha sivet litt inn i meg fra de aviser jeg leste." Ibid., 148–49.

34 "Som vi alle trodde på, mer eller mindre, men alle trodde på det. Jeg trodde på det, derfor skrev jeg som jeg gjorde." Ibid., 149.

35 Ibid., 150.

36 See Ferguson, *Enigma*, 415.

37 "Det var ikke galt da jeg skrev det. Det var rett, og det jeg skrev var rett." Hamsun, *Paa gjengrodde stier*, 151.

38 "Jeg telegraferte natt og dag når tiden var knapp og det gjaldt liv eller død for mine landsmenn." Ibid., 151.

39 "Hengende mellom himmel og jord." Ibid., 153.

40 "Jeg er gammel nok til å ha en rettesnor for meg selv, og dette er min." Ibid., 154.

41 "Aaret er 1945. Den 26. Mai kom Politimesteren i Arendal til Nørholm og forkyndte Husarrest for min kone og mig for 30 Dager. Jeg blev ikke varslet." Ibid., 5.

42 "St. Hans 1948. Idag har Høiesteret dømt, og jeg ender min skrivning." Ibid., 185.

43 "Hvad skal jeg gjøre da? Jeg er snudd op ned paa, det er Saken, jeg er lei av mig selv, har ingen Ønsker, ingen Interesser, ingen Glæder. Fire eller fem gode Sanser i Dvale og den sjette Sans borttusket for mig. Det kan jeg takke Riksadvokaten for." Ibid., 59.

44 Ibid., 66.

45 For the role of the press in post-war Norway, see Stein Ugelvik Larsen's "Nazismen i Norge" (Nazism in Norway), in *Nazismen og norsk litteratur*, ed. Bjarte Birkeland et al., which shows rather convincingly that the media had indeed played an important role in coloring public opinion.

46 "Vi har faat den politiske Arrestant i Norge . . . Thranerøra, Kristian Lofthus, Hans Nielsen Hauge tæller ikke. Men idag har vi faat en som

tæller, han gaar i Flokker over Landet Norge, han er i firti, femti, seksti Tusen Eksemplarer, sies det. Og kanske i mange Tusen flere." Hamsun, *Paa gjengrodde stier*, 14.

47   Marie, in spite of her initial suspicion of the necessity of Langfeldt's questions, revealed many details about the Hamsuns' intimate relations. Knut, in fact, contemplated divorcing her.

48   "Aaret er 1946 den 11. Februar. Jeg er ute igjen av Anstalten. Dermed menes ikke at jeg er fri, men jeg kan puste igjen." Hamsun, *Paa gjengrodde stier*, 56.

49   Hamsun, *On Overgrown Paths*, v.

50   Næss, *Knut Hamsun*, 154.

51   Johs. Andenæs, *Det vanskelige oppgjøret: Rettsoppgjøret etter okkupasjonen* (Oslo: Tanum-Norli, 1979).

52   L. Børsum, *Fange i Ravensbrück* (Oslo: Gyldendal, 1946); P. Moen, *Dagbok* (Oslo: Cappelen, 1949); J. Borgen, *Dager på Grini* (Oslo: Gyldendal, 1945); K. Ottosen, *I slik en natt: Historien om deportasjonen av jøder fra Norge* (Oslo: Aschehough, 1994) and *Bak lås og slå: norske kvinner og menn i Hitlers fengsler og tukthus* (Oslo: Aschehough, 1993); and V. Komissar, *Nådetid: Norske jøder på flukt 1942* (Oslo, Aschehough, 1992).

53   "Aa, det uendelig smaa midt i det uendelig store i denne makeløse Verden." Hamsun, *Paa gjengrodde stier*, 87.

54   "Jeg er en Kran som staar og drypper, en, to, tre, fire." Ibid., 69.

55   Ibid., 128.

56   "Jeg stryker Johannes' Hode paa et Fat. Det var ikke godt heller." Ibid., 134; "Der strøk du jo ut Herodias Datter ogsaa." Ibid., 136.

57   Atle Kittang, *Luft, vind, ingenting*, 13 and footnote 3.

58   However, when Kittang discusses those Hamsun novels that are harder to place in the category of "ironic undermining" he uses the "real life" argument. Kittang essentially reads *Markens grøde* through the dialectic between Isak and Geissler and identifies in the novel a "merciless distance" between the narrator and Hamsun. He concludes his discussion of *Markens grøde* by referring to Hamsun's life; Hamsun's pattern of writing in boarding houses and hotels undermines the idyllic messages of *Markens grøde* (Kittang, *Luft, vind, ingenting*, 207). This presumably says that Hamsun's life *has* something to do with his fiction. But if we argue that life undermines fiction, we can also argue the opposite and claim that life sometimes confirms fiction. For instance, we could

argue that Hamsun's real aversion to feminism led him to create certain types of women protagonists, or we could claim that his real distaste for democratic institutions translated into disparaging or ironic depictions of protagonists who insist on equality.

59 Mosse, *Nazi Culture*, xxxviii.

60 "Sett med ettertidas klokskap ville det nok vært ryddigere og greiere med en straffesak. Den kunne belyst Hamsun-saken bedre enn den sivil-rettslige prosessen vi fikk, og i en straffesak hadde ikke diskusjonen om Hamsun NS-medlemskap fått noen avgjørende betydning." See Andreas Wiese, "Legg fram Hamsun-notatet" (Show us the note on Hamsun), in *Dagbladet*, September 11, 1998. The article was part of a wider discussion in the Norwegian media in 1998, following a statement by Knut P. Langfeldt, Gabriel Langfeldt's son, that he was in possession of a note from his father that proved that the psychiatric report on Hamsun was ordered by then-president Einar Gerhardsen. The statement turned out to be a false one. Although such speculations have persisted, and there is some circumstantial evidence that that might have been true, the definitive proof has been elusive and the question remains a hypothetical one.

61 Jon Langdal calls such strategy "the apologist's last saving grace in Hamsun research" (*apologetens siste skanse i Hamsunsforskningen*), namely the claim that Hamsun's irony makes it impossible to definitively pinpoint his messages. Langdal, "Hvordan trylle bort det ubehaglige?" (How to conjure away the uncomfortable), *Agora* 1–2 (1999): 232–64, 252.

62 Ferguson, *Enigma*, 422.

63 Atle Kittang, "Knut Hamsun og nazismen" (Knut Hamsun and Nazism), in *Nazismen og norsk litteratur*, ed. Bjarte Birkeland et al. (Oslo: Universitetsforlaget, 1995), 254–67. The article is divided into three sections with self-explanatory titles: "Dilemmaet" (The dilemma), "Det strafferettslege spørsmålet" (The legal/penal question), "Forfattaren Hamsun og nazismen" (The writer Hamsun and Nazism).

64 Ibid., 260.

65 Ibid., 263.

66 "Postmesteren blir på denne måten eit ironisk symbol på ein djupareliggande dissonans i verket: konflikten mellom illusjon og røyndom, lære og liv." Ibid., 263.

67 "Men kastraten representerar samstundes fantasien, evna til å førestille seg det som ikkje er. . . . Nettopp fordi han er kastrert—tom, uthulla—må

han byggje seg sitt eige fantasitilvære, og det er det som opprettheld livskrafta i han." Ibid., 264.

68 Ulrich Kriehn, "Auf den Spuren einer Kindheit" (In the footsteps of a childhood). Lecture given on October 14, 2006, in Duderstadt, Germany. See also http//www.kulturasyl.de/1261099.htm.

69 Aasmund Brynildsen, *Svermeren og hans demon: Fire essays om Knut Hamsun, 1952–1972* (The dreamer and his demon: Four essays on Knut Hamsun, 1952–1972). (Oslo: Dreyer, 1973.)

Epilogue

1 Mark Deavin, "Knut Hamsun and the Cause of Europe," *National Vanguard Magazine* 116 (August–September 1996), http//www.natvan.com/national-vanguard/116/hamson.html Hamsun is misspelled as Hamson in the Web address.

2 Braatøy, *Livets cirkel*, 94.

BIBLIOGRAPHY

Aaslestad, Petter. *Narratologi: En innføring i anvendt fortelleteori*. Oslo: Cappelen, 1999.

Abrahamsen, Samuel. *Norway's Response to the Holocaust*. New York: Holocaust Library, 1991.

Ager, W. T. "Fra Hamsuns Amerika-Ophold." In *Kvartalskrift*. Eau Claire, WI: Det norske selskab i Amerika, 1916.

Akçam, Taner. *A Shameful Act: The American Genocide and the Question of Turkish Responsibility*. Translated by Paul Bessemer. New York: Metropolitan Museum Books, 2006.

Andenæs, Johannes. "Knut Hamsun og landssvikoppgjøret." In *Det uskyldige geni? Fra debatten om "Prosessen mot Hamsun,"* edited by Simen Skjønsberg. Oslo: Gyldendal, 1979.

———. *Det vanskelige oppgjøret: Rettsoppgjøret etter okkupasjonen*. Oslo: Tanum–Norli, 1979.

Andersen, Britt. "Det hjemlige og det fremmede i Hamsuns *Pan*." In *Hamsun 2000: 8 foredrag fra Hamsun-dagene på Hamarøy*. Hamarøy: Hamsun-Selskapet, 2000.

Andersen, Per Thomas. *Dekadanse i nordisk litteratur 1880–1900*. Oslo: Aschehoug, 1992.

Appiah, Kwame Anthony. "Race." In *Critical Terms for Literary Study*, edited by Frank Lentricchia and Thomas McLaughlin. Chicago: University of Chicago Press, 1990.

Arneberg, Per. "Brekkesaga." In *Norsk skrivekunst: En essay-antologi*, edited by Erling Nielsen. Copenhagen: Hans Reitzel Publishing House, 1958.

Arntzen, Even, and Henning H. Wærp, eds. *Hamsun. Tromsø III: Rapport fra den 3. internasjonale Hamsun-konferanse, 2003. Tid og rom i Hamsuns prosa.* Hamaroy: Hamsun-Selskapet, 2003.

Arppe, Wilhelm, et al. *Norwegen: Geschichte—Kultur—Wirtschaft—in Wort und Bild.* Oslo: Die Hauptabteilung für Volkslaufklarung und Propaganda beim Reichskommissar für die besetzten norwegischen Gebiete, Kamban forlag and Das bibliographische Institut A.G. Leipzig, 1943.

Avdem, Anna Jorunn. "Bondekvinna og 'hamskiftet'." *Kvinnenes kulturhistorie,* vol. 2: *Fra år 1800 til vår tid.* Oslo: Universitetsforlaget, 1985.

Axtell, James. *Natives and Newcomers: The Cultural Origins of North America.* Oxford: Oxford University Press, 2001.

Bache-Wiig, Harald, and Astrid Sæther, eds. *100 år etter: Om det litterære livet i Norge i 1890-åra.* Oslo: Aschehoug, 1993.

Baird, Frank Pierce. "A History of Education in Idaho through Territorial Days." Master's thesis, University of Washington, 1928.

Barnouw, Dagmar. "The Threatened Self: Walter Rathenau and the Politics of Wholeness." In *Weimar Intellectuals and the Threat of Modernity.* Bloomington: Indiana University Press, 1988.

Bell, Susan Groag, and Karen M. Offen, eds. *Women, the Family, and Freedom: The Debate in Documents,* vol. 2: *1880–1950.* Stanford: Stanford University Press, 1983.

Bennet, Steichen, Metzker. *The Wisconsin Heritage in Photography.* Exhibition catalogue. Milwaukee: Milwaukee Art Center, 1970.

Berg, Roald. "Nation-building, State Structure, and Ethnic Groups: The Scandinavian Samis, 1905–1919." *Scandinavian Journal of History* 20: 61–69.

Berggreen, Brit. "Fra kvinnebonde til bondekvinne." In *Kvinnenes kulturhistorie,* vol. 2: *Fra år 1800 til vår tid.* Oslo: Universitetsforlaget, 1985.

Bergland, Betty. "Norwegian Immigrants and 'Indianerne' in the Landtaking, 1838–1862." *Norwegian-American Studies 35.* Northfield, MN: Norwegian-American Historical Association, 2000.

———. "Indigenous Peoples and Norwegian Immigrants: Imagining *Vesterheimen* after the Dakota Conflict." Paper presented at the 42nd annual meeting of the Western History Association, Colorado Springs, 2002.

———. "Norwegian Immigrants and the Dakota Conflict." Paper presented at 93rd annual meeting of the Society for the Advancement of Scandinavian Studies. Minneapolis, 2003.

Berman, Marshall. *All That Is Solid Melts into Air*. New York: Penguin Books, 1988.

Berman, Patricia. *Munch and Women: Image and Myth*. Alexandria, VA: Art Services International, 1997.

Bettyruth, Walter. *The Jury Summation as Speech Genre*. Amsterdam/Philadelphia: John Benjamins Publishing Company, 1988.

Birmingham, Robert A., and Leslie E. Eisenberg. *Indian Mounds of Wisconsin*. Madison: University of Wisconsin Press, 2000.

Bjørby, Pål. "Eros and Subjectivity: Knut Hamsun's *Pan* and Ragnhild Jølsen's *Rikka Gan*." In *Fin(s) de Siècle in Scandinavian Perspective: Studies in Honor of Harald S. Næss*. Columbia, SC: Camden House, 1993.

Blaisdell, Robert, ed. *Great Speeches by Native Americans*. Mineola, NY: Dover Thrift Editions, 2000.

Blegen, Theodore. *Norwegian Migration to America 1825–1860*. Northfield, MN: Norwegian-American Historical Association, 1931.

Blom, Ida. "Kvinnen: Et likeverdig menneske?" In *Norges Kulturhistorie*, vol. 5: *Brytningsår-blomstringstid*, edited by Ingrid Semmingsen. Oslo: Aschehoug, 1980.

———. *Barnebegrensning: Synd eller sunn fornuft*. Oslo: Universitetsforlaget, 1984.

Borgen, Johan. *Dager på Grini*. Oslo: Gyldendal, 1945.

Børsum, Lise. *Fange i Ravensbrück*. Oslo: Gyldendal, 1946.

Bouquet, Mary. *Sans og samling/Bringing It All Back Home*. Oslo: Universitetsforlaget, 1996.

Braatøy, Trygve. *Livets cirkel: Bidrag til analyse av Knut Hamsuns diktning*. Oslo: Fabritius och Sønners, 1929.

Brinker-Gabler, Gisela. "Introduction." In *Encountering the Other(s): Studies in Literature, History, and Culture*. Albany, NY: SUNY Press, 1995.

Broberg, Gunnar, Harald Runblom, and Mattias Tydén. *Judiskt Liv i Norden*. Studia multiethnica Upsaliensia 6. Uppsala: Acta Universitatis Upsaliensis, 1988.

Bruknapp, Dag O. "Idéene splitter partiet: Rasespørsmålets betydning i NS's utvikling." In *Fra idé til dom*, edited by Rolf Danielsen and Stein Ugelvik Larsen. Bergen: Universitetsforlaget, 1976.

Brynildsen, Aasmund. *Svermeren og hans demon: Fire essays om Knut Hamsun, 1952–1972*. Oslo: Dreyer, 1973.

Bull, Francis, ed. *Knut Hamsun: Artikler i utvalg*. Oslo: Gyldendal, 1939.

———. *Knut Hamsun: Artikler 1889–1928*. Oslo: Gyldendal, 1965.

Caspari, Theodor. *Norsk naturfølelse i det nittende aarhundrede*. Kristiania: Aschehoug, 1917.

Chamberlin, J. Edward, and Sander L. Gilman. *Degeneration: The Dark Side of Progress*. New York: Columbia University Press, 1985.

Christensen, Olav, and Anne Eriksen. *Hvite løgner: Stereotype forestillinger om svarte*. Oslo: Aschehoug, 1992.

Cohn, Dorrit. *The Distinction of Fiction*. Baltimore, MD: Johns Hopkins University Press, 1999.

Dahl, Hans Fredrik. "Hamsun, Quisling og det norske rettsoppgjøret." In *Hamsun i Tromsø: 11 foredrag fra Hamsun-konferansen i Tromsø 1995*, edited by Nils M. Knutsen. Hamarøy: Hamsun-Selskapet, 1996.

———. "Fascistisk fare for Norge?" In *Norsk idéhistorie*, vol. 5: *De store ideologienes tid*, edited by Trond Berg Eriksen and Øystein Sørensen. Oslo: Aschehoug, 2001.

———. "Marie, Knut og de 55000 andre." Theater program for *Jeg kunne gråte blod*. Oslo: Riksteatret, September 2004.

Dahlerup, Pil. *De moderne gennembruds kvinder*. Copenhagen: Gyldendal, 1983.

Danielsen, Dyrik, et al. *A History of Norway: From the Vikings to Our Own Time*. Oslo: Universitetsforlaget, 1995.

Darwin, Leonard. *The Need for Eugenic Reform*. New York: Appleton, 1926.

Deavin, Mark. "Knut Hamsun and the Cause of Europe," *National Vanguard Magazine* 116 (August–September 1996). http//www.natvan.com/national-vanguard/116/hamson.html.

Deloria, Philip Joseph. *Playing Indian*. New Haven: Yale University Press, 1998.

Derry, T. K. *A History of Scandinavia: Norway, Sweden, Denmark, Finland, and Iceland*. Minnneapolis: University of Minnesota Press, 1979.

Diedrich, Mark, ed. *Winnebago Oratory: Great Moments in the Recorded Speech of the Hochungra, 1742–1887*. Rochester, MN: Coyote Books, 1991.

Dijkstra, Bram. *Evil Sisters: The Threat of Female Sexuality and the Cult of Manhood*. New York: Knopf, 1996.

———. *Idols of Perversity: Fantasies of Feminine Evil in Fin-de-Siècle Culture*. New York: Oxford University Press, 1986.

Dinesen, Wilhelm. *Boganis jagtbreve*. Copenhagen: Gyldendal, 1935. Originally published as *Jagtbreve* (1889) and *Nye Jagtbreve* (1892).

Dinesen, Wilhelm. *Boganis: Letters from the Hunt*. Translated by Lise Lange Striar and Myles Striar. Boston: Rowan Tree Press, 1987.

Dingstad, Ståle. *Hamsuns strategier: Realisme, humor og kynisme*. Oslo: Gyldendal, 2003.

Eco, Umberto. "Tåkete totalitarisme og urfascisme." *Samtiden* 5 (1995): 49–59.

———. "Ur-Fascism." *New York Review of Books*, June 22, 1995.

Evang, Karl. *Rasepolitik og reaksjon: Tillegg; Det norske forslag til sterilisasjonslov*. Sosialistiske lægers forenings småskr 2. Oslo: Fram Forlag, 1934.

Facos, Michelle. *Nationalism and the Nordic Imagination.* Berkeley: University of California Press, 1980.

Farley, Harold. "An Unpublished History of Idaho Education." Boise, Idaho, 1974.

Felski, Rita. *The Gender of Modernity.* Cambridge, MA: Harvard University Press, 1995.

———. "Tragic Women." Address to a conference at the University of Minnesota, April 25–27, 2002, "After the Decline of the 'Master Narrative': Rethinking Modernism, Art, and Politics in Germany and Scandinavia, 1890–1950."

Ferguson, Robert. *Enigma: The Life of Knut Hamsun.* New York: Farrar, Straus and Giroux, 1987.

Fox-Genovese, Elizabeth. "Within the Plantation Household: Women in a Paternalist System." In *Society and Culture in the Slave South,* edited by William J. Harris. London: Routledge, 1992.

Fure, Odd-Bjørn. *Kampen mot glemselen: Kunnskapsvakuum i mediesamfunnet.* Oslo: Universitetsforlaget, 1997.

Gaski, Harald, ed. *In the Shadow of the Midnight Sun: Contemporary Sami Prose and Poetry.* Kárásjohka, Norway: Davvi Girji, 1996.

Genovese, Eugene, and Elizabeth Fox-Genovese. "The Fruits of Merchant Capital: The Slave South as a Paternalist Society." In *Society and Culture in the Slave South,* edited by William J. Harris. New York: Routledge, 1992.

Gierløff, Christian. *Knut Hamsuns Egen Røst.* Oslo: Gyldendal, 1961.

Giersing, Morten, et al. *Det reaktionære oprør: Om fascismen i Hamsuns forfatterskap,* Skriftrække fra Institutt for Litteraturvidenskap 5. Copenhagen: GMT, 1975.

Gilman, Sander L. "Sexology, Psychoanalysis, and Degeneration: From a Theory of Race to a Race to Theory." In *Degeneration: The Dark Side of Progress,* edited by Edward J. Chamberlin and Sander L. Gilman. New York: Columbia University Press, 1985.

Gjernes, Birgit. *Marie Hamsun: Et livsbilde.* Oslo: Aschehoug, 1994.

Glambek, Ingeborg. *Det nordiske i arkitektur og design: Sett utenfra.* Oslo: Arkitektens Forlag og Norsk Arkitekursforlag, 1997.

Gobineau, Joseph Arthur, and Adrian Collins. *The Inequality of Human Races.* New York: Putnam, 1915.

Goldberg, David Theo. "The Social Formation of Racist Discourse." In *"Race," Writing, and Difference,* edited by Henry Louis Gates Jr. Chicago: University of Chicago Press, 1986.

Goldwater, Robert. *Primitivism in Modern Painting.* New York: Harper and Brothers, 1938. (Reprinted as *Primitivism in Modern Art.* Cambridge, MA: Belknap Press, 1986.)

Grabowski, Simon. "Kareno in Nordland: A Study of *Livets Spil.*" *Edda* 21 (1969): 297–321.

Grimley, O. B. *The New Norway: A People with the Spirit of Cooperation.* Oslo: Griff-Forlaget, 1937.

Gujord, Heming. "Norske forfattere i historiens tjeneste." *Edda* 2 (2000): 158–70.

Hamsun, Knut. See separate entry for Knut Hamsun at the end of the Bibliography, pp. 326–29.

Hamsun, Marie. *Regnbuen.* Oslo: Aschehoug, 1953.

Hamsun, Tore. *Knut Hamsun: Lebensbericht in Bildern.* München: Deutscher Kunstverlag, 1956.

Hansen, Andreas Martin. *Norsk folkepsykologi.* Kristiania: Jacob Dybwads Forlag, 1899.

Hansen, Lars Ivar, and Bjørnar Olsen. *Samenes historie fram til 1750.* Oslo: Cappelen Akademisk Forlag, 2004.

Hansen, Thorkild. *Prosessen mot Hamsun.* Oslo: Gyldendal, 1978.

Hartmann-Johnsen, Olaf Johan. "Knut Hamsun fortjente vår avsky." *Aftenposten,* October 30, 2004.

Haugan, Jørgen. *Solgudens fall: Knut Hamsun-en litterær biografi.* Oslo: Aschehoug, 2004.

Herf, Jeffrey. *Reactionary Modernism.* Cambridge, MA: Cambridge University Press, 1984.

Hermundstad, Gunvald, ed. *Hamsuns polemiske skrifter.* Oslo: Gyldendal, 1998.

Herzog, Dagmar. *Sex after Fascism: Memory and Morality in Twentieth-Century Germany.* Princeton: Princeton University Press, 2005.

Hirn, Yrjö. "Kalevalaromantiken och Axel Gallen-Kallela." In *Lärt folk och landstrykare i det finska Finlands kulturliv.* Helsinki: Wahlström och Widstrand, 1939.

Hitler, Adolf. "Adolf Hitler om den tyske kvinne." Oslo: Der Reichsführer SS-Hauptamt.

Holand, Hjalmar Rued. *Norwegians in America: The Last Migration.* Translated by Helmer M. Blegen. Sioux Falls, ID: Center for Western Studies, 1978.

Holm, Birgitta. "Den manliga läsningens mysterier: Knut Hamsuns roman 100 år efteråt." *Edda* 3 (1992): 261–70.

Hult, Marte H. *Framing a National Narrative: The Legend Collections of Peter Christen Asbjørnsen.* Detroit: Wayne State University Press, 2003.

Høidal, Oddvar K. "Vidkun Quisling and the Deportation of Norway's Jews." Manuscript.

Ingwersen, Faith, and Mary Kay Norseng, eds. *Fin(s) de Siècle in Scandinavian*

Perspective: Studies in Honor of Harald S. Næss. Columbia, SC: Camden House, 1993.

Jernsletten, Kristin. "Det samiske i *Markens grøde*: Erfaringer formidlet og fornektet i teksten." *Nordlit:Arbeidstidsskrift i litteratur* 12 (2003): 41–57.

Jochens, Jenny. "Race and Ethnicity in the Old Norse World." *Viator* 30 (1999): 79–103.

——. "Vikings Westward to Vínland: The Problem of Women." In *Cold Counsel: Women in Old Norse Literature and Myth*, edited by Sarah M. Anderson, with Karen Swenson. New York: Routledge, 2002.

Johansen, Per Ole. "Norsk Embedsverk og jødiske innvandrere og flyktninger 1914–1940." In *Judiskt liv i Norden*, edited by Gunnar Broberg, Harald Runblom, and Mattias Tyden. *Studie Multiethnica Upsaliensia 6*. Uppsala: Acta Universitatis Upsaliensis, 1988.

Joll, James. "Walther Rathenau: Prophet without a Cause." In Joll, *Three Intellectuals in Politics*. New York: Pantheon Books, 1960.

Jordan, Winthrop D. *White over Black: American Attitudes toward the Negro, 1550–1812*. Chapel Hill: University of North Carolina Press, 1968.

Kent, Neil. *The Soul of the North: A Social, Architectural and Cultural History of the Nordic Countries, 1700–1940*. London: Reaktion Books, 2001.

Key, Ellen. *The Century of the Child*. New York: G. P. Putnam's Sons, 1909.

——. "A New Marriage Law." Reprinted in *Women, the Family, and Freedom: The Debate in Documents*, vol. 2: *1880–1950*, edited by Susan Groag Bell and Karen M. Offen. Stanford: Stanford University Press, 1983.

Kierulf, Anine, and Cato Schiotz. *Høyesterett og Knut Hamsun*. Oslo: Gyldendal, 2004.

Kirkegaard, Peter. *Knut Hamsun som modernist*. Copenhagen: Medusa, 1975.

Kittang, Atle. "Jeger, elskar, forteljar. Moderniteten in Knut Hamsun's *Pan*." In *Hamsun i Tromsø: 11 foredrag fra Hamsun-konferansen i Tromsø 1995*. Hamarøy: Hamsun-Selskapet, 1996.

——. *Luft, vind, ingenting: Hamsuns desillusjonsromanar fra Sult til Ringen sluttet*. Oslo: Gyldendal, 1984.

——. "Knut Hamsun og nazismen." In *Nazismen og norsk litteratur*, edited by Bjarte Birkeland, Atle Kittang, Stein Ugelvik Larsen, and Leif Longum. Oslo: Universitetsforlaget, 1995.

Kjerland, Kirsten Alsaker, and Anne K. Bang, eds. *Nordmenn i Afrika: Afrikanere i Norge*. Bergen: Vigmostad & Bjørke, 2002.

Kluge, Friedrich. *An Etymological Dictionary of the German Language*. Translated by John Francis Davis. London: George Bell and Sons, 1891.

Knutsen, Nils M. *Knut Hamsun og Nordland: Den lange veien hjem*. Tromsø: Angelica Forlag, 2006.

Kolloen, Ingar Sletten. *Hamsun Svermeren*. Oslo: Gyldendal, 2003.

———. *Hamsun Erobreren.* Oslo: Gyldendal, 2004.

Komissar, Vera. *Nådetid: Norske jøder på flukt 1942.* Oslo: Aschehoug 1992.

Kriehn, Ulrich. "Auf den Spuren einer Kindheit." (Duderstadt, October 14, 2006.) http//www.kulthrasyl.de/1261099.htm.

Kringlen, Einar. "Knut Hamsuns personlighet." *Nytt norsk tidskrift* 1 (2005): 18–29.

Kristeva, Julia. *Language the Unknown: An Initiation into Linguistics.* Translated by Anne M. Menke. New York: Columbia University Press, 1989.

Kuutma, Kristin. "Collaborative Ethnography Before Its Time: Johan Turi and Emilie Demand Hatt." *Scandinavian Studies* 75 (Summer 2003): 165–80.

Kvideland, Reimund, and Henning K. Sehmsdorf. *Scandinavian Folk Belief and Legend.* Minneapolis: University of Minnesota Press, 1988.

Kyllingstad, Jon Røyne. *Kortskaller og longskaller: Fysisk antropologi i Norge og striden om det nordiske herremennesket.* Oslo: Scandinavian Academic Press/Spartacus Forlag, 2004.

Langdal, Jon. "Hvordan trylle bort det ubehaglige?" *Agora* 1–2 (1999): 232–64.

Langfeldt, Gabriel, and Ørnulv Ødegård. *Den rettspsykiatriske erklæring om Knut Hamsun.* Oslo: Gyldendal, 1978.

Larsen, Lars Frode. *Over havet.* Oslo: Gyldendal, 1990.

———. *Den unge Hamsun.* Oslo: Schibsted, 1998.

———. *Radikaleren. Hamsun ved gjennombruddet, 1888–1891.* Oslo: Schibsted, 2001.

Larsen, Stein Ugelvik. "Nazismen i Norge." In *Nazismen og norsk litteratur*, edited by Bjarte Birkeland and Stein Ugelvik Larsen. Oslo: Universitetsforlaget, 1975.

Lindemann, Albert S. *Anti-Semitism Before the Holocaust.* Harlow, UK: Longman, 2000.

Lindow, John. "Supernatural Others and Ethnic Others: A Millennium of World View." *Scandinavian Studies* 67 (Winter 1995): 8–31.

Linneberg, Arild. "Hamsuns *Pan* og fascismen." In *Søkelys på Knut Hamsuns 90-års diktning*, edited by Øystein Rottem. Oslo: Universitetsforlaget, 1979.

Lintelman, Joy, and Betty Bergland. "Scandinavian Immigrants and Indigenous Peoples: Ethnicity, Gender and Colonial Encounters in Midwestern Regions of the United States, 1830–1930." Paper submitted to the International Federation for Research in Women's History at the 19th International Congress of Historical Sciences, Oslo 2000.

Lorentzen, Jørgen. *Mannlighetens muligheter.* Oslo: Aschehoug, 1998.

Lovoll, Odd. *The Promise of America: A History of the Norwegian-American People.* Minneapolis: University of Minnesota Press, in cooperation with the Norwegian-American Historical Association, 1984.

———. *The Promise Fulfilled: A Portrait of Norwegian Americans Today*. Minneapolis: University of Minnesota Press, 1998.

Löwenthal, Leo. "Knut Hamsun, 1860–1952." In *Literature and the Image of Man*. Boston: Beacon Press, 1957.

Lucas, Richard H., and K. Byron McCoy. *The Winning Edge: Effective Communication and Persuasion Techniques for Lawyers*. New York: Wiley Law Publications, 1993.

Marken, Amy van. "Review of Bolckman's Dissertation." *Edda* 56 (1969): 63.

McClintock, Anne. *Imperial Leather: Race, Gender, and Sexuality in the Colonial Contest*. New York: Routledge, 1995.

McFarlane, J. W. "The Whisper of the Blood: A Study of Knut Hamsun's Early Novels." *Modern Languages Association Papers* 71 (1956): 563–94.

Mendelsohn, Oskar. "Jødene i Norge." In *Judiskt Liv i Norden*, edited by Gunnar Broberg, Harald Runblom, and Mattias Tydén. Uppsala: Acta Universitatis Upsaliensis, 1988.

Milwaukee Art Center. *Bennett, Steichen, Metzker: The Wisconsin Heritage in Photography*. Catalogue, 1970.

Mjøen, Jon Alfred. *Racehygiene*. Kristiania: Jacob Dybwads Forlag, 1914.

———. "Harmonic and Disharmonic Race-crossings." In *Eugenics in Race and State: Scientific Papers of the Second International Congress of Eugenics*. New York: Garland, 1922.

Mjøen, Sonja. *Da mor var ung: Samtaler og minner*. Oslo: Cappelen, 1975.

Moen, Petter. *Dagbok*. Oslo: Cappelen, 1949.

Mohr, Otto Lous. *Arvelærens Grundtrek*. Kristiania: Norli, 1923.

———. "Menneskeavlen under kultur." *Samtiden* 37 (1926): 22–48.

Moray, Gerta. "Emily Carr and the Traffic in Native Images." In *Antimodernism and Artistic Experience: Policing the Boundaries of Modernity*, edited by Lynda Jessup. Toronto: University of Toronto Press, 2001.

Morgridge, Barbara Gordon. "Editor's Introduction" to Hamsun, *The Cultural Life of Modern America*. Cambridge, MA: Harvard University Press, 1969.

Mosse, George L. *Nazi Culture: Intellectual, Cultural and Social Life in the Third Reich*. Madison: University of Wisconsin Press, 1966.

Myers, Fred R. "Introduction—Around and About Modernity: Some Comments on Themes of Primitivism and Modernism." In *Antimodernism and Artistic Experience: Policing the Boundaries of Modernity*, edited by Lynda Jessup. Toronto: University of Toronto Press, 2001.

Næss, Harald S. *Knut Hamsun og Amerika*. Oslo: Gyldendal, 1969.

———. *Knut Hamsun*. Boston: Twayne Publishers, 1984.

———. "Ringen sluttet: In Defence of Abel Brodersen." In *Facets of European Modernism: Essays in Honor of James McFarlane*, edited by Janet Garton. Norwich, UK: University of East Anglia Press, 1985.

――. "Knut Hamsun and *Growth of the Soil.*" *Scandinavica* 25 (May 1986): 5–17.

――. *Knut Hamsuns brev.* 7 vols. Oslo: Gyldendal, 1994– 2001.

Nasgaard, Roald. *The Mystic North: Symbolist Landscape Painting in Northern Europe and North America 1890–1940.* Toronto: University of Toronto Press, in association with the Art Gallery of Toronto, 1984.

Nelson, Oscar. *History of the Schools.* Boise, Idaho, 1990.

Nettum, Rolf Nyboe. *Konflikt og visjon: Hovedtemaer i Knut Hamsuns forfatterskap 1890–1912.* Oslo: Gyldendal, 1970.

Niemi, Einar. "Sami History and the Frontier Myth." In *Sami Culture in a New Era: The Norwegian Sami Experience,* edited by Harald Gaski. Kárásjohka: Davvi Girji Press, 1997.

Nilson, Sten Sparre. *En ørn i uvær.* Oslo: Gyldendal, 1960.

Ostby, Arvid. *Knut Hamsun: En bibliografi.* Oslo: Gyldendal, 1972.

Ottosen, Kristian. *Bak lås og slå: Historien om norske kvinner og menn i Hitlers fengsler og tukthus.* Oslo: Aschehoug, 1993.

――. *I slik en natt: Historien om deportasjonen av jøder fra Norge.* Oslo: Aschehoug, 1994.

Oxfeldt, Elisabeth. "Orientalism on the Periphery: The Cosmopolitan Imagination in Nineteenth-Century Danish and Norwegian Literature and Culture." Ph.D. diss., University of California at Berkeley, 2002.

Øyslebø, Olaf. *Hamsun gjennom stilen: En studie i kunstnerisk utvikling.* Oslo: Gyldendal, 1964.

Pagden, Anthony. *European Encounters with the New World.* New Haven: Yale University Press, 1993.

Perelman, Chaim, and L. Olbrechts-Tyteca. *The New Rhetoric: A Treatise on Argumentation.* Notre Dame, IN: University of Notre Dame Press, 1969.

Pollan, Sonja. *Vi selv og de andre: Raseteorier i Norge for hundre år siden.* Oslo: Universitetsforlaget, 1978.

Popperwell, Ronald G. "Knut Hamsun's *Livet ivold.*" In *20th Century Drama in Scandinavia.* Proceedings of the 12th IASS Study Conference. Helsinki: University of Helsinki, 1979.

Rediess, Wilhelm, ed., "Norwegen und die Norweger." In *SS: Für ein Grossgermanien, Schwert und Wiege.* Oslo: SS-Hefte, 1944.

Reiersen, Johan Reinert. *Veiviseren for norske emigranter til De forenede nordamerikanske stater og Texas.* Christiania, 1844.

――. *Pathfinder for Norwegian Emigrants.* Translated by Frank G. Nelson. Northfield, MN: Norwegian-American Historical Association, 1981.

Rekdal, Per Bjørn. *Norsk museumsformidling og den flerkulturelle utfordringen.* Oslo: Norsk museumsutvikling 7, 1999.

Rhodes, Anthony. *Propaganda, the Art of Persuasion: World War II, An Allied and Axis Visual Record, 1933–1945.* Secaucus, NJ: Wellfleet Press, 1987.

Rhodes, Colin. *Primitivism and Modern Art.* London: Thames and Hudson, 1994.

Ritchie, Grace. *The Way We Were: The Early Schools of Idaho.* Idaho Falls, ID: Retired Teachers Association, 1976.

Roll-Hansen, Nils. "Eugenic Sterilization: A Preliminary Comparison of the Scandinavian Experience to that of Germany." *Genome* 31 (1989).

———. "Norwegian Eugenics: Sterilization as a Social Reform." In *Eugenics and the Welfare State: Sterilization Policy in Denmark, Sweden, Norway and Finland*, edited by Gunnar Broberg and Nils Roll-Hansen. East Lansing: Michigan State University Press, 1996.

Ross, Peter, and Blanche Hampton. "Don't Trust the Locals: European Explorers in the Amazon." In *Literature and Travel*, edited by Michael Hanne. Amsterdam, 1993.

Rossel, Sven H. "The Image of the United States in Danish Literature: A Survey with Scandinavian Perspectives." In *Images of America in Scandinavia*, edited by Poul Houe and Sven Rossel. Amsterdam: Rodopi Press, 1998.

Rottem, Øystein. "Gåten Hamsun er en konstruksjon." *Dagbladet*, July 24, 2000.

Rubin, Gayle. "Woman as Nigger." In *Masculine/Feminine: Readings in Sexual Mythology and the Liberation of Women*, edited by Betty Roszak and Theodore Roszak. New York: Harper and Row, 1969.

Rynning, Ole. *Sandfærdig beretning om Amerika, Til oplysning og nytte for bonde og menigmand.* Christiania, 1838.

Rynning, Ole. *Ole Rynning's True Account of America.* Translated and edited by Theodore C. Blegen. Minneapolis, MN: Norwegian-American Historical Association, 1926.

Ræder, Ole Munch. *America in the Forties: The Letters of Ole Munch Ræder.* Translated and edited by Gunnar J. Malmin. Minneapolis: University of Minnesota Press, 1929.

Said, Edward. *Culture and Imperialism.* New York: Knopf, 1993.

———. *Orientalism.* New York: Vintage, 1994.

Salversen, Helge. "Sami Ædnan: Four States-One Nation? Nordic Minority Policy and the History of the Sami." In *Ethnicity and Nation Building in the Nordic World,* edited by Sven Tägil. Carbondale: Southern Illinois University Press, 1995.

Sandberg, Mark. "Writing on the Wall: The Language of Advertising in Knut Hamsun's *Sult.*" *Scandinavian Studies* 71 (Fall 1999): 265–96.

Scharffenberg, Johan. *Hovedpunkter i Arvelæren.* Oslo: Der Norske Arbeiderpartis Forlag, 1932.

Schnurbein, Stefanie von. *Krisen de Männlichkeit: Schreiben und Geschlechterdiskurs in skandinavischen Romanen seit 1890.* Göttingen: Wallstein Verlag, 2001.

Schiøtz, Carl. *Lærebok i hygiene.* Oslo, 1937.

Schoolfield, George C. *A Baedeker of Decadence: Charting a Literary Fashion, 1884– 1927.* New Haven: Yale University Press, 2003.

Schorske, Carl E. *Fin de Siècle Vienna: Politics and Culture.* New York: Knopf, 1980.

Schreiner, Kristian Emil. *Zur Osteologie der Lappen.* Vols. 1 and 2. Oslo: Aschehoug, 1931–35.

Sehmsdorf, Henning K. *Short Stories from Norway 1850–1900.* Translated by Henning K. Sehmsdorf. Department of Scandinavian Studies, University of Wisconsin at Madison, 1986.

Showalter, Elaine. *Sexual Anarchy: Gender and Culture at the Fin de Siècle.* New York: Penguin-Viking, 1990.

Simonsen, Konrad. *Georg Brandes: Jødisk aand i Danmark.* Copenhagen: Nationale Forfatterres Forlag, 1913.

———. *Den Moderne Mennesketype.* Kristiania: Aschehoug, 1918.

Simpson, Allen. "Knut Hamsun's Anti-Semitism." *Edda* 5 (1977): 273–93.

———. "Midt i Forgjængelsens Karneval: *Markens Grøde* in Knut Hamsun's Authorship." *Scandinavian Studies* 56 (1984): 1–35.

Skrødal, Marit Elin. "Samene i Knut Hamsuns diktning: En gjennomgang av samene og noen tatere i Hamsuns litterære verker." Ph.D. diss., University of Tromsø, 1995.

Slagstad, Rune. *De nasjonale strateger.* Oslo: Pax Forlag, 1998.

Sogner, Sølvi. "Fra flerbarns—til fåbarnsfamilier." *Kvinnenes kulturhistorie,* vol. 2: *Fra år 1800 til vår tid.* Oslo: Universitetsforlaget, 1985.

Sollors, Werner. "Ethnicity." In *Critical Terms for Literary Study,* edited by Frank Lentricchia and Thomas McLaughlin. Chicago: University of Chicago Press, 1990.

Sontag, Susan. *Illness as Metaphor.* New York: Farrar, Straus, and Giroux, 1978.

Stepan, Nancy Leys. "Biological Degeneration: Races and Proper Places." In *Degeneration: The Dark Side of Progress,* edited by Edward J. Chamberlain and Sander L. Gilman. New York: Columbia University Press, 1985.

———. "Race and Gender: The Role of Analogy in Science." In *Anatomy of Racism,* ed. David Theo Goldberg. Minneapolis: University of Minnesota Press, 1990.

———. "Introduction: Science and Social Knowledge." In *The Hour of Eugenics: Race, Gender, and Nation in Latin America.* Ithaca, NY: Cornell University Press, 1991.

Stern, Fritz. "Walther Rathenau and the Vision of Modernity." In *Einstein's German World.* Princeton: Princeton University Press, 1999.

Stjernfelt, Frederik. "Hvad blir vi som ikke blir noget? Anerkendelsens strukturer i Hamsuns Ringen sluttet." *Norskrift* 57 (1989): 20–60.

Stokker, Kathleen. *Folklore Fights the Nazis: Humor in Occupied Norway 1940–1945*. Madison: University of Wisconsin Press, 1995.

Storfjell, Troy. "Samene i *Markens grøde*—kartlegging av en (umulig) idyll." In *Hamsun i Tromsø III: Rapport fra den 3. internasjonale Hamsun-konferanse, 2003; Tid og rom i Hamsuns prosa*," edited by Even Arntzen and Henning H. Wærp. Hamarøy: Hamsun-Selskapet, 2003.

———. "Mapping a Space for Sámi Studies in North America." *Scandinavian Studies* 75 (Summer 2003): 153–64.

Streese, Konstanze. "Writing the Other's Language: Modes of Linguistic Representation in German Colonial and Anti-Colonial Literature." In *Encountering the Other(s): Studies in Literature, History, and Culture*, edited by Gisela Brinker-Gabler. Albany, NY: SUNY Press, 1995.

Szobar, Patrizia. "Telling Sexual Stories in the Nazi Courts of Law: Race Defilement in Germany, 1933 to 1945." In *Sexuality and German Fascism*, edited by Dagmar Herzog. New York: Berghahn Books, 2005.

Thomas, William Hannibal. *The American Negro: What He Was, What He Is, and What He May Become, a Critical and Practical Discussion*. New York: Macmillan, 1901.

Tiemroth, Jørgen E. *Illusionens vej: Knut Hamsuns forfatterskab*. Copenhagen: Gyldendal, 1974.

Tinker, George E. *Missionary Conquest: The Gospel and Native American Cultural Genocide*. Minneapolis: Augsburg Fortress Press, 1993.

Todorov, Tzvetan. *The Conquest of America: The Question of the Other*. Translated by Richard Howard. New York: Harper Perennial, 1992.

Torgovnick, Marianna. *Gone Primitive: Savage Intellects, Modern Lives*. Chicago: University of Chicago Press, 1990.

Turi, Johan. *Turi's Book of Lappland*. Translated by E. Gee Nash. New York: Harper and Brothers, 1931.

Varnedoe, Kirk. *Northern Light: Nordic Art at the Turn of the Century*. Oslo: J. M. Stenersens Forlag, 1988.

Vowles, Richard B. "Boganis, Father of Osceola; or Wilhelm Dinesen in America 1872–1874." *Scandinavian Studies* 48 (1976): 369–83.

Waal, Carla. "The Plays of Knut Hamsun." *Quarterly Journal of Speech* 57 (February 1971): 75–82.

Westlie, Bjørn. "Still No Peace for the Jews of Norway: The Unresolved Restitution Claims." Jerusalem: Institute of the World Jewish Congress, Policy Forum no. 12, 1996.

———. *Oppgjør i skyggen av Holocaust*. Oslo: Aschehoug, 2002.

Wiese, Andreas. "Legg fram Hamsun-notatet." *Dagbladet*, September 11, 1998.

Witoszek, Nina. "Der Kultur møter Natur: Tilfellet Norge." *Samtiden* 4 (1991): 11–19.

——. *Norske naturmytologier.* Oslo: Pax Forlag, 1998.

Zantop, Susanne. "Domesticating the Other: European Colonial Fantasies 1770–1830." In *Encountering the Other(s): Studies in Literature, History, and Culture*, edited by Gisela Brinker-Gabler. Albany, NY: SUNY Press, 1995.

——. *Colonial Fantasies: Conquest, Family, and Nation in Precolonial Germany, 1770–1870.* Durham, NC: Duke University Press, 1997.

Žagar, Monika. "Hamsun's Black Man or Lament for Paternalist Society: A reading of Hamsun's play *Livet ivold* through *Fra det moderne Amerikas aandsliv.*" *Edda* 4 (1997): 364–79.

——. "'Nu var hun fanget': Kvinner, barn og fruktbarhet i Knut Hamsuns roman *Markens grøde*" (Now she was caught: Women, children, and fertility in Knut Hamsun's novel *Growth of the Soil*). *Hamsun i Tromsø II: Rapport fra den 2. internasjonale Hamsun-konferanse*, 171–93. Hamarøy: Hamsun-Selskapet, 1999.

——. "Hamsun's Dronning Tamara." *Scandinavian Studies* 70 (1998): 337–58.

——. "The Rhetoric of Defense in Hamsun's *Paa gjengrodde stier* (On overgrown paths)." Edda 3 (1999): 252–61.

——. "Imagining the Red-Skinned Other: Hamsun's Article 'Fra en Indianerleir' (1885)." *Edda* 4 (2001): 385–95.

——. "How Knut Hamsun Imagines Juliane and Her Speech: Hamsun's Play *Livet ivold* [In the grip of life]." In *Gender-Power-Text, Nordic Culture in the Twentieth Century*, edited by Helena Forsås-Scott. Norwich, UK: Norvik Press, 2004.

Works by Knut Hamsun

Articles

"Adolf Hitler." *Aftenposten*, May 7, 1945. Reprinted in *Hamsuns polemiske skrifter.* Oslo: Gyldendal, 1998.

"Barnet." *Morgengladet*, January 16, 1915. Reprinted in *Hamsuns polemiske skrifter.* Oslo: Gyldendal, 1998.

"Bonde-." *Aftenposten*, March 9, 1918. Reprinted in *Hamsuns polemiske skrifter.* Oslo: Gyldendal, 1998.

"Det amerikanske overmot." *SS-Germanske Budstikke* 3 (5–7), 1943.

"En Bok om Lappernes Liv." Review of *En bok om Lappernes liv* by Johan Thri. *Verdens Gang*, 1911. Reprinted in *Hamsuns polemiske skrifter.* Oslo: Gyldendal, 1998.

"Et brev fra Knut Hamsun." *SS-Heftet* 1, 1944.

"Festina lente." Reprinted as part of "Fra Amerika," in *Hamsuns polemiske skrifter.* Oslo: Gyldendal, 1998.

"Fra det ubevidste Sjæleliv." Reprinted in *Knut Hamsun Artikler,* edited by Francis Bull. Oslo: Gyldendal, 1939.

"Fra en Indianerleir." Reprinted in *Hamsuns polemiske skrifter.* Oslo: Gyldendal, 1998.

"Grønland." *Ragnarok* 9–10, Jubileumsnummer, 1944.

Hamsuns polemiske skrifter. Hermundstad, Gunvald, ed. Oslo: Gyldendal, 1998.

"Hilsningstelegram til Presseklubbens Finnlandskveld." *Aftenposten,* February 23, 1944. Reprinted in *Hamsuns polemiske skrifter.* Oslo: Gyldendal, 1998.

"Jeg bier på at våre studenter skal storme fram og være med." *Bergens Tidende,* March 30, 1942. Reprinted in *Hamsuns polemiske skrifter.* Oslo: Gyldendal, 1998.

Knut Hamsun:Artikler i utvalg. Frances Bull, ed. Oslo: Gyldendal, 1939.

"Knut Hamsun om englenderne." *Ideologisk Månedshefte for Hirden* 2, May 1941.

"Knut Hamsun svarer på to spørsmål." *Grimstad Adressetidende,* January 30, 1941. Reprinted in *Hamsuns polemiske skrifter.* Oslo: Gyldendal, 1998.

"Kvindeseier." *Stridende liv,* 1905.

"Nabobyen." In *Knut Hamsun: Artikler, 1889–1928,* edited by Francis Bull. Oslo: Gyldendal, 1965.

"Ossietzky." *Tidens Tegn,* November 22, 1935. Reprinted in *Hamsuns polemiske skrifter.* Oslo: Gyldendal, 1998.

"Røde, sorte og hvide." *Verdens Gang, 1891.* Reprinted in *Hamsuns polemiske skrifter.* Oslo: Gyldendal, 1998.

"Utvandrerne." *Grimstad Adressetidende,* December 1, 1927. Reprinted in *Hamsuns polemiske skrifter.* Oslo: Gyldendal, 1998.

"Virkeliggjort kameratskap." *Berlin-Rom-Tokio* 2, 1942. Reprinted in *Hamsuns polemiske skrifter.* Oslo: Gyldendal, 1998.

Short stories, novels, and plays in Norwegian

Børn av tiden. Copenhagen: Gyldendal, 1913.

Dronning Tamara. In *Samlede verker,* vol. 15. Oslo: Gyldendal, 1955.

Den siste glæde. In *Samlede verker,* vol. 7. Oslo: Gyldendal, 1992.

Fra det moderne Amerikas aandsliv. Oslo: Gyldendal, 1962.

I Æventyrland. In *Samlede verker,* vol. 4. Copenhagen: Gyldendal, 1916.

Livet ivold. In *Samlede verker,* vol. 15. Oslo: Gyldendal, 1964.

Livets spil. In *Samlede verker,* vol. 14. Oslo: Gyldendal, 1964.

Markens grøde. In *Samlede verker,* vol. 7. Oslo: Gyldendal, 1963.

Men livet lever. In *Samlede verker,* vol. 12. Oslo: Gyldendal, 1992.

Munken Vendt. In *Samlede verker,* vol. 14. Oslo: Gyldendal, 1964.

Ny jord. Oslo: Gyldendal, 1992.

Paa gjengrodde stier. Oslo: Gyldendal, 1949.

Pan. In *Samlede verker,* vol. 2. Oslo: Gyldendal, 1963.

Ringen sluttet. In *Samlede verker.* Oslo: Gyldendal, 1964.

Rosa. In *Samlede verker,* vol. 5. Oslo: Gyldendal, 1963.

Segelfoss by. Oslo: Gyldendal, 1995.

"Under halvmaanen." In *Samlede verker,* vol. 4. Oslo: Gyldendal, 1955.

Short stories, novels, and plays in English translation

Children of the Age. Translated by J. S. Scott. New York: Knopf, 1924.

The Cultural Life of Modern America. Translated by Barbara Gordon Morgridge. Cambridge, MA: Harvard University Press, 1969.

"A Fragment of Life," in *Night Roamers and Other Stories.* Translated by Tiina Nunnally. Seattle: Fjord Press, 1992.

Growth of the Soil. Translated by W. W. Wurster. New York: Vintage, 1972.

Hunger. Translated and introduced by Robert Bly and Isaac Bashevis Singer. New York: Farrar, Straus and Giroux, 1967.

In the Grip of Life. Translated by Graham and Tristan Rawson. New York: Knopf, 1924.

The Last Chapter. Translated by Arthur G. Charter. New York: Knopf. 1929.

Mysteries. Translated by Gerry Bothmer. New York: Farrar, Straus and Giroux, 1971.

On Overgrown Paths. Translated and introduced by Carl L. Anderson. New York: P. S. Eriksson, 1967.

On the Prairie: A Sketch of the Red River Valley. Translated by John Christianson. St. Paul: Minnesota Historical Society, 1961.

Segelfoss town. Translated by J. S. Scott. New York: Knopf; Toronto: Macmillan, 1925.

Shallow Soil. Translated by Carl Christianson Hyllested. New York: Knopf, 1921.

"Slaves of Love," in *Slaves of Love and Other Short Norwegian Stories.* Selected and edited by James McFarlane. Oxford and New York: Oxford University Press, 1982.

Tales of Love and Loss. Translated by Robert Ferguson. London: Souvenir Press, 1997.

Under the Autumn Star. Los Angeles: Sun and Moon Press, 1998.

Vagabonds. Translated by Eugene Gay-Tifft. New York: Coward-McCann, 1930.

Victoria. Translated by Oliver Stallybrass. London: Souvenir Press, 1974.

The Women at the Pump. New York: Farrar, Straus and Giroux, 1978.

Letters

Knut Hamsuns brev, 1896–1907, vol. 2. Edited by Harald S. Næss. Oslo: Gyldendal, 1995.

Knut Hamsuns brev, 1908–1914, vol. 3. Edited by Harald S. Næss. Oslo: Gyldendal, 1996.

Knut Hamsuns brev, 1915–1924, vol. 4. Edited by Harald S. Næss. Oslo: Gyldendal, 1997.

Knut Hamsuns brev, 1921–1933, vol. 5. Edited by Harald S. Næss. Oslo: Gyldendal, 1998.

Knut Hamsuns brev, 1934–1950, vol. 6. Edited by Harald S. Næss. Oslo: Gyldendal, 1999.

Selected Letters. Selected and edited by Harald Naess and James McFarlane. Norwich, UK: Norvik Press, 1990–98.

INDEX

B

banality, 5, 8
Bang, Herman, 55
Battle of the sexes, 145, 227
Benedictsson, Victoria, 58
Bennett, Henry Hamilton, 84–85
Benoni og Rosa (Benoni and Rosa), 178
Berg, Roald, 170
Berggreen, Brit, 76–77
Bergland, Betty, 32, 87, 90
Berman, Marshall, 10
Beyer, Harald, 194
Birmingham, Robert, 90, 94
birth control. *See* contraception
Bjørby, Pål, 60
Bjørnson, Bjørnstjerne, 33, 34, 53, 87, 120, 125, 200
Black race, 38
Blom, Ida, 65–66
Bolckman, Alex, 79
Bolshevism, 17, 182, 303n58
Bonnevie, Kristine, 25, 38
Børn av tiden (Children of the age), 41, 107–10; race in, 109–10
Braatøy, Trygve, 146–47, 150, 234
Brandes, Georg, 34–35, 39, 53, 56, 142
Bremer, Fredrika, 52, 86
Brenna, Brita S., 117–18
"Brev om kvinden" (A letter about woman), 67
Brox, Ottar, 170
Bryn, Halfdan, 27–28, 184–85
Bull, Ole, 35

C

Castberg, Johan, 25, 34, 35
Castberg Law, 25
castration, 182, 201, 230
Celts, 29, 31

chastity, 53
children, 38, 63, 230. *See also* Hamsun, Knut
Christensen, Olav, 115
Clauss, Ludwig Ferdinand, 183
Cohn, Dorrit, 217
Collett, Camilla Wergeland, 52
Collin, Christen, 181
colonial ambivalence, 85
Combüchen, Sigrid, 6
Communist Manifesto, 10
contraception, 25, 38, 65–66; in *Markens grøde*, 73–74
creativity and gender, 60
The Cultural Life of Modern America (ed. Barbara Morgridge), 121

D

Dahl, Hans Fredrik, 6–8, 191, 239
Dahlerup, Pil, 56
Dangerous Woman, 57
darkness, 14
Darwin, Charles, 22
Darwin, Leonard, 22
Deavin, Mark, 232
decadence, 56
degeneration, 13, 19, 26, 38, 52; artists' articulation of, 48; family structure and, 63–67; and geography and climate, 20, 89–90; and race-mixing, 41, 111. *See also* eugenics; women
Deloria, Philip, 83, 86
democracy, 13, 31, 39, 187, 200, 223, 233; American, 70, 118–20, 126, 186–87; and outsiders, 31
demographics, 13
Den gaadefulle (The enigmatic one), 128
Denmark, 141–42

Finns, 28, 38, 132
Fischer, Eugen, 28, 183–84
"Forord til 'Revolusjonspolitikk og
    Norsk lov" (Preface to *Revolution-
    ary Politics and Norwegian Law*),
    187
"Fra en Indianerleir" (From an Indian
    camp), 38, 84–85, 90, 101–2, 178;
    myth of the "lost race," 94; race
    and race-mixing in, 89–90, 95–96;
    view of Native women, 100–101
Fra det modern Amerikas aandsliv
    (From the cultural life of modern
    America), 21, 33, 38, 86, 98–99,
    125, 127–28; eugenics in, 121;
    portrayal of women in, 68–71, 80,
    112, 119; promiscuity in, 132; race
    in, 112, 118, 121–22, 128; rela-
    tionship to *Ringen sluttet*, 128–29;
    sexuality in, 118–19; sources in,
    157; on southern United States,
    119–20
"Fra det ubevidste Sjæleliv" (From
    the unconscious life of the soul),
    11, 99
Friar Vendt, 166
Friis, Jens Andreas, 165
folk narratives, 175
Fox-Genovese, Elizabeth, 120

G

Gallen-Kallela, Akseli, 48
Galton, Francis, 21
Gauguin, 15, 48, 98
gender, 9–11, 115, 158; artists and,
    55–57, 126; imbalance of, 137;
    modernity and, 133; patriarchy
    and, 104, 146, 158. *See also* race:
    and gender
gender roles, 26, 54, 174–76;

Hamsun's depiction of, 72, 77,
    124, 149–51
Genovese, Eugene, 120
German civilization, 39
Germanic race, 39–40
Germany, 4, 10, 17; anthropological/
    race research in, 183–84; Nor-
    wegian artists and, 140; view of
    Norway, 201–4
Giersing, Morten, 4
globalization, 129–30
Goebbels, Joseph, 18, 196, 226. *See
    also* Nobel prize for literature
Goepfert, Bergljot, 61, 137, 146, 151
"Gravsted" (Grave site), 99
Great Britain, 17, 140, 182, 201. *See
    also* Hamsun, Knut
"great morality debate," 53
Greenland, 19, 20, 201
Greenland colony, 30–31
Grieg, Edvard, 35
Grieg, Nordahl, 34
Grimley, O. B., 165–66
Grimstad Municipal Court, 211
Günther, Hans F. K., 183
Gyldendal Publishing house, 39, 187

H

Hambro, Carl Joachim, 188
Hamsun (1996 film), 3, 4, 5, 197, 214
Hamsun, Arild, 186, 196
Hamsun, Knut: account of meeting
    a Native Indian, 95–97; anti-
    modernism and, 43; anti-Semitism
    of, 194–95; apologists for, 225–26,
    228–29; attraction to NS party,
    185–86; belief in Third Reich,
    195–97, 229; canon of, 15–17, 150,
    227, 231, 234; children of, 61–64,
    151; as collaborator, 2, 6–8,

speech, 218–22; gender in, 227; Hamsun's perceived audience, 214–15; purpose of, 226–31; reception of, 216, 224, 226; responses to claims of treason, 223; rhetorical strategy of, 217, 222, 224–26

"Paa turnee" (On tour), 126

Pan, 15, 50, 58, 60, 79, 99–100, 125; narrator, 217; view of nature in, 102–3, 166; view of Sami in, 176

Paris, 50

patriarchy, 26, 57, 112, 126

Peer Gynt (Henrik Ibsen), 141

Picasso, 98

Picts, 31

Ploetz, Alfred, 22

popular trivial literature, 85

population decline 25, 38

Pratt, Mary Louise, 45

Press Internationale congress, 196

primitivism, 14–15, 19, 40, 89–90, 129–30; art and, 98; demise and, 145; discourse of, 43–44; gender and, 100–101; in Hamsun's literature, 99–100; modernity and, 130; North Norway, 46; primitive cultures, 14–15; Scandinavian, 49, 234; United States and, 43

promiscuity, 40, 114, 132, 142

Prosessen mod Hamsun (The trial against Hamsun) (Thorkild Hansen), 214

prostitution, 36, 53

protagonists. *See* female protagonists; male protagonists

Q

Queen Tamara, 59

Quisling, Vidkun, 7, 154, 182, 186–87, 229

Quisling government, 193–94, 197

R

race, 10, 21, 132; biology and, 114–15; degeneration, 19, 120–21; evolution, 26–27; and gender, 10, 11, 128, 129; Nordic ideal, 183–85; in old Norse texts, 29–31; research on, 183–85; sexuality and, 124; women and, 30–31

race biology, 13, 20–21

race-crossing, 37–38, 40, 55, 96, 111, 126, 184, 235

Racehygiene (Jon Alfred Mjøen), 22, 24–25

race-mixing. *See* race-crossing

racism, 12, 123, 198, 206; of Knut Hamsun, 127, 132, 179, 191–92; literary critics' handling of, in Knut Hamsun's writings, 113, 121

Ræder, Ole Munch, 92

Rathenau, Walter, 39

Redaktør Lynge (Editor Lynge), 231

"Realisert kameratskap" (Realized camaraderie), 201. *See also* "Virkeliggjort kameratskap"

realism, 5, 57

Regnbuen (The rainbow), 61–63

Reiersen, Johan Reinert, 92

reproduction, 25, 30, 64–66. *See also* contraception

Rhodes, Anthony R. E., 125

Riksmål (the language of the realm), 49

Riksteatret, 6

Ring, Barbara, 34

Ringen sluttet (The ring is closed), 38, 58, 126–35, 182; modernity in, 127; promiscuity in, 132; race in, 127; relationship to *Fra*

Wollstonecraft, Mary, 45

women, 12; arts and, 68–70; artists
depiction of, 55–57; degeneration and, 53–54, 68; in Hamsun
scholarship, 9; Hamsun's depiction
of, 57–61, 67–68; mannish, 53;
modernity and, 11; Nazi view of,
208–9; roles of, 13; sexual desires
of, 58–59, 75, 176; urban, 75, 66,
72

women's rights, 26, 51–52, 147,
252n1; responses to, in Norway,
52–57; and suffrage, 34, 51

World War I, 40, 46, 71, 169, 181,
196, 202, 233

World War II, 7, 25, 125, 207, 215,
225, 236

Z

Zantop, Susanne, 8, 10, 93

Züchner, Ernst Edmund, 197

Monika Žagar is associate professor of Scandinavian studies and director of undergraduate studies for the Department of German, Scandinavian, and Dutch at the University of Minnesota. She received her Ph.D. from the University of California at Berkeley.